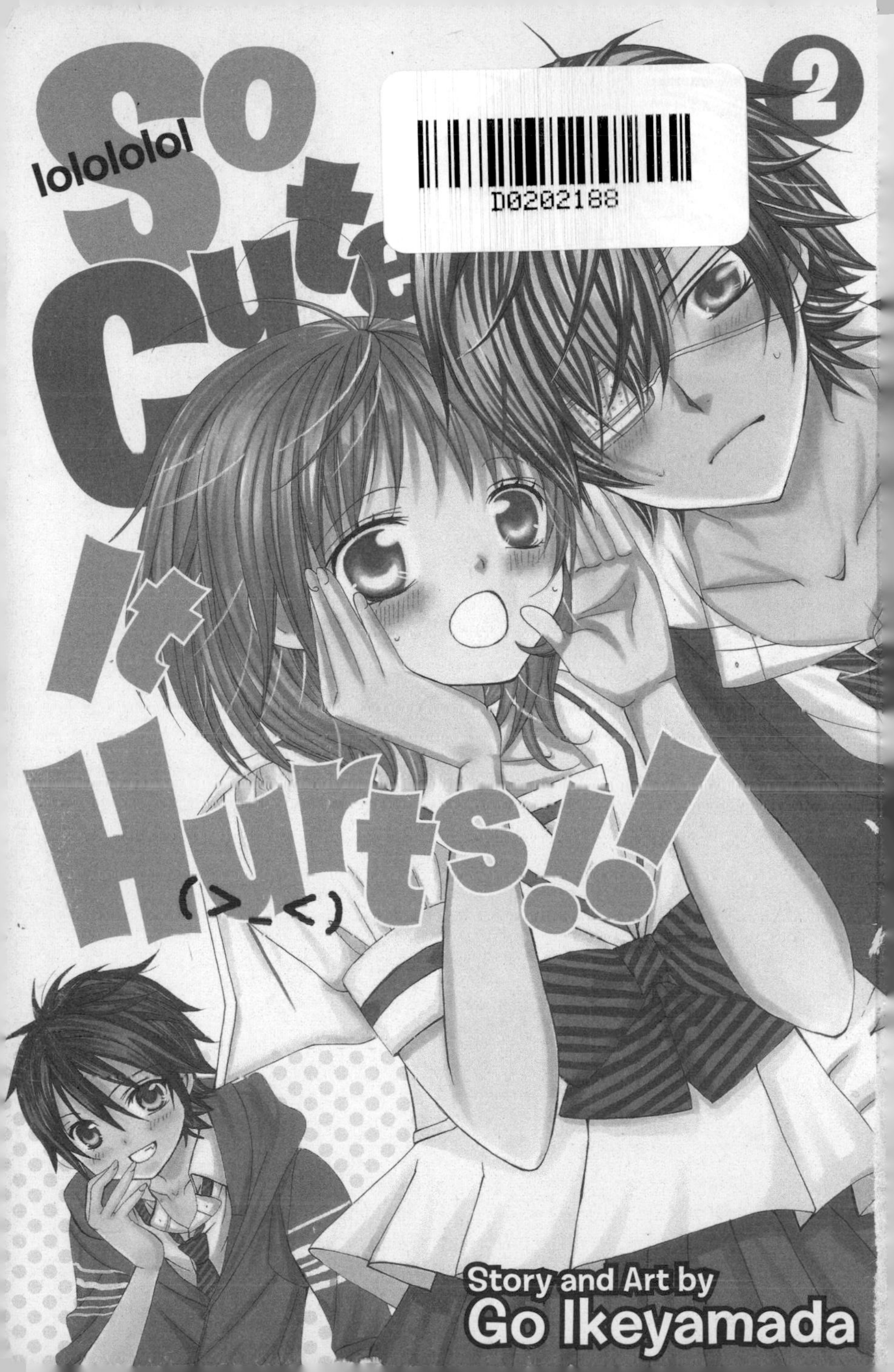
So Cute
lolololol
It
Hurts!!
(>_<)
2
Story and Art by
Go Ikeyamada

CHARACTERS

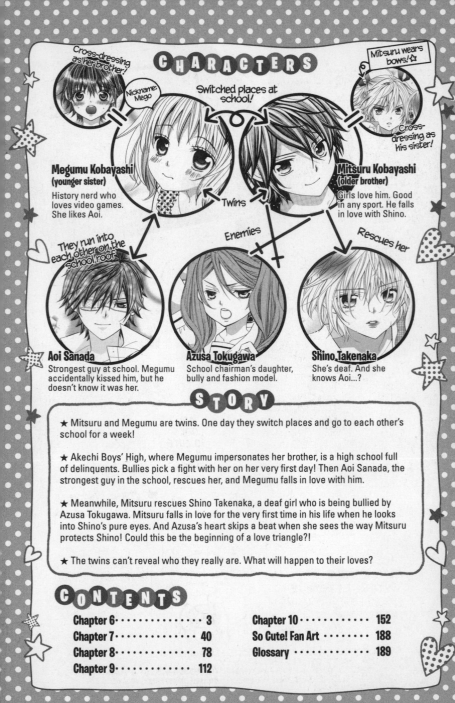

Cross-dressing as her brother!
Nickname: Mego
Switched places at school!
Mitsuru wears bows!☆
Cross-dressing as his sister!
Twins
Enemies
Rescues her
They run into each other on the school roof

Megumu Kobayashi
(younger sister)
History nerd who loves video games. She likes Aoi.

Mitsuru Kobayashi
(older brother)
Girls love him. Good in any sport. He falls in love with Shino.

Aoi Sanada
Strongest guy at school. Megumu accidentally kissed him, but he doesn't know it was her.

Azusa Tokugawa
School chairman's daughter, bully and fashion model.

Shino Takenaka
She's deaf. And she knows Aoi...?

STORY

★ Mitsuru and Megumu are twins. One day they switch places and go to each other's school for a week!

★ Akechi Boys' High, where Megumu impersonates her brother, is a high school full of delinquents. Bullies pick a fight with her on her very first day! Then Aoi Sanada, the strongest guy in the school, rescues her, and Megumu falls in love with him.

★ Meanwhile, Mitsuru rescues Shino Takenaka, a deaf girl who is being bullied by Azusa Tokugawa. Mitsuru falls in love for the very first time in his life when he looks into Shino's pure eyes. And Azusa's heart skips a beat when she sees the way Mitsuru protects Shino! Could this be the beginning of a love triangle?!

★ The twins can't reveal who they really are. What will happen to their loves?

CONTENTS

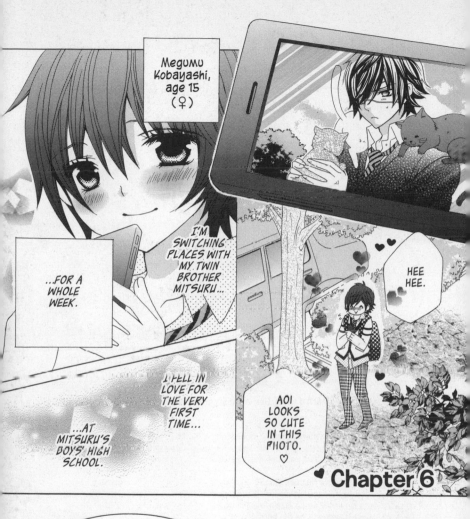

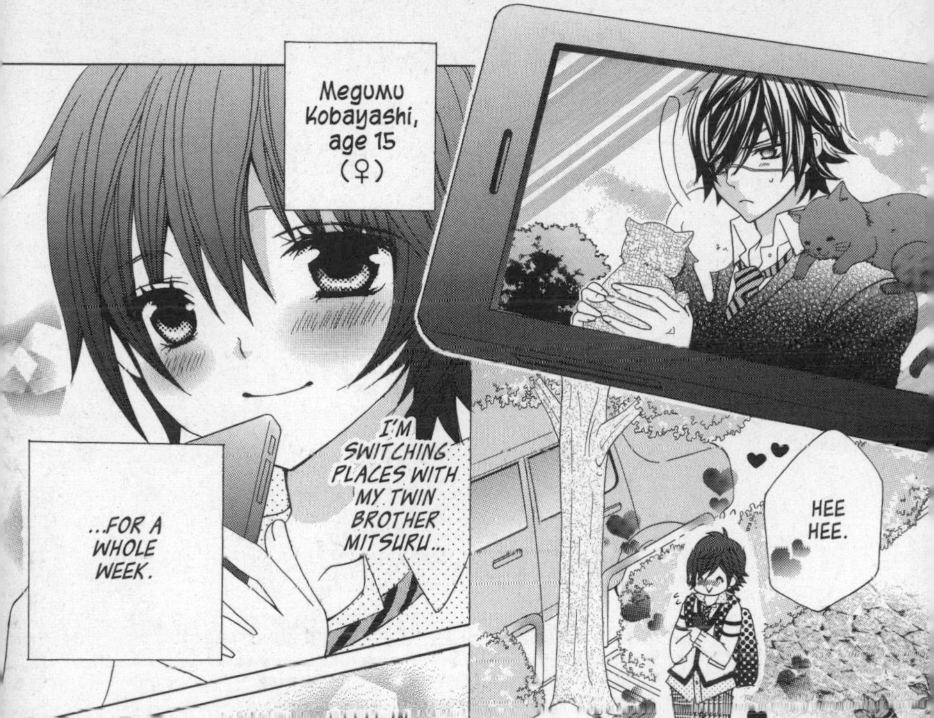
HEE HEE.
AOI LOOKS SO CUTE IN THIS PHOTO. ♡
Chapter 6
Megumu Kobayashi, age 15 (♀)
I'M SWITCHING PLACES WITH MY TWIN BROTHER MITSURU...
...FOR A WHOLE WEEK.
I FELL IN LOVE FOR THE VERY FIRST TIME...
...AT MITSURU'S BOYS' HIGH SCHOOL.

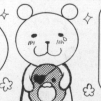

HELLO.
I'M GO IKEYAMADA.
THANK YOU FOR PICKING UP VOLUME 2 OF *SO CUTE IT HURTS!!*, MY 45TH BOOK!!

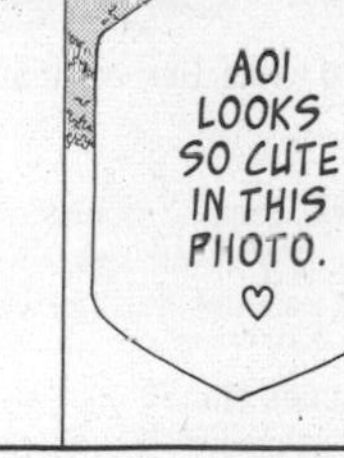

THE MANGA NOW HAS ITS OFFICIAL TWITTER ACCOUNT!
↓
(@KOBAKAWA_INFO)♡
SO DO TAKE A LOOK.♡

I RECEIVED MANY NEW YEAR'S CARDS, LETTERS AND DRAWINGS AFTER VOLUME 1 CAME OUT. THANK YOU SO MUCH!! (^0^)
I'M SO HAPPY I HAVE A GOOFY SMILE ON MY FACE AS I'M READING THEM. (*SMILE*)
THANKS TO EVERYONE, VOLUME 3 WILL BE ON SALE IN JAPAN IN THE SUMMER, AND FUN PROJECTS ARE IN PROGRESS! PLEASE LOOK FORWARD TO THEM.♡♡
VOLUME 2 REVEALS ONE OF AOI'S SECRETS AND HIS RELATIONSHIP WITH SHINO. THE TWINS' LOVES ZOOM TO A NEW PHASE AS WELL.
I HOPE EVERYONE ENJOYS READING THE MANGA.

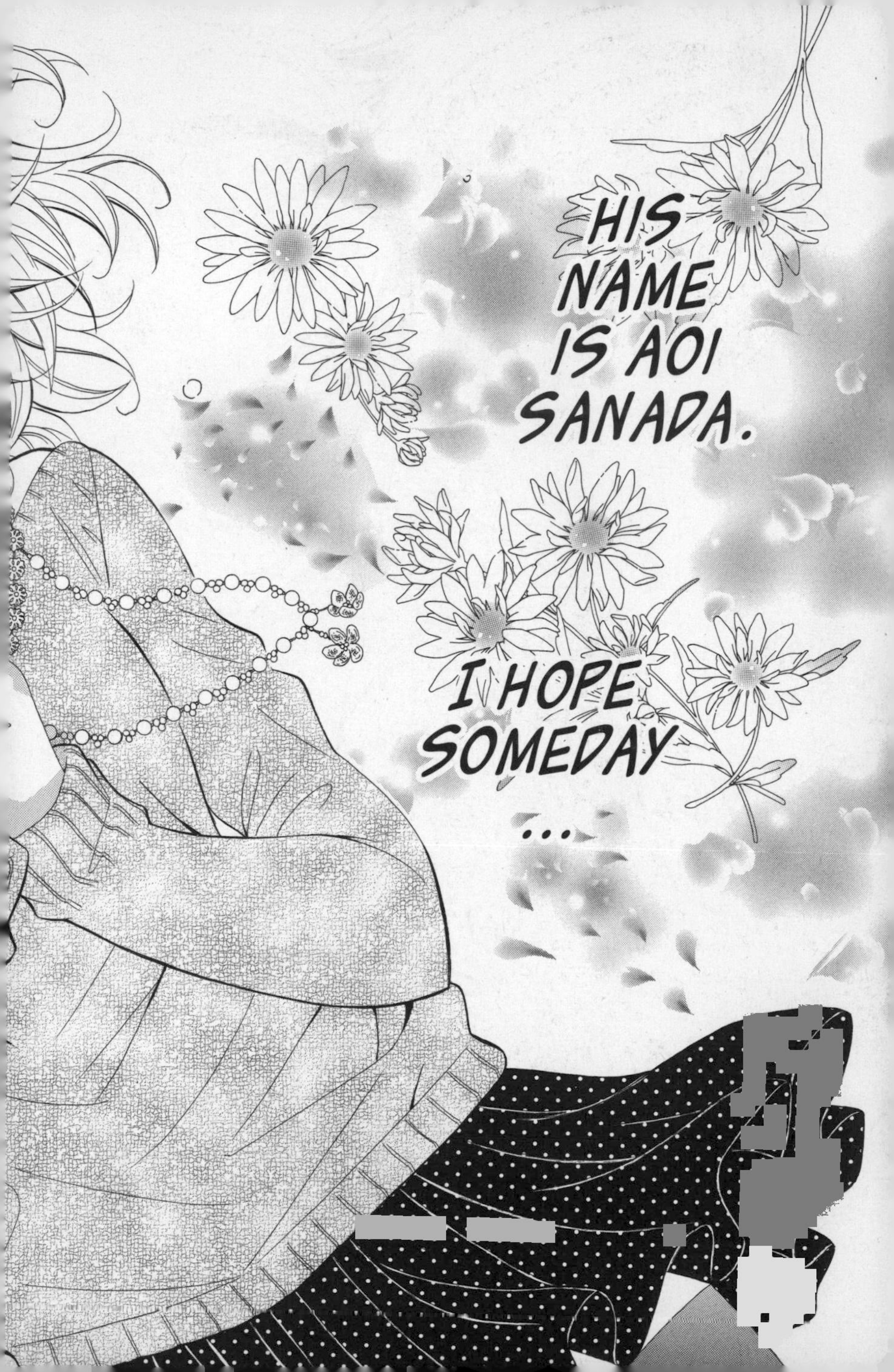
HIS NAME IS AOI SANADA.
I HOPE SOMEDAY...

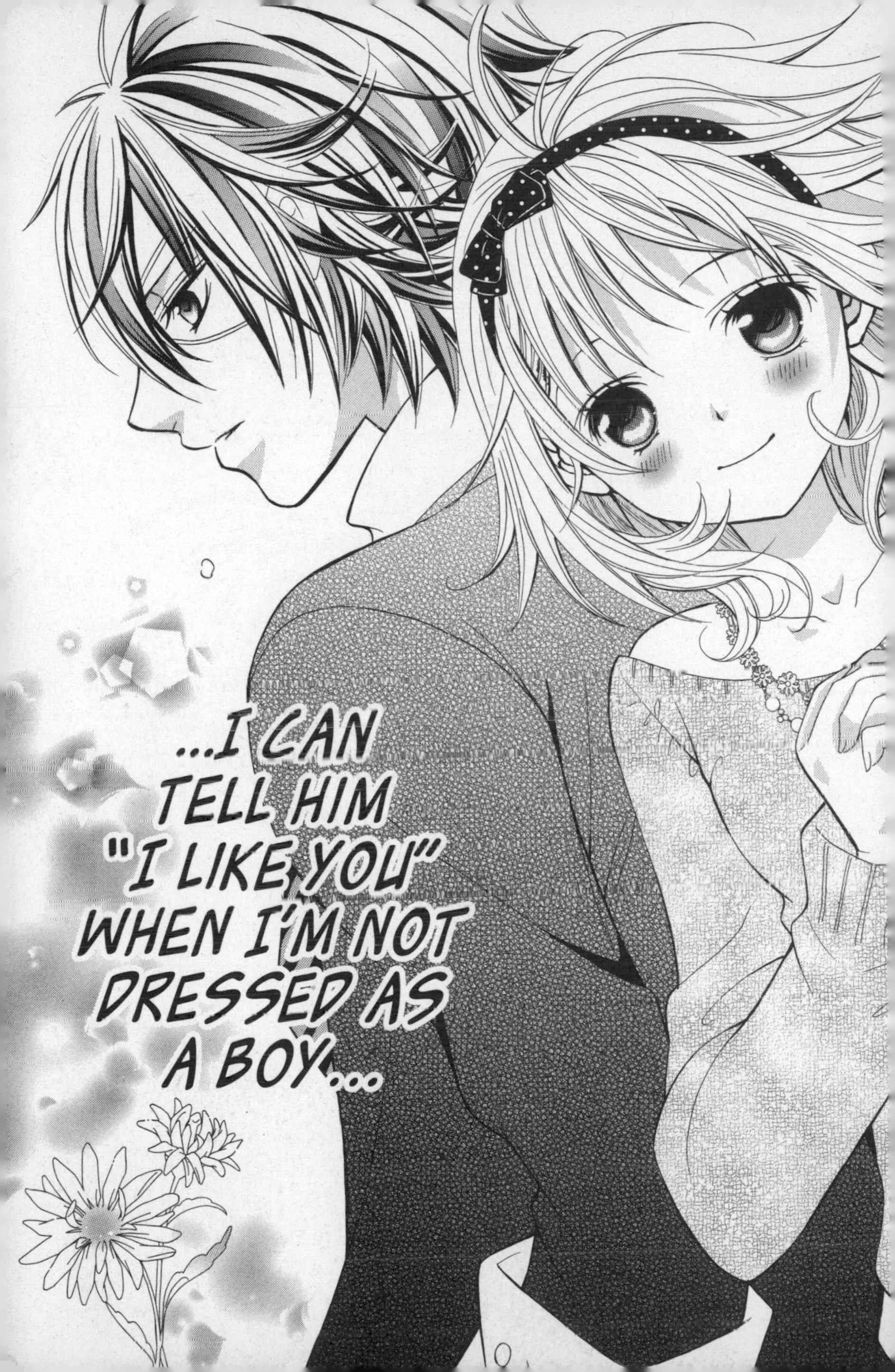
...I CAN TELL HIM "I LIKE YOU" WHEN I'M NOT DRESSED AS A BOY...

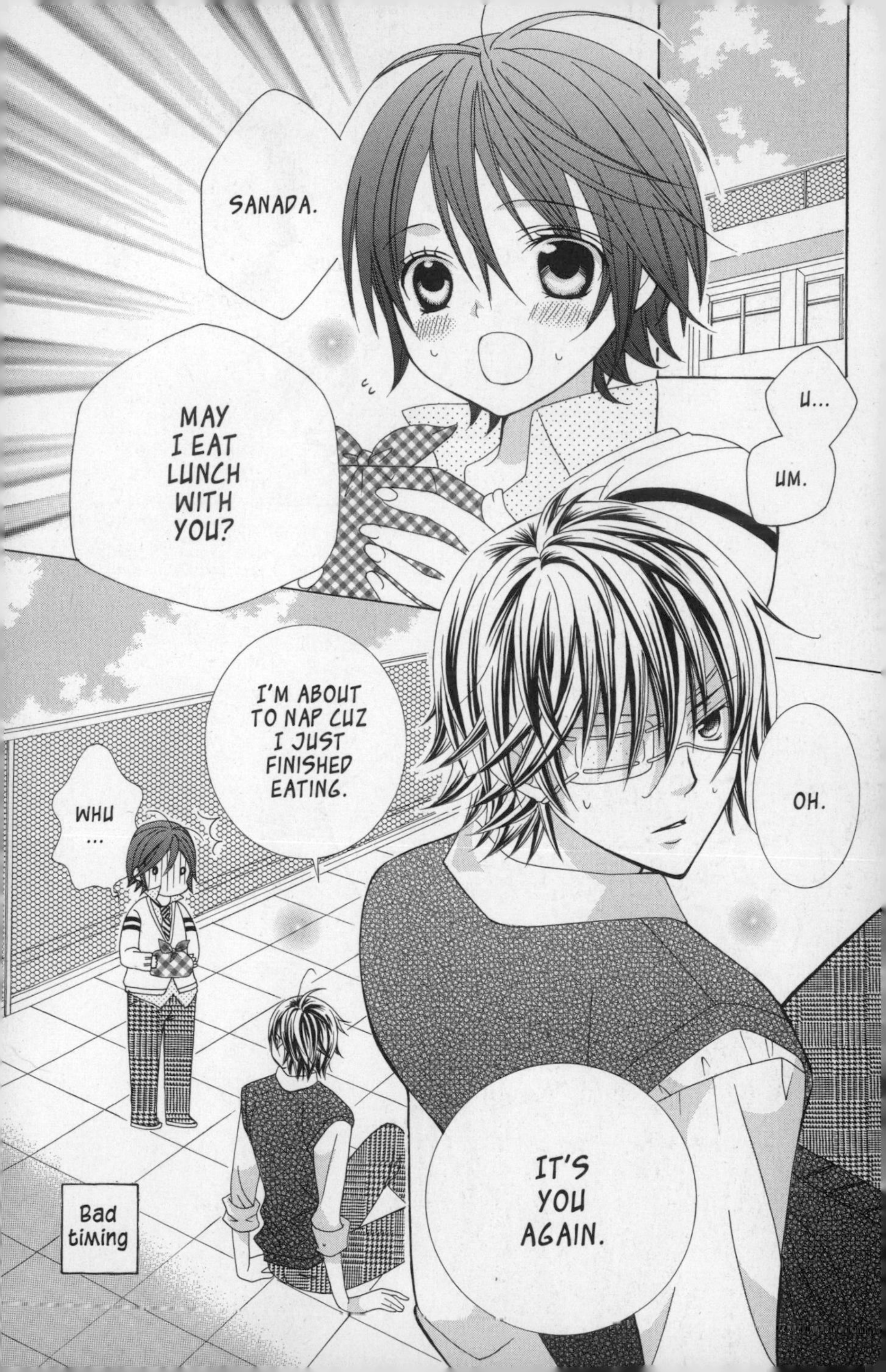
U...
UM.
SANADA.
MAY I EAT LUNCH WITH YOU?
OH.
IT'S YOU AGAIN.
I'M ABOUT TO NAP CUZ I JUST FINISHED EATING.
WHU ...
Bad timing

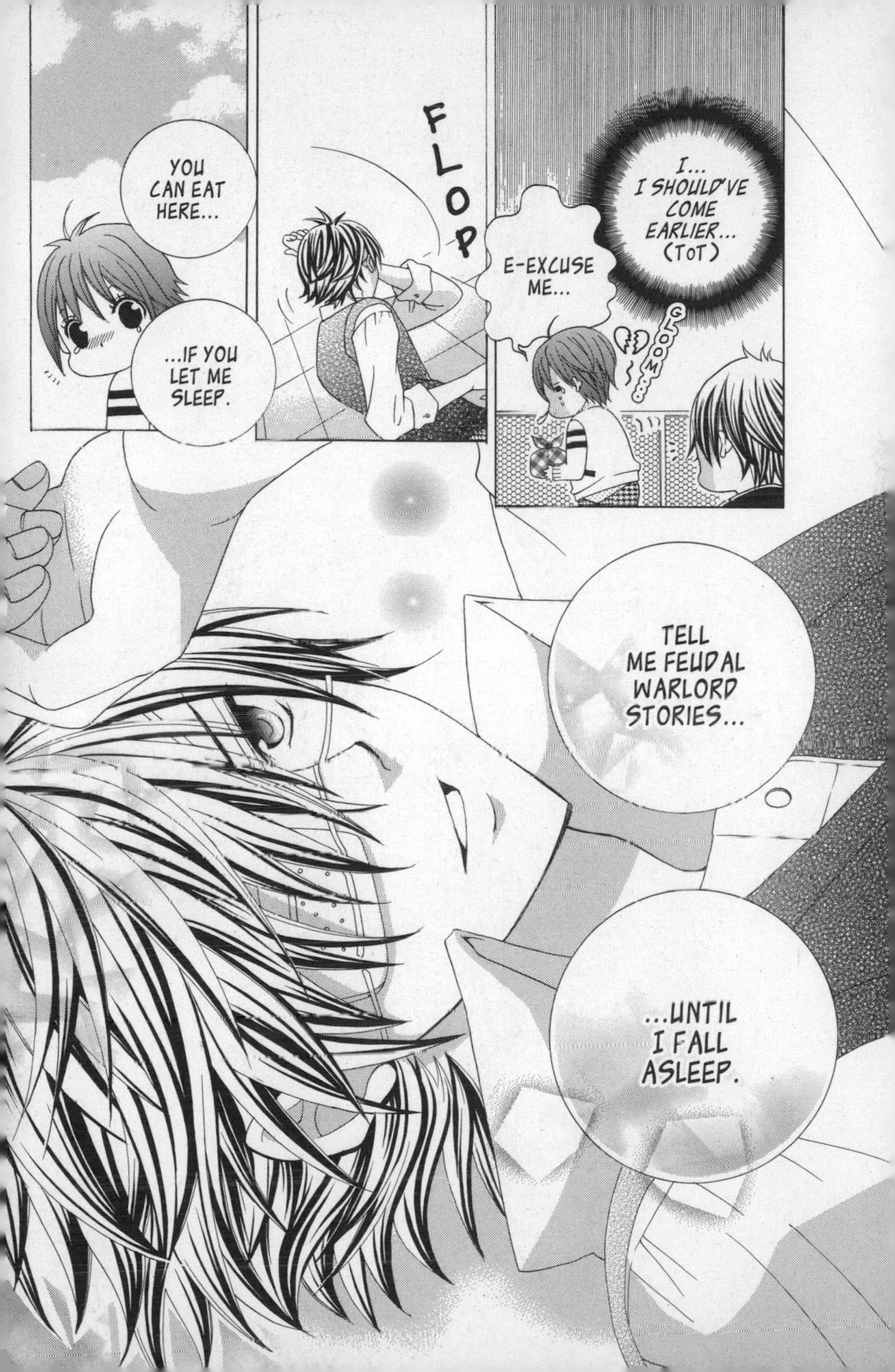
I... I SHOULD'VE COME EARLIER... (TOT)
E-EXCUSE ME...
GLOOM...
FLOP
YOU CAN EAT HERE...
...IF YOU LET ME SLEEP.
TELL ME FEUDAL WARLORD STORIES...
...UNTIL I FALL ASLEEP.

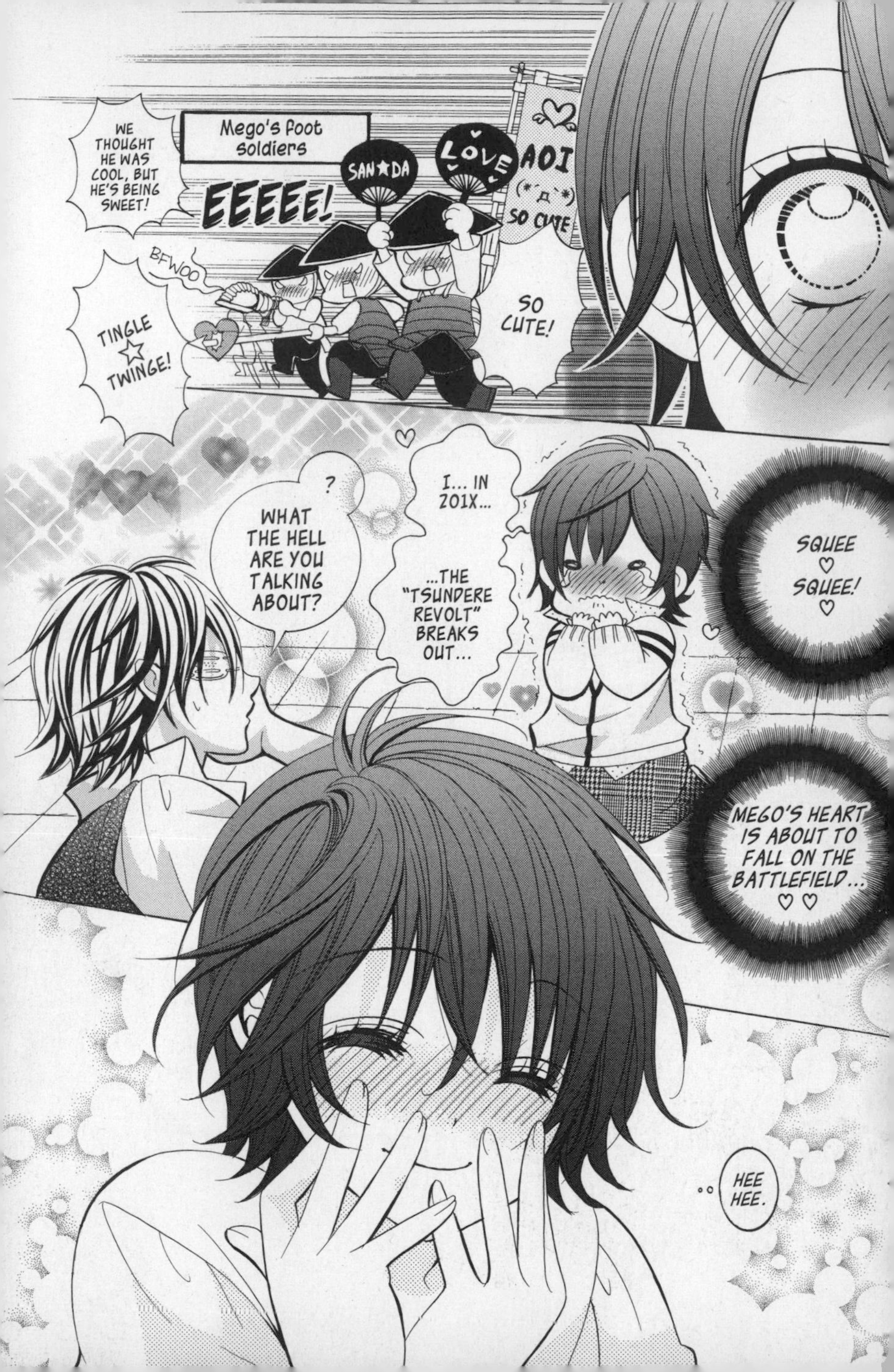

AOI (*´д`*) SO CUTE
LOVE
SAN★DA
Mego's foot soldiers
WE THOUGHT HE WAS COOL, BUT HE'S BEING SWEET!
EEEEE!
SO CUTE!
BFWOO
TINGLE ☆ TWINGE!
SQUEE ♡ SQUEE! ♡
I... IN 201X...
...THE "TSUNDERE REVOLT" BREAKS OUT...
?
WHAT THE HELL ARE YOU TALKING ABOUT?
MEGO'S HEART IS ABOUT TO FALL ON THE BATTLEFIELD... ♡ ♡
HEE HEE.

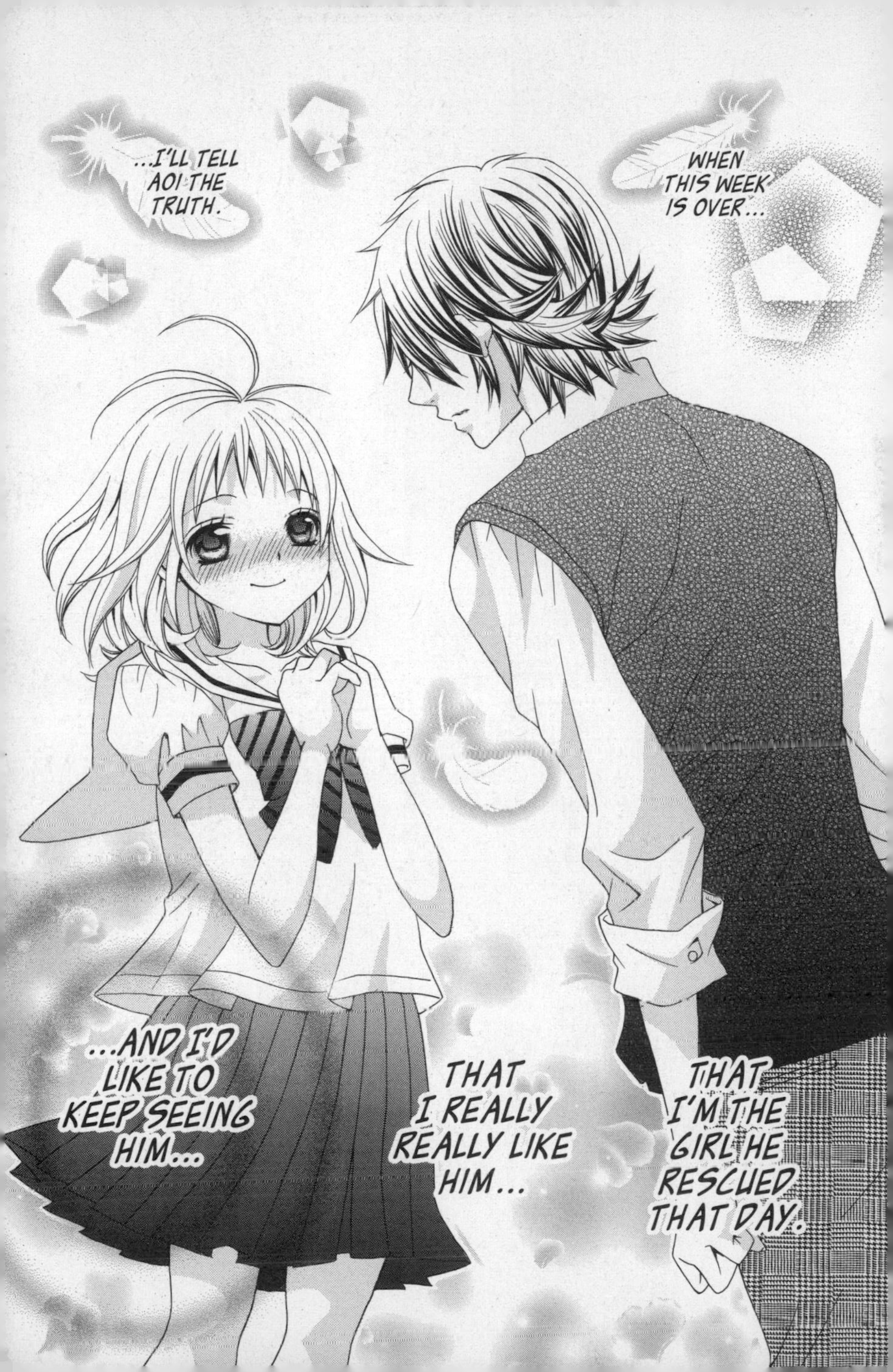
WHEN THIS WEEK IS OVER...
...I'LL TELL AOI THE TRUTH.
THAT I'M THE GIRL HE RESCUED THAT DAY.
THAT I REALLY REALLY LIKE HIM...
...AND I'D LIKE TO KEEP SEEING HIM...

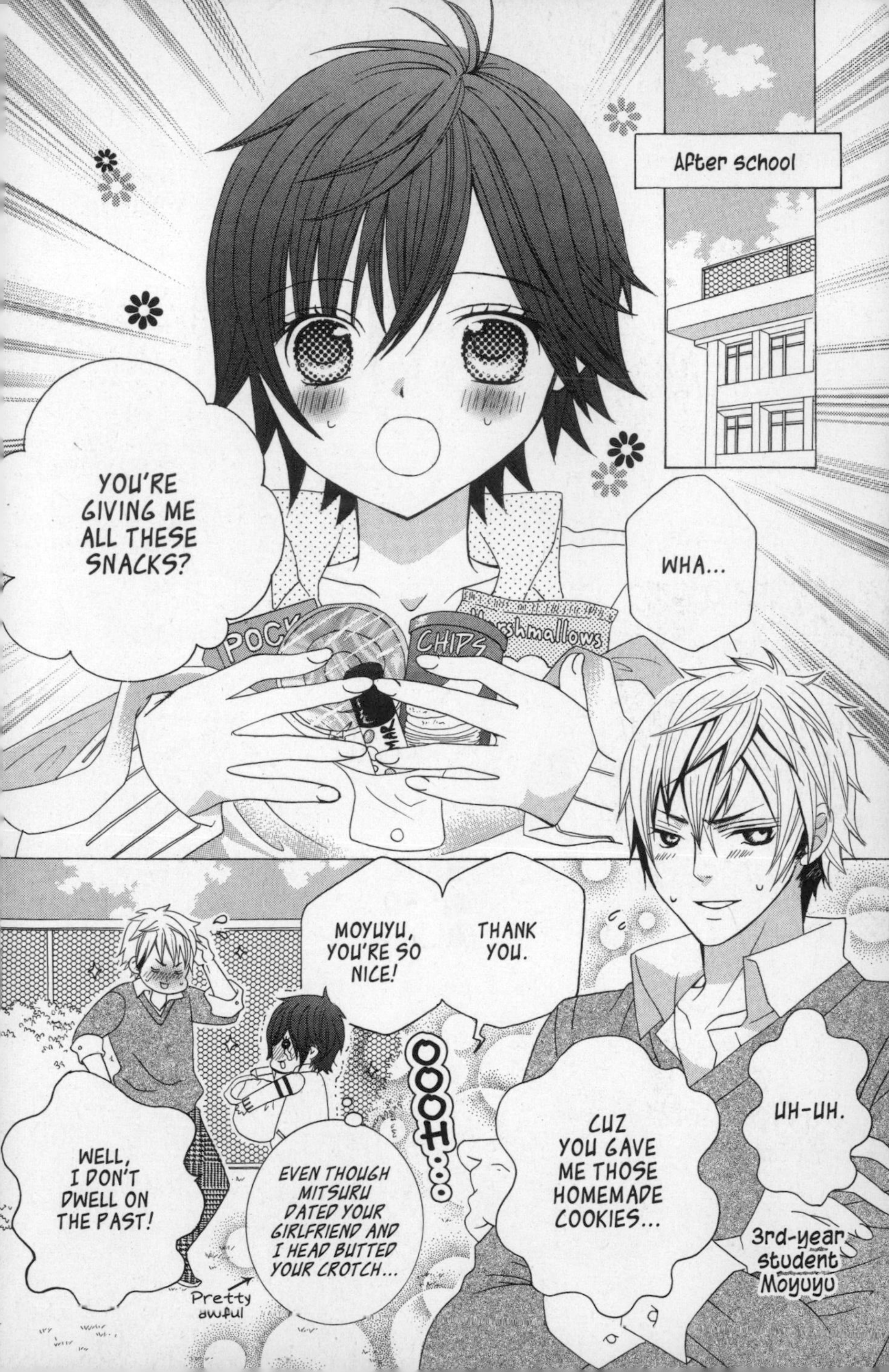
After school
YOU'RE GIVING ME ALL THESE SNACKS?
WHA...
POCK
CHIPS
Marshmallows
MOYUYU, YOU'RE SO NICE! THANK YOU.
UH-UH.
CUZ YOU GAVE ME THOSE HOMEMADE COOKIES...
3rd-year student Moyuyu
OOOH...
EVEN THOUGH MITSURU DATED YOUR GIRLFRIEND AND I HEAD BUTTED YOUR CROTCH...
Pretty awful
WELL, I DON'T DWELL ON THE PAST!

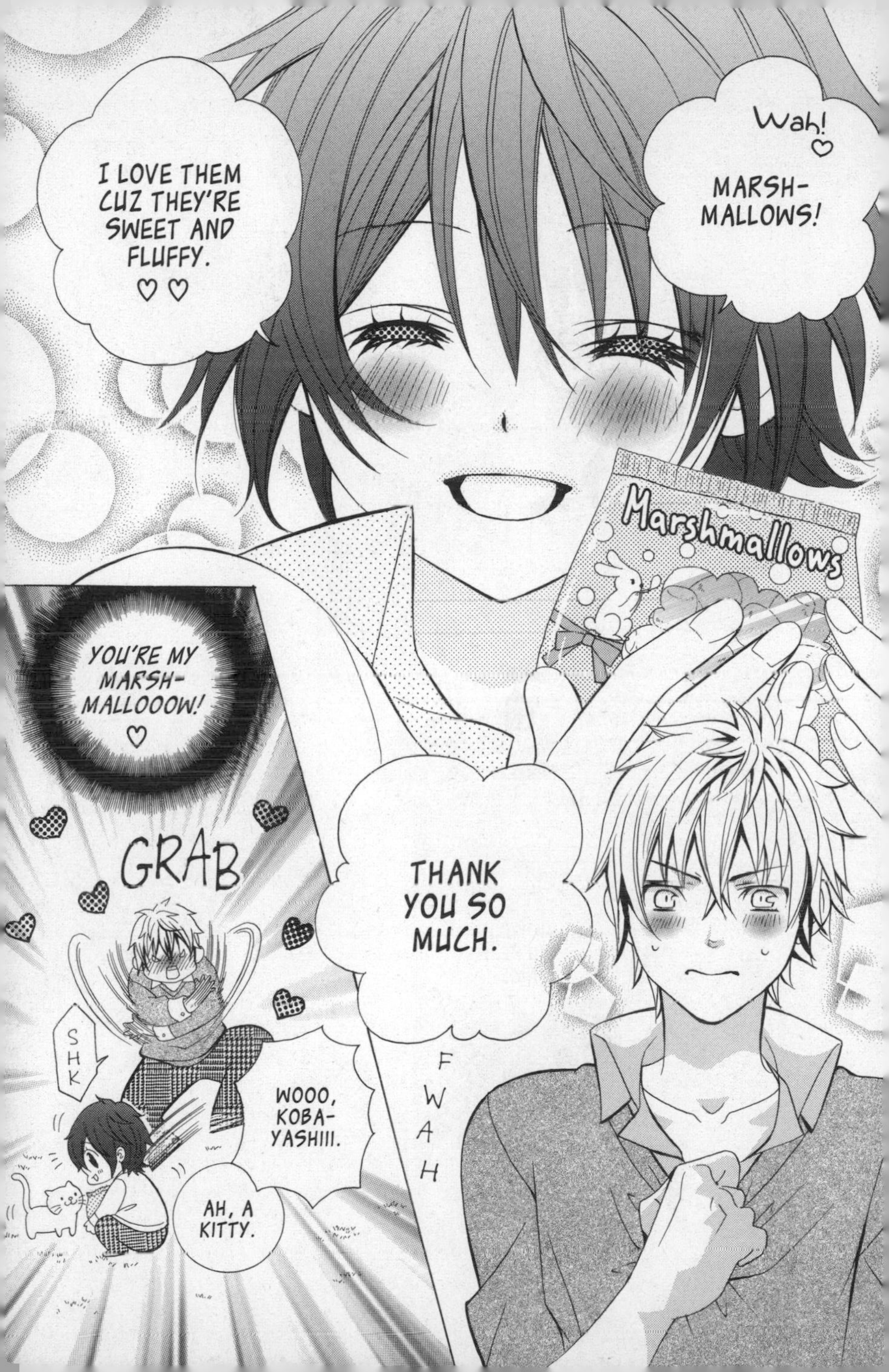
Wah! ♡
MARSH-MALLOWS!
I LOVE THEM CUZ THEY'RE SWEET AND FLUFFY. ♡ ♡
Marshmallows
THANK YOU SO MUCH.
FWAH
YOU'RE MY MARSH-MALLOOOW! ♡
GRAB
SHK
WOOO, KOBA-YASHIII.
AH, A KITTY.

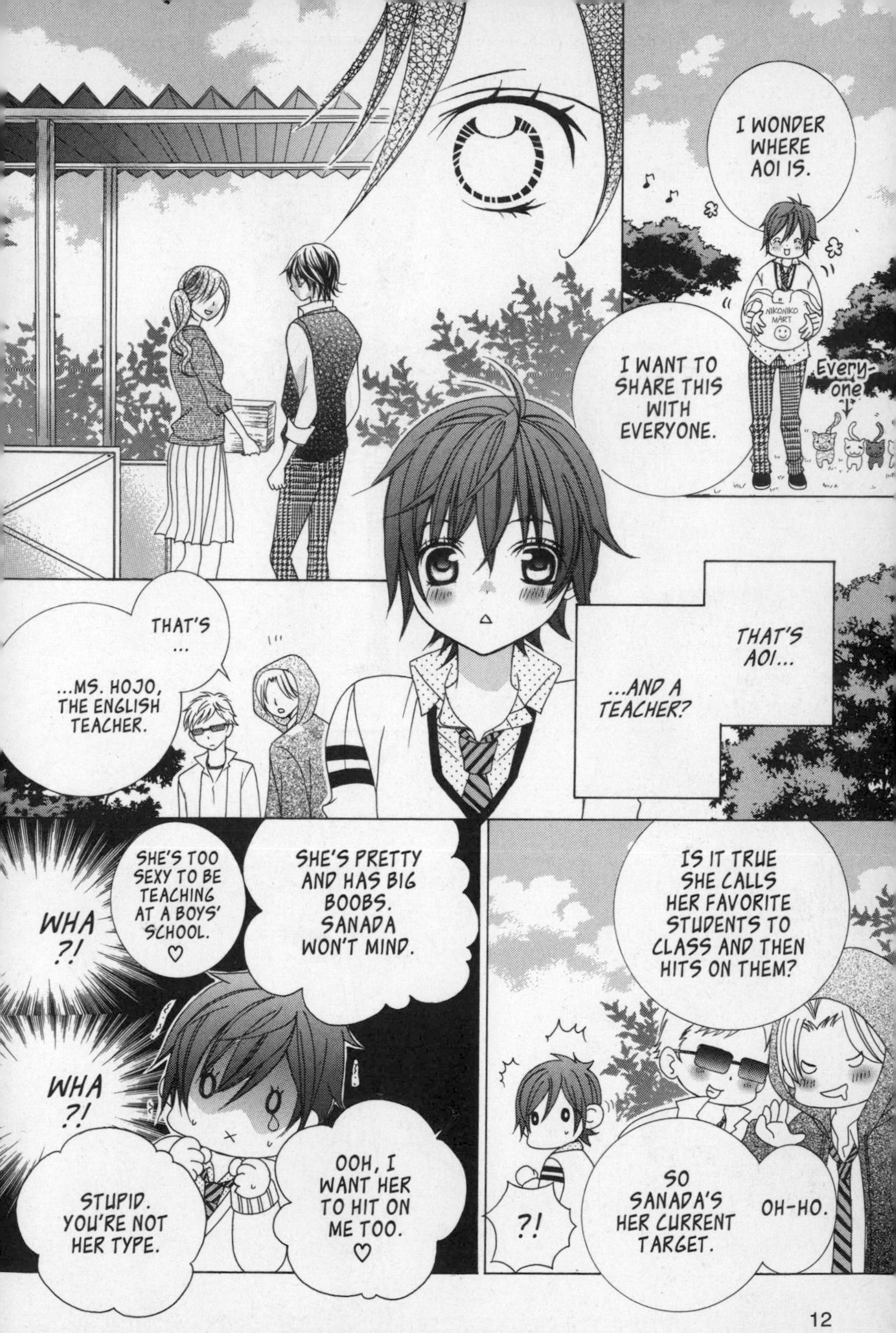
I WONDER WHERE AOI IS.
I WANT TO SHARE THIS WITH EVERYONE.
NIKONIKO MART
Every-one
THAT'S AOI...
...AND A TEACHER?
THAT'S ...
...MS. HOJO, THE ENGLISH TEACHER.
IS IT TRUE SHE CALLS HER FAVORITE STUDENTS TO CLASS AND THEN HITS ON THEM?
OH-HO.
SO SANADA'S HER CURRENT TARGET.
?!
SHE'S PRETTY AND HAS BIG BOOBS. SANADA WON'T MIND.
SHE'S TOO SEXY TO BE TEACHING AT A BOYS' SCHOOL. ♡
WHA ?!
WHA ?!
OOH, I WANT HER TO HIT ON ME TOO. ♡
STUPID. YOU'RE NOT HER TYPE.

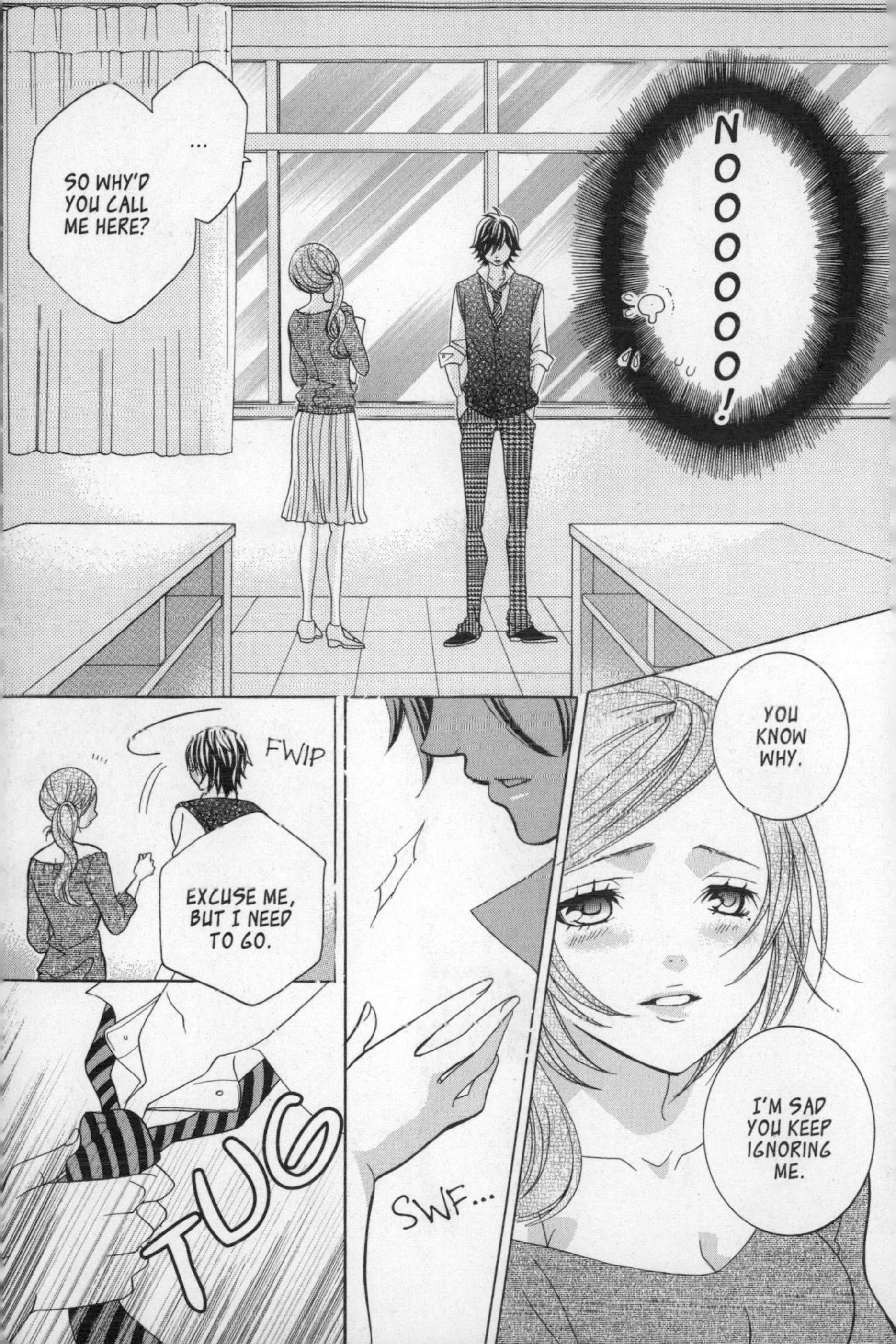
NOOOOOO!
...
SO WHY'D YOU CALL ME HERE?
YOU KNOW WHY.
I'M SAD YOU KEEP IGNORING ME.
SWF...
FWIP
EXCUSE ME, BUT I NEED TO GO.
TUG

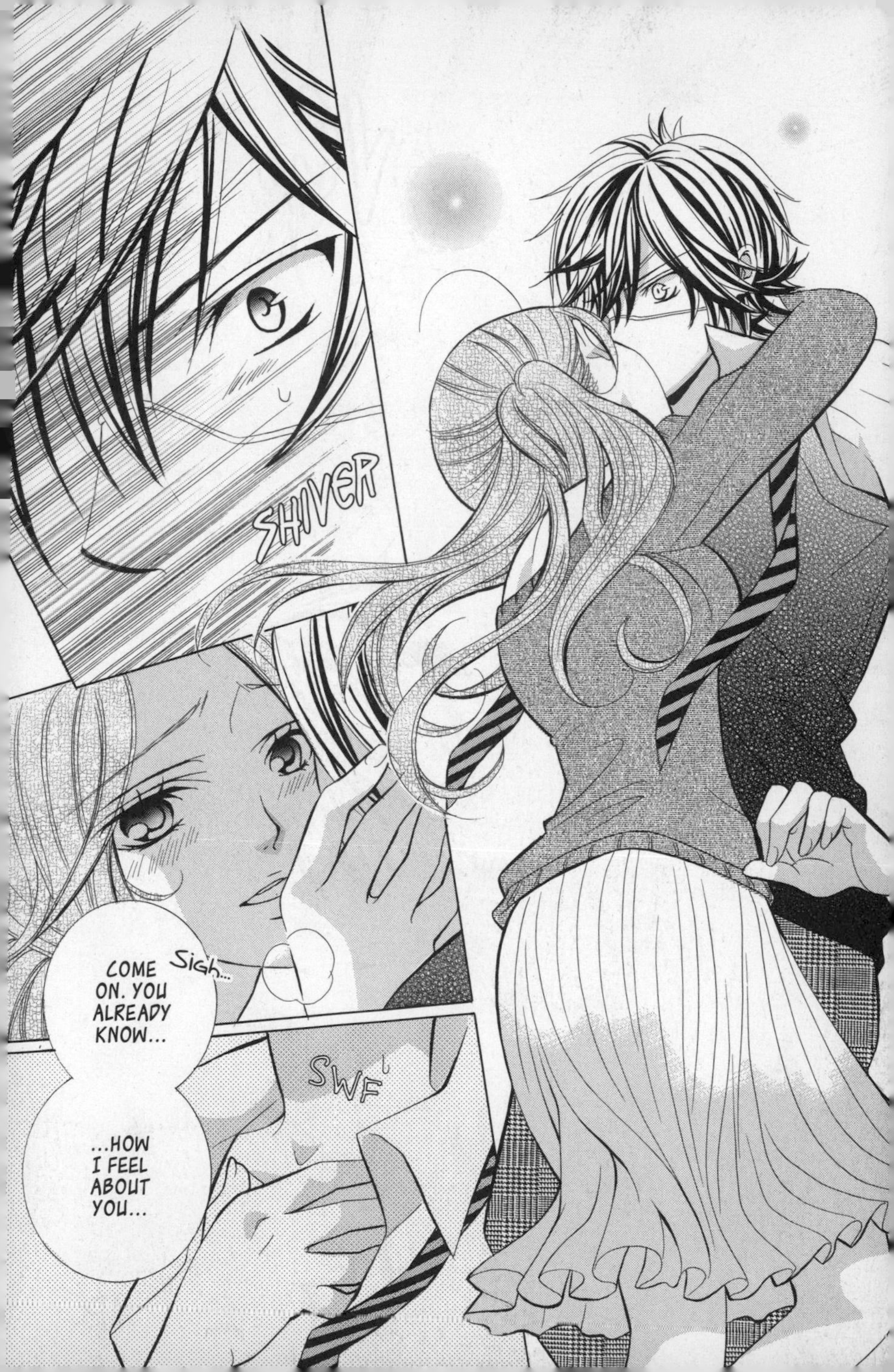
SHIVER
Sigh...
COME ON. YOU ALREADY KNOW...
SWF
...HOW I FEEL ABOUT YOU...

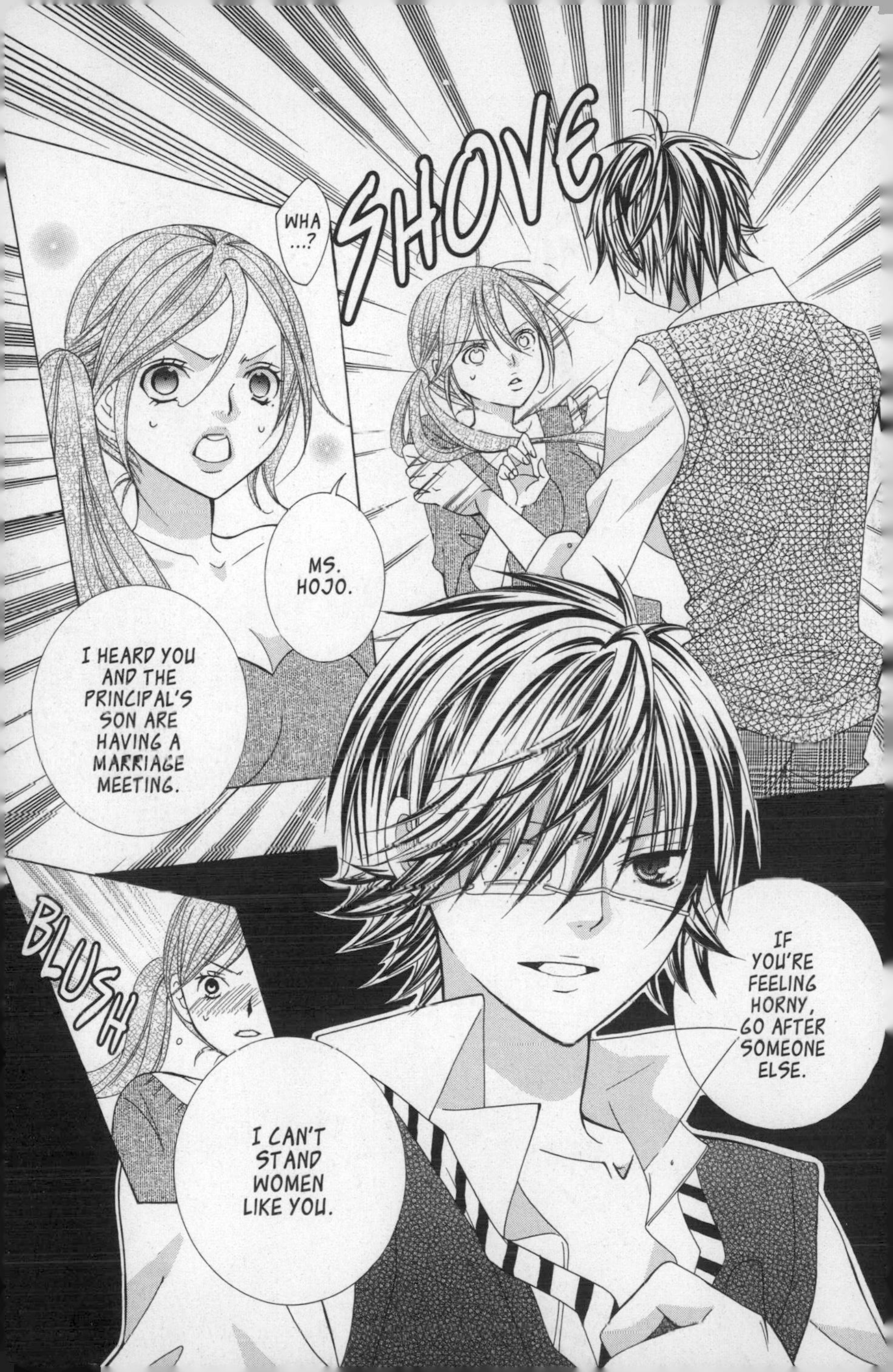
SHOVE
WHA ...?
MS. HOJO.
I HEARD YOU AND THE PRINCIPAL'S SON ARE HAVING A MARRIAGE MEETING.
IF YOU'RE FEELING HORNY, GO AFTER SOMEONE ELSE.
BLUSH
I CAN'T STAND WOMEN LIKE YOU.

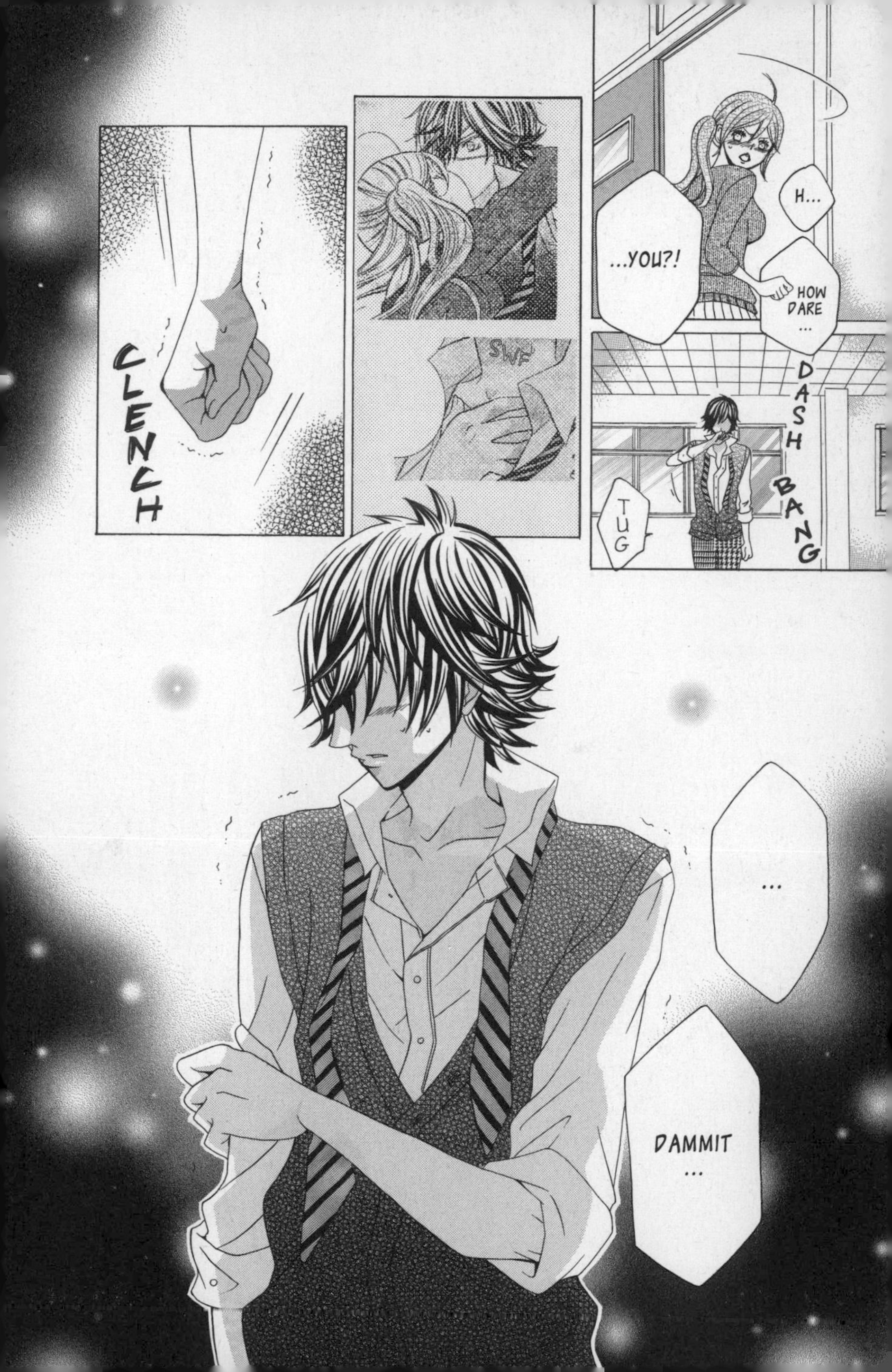
H...
HOW DARE ...
...YOU?!
DASH
BANG
TUG
SWF
CLENCH
...
DAMMIT ...

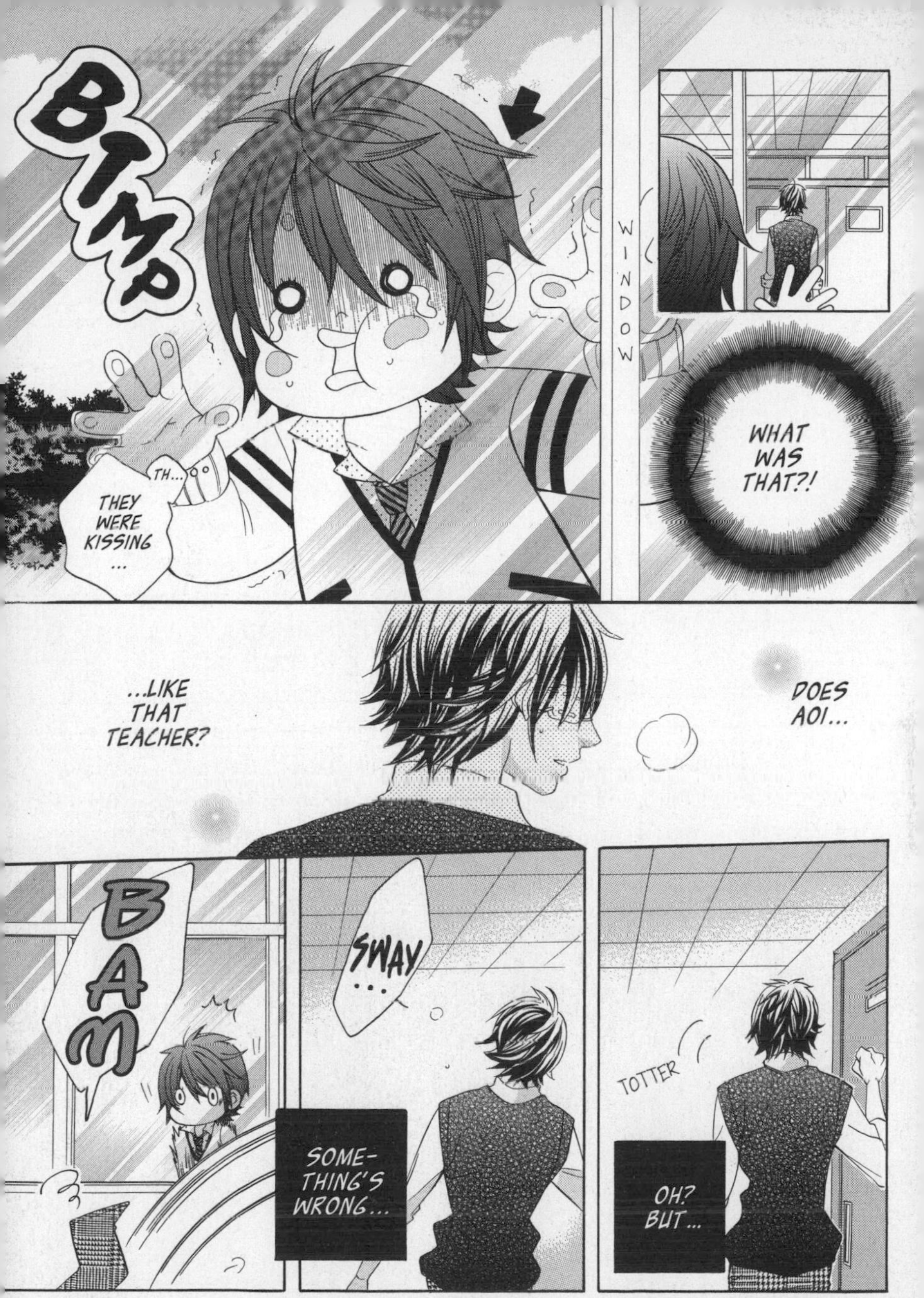
WHAT WAS THAT?!
WINDOW
BIMP
TH...
THEY WERE KISSING...
DOES AOI...
...LIKE THAT TEACHER?
TOTTER
OH? BUT...
SWAY...
SOMETHING'S WRONG...
BAM

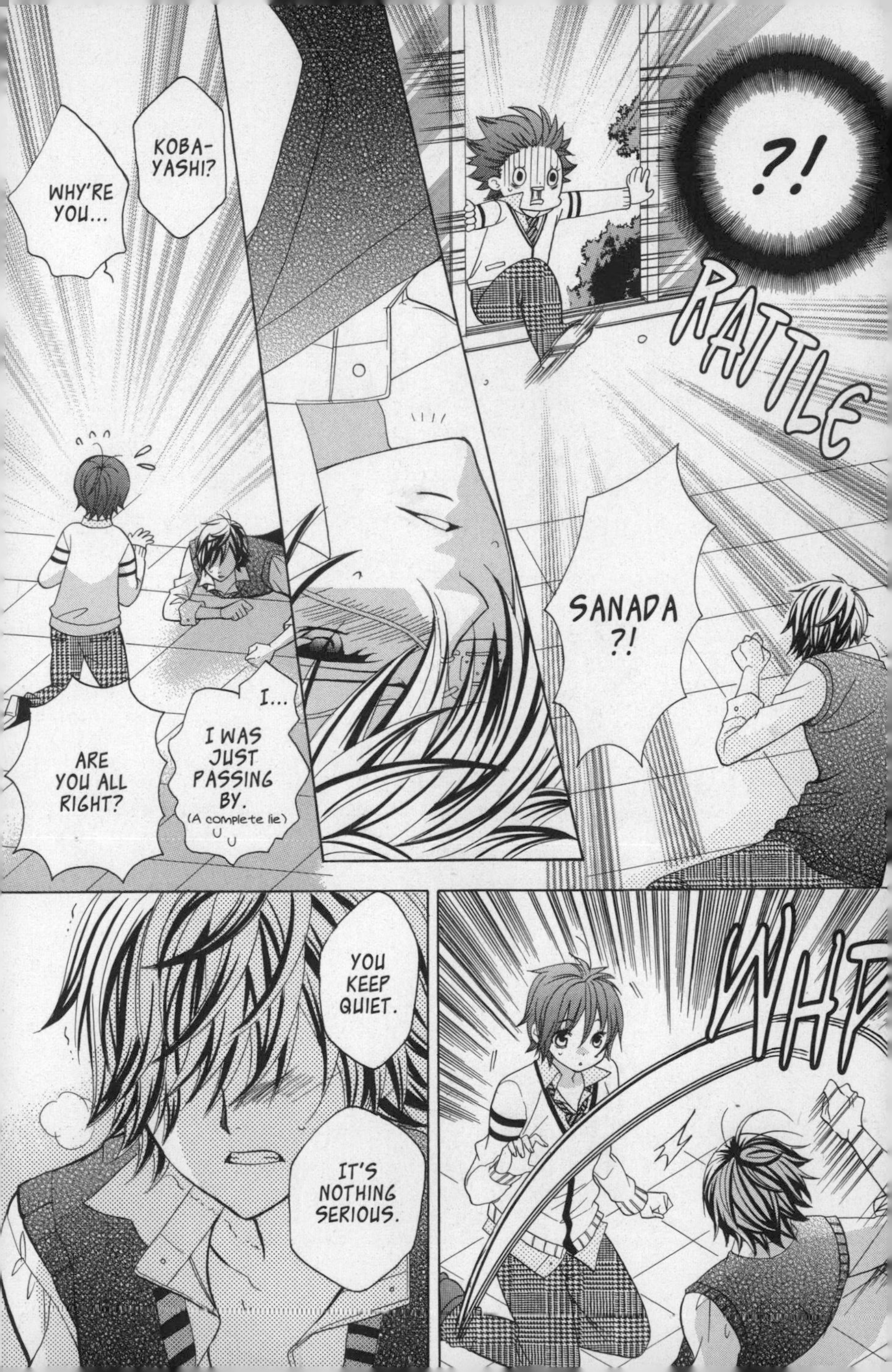

?!
RATTLE
SANADA ?!
KOBA-YASHI?
WHY'RE YOU...
I...
I WAS JUST PASSING BY.
(A complete lie)
ARE YOU ALL RIGHT?
YOU KEEP QUIET.
IT'S NOTHING SERIOUS.

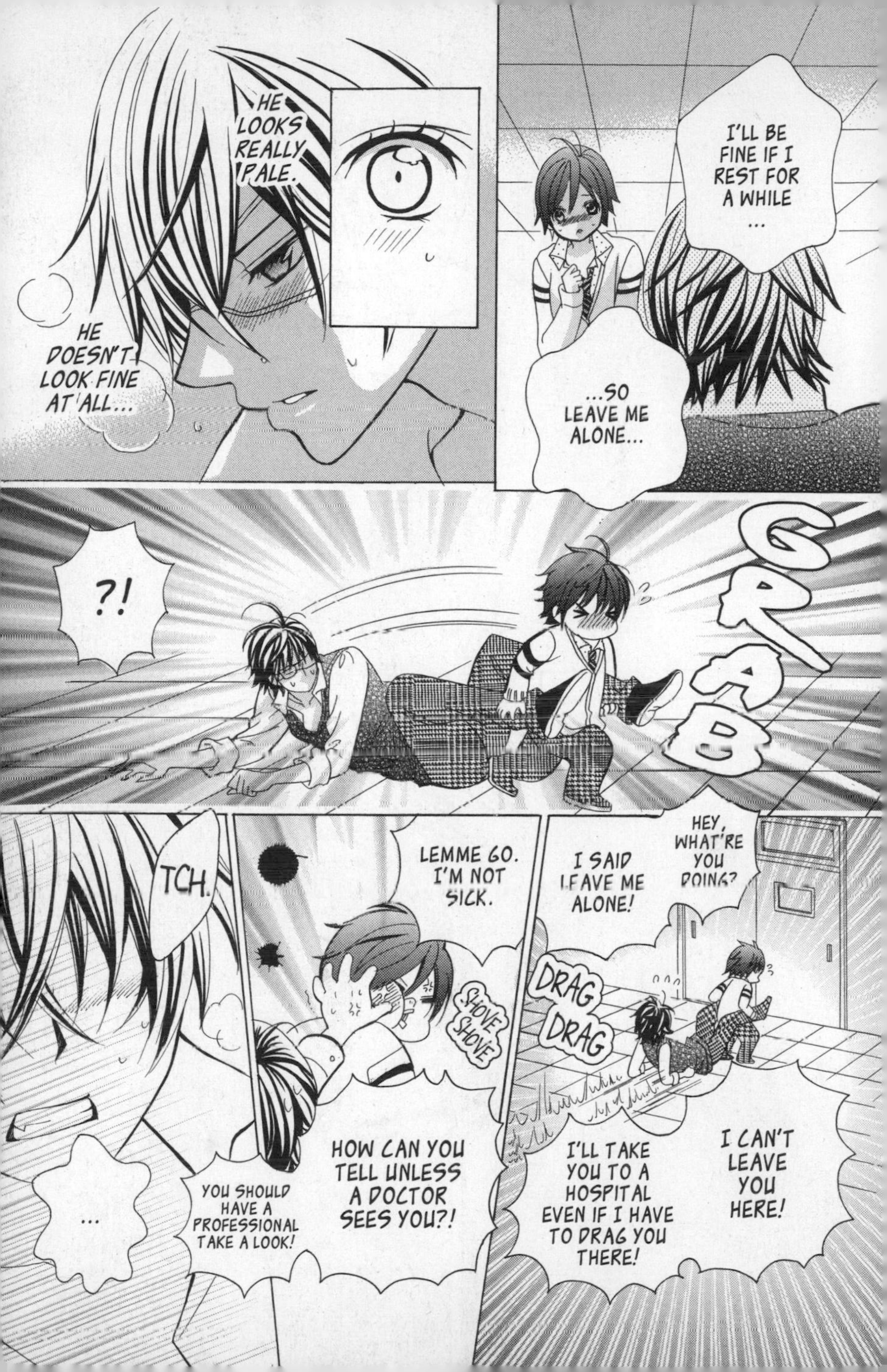
I'LL BE FINE IF I REST FOR A WHILE ...
...SO LEAVE ME ALONE...
HE LOOKS REALLY PALE.
HE DOESN'T LOOK FINE AT ALL...
GRAB
?!
HEY, WHAT'RE YOU DOING?
I SAID LEAVE ME ALONE!
DRAG DRAG
I CAN'T LEAVE YOU HERE!
I'LL TAKE YOU TO A HOSPITAL EVEN IF I HAVE TO DRAG YOU THERE!
LEMME GO. I'M NOT SICK.
SHOVE SHOVE
HOW CAN YOU TELL UNLESS A DOCTOR SEES YOU?!
YOU SHOULD HAVE A PROFESSIONAL TAKE A LOOK!
TCH.
...

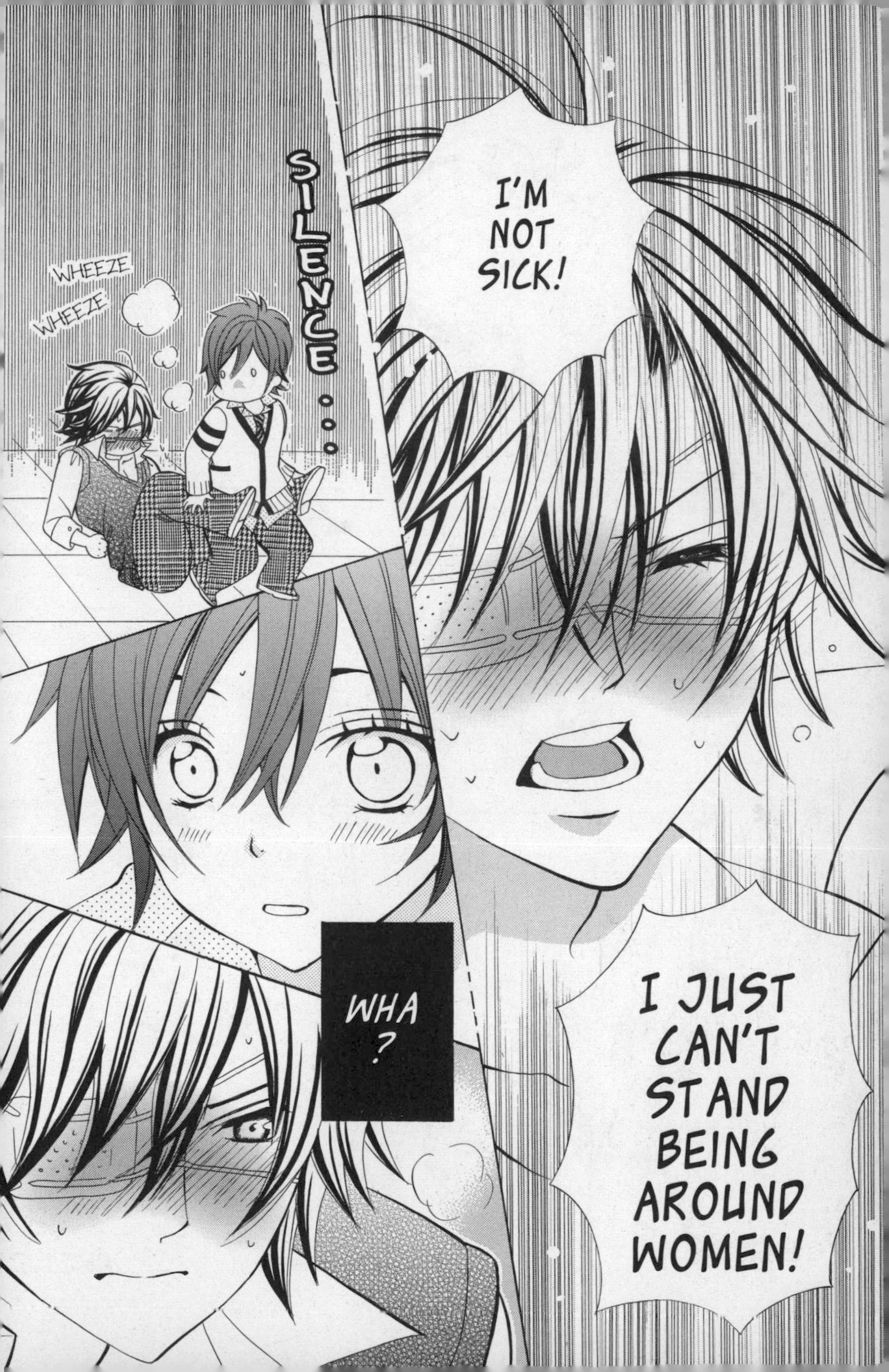
I'M NOT SICK!
I JUST CAN'T STAND BEING AROUND WOMEN!
SILENCE...
WHEEZE
WHEEZE
WHA ?

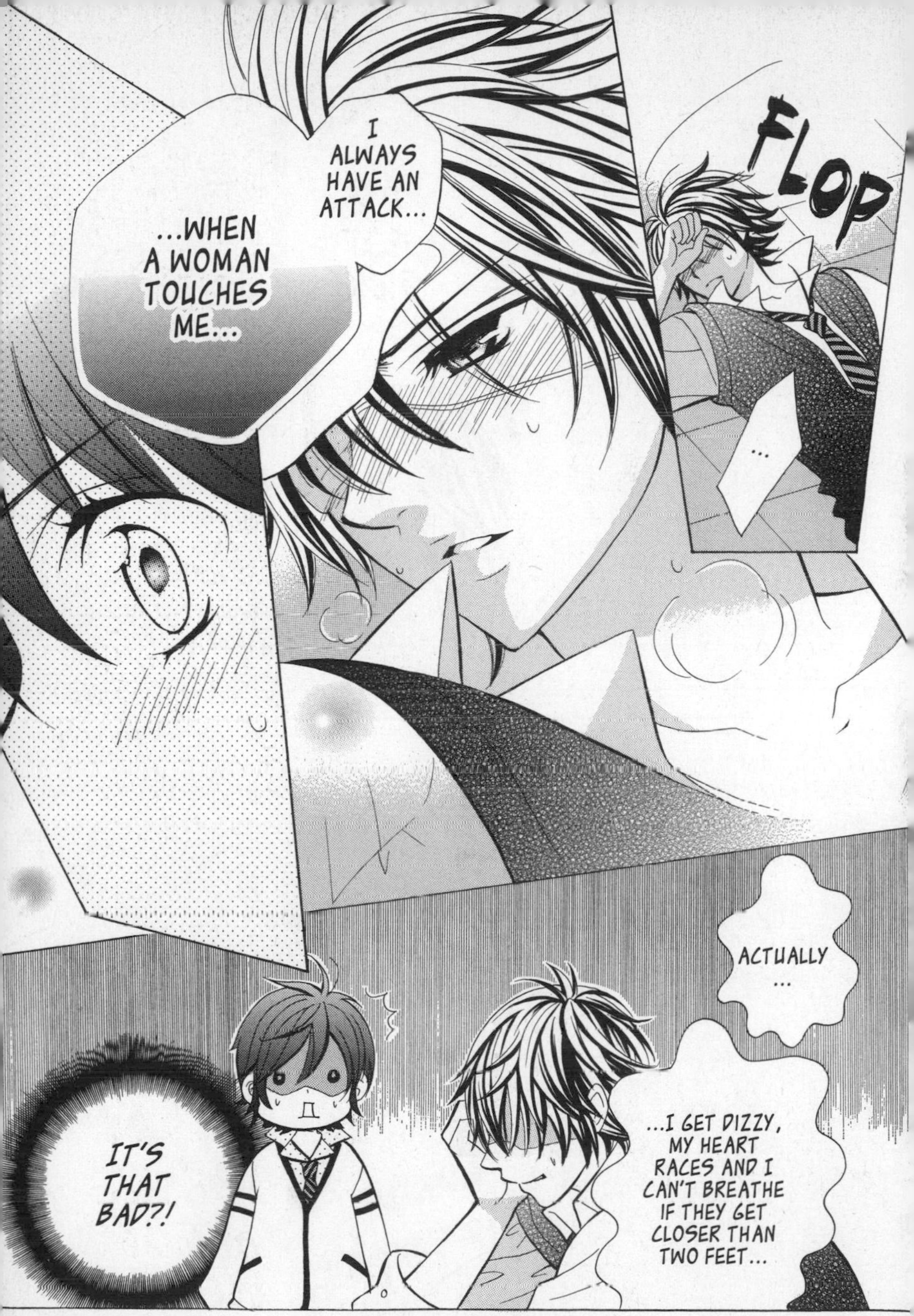
FLOP
...
I ALWAYS HAVE AN ATTACK...
...WHEN A WOMAN TOUCHES ME...
ACTUALLY...
...I GET DIZZY, MY HEART RACES AND I CAN'T BREATHE IF THEY GET CLOSER THAN TWO FEET...
IT'S THAT BAD?!

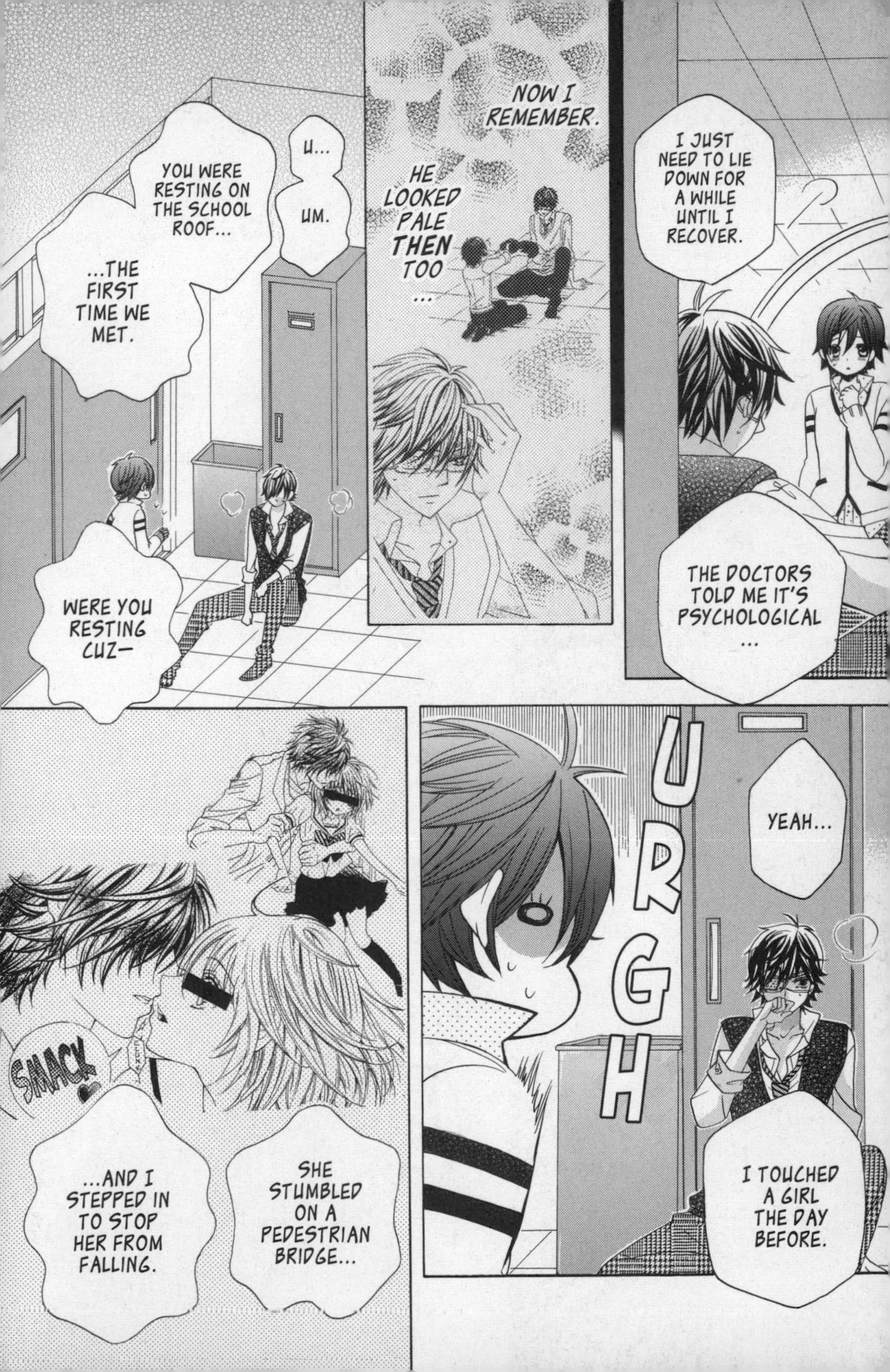
I JUST NEED TO LIE DOWN FOR A WHILE UNTIL I RECOVER.
THE DOCTORS TOLD ME IT'S PSYCHOLOGICAL ...
NOW I REMEMBER.
HE LOOKED PALE THEN TOO ...
U...
UM.
YOU WERE RESTING ON THE SCHOOL ROOF...
...THE FIRST TIME WE MET.
WERE YOU RESTING CUZ—
YEAH...
URGH
I TOUCHED A GIRL THE DAY BEFORE.
SMACK
SHE STUMBLED ON A PEDESTRIAN BRIDGE...
...AND I STEPPED IN TO STOP HER FROM FALLING.

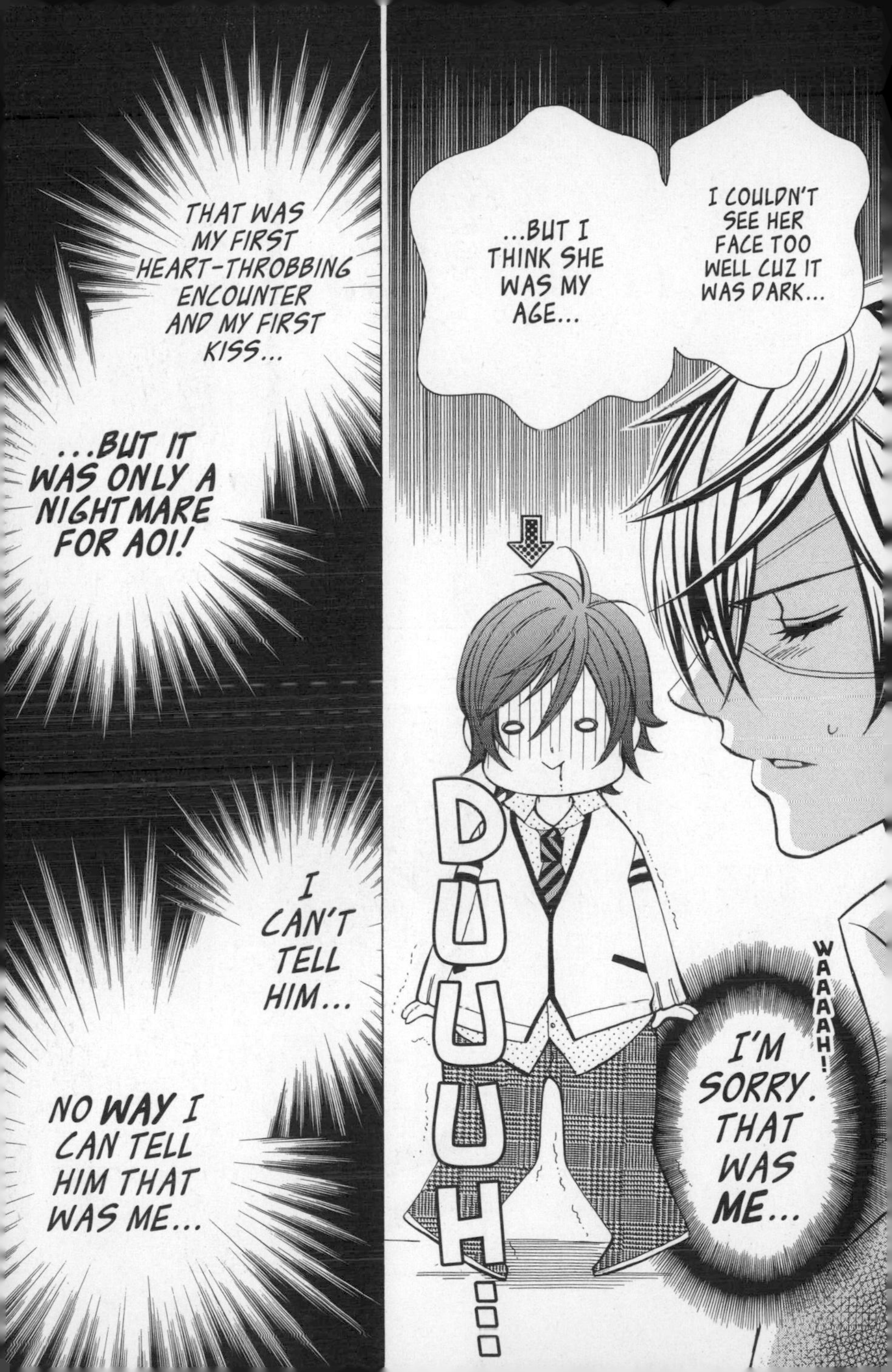
I COULDN'T SEE HER FACE TOO WELL CUZ IT WAS DARK...
...BUT I THINK SHE WAS MY AGE...
WAAAAAH!
I'M SORRY. THAT WAS ME...
DUUUUH...
THAT WAS MY FIRST HEART-THROBBING ENCOUNTER AND MY FIRST KISS...
...BUT IT WAS ONLY A NIGHTMARE FOR AOI!
I CAN'T TELL HIM...
NO WAY I CAN TELL HIM THAT WAS ME...

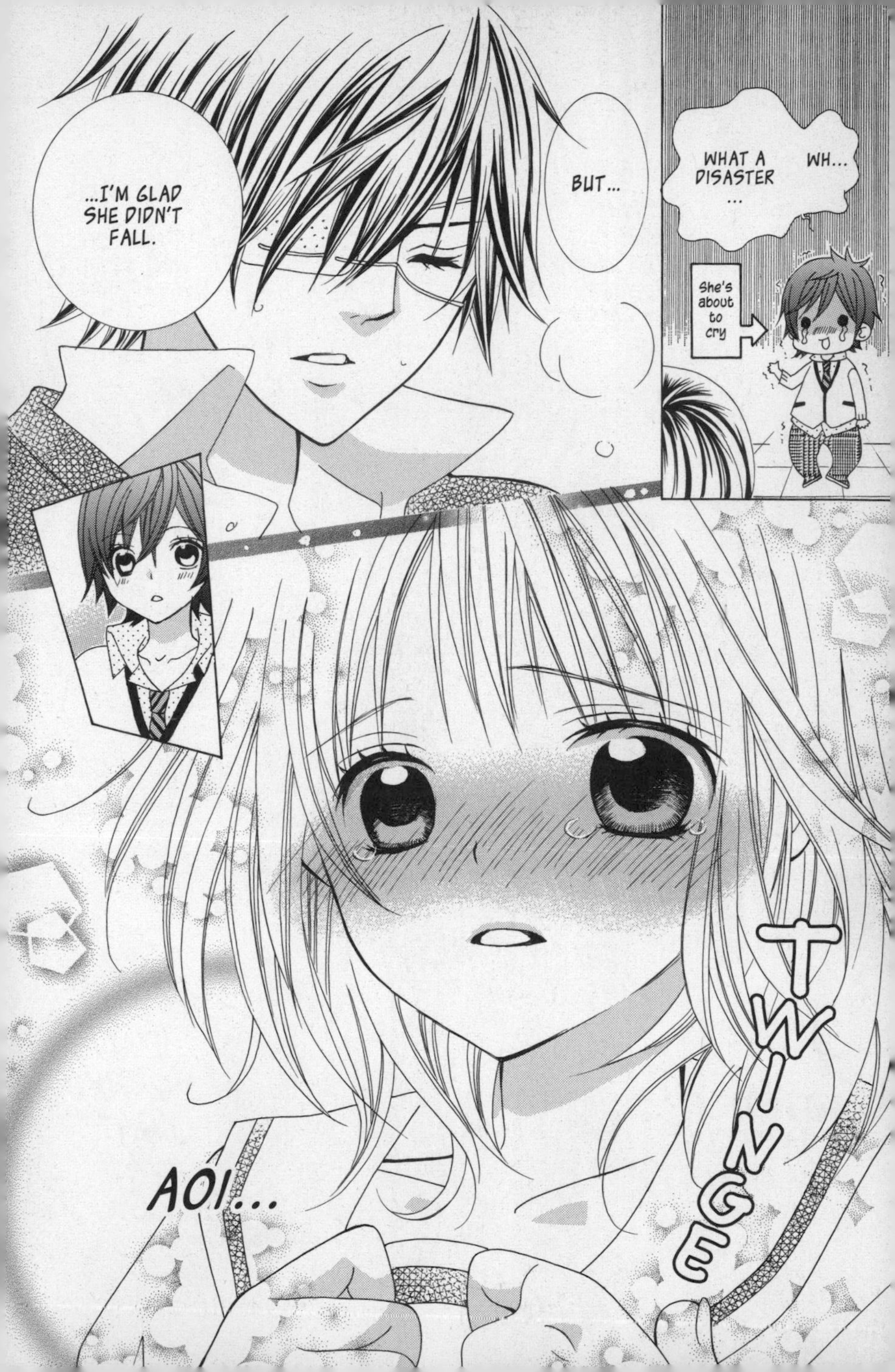
WH...
WHAT A DISASTER ...
She's about to cry
BUT...
...I'M GLAD SHE DIDN'T FALL.
TWINGE
AOI...

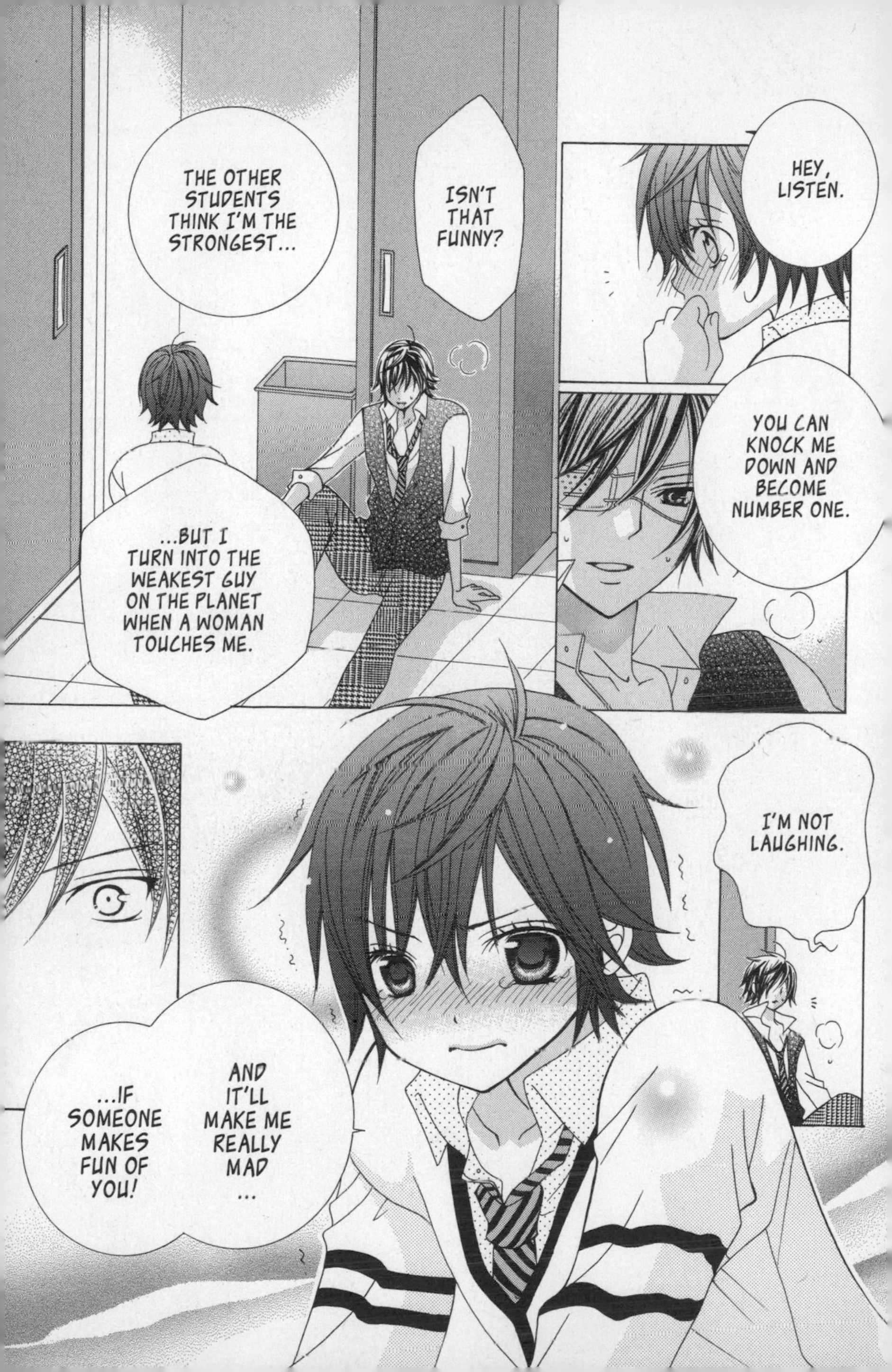
HEY, LISTEN.
YOU CAN KNOCK ME DOWN AND BECOME NUMBER ONE.
ISN'T THAT FUNNY?
THE OTHER STUDENTS THINK I'M THE STRONGEST...
...BUT I TURN INTO THE WEAKEST GUY ON THE PLANET WHEN A WOMAN TOUCHES ME.
I'M NOT LAUGHING.
AND IT'LL MAKE ME REALLY MAD ...
...IF SOMEONE MAKES FUN OF YOU!

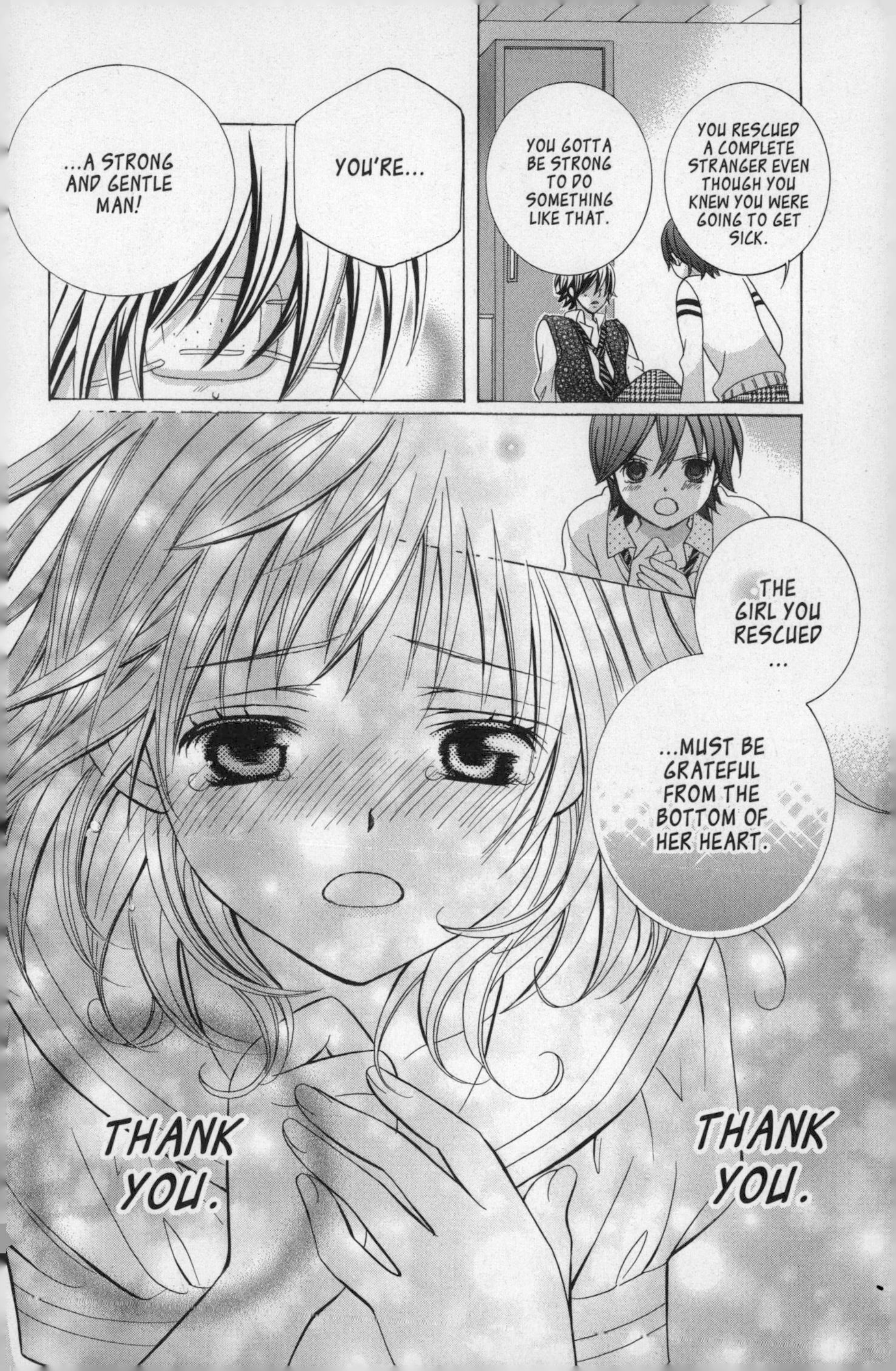
YOU RESCUED A COMPLETE STRANGER EVEN THOUGH YOU KNEW YOU WERE GOING TO GET SICK.
YOU GOTTA BE STRONG TO DO SOMETHING LIKE THAT.
YOU'RE...
...A STRONG AND GENTLE MAN!
THE GIRL YOU RESCUED ...
...MUST BE GRATEFUL FROM THE BOTTOM OF HER HEART.
THANK YOU.
THANK YOU.

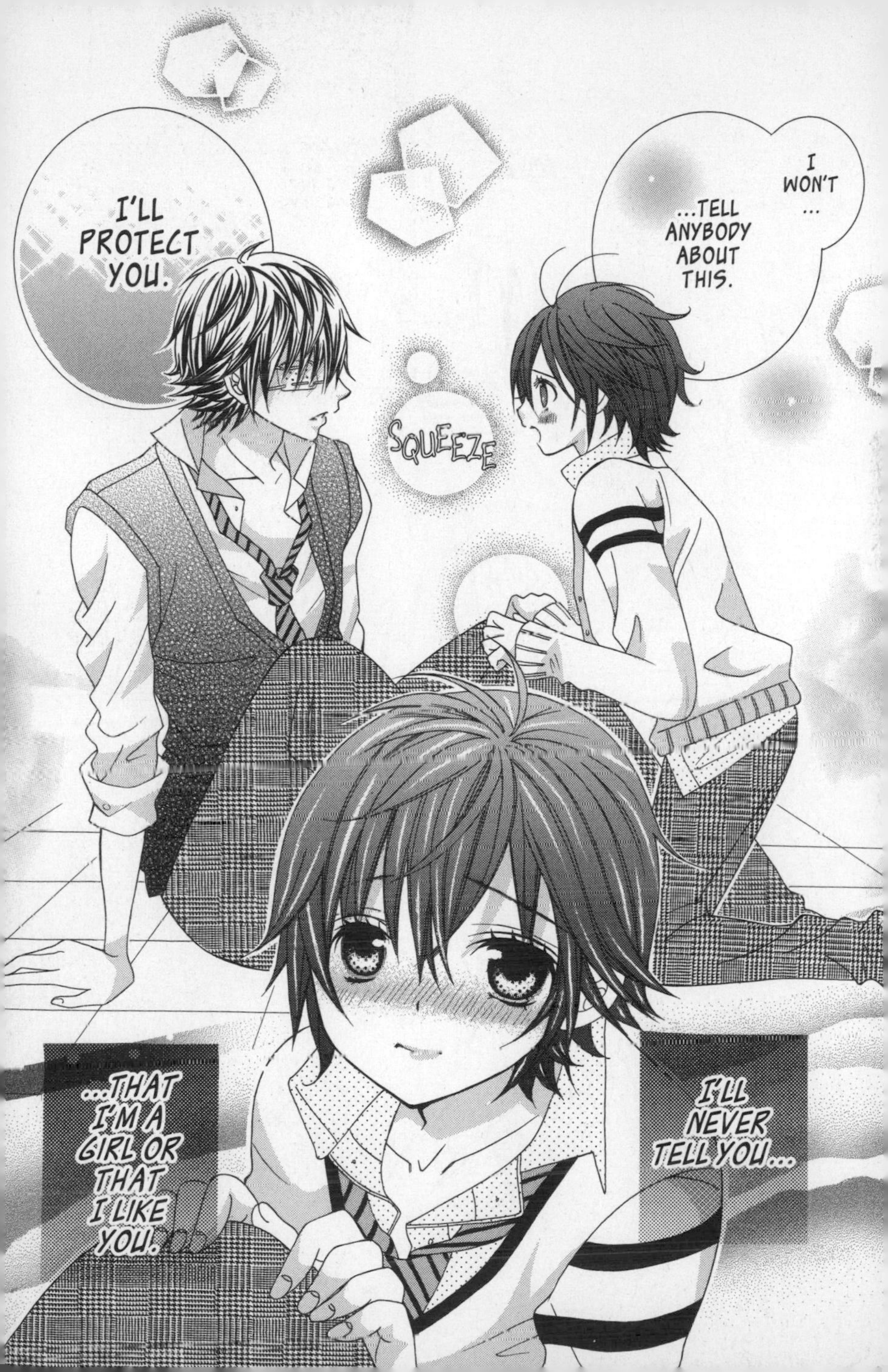
I WON'T ...
...TELL ANYBODY ABOUT THIS.
I'LL PROTECT YOU.
SQUEEZE
I'LL NEVER TELL YOU...
...THAT I'M A GIRL OR THAT I LIKE YOU.

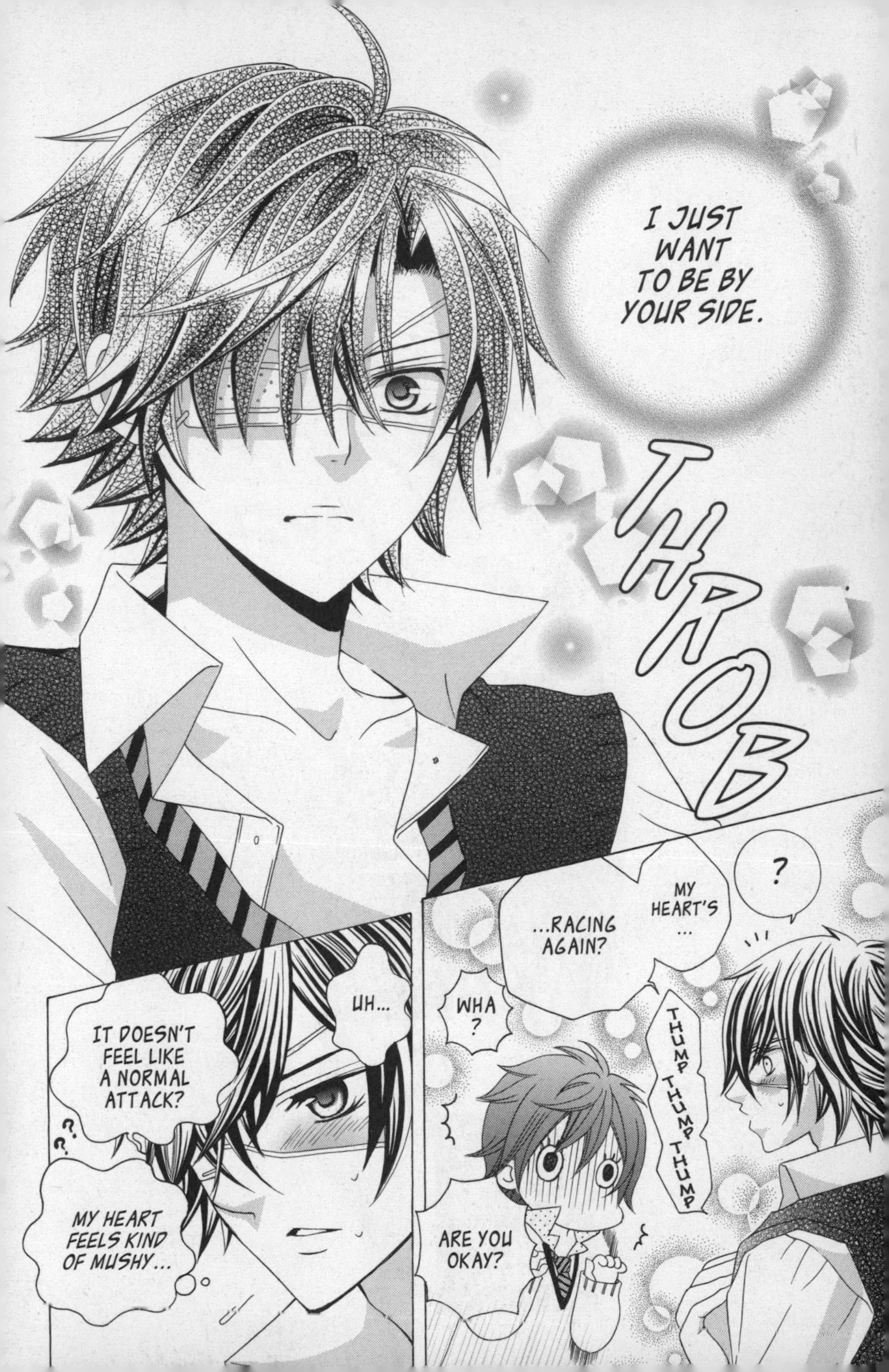
I JUST WANT TO BE BY YOUR SIDE.
THROB
?
MY HEART'S ...
...RACING AGAIN?
THUMP THUMP THUMP THUMP
WHA ?
ARE YOU OKAY?
UH...
IT DOESN'T FEEL LIKE A NORMAL ATTACK?
MY HEART FEELS KIND OF MUSHY...

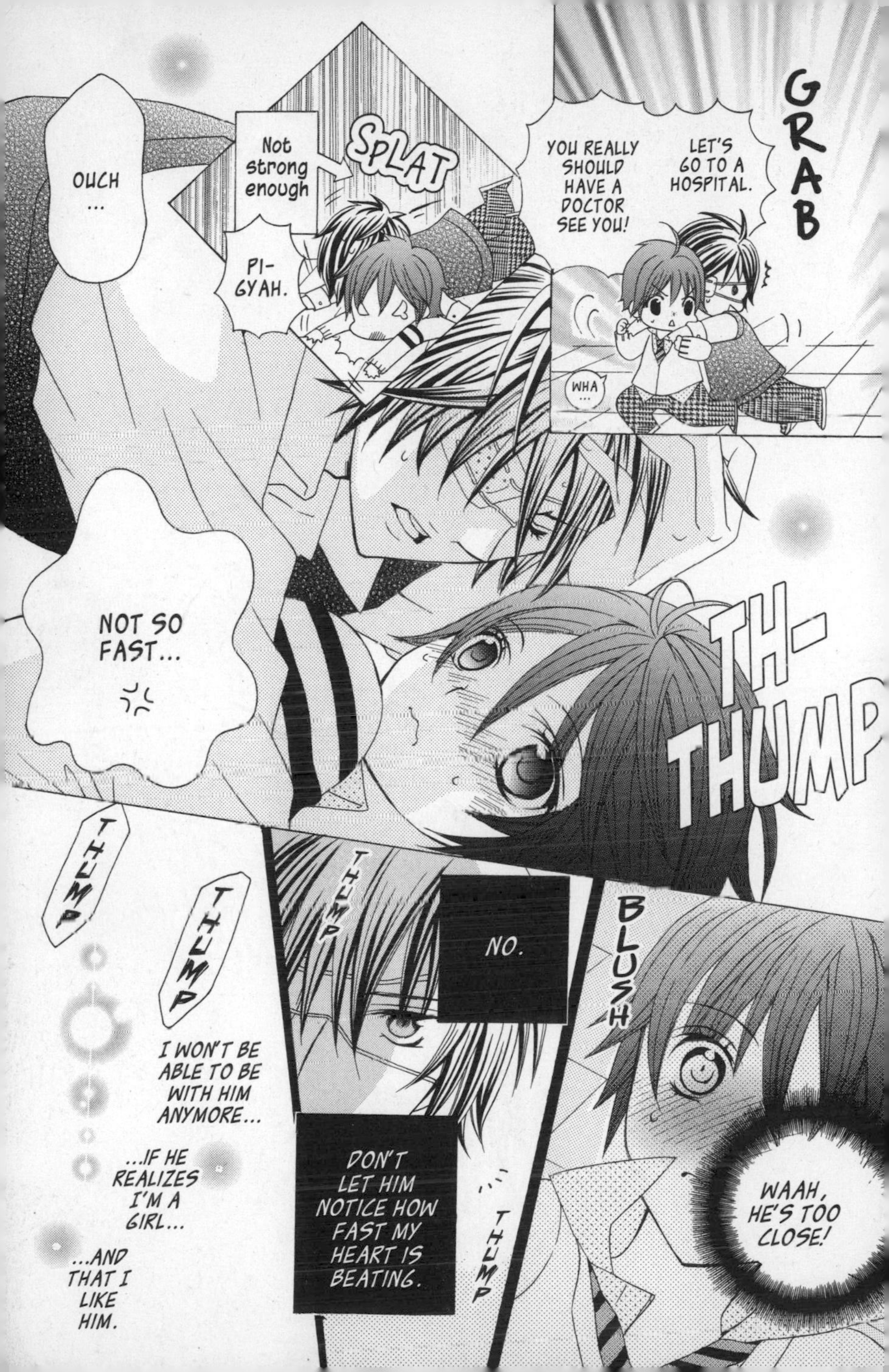
GRAB
LET'S GO TO A HOSPITAL.
YOU REALLY SHOULD HAVE A DOCTOR SEE YOU!
WHA ...
SPLAT
Not strong enough
PI-GYAH.
OUCH ...
TH-THUMP
NOT SO FAST...
BLUSH
WAAH, HE'S TOO CLOSE!
THUMP
NO.
DON'T LET HIM NOTICE HOW FAST MY HEART IS BEATING.
THUMP
THUMP
THUMP
I WON'T BE ABLE TO BE WITH HIM ANYMORE...
...IF HE REALIZES I'M A GIRL...
...AND THAT I LIKE HIM.

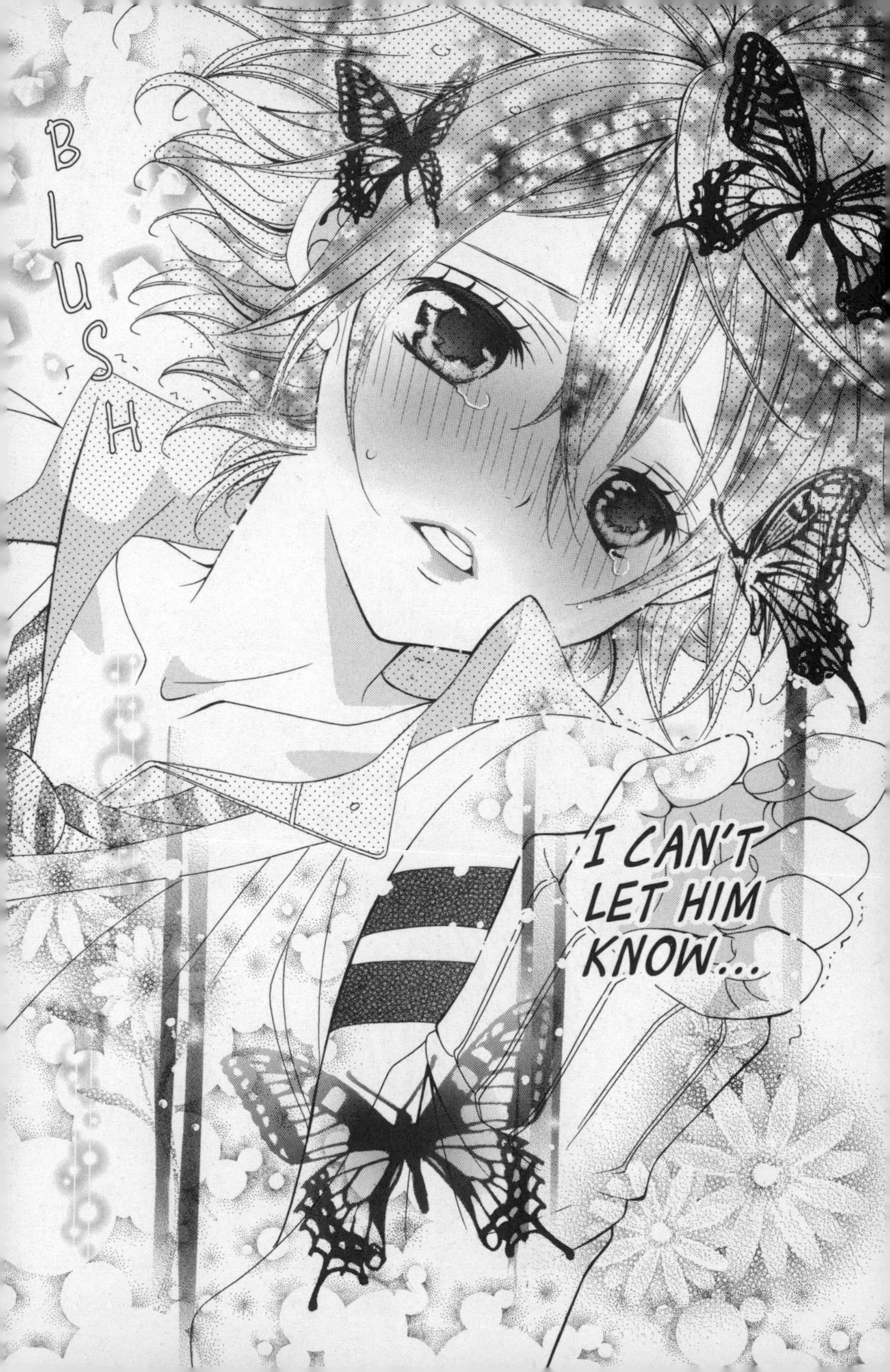
BLUSH
I CAN'T LET HIM KNOW...

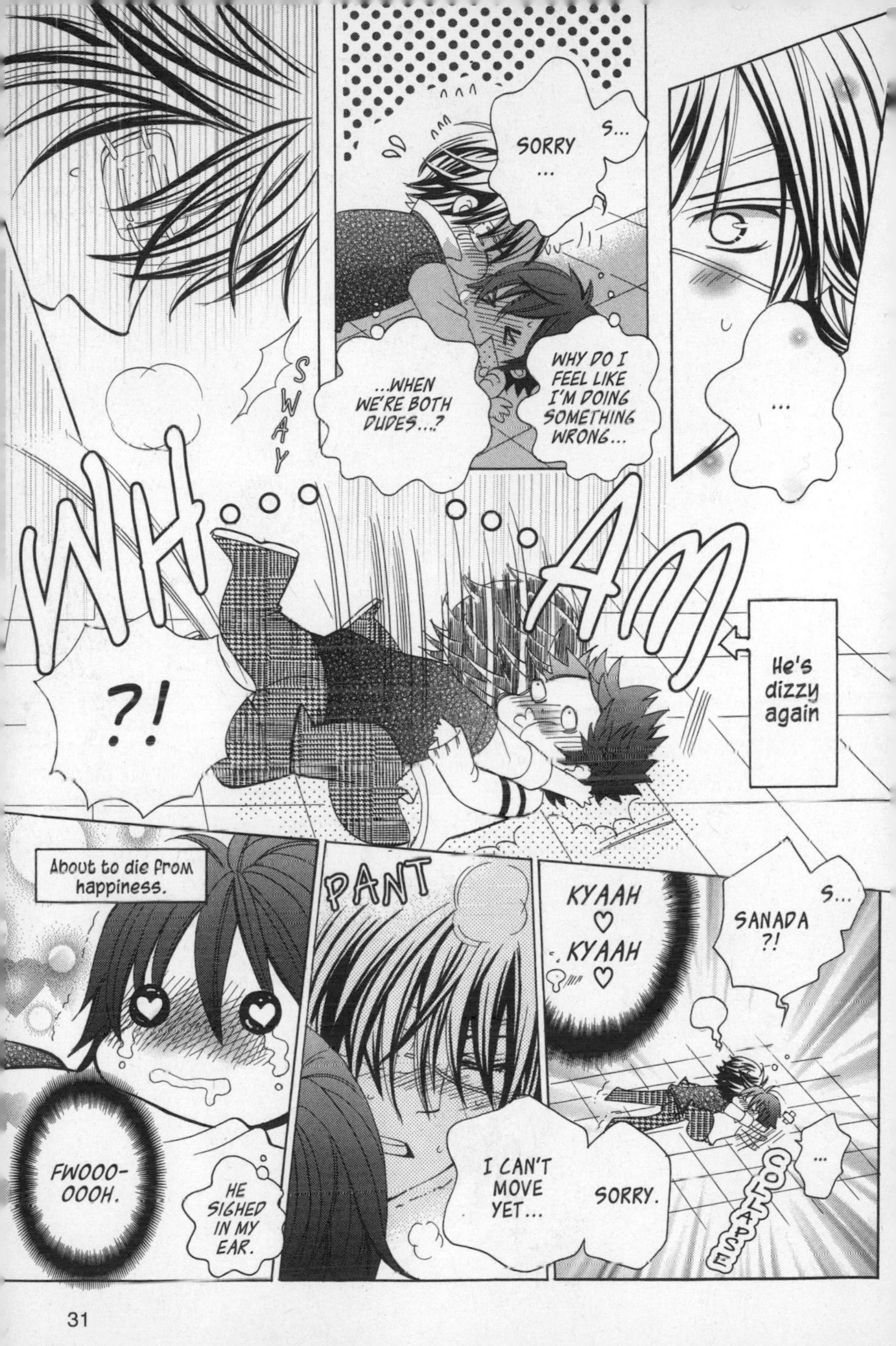
...
S... SORRY ...
WHY DO I FEEL LIKE I'M DOING SOMETHING WRONG...
...WHEN WE'RE BOTH DUDES...?
SWAY
He's dizzy again
WH...AM
?!
S... SANADA ?!
KYAAH ♡ KYAAH ♡
...
COLLAPSE
PANT
SORRY.
I CAN'T MOVE YET...
About to die from happiness.
FWOOO-OOOH.
HE SIGHED IN MY EAR.

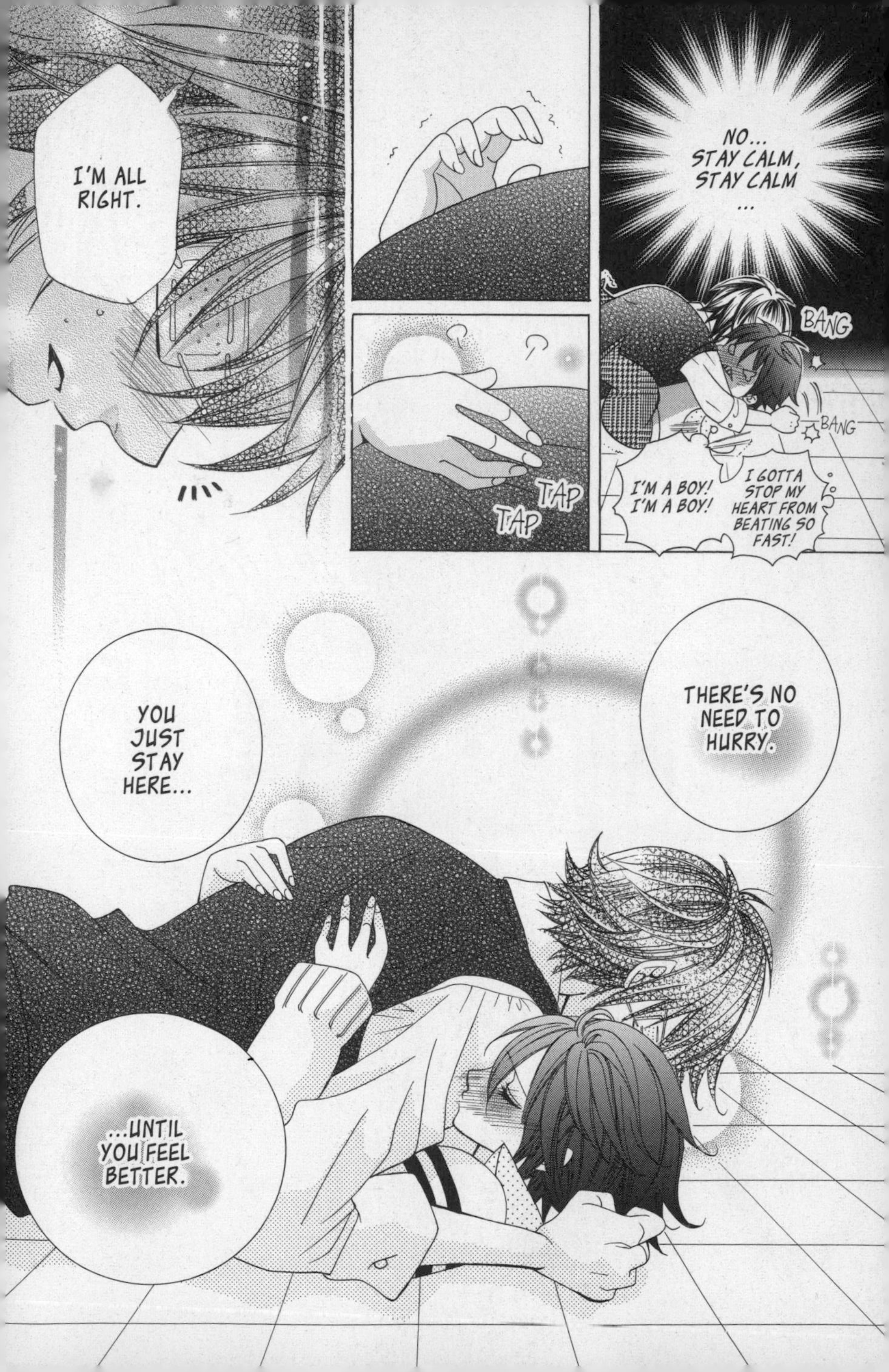
NO... STAY CALM, STAY CALM ...
BANG
BANG
I GOTTA STOP MY HEART FROM BEATING SO FAST!
I'M A BOY! I'M A BOY!
TAP
TAP
I'M ALL RIGHT.
THERE'S NO NEED TO HURRY.
YOU JUST STAY HERE...
...UNTIL YOU FEEL BETTER.

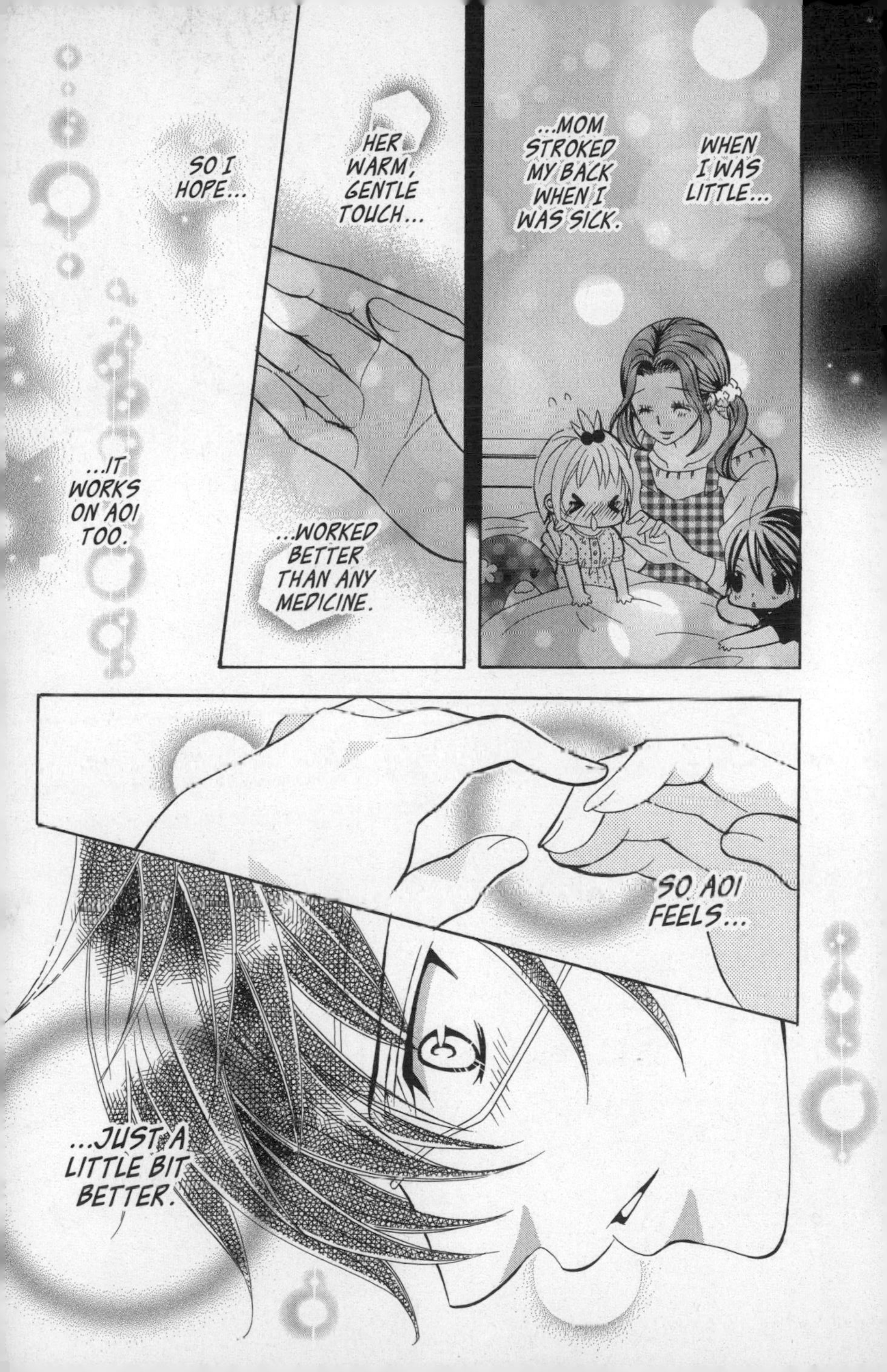
WHEN I WAS LITTLE...
...MOM STROKED MY BACK WHEN I WAS SICK.
HER WARM, GENTLE TOUCH...
...WORKED BETTER THAN ANY MEDICINE.
SO I HOPE...
...IT WORKS ON AOI TOO.
SO AOI FEELS...
...JUST A LITTLE BIT BETTER.

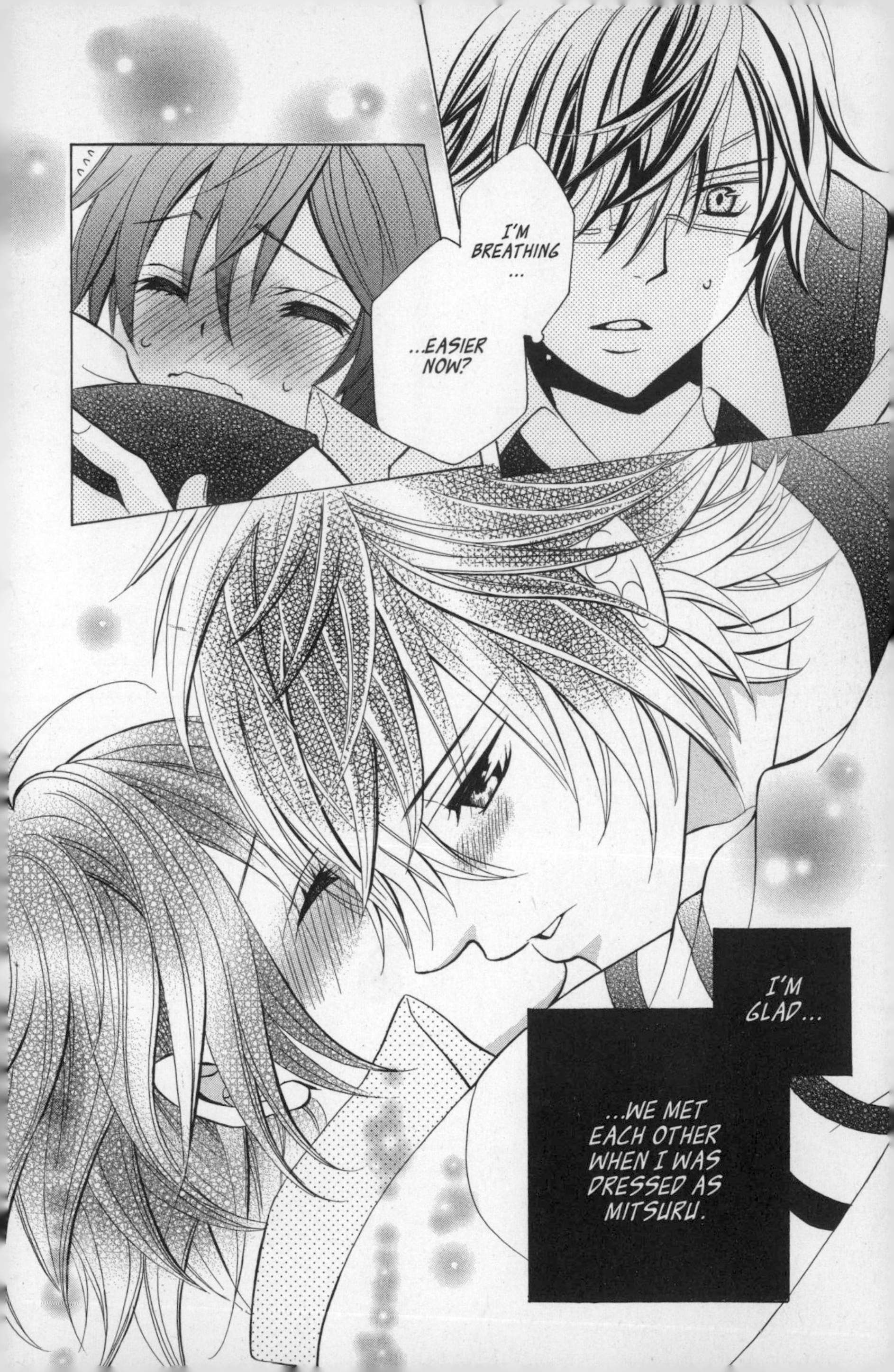
I'M BREATHING ...
...EASIER NOW?
I'M GLAD...
...WE MET EACH OTHER WHEN I WAS DRESSED AS MITSURU.

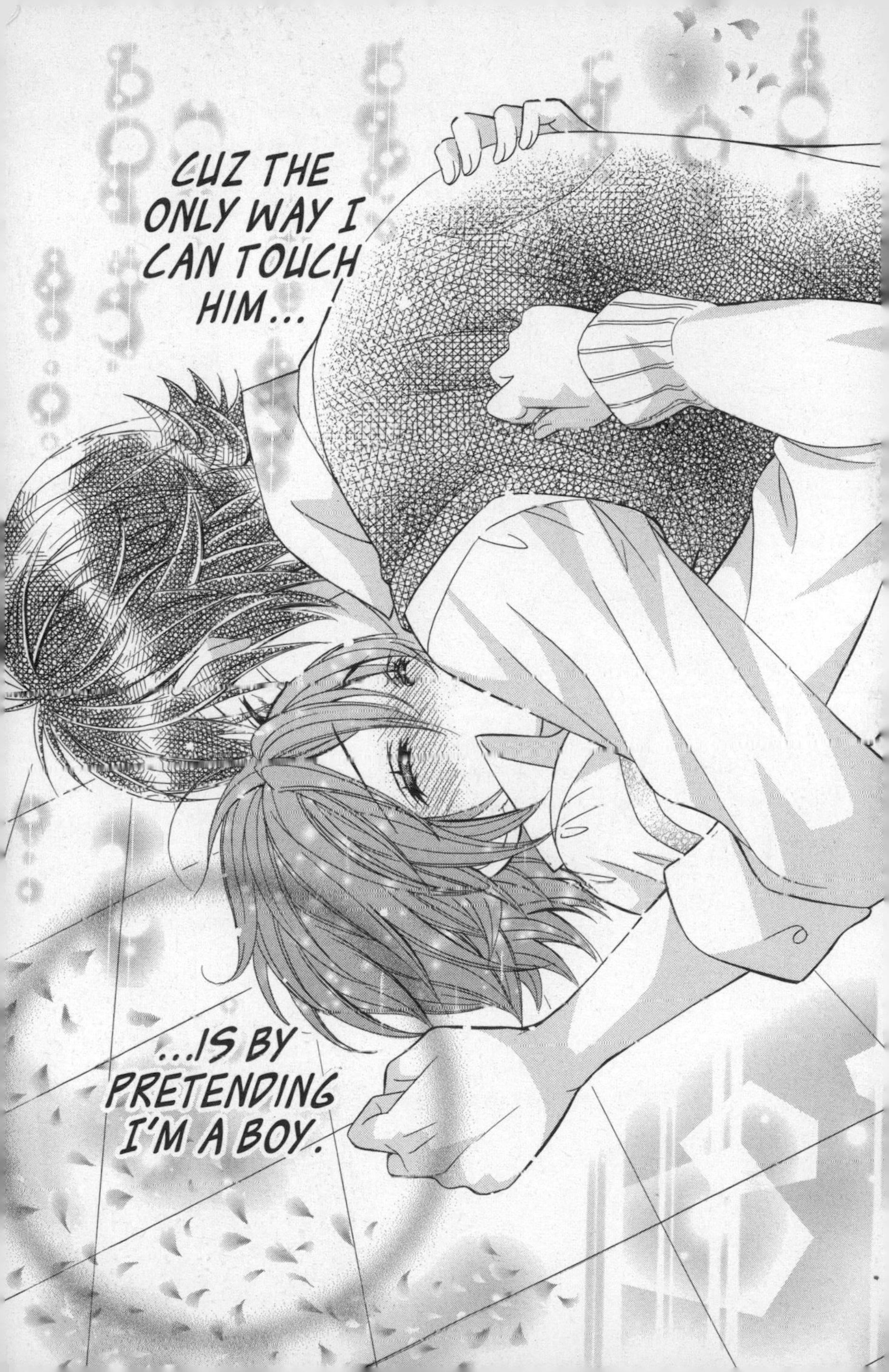
CUZ THE ONLY WAY I CAN TOUCH HIM...
...IS BY PRETENDING I'M A BOY.

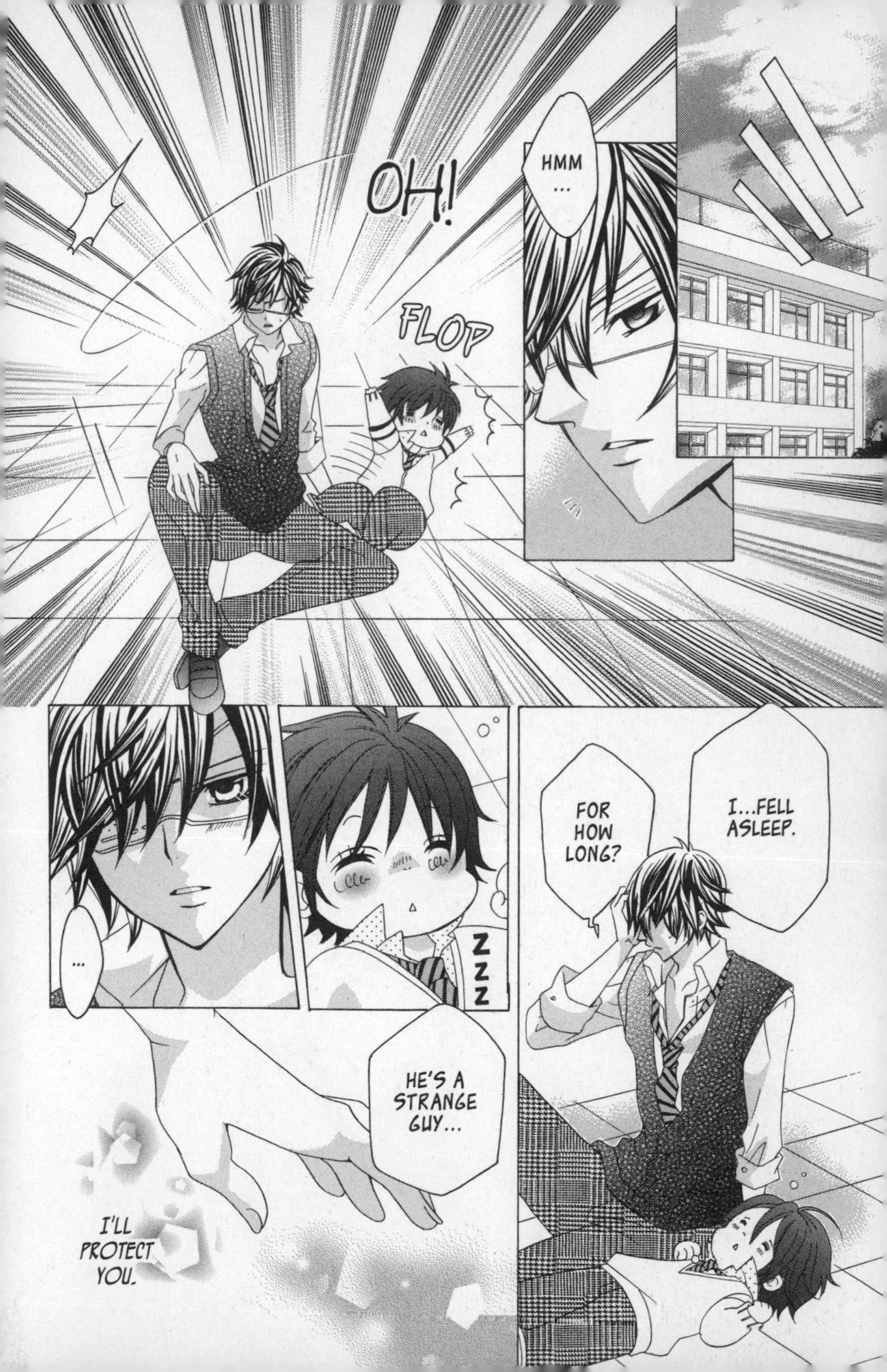
HMM ...
OH!
FLOP
I...FELL ASLEEP.
FOR HOW LONG?
ZZZ
...
HE'S A STRANGE GUY...
I'LL PROTECT YOU.

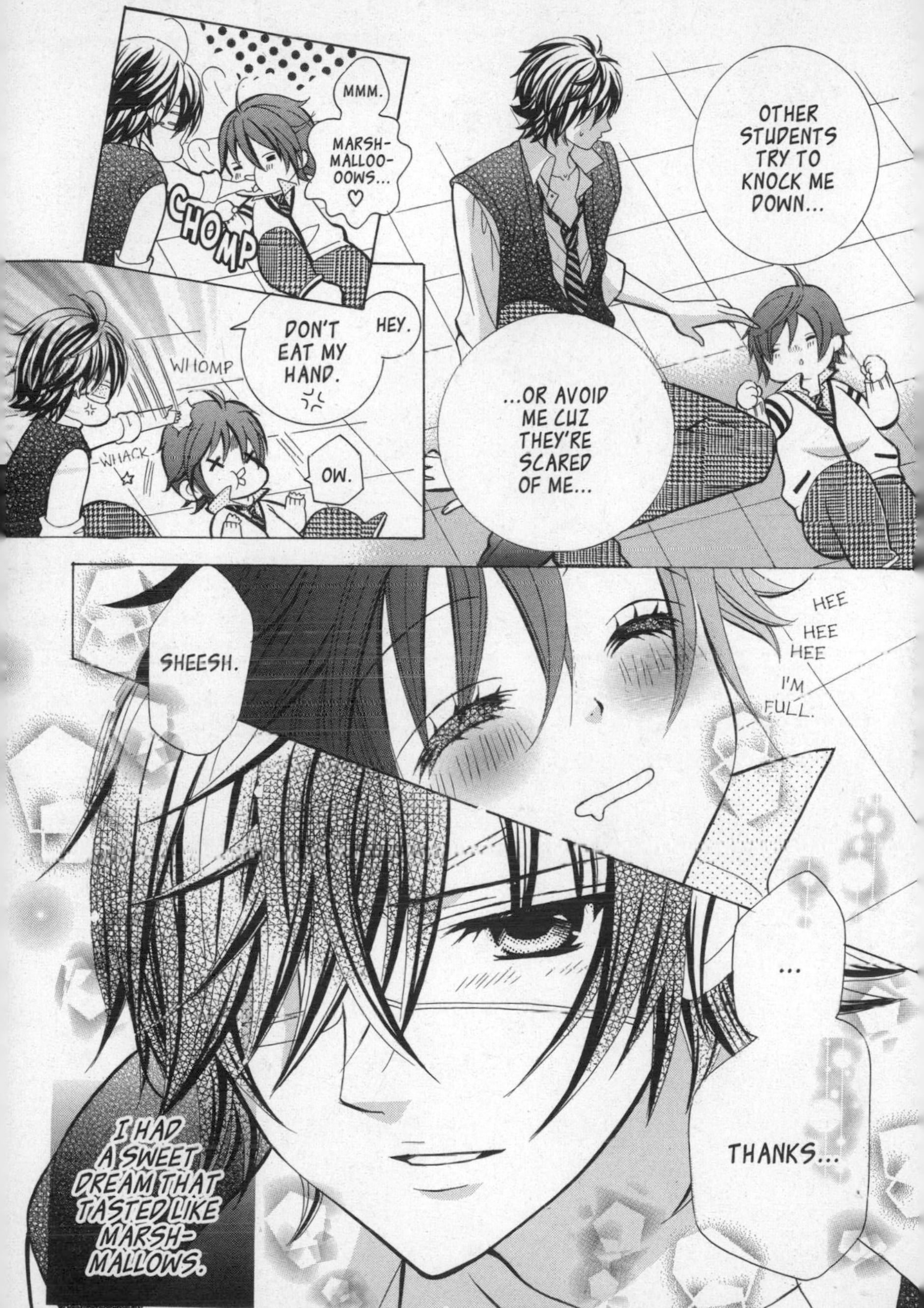
OTHER STUDENTS TRY TO KNOCK ME DOWN...
...OR AVOID ME CUZ THEY'RE SCARED OF ME...
MMM.
MARSH-MALLOOOOWS... ♡
CHOMP
HEY.
DON'T EAT MY HAND.
WHOMP
WHACK
OW.
HEE HEE HEE
I'M FULL.
SHEESH.
...
THANKS...
I HAD A SWEET DREAM THAT TASTED LIKE MARSH-MALLOWS.

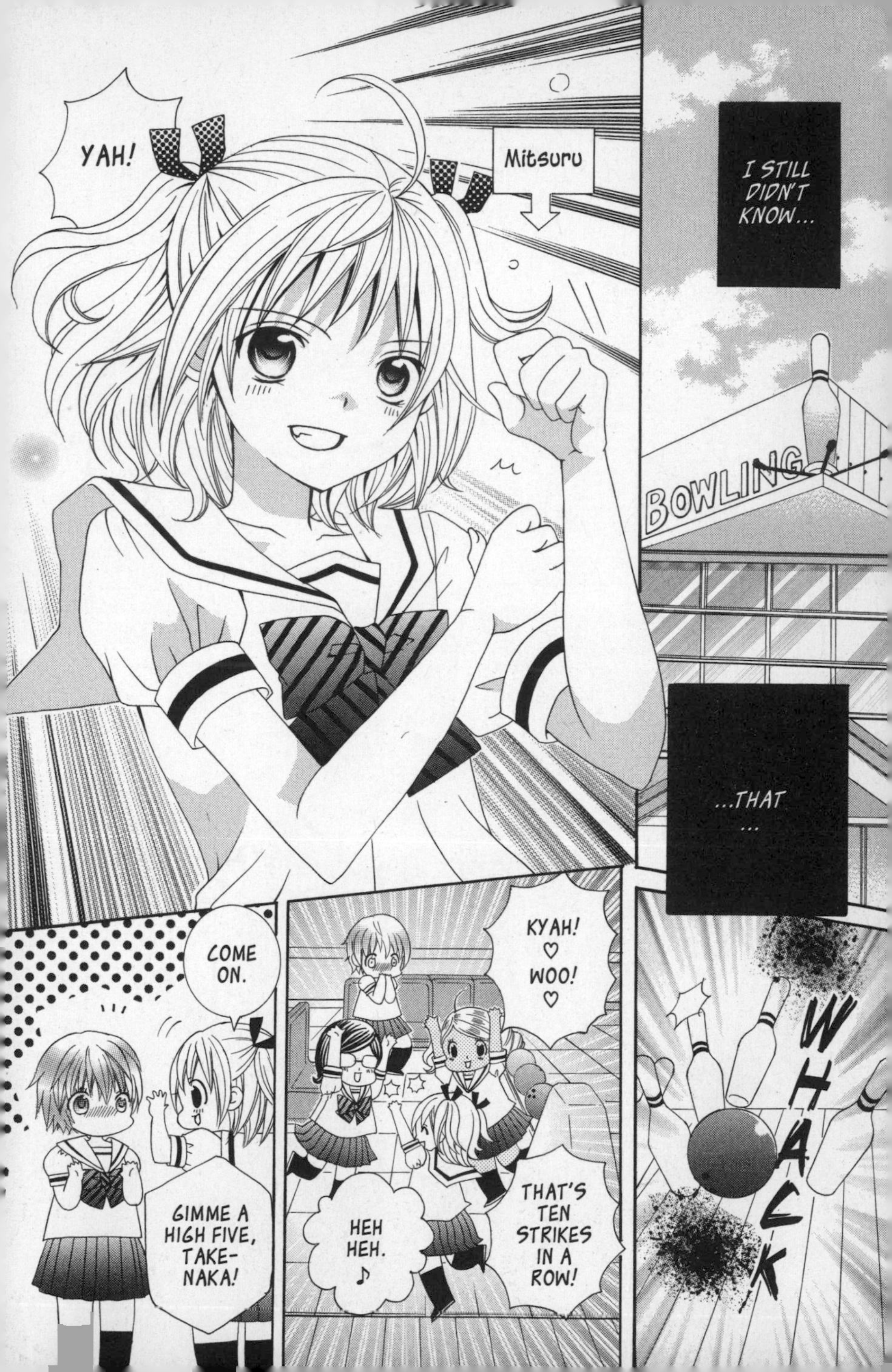
I STILL DIDN'T KNOW...
...THAT ...
YAH!
Mitsuru
BOWLING
WHACK
KYAH! ♡ WOO! ♡
THAT'S TEN STRIKES IN A ROW!
HEH HEH. ♪
COME ON.
GIMME A HIGH FIVE, TAKE-NAKA!

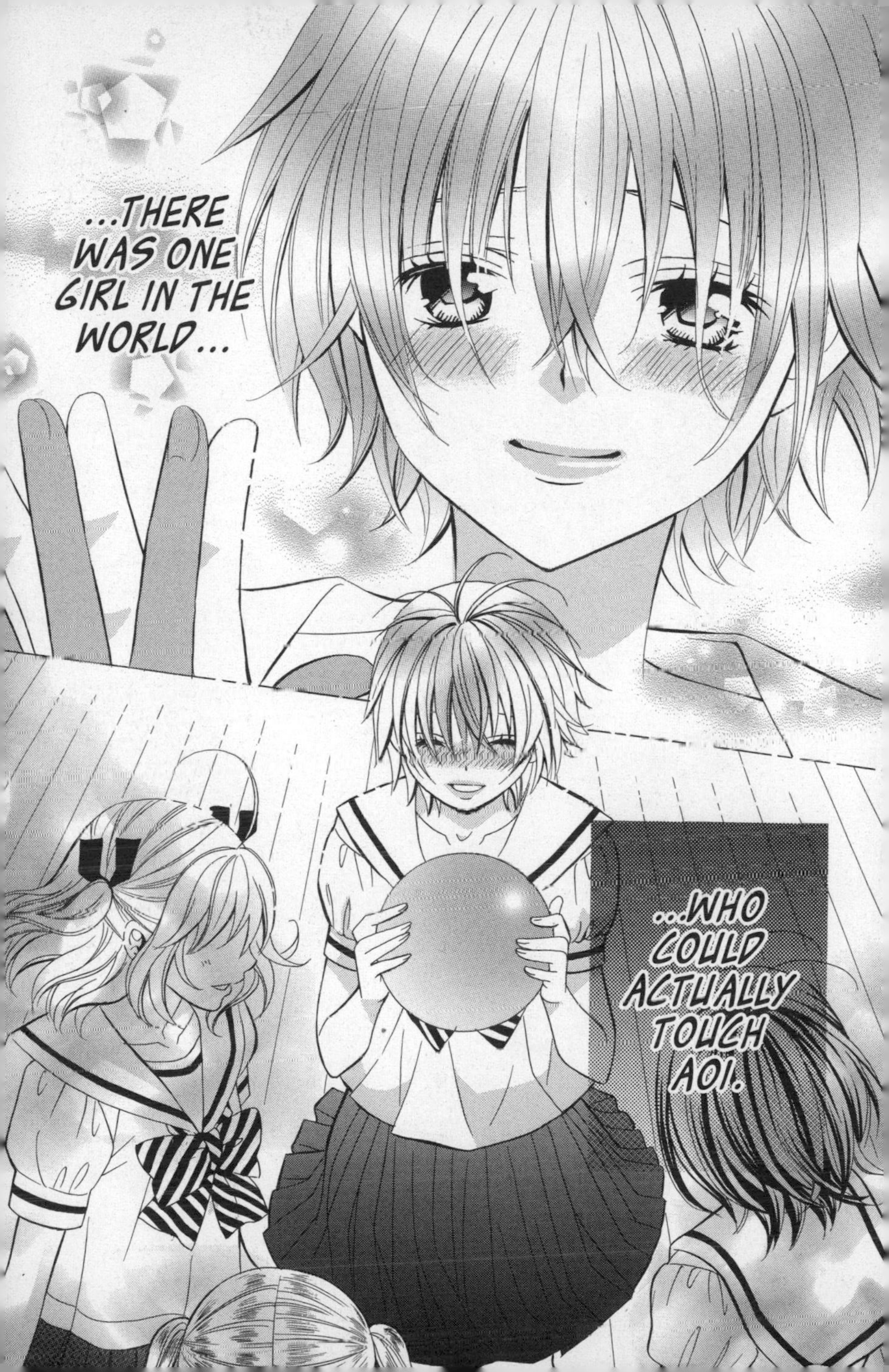
...THERE WAS ONE GIRL IN THE WORLD...
...WHO COULD ACTUALLY TOUCH AOI.

Chapter 7

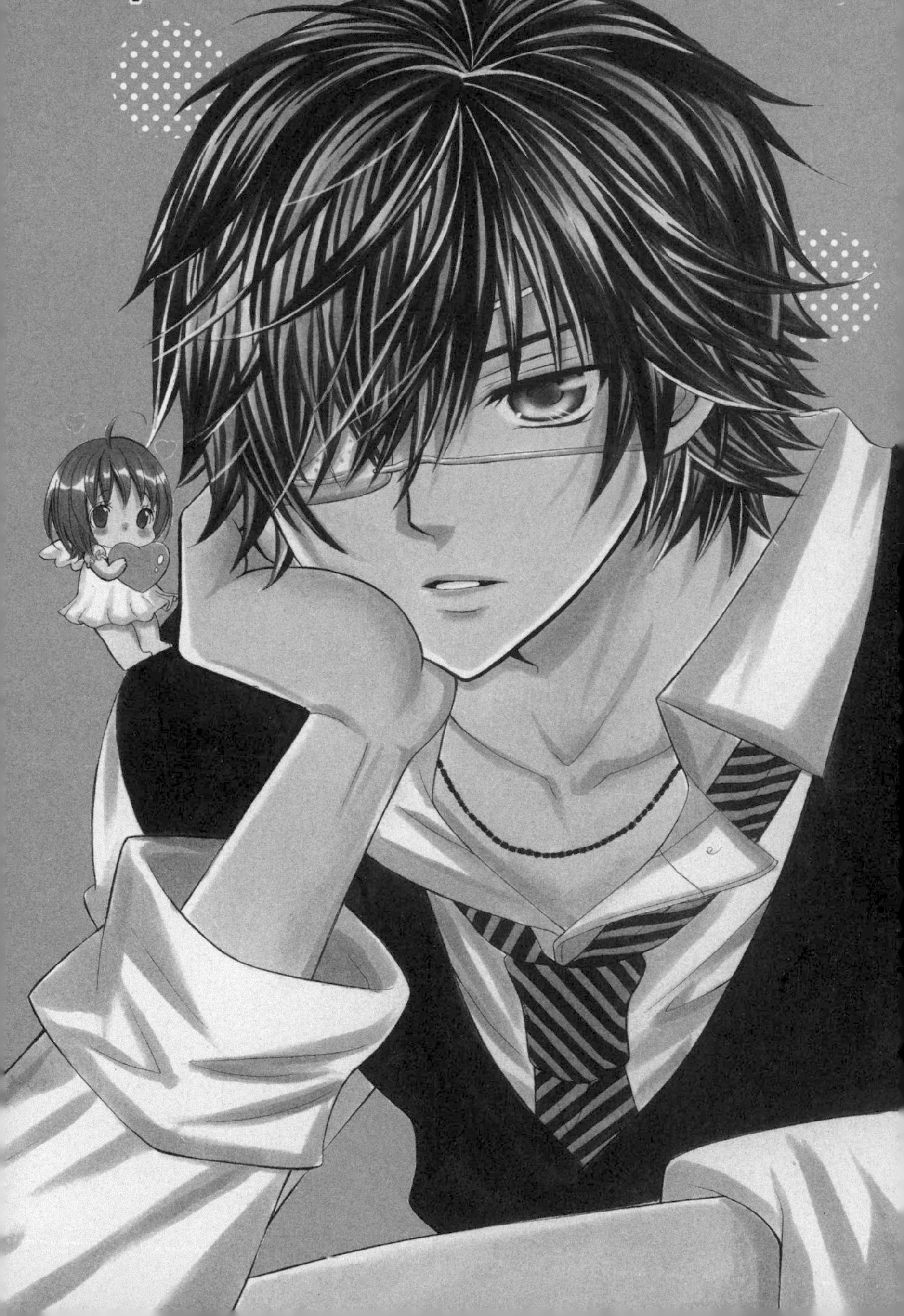

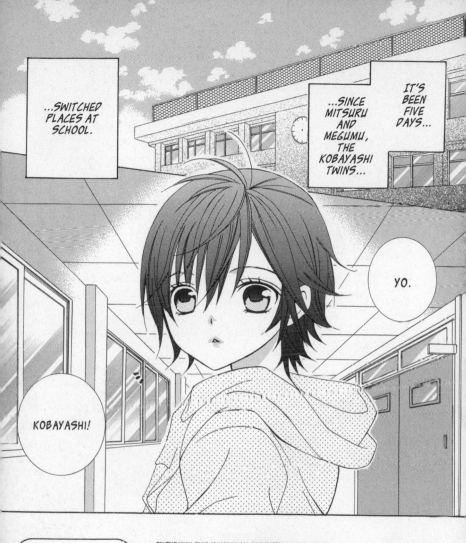

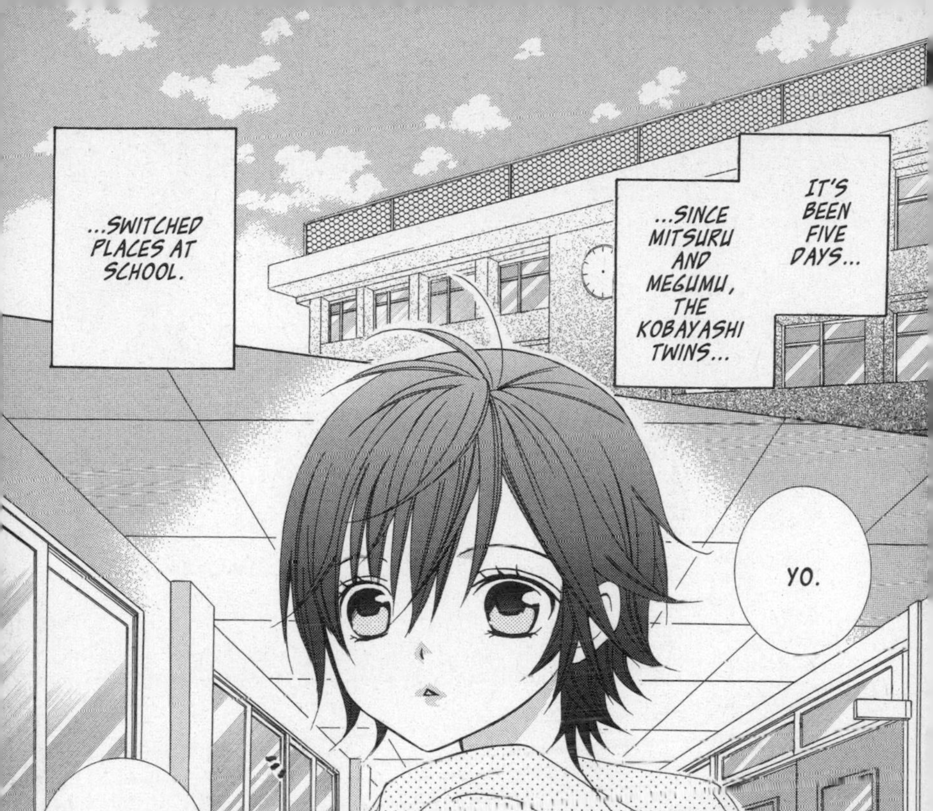
IT'S BEEN FIVE DAYS...
...SINCE MITSURU AND MEGUMU, THE KOBAYASHI TWINS...
...SWITCHED PLACES AT SCHOOL.
YO.
KOBAYASHI!

I DREW FOUR COLOR CHAPTER TITLE PAGES IN SUCCESSION, CHAPTER 7 THROUGH CHAPTER 10!! I ENJOYED THINKING ABOUT WHO TO DRAW EACH TIME.♡♡

BY THE WAY, THIS IS HOW YOU CAN DISTINGUISH MITSURU CROSS-DRESSING FROM MEGO. MITSURU WEARS TWO BOWS ON HIS WIG AND CARRIES HIS BAMBOO SWORD AROUND. MEGO DOESN'T WEAR ANY BOWS.

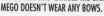

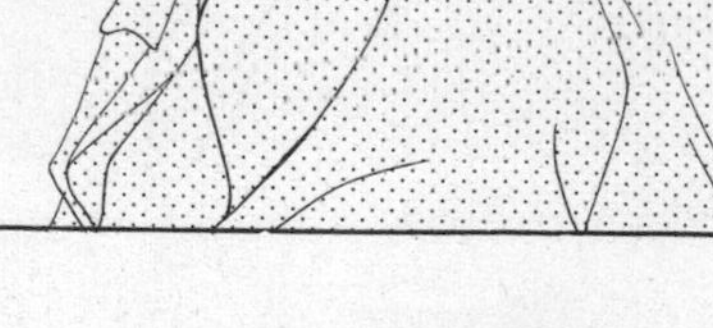
Mitsuru
Mego

SO THE VOLUME 1 COVER FEATURES THE TWO HEROES, MITSURU (AS MEGO) AND AOI. I'M SORRY IF YOU DIDN'T NOTICE! THE VOLUME 2 COVER FEATURES MEGO AND AOI. (*SMILE*)

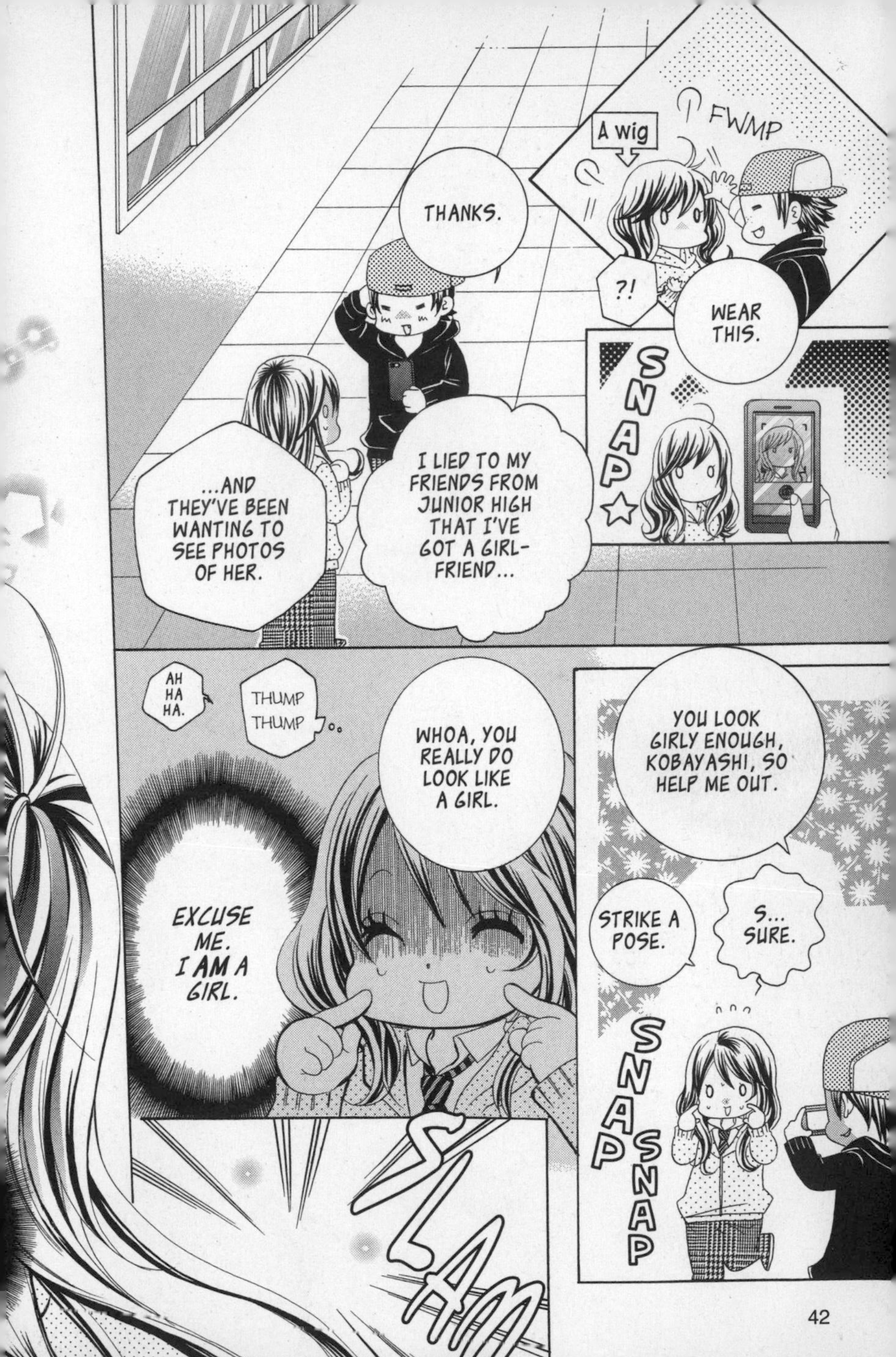
FWMP
A wig
?!
WEAR THIS.
SNAP ☆
THANKS.
I LIED TO MY FRIENDS FROM JUNIOR HIGH THAT I'VE GOT A GIRL-FRIEND...
...AND THEY'VE BEEN WANTING TO SEE PHOTOS OF HER.
YOU LOOK GIRLY ENOUGH, KOBAYASHI, SO HELP ME OUT.
S... SURE.
STRIKE A POSE.
SNAP SNAP
SNAP
WHOA, YOU REALLY DO LOOK LIKE A GIRL.
THUMP THUMP
AH HA HA.
EXCUSE ME. I AM A GIRL.
SLAM

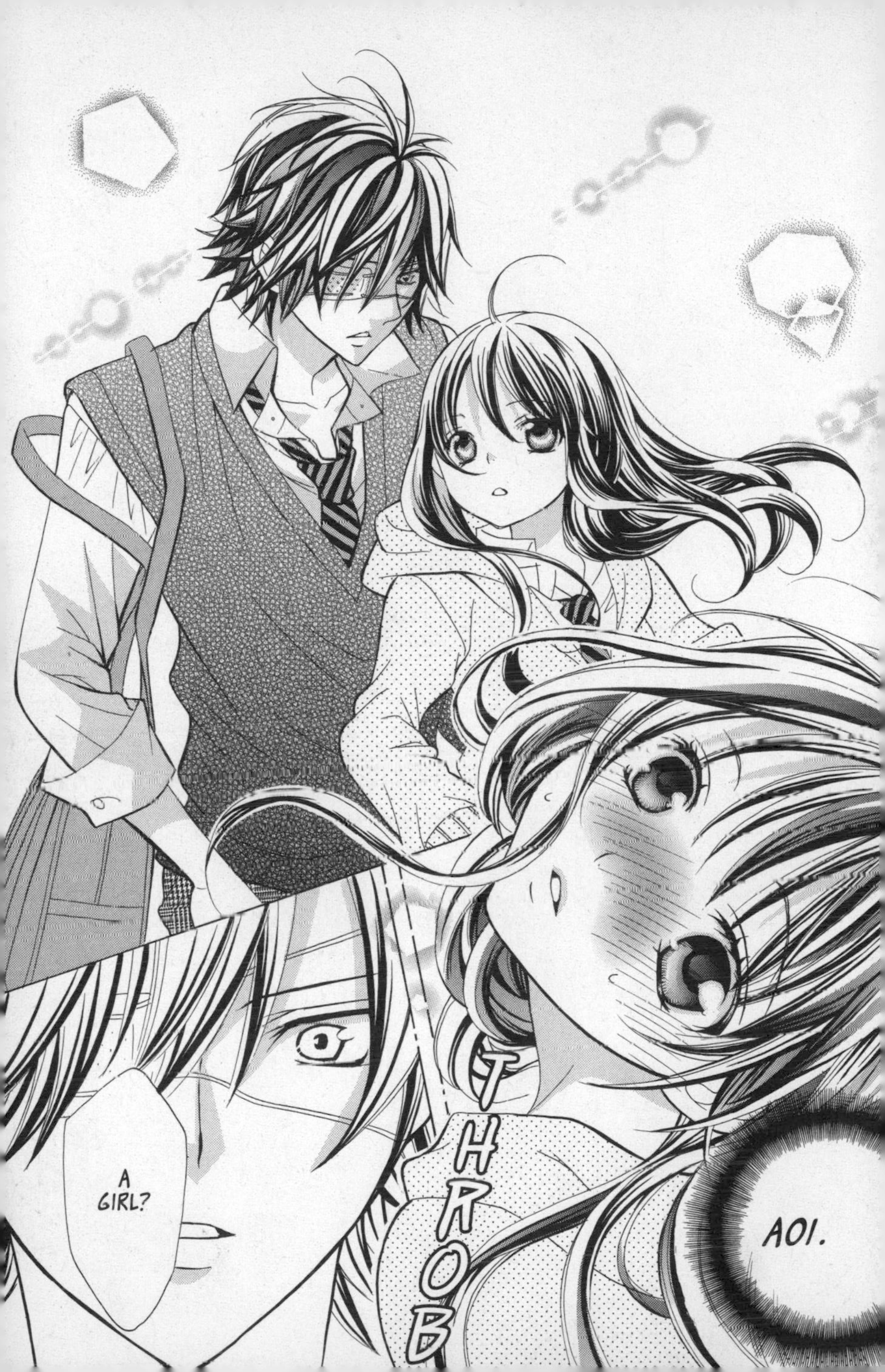
AOI.
THROB
A GIRL?

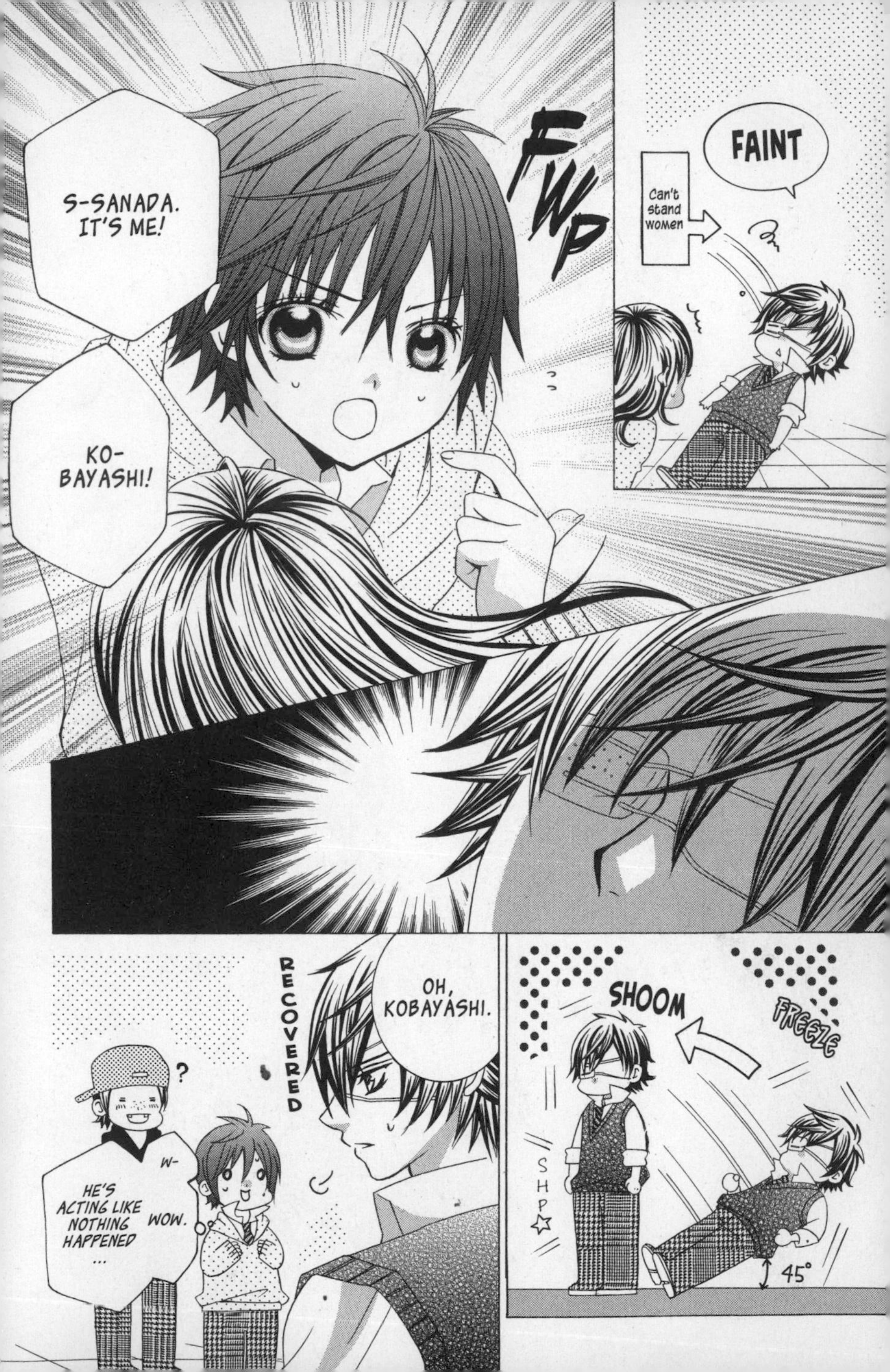
FAINT
Can't stand women
FWP
S-SANADA. IT'S ME!
KO-BAYASHI!
SHOOM
FREEZE
SHP☆
45°
OH, KOBAYASHI.
RECOVERED
?
W- WOW.
HE'S ACTING LIKE NOTHING HAPPENED ...

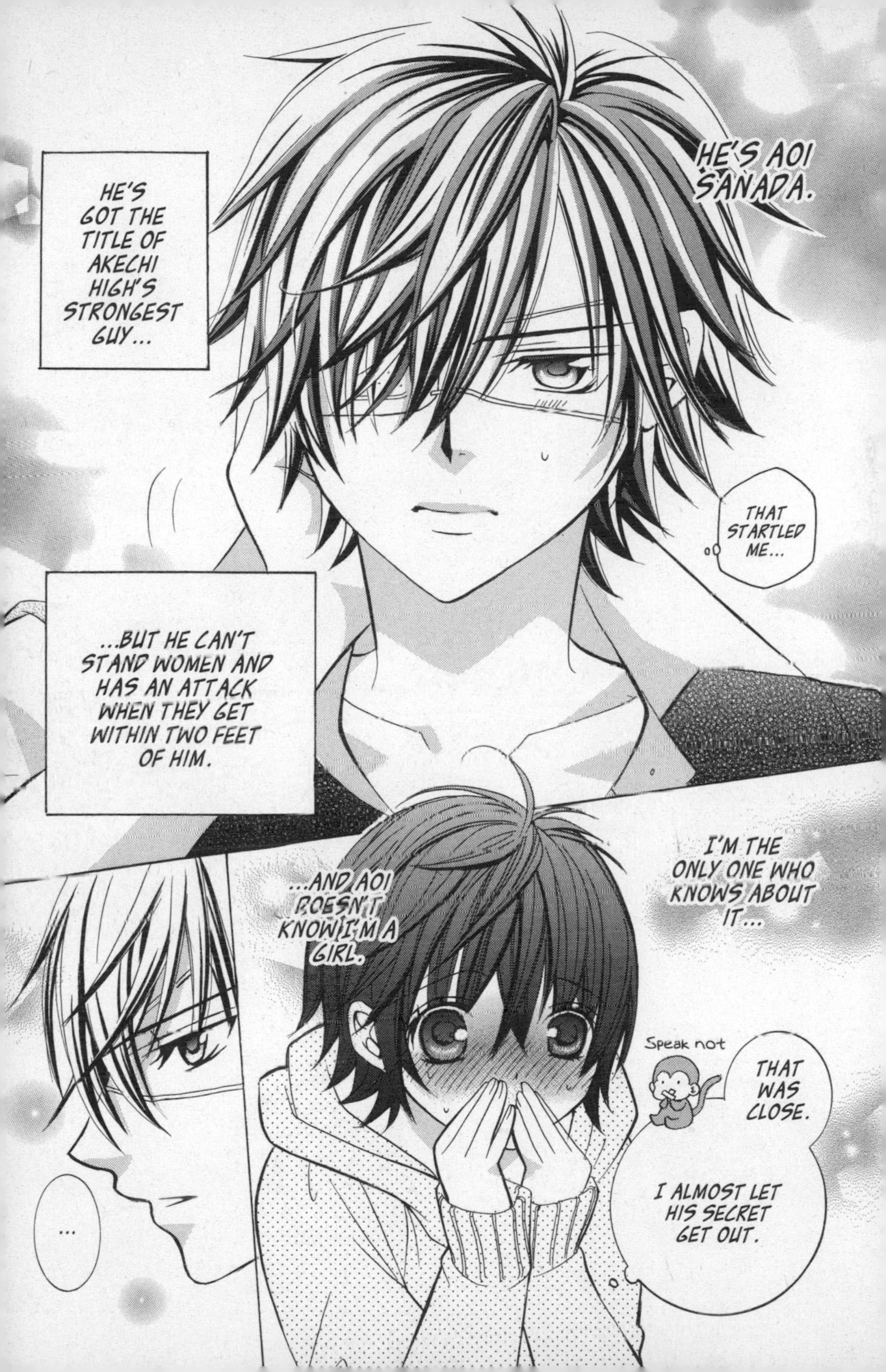
HE'S AOI SANADA.
HE'S GOT THE TITLE OF AKECHI HIGH'S STRONGEST GUY...
THAT STARTLED ME...
...BUT HE CAN'T STAND WOMEN AND HAS AN ATTACK WHEN THEY GET WITHIN TWO FEET OF HIM.
I'M THE ONLY ONE WHO KNOWS ABOUT IT...
...AND AOI DOESN'T KNOW I'M A GIRL.
Speak not
THAT WAS CLOSE.
I ALMOST LET HIS SECRET GET OUT.
...

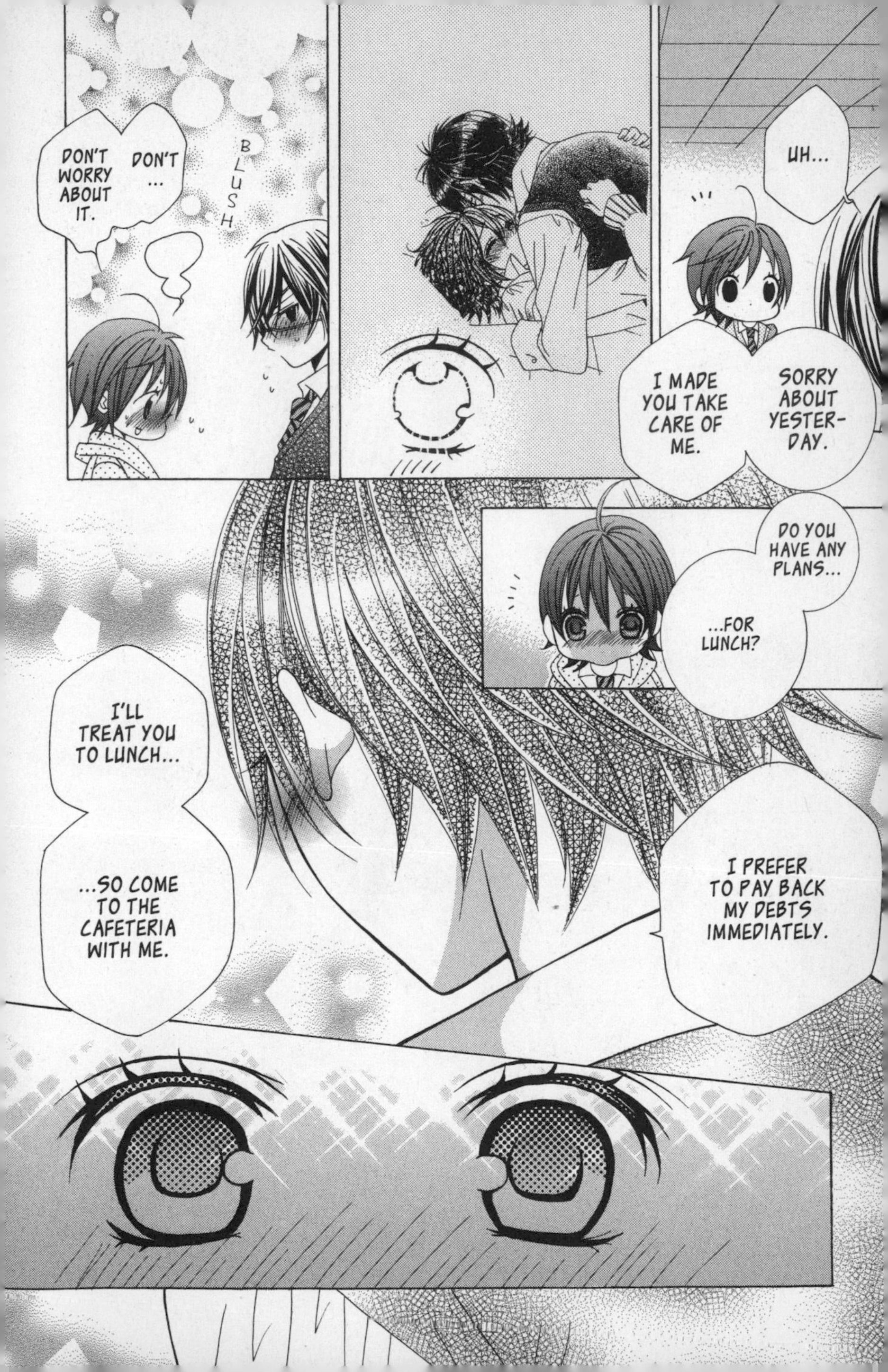
UH...
SORRY ABOUT YESTER-DAY.
I MADE YOU TAKE CARE OF ME.
DON'T ...
BLUSH
DON'T WORRY ABOUT IT.
DO YOU HAVE ANY PLANS...
...FOR LUNCH?
I PREFER TO PAY BACK MY DEBTS IMMEDIATELY.
I'LL TREAT YOU TO LUNCH...
...SO COME TO THE CAFETERIA WITH ME.

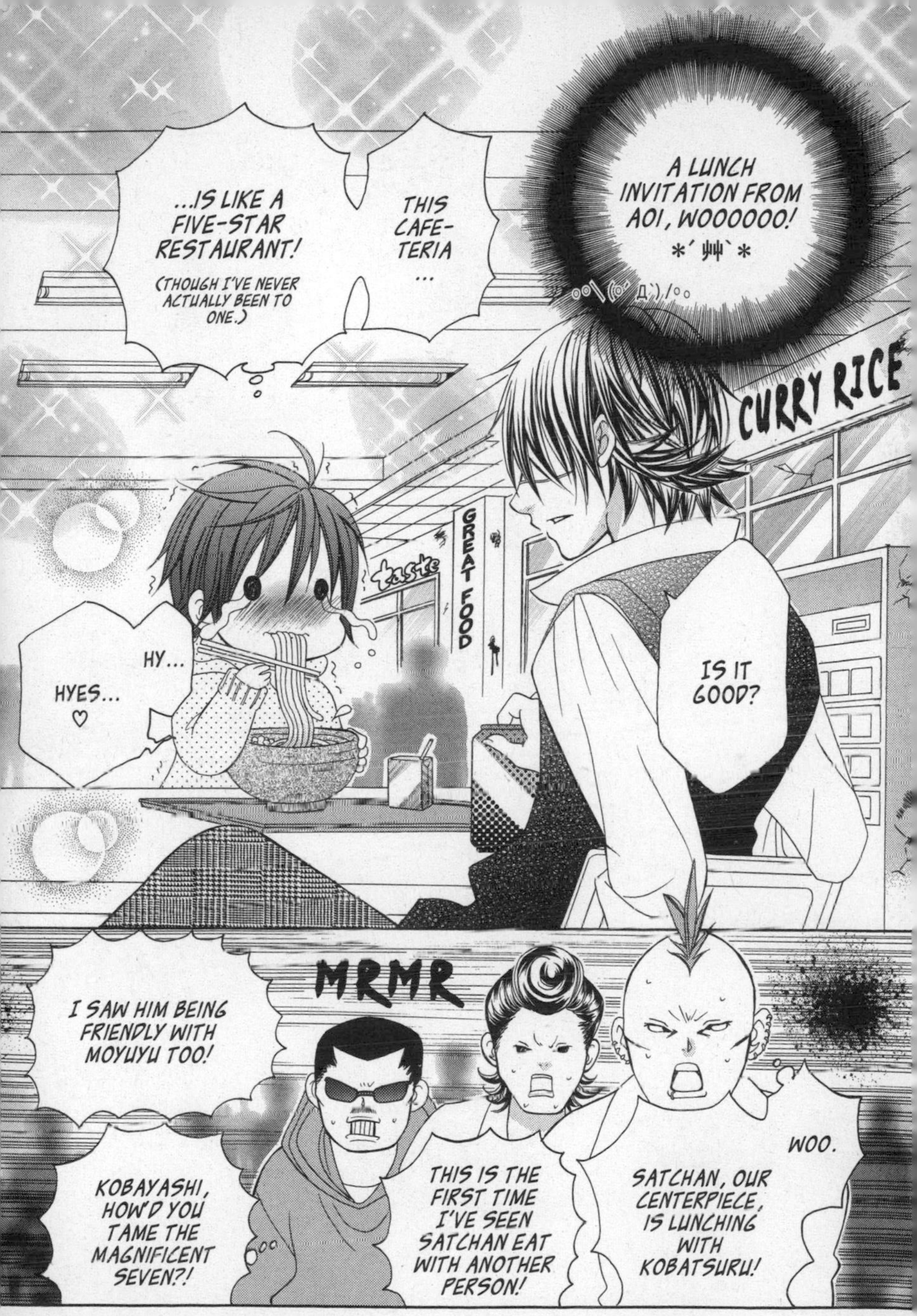
A LUNCH INVITATION FROM AOI, WOOOOOO!
´艸`
THIS CAFETERIA...
...IS LIKE A FIVE-STAR RESTAURANT!
(THOUGH I'VE NEVER ACTUALLY BEEN TO ONE.)
CURRY RICE
GREAT FOOD
taste
IS IT GOOD?
HY...
HYES... ♡
WOO.
MRMR
SATCHAN, OUR CENTERPIECE, IS LUNCHING WITH KOBATSURU!
THIS IS THE FIRST TIME I'VE SEEN SATCHAN EAT WITH ANOTHER PERSON!
I SAW HIM BEING FRIENDLY WITH MOYUYU TOO!
KOBAYASHI, HOW'D YOU TAME THE MAGNIFICENT SEVEN?!

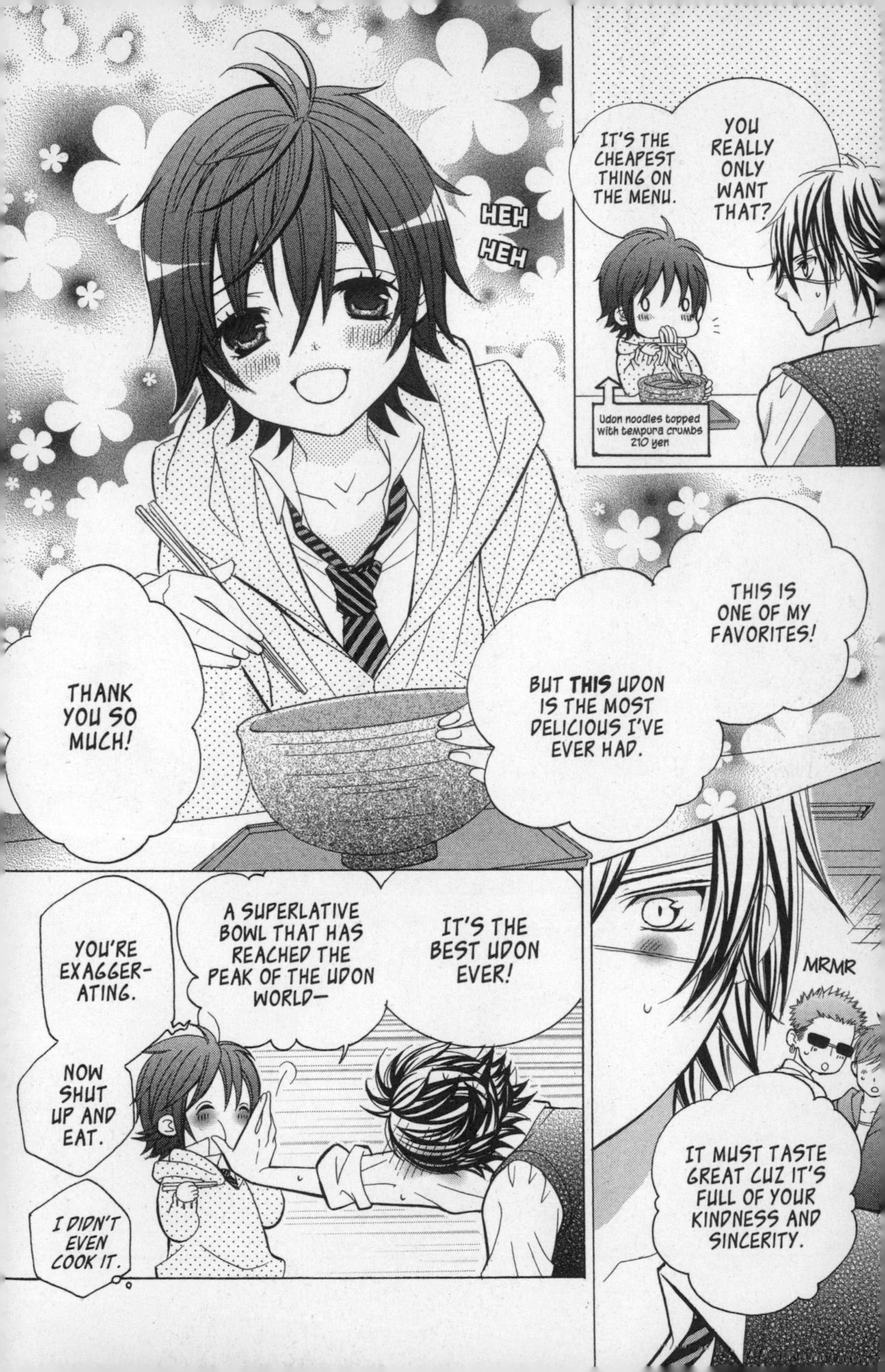
YOU REALLY ONLY WANT THAT?
IT'S THE CHEAPEST THING ON THE MENU.
Udon noodles topped with tempura crumbs 210 yen
HEH HEH
THIS IS ONE OF MY FAVORITES!
BUT THIS UDON IS THE MOST DELICIOUS I'VE EVER HAD.
THANK YOU SO MUCH!
MRMR
IT MUST TASTE GREAT CUZ IT'S FULL OF YOUR KINDNESS AND SINCERITY.
IT'S THE BEST UDON EVER!
A SUPERLATIVE BOWL THAT HAS REACHED THE PEAK OF THE UDON WORLD—
YOU'RE EXAGGER-ATING.
NOW SHUT UP AND EAT.
I DIDN'T EVEN COOK IT.

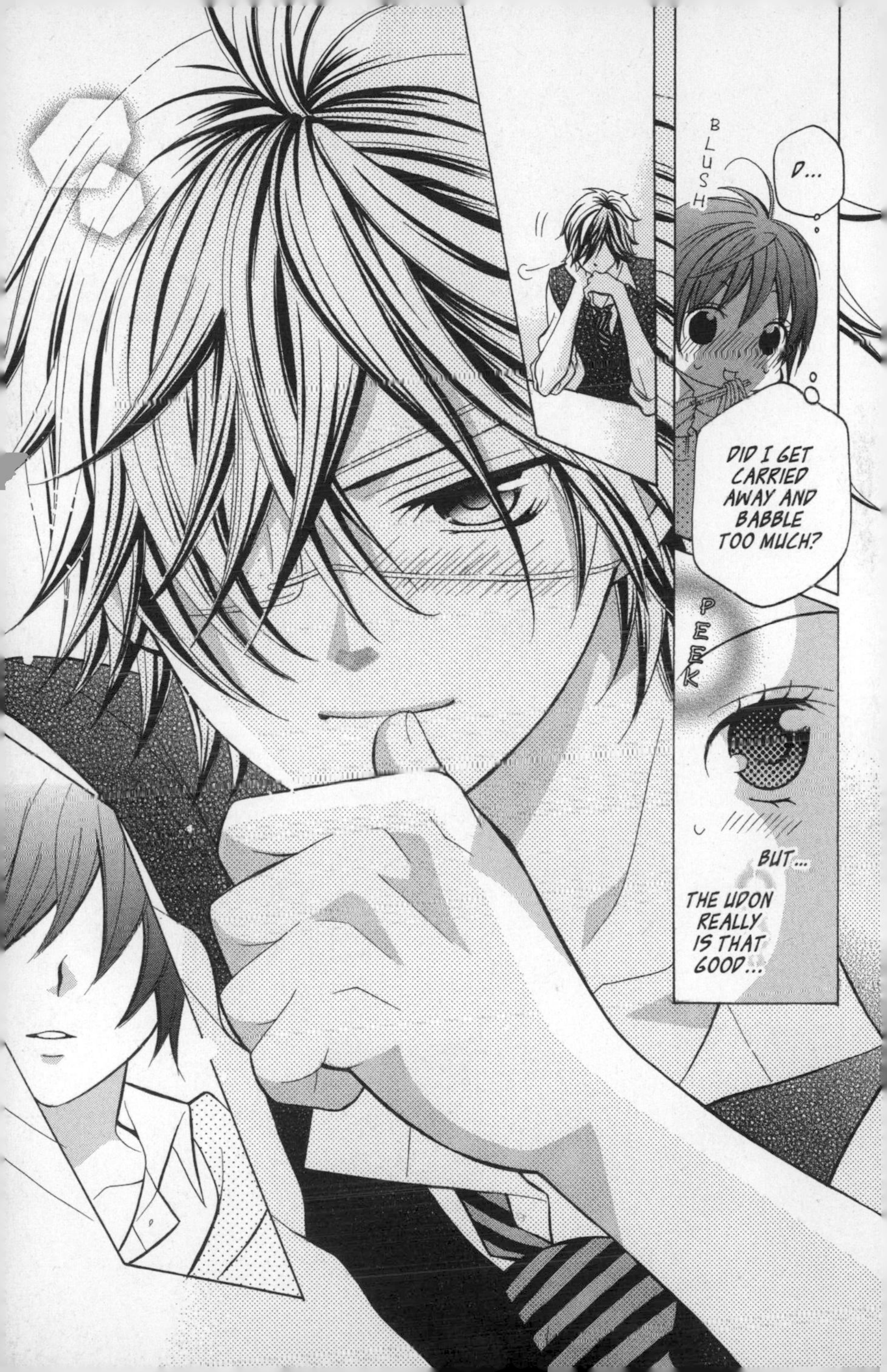
D...
DID I GET CARRIED AWAY AND BABBLE TOO MUCH?
BLUSH
PEEK
BUT...
THE UDON REALLY IS THAT GOOD...

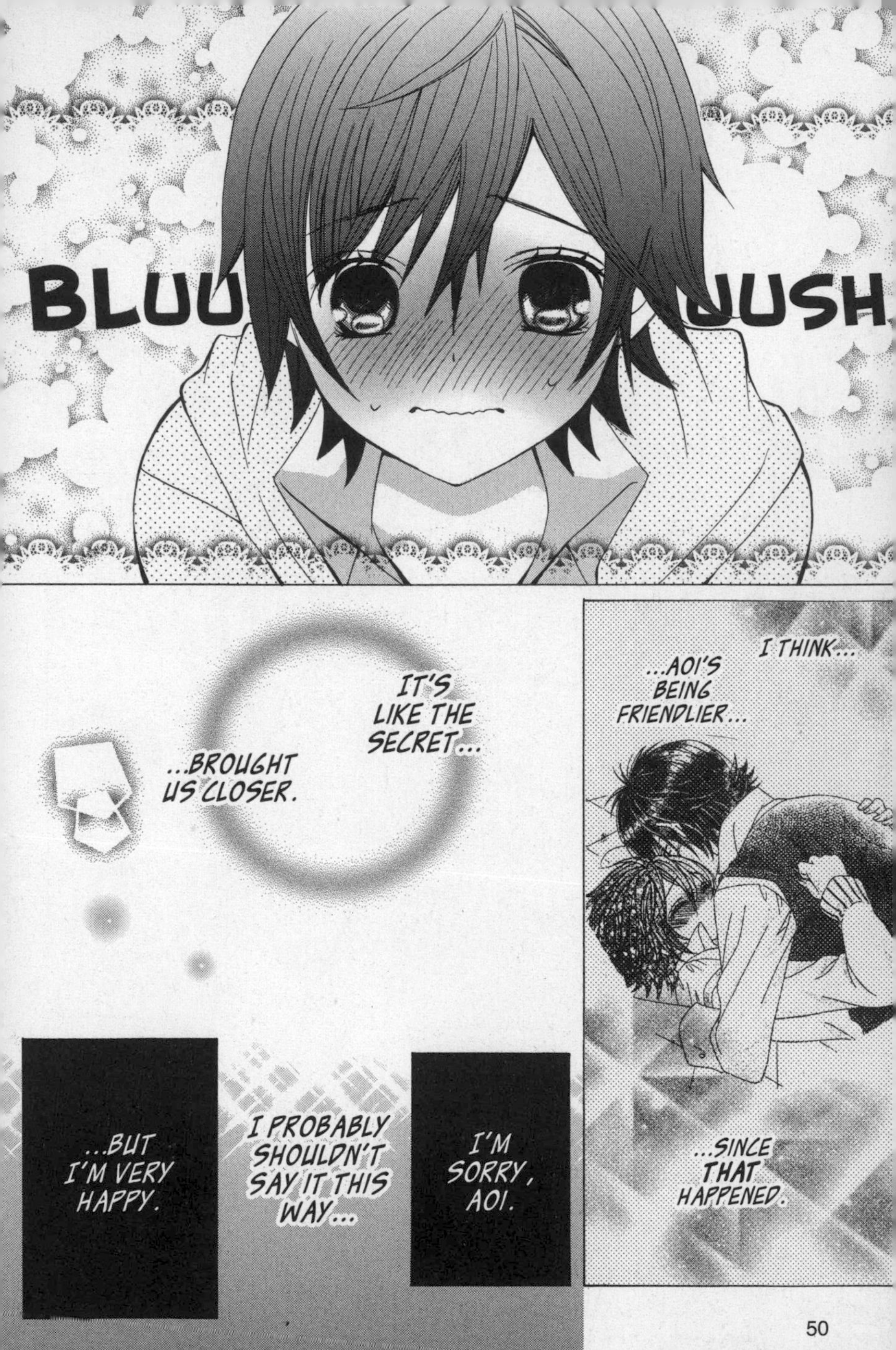
BLUU UUSH
I THINK...
...AOI'S BEING FRIENDLIER...
...SINCE THAT HAPPENED.
IT'S LIKE THE SECRET...
...BROUGHT US CLOSER.
I'M SORRY, AOI.
I PROBABLY SHOULDN'T SAY IT THIS WAY...
...BUT I'M VERY HAPPY.

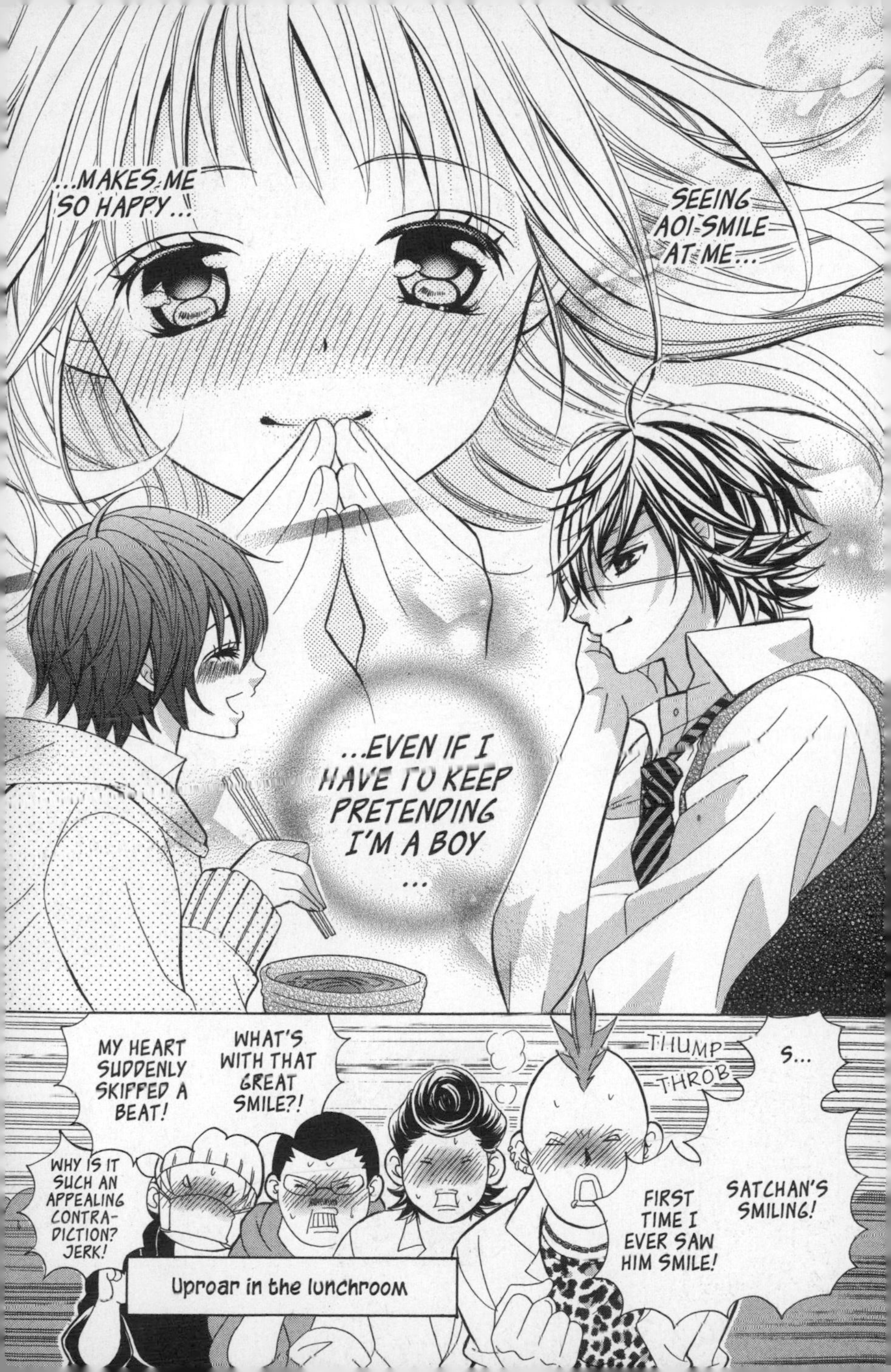
SEEING AOI SMILE AT ME...
...MAKES ME SO HAPPY...
...EVEN IF I HAVE TO KEEP PRETENDING I'M A BOY ...
S...
THUMP
THROB
SATCHAN'S SMILING!
FIRST TIME I EVER SAW HIM SMILE!
WHAT'S WITH THAT GREAT SMILE?!
MY HEART SUDDENLY SKIPPED A BEAT!
WHY IS IT SUCH AN APPEALING CONTRA-DICTION? JERK!
Uproar in the lunchroom

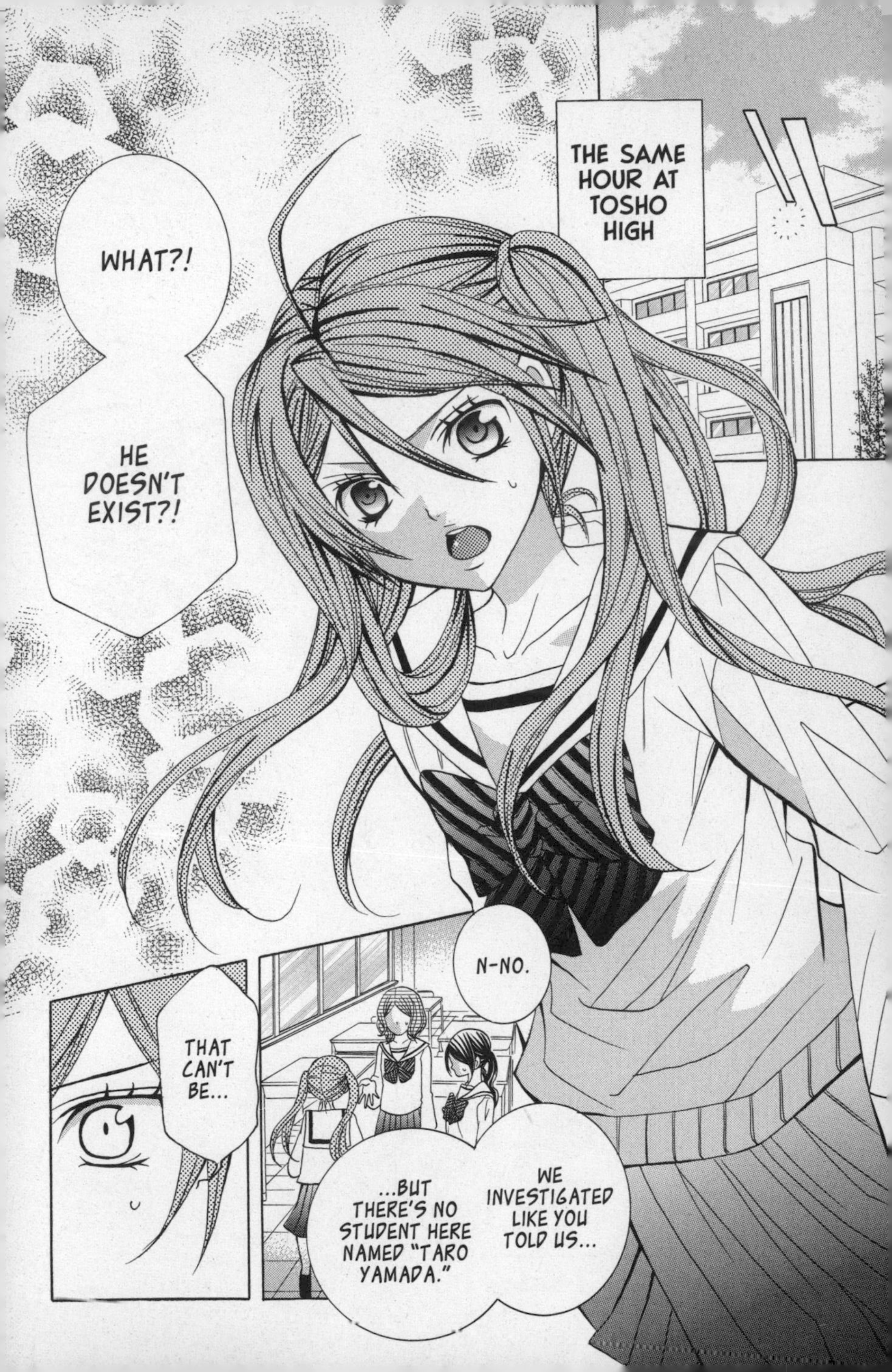
THE SAME HOUR AT TOSHO HIGH
WHAT?!
HE DOESN'T EXIST?!
N-NO.
WE INVESTIGATED LIKE YOU TOLD US...
...BUT THERE'S NO STUDENT HERE NAMED "TARO YAMADA."
THAT CAN'T BE...

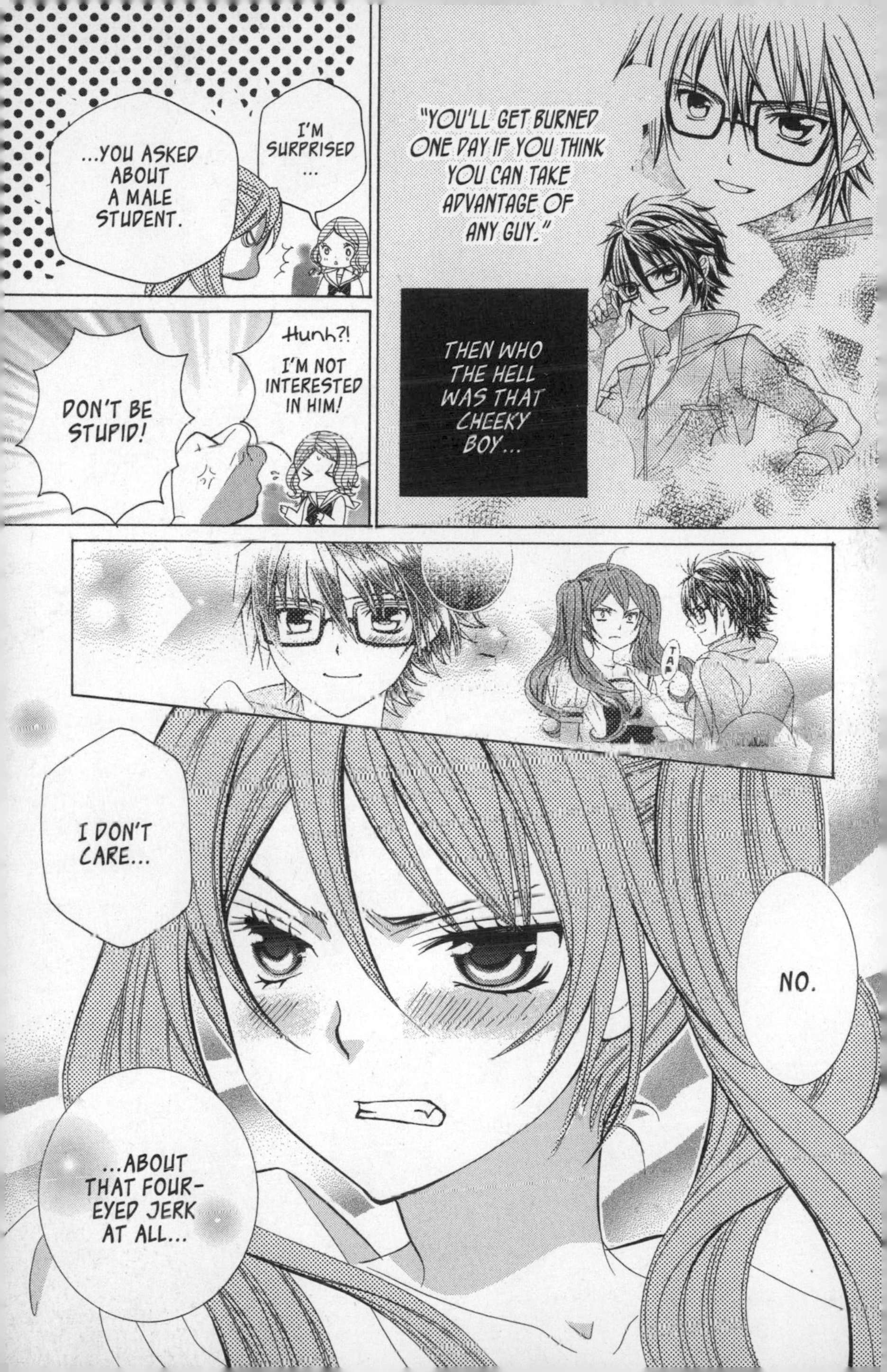
"YOU'LL GET BURNED ONE DAY IF YOU THINK YOU CAN TAKE ADVANTAGE OF ANY GUY."
THEN WHO THE HELL WAS THAT CHEEKY BOY...
I'M SURPRISED...
...YOU ASKED ABOUT A MALE STUDENT.
Hunh?!
I'M NOT INTERESTED IN HIM!
DON'T BE STUPID!
TAP
NO.
I DON'T CARE...
...ABOUT THAT FOUR-EYED JERK AT ALL...

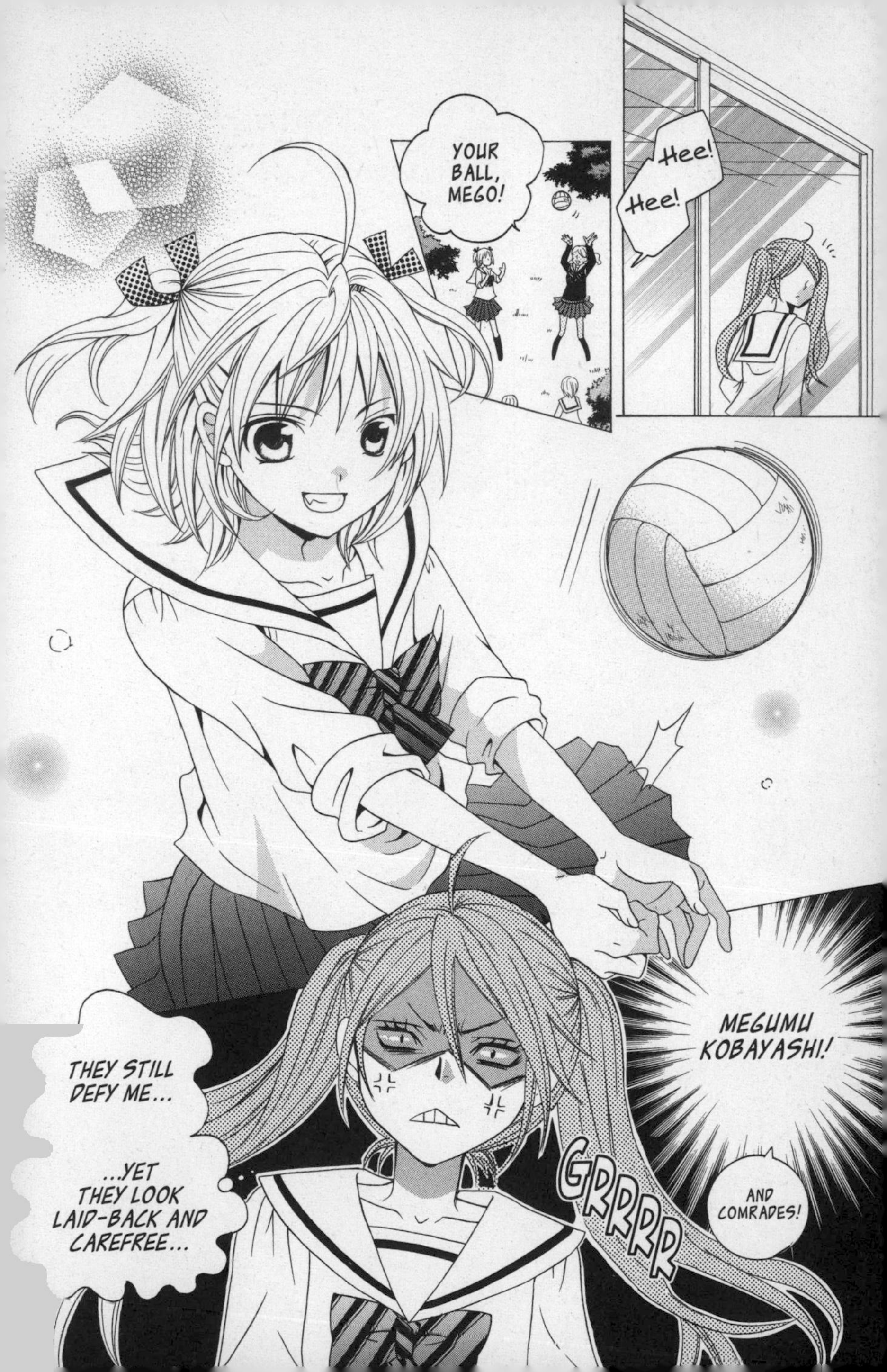
Hee!
Hee!
YOUR BALL, MEGO!
MEGUMU KOBAYASHI!
AND COMRADES!
GRRRR
THEY STILL DEFY ME...
...YET THEY LOOK LAID-BACK AND CAREFREE...

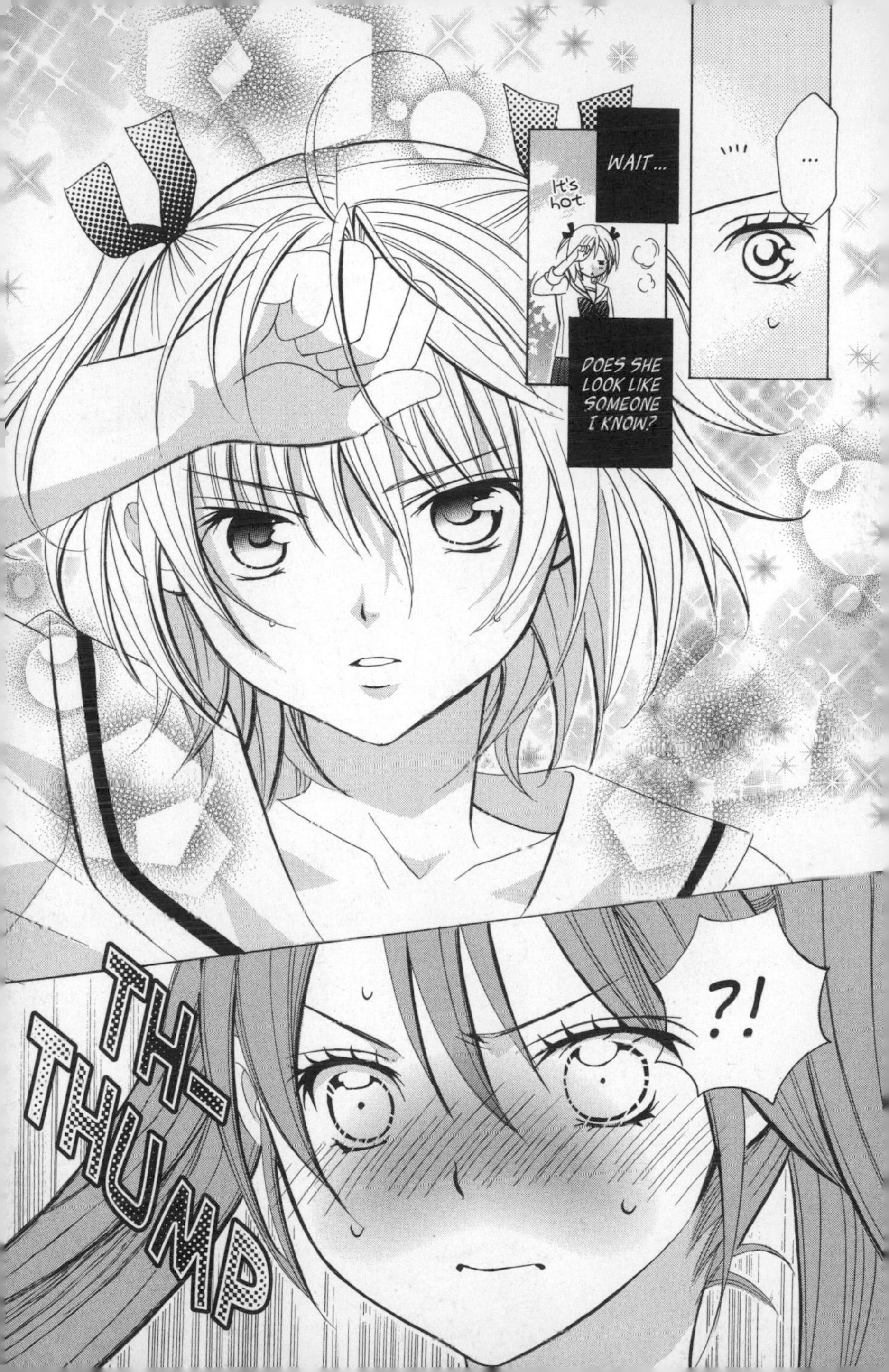

...
WAIT...
It's hot.
DOES SHE LOOK LIKE SOMEONE I KNOW?
?!
TH-THUMP

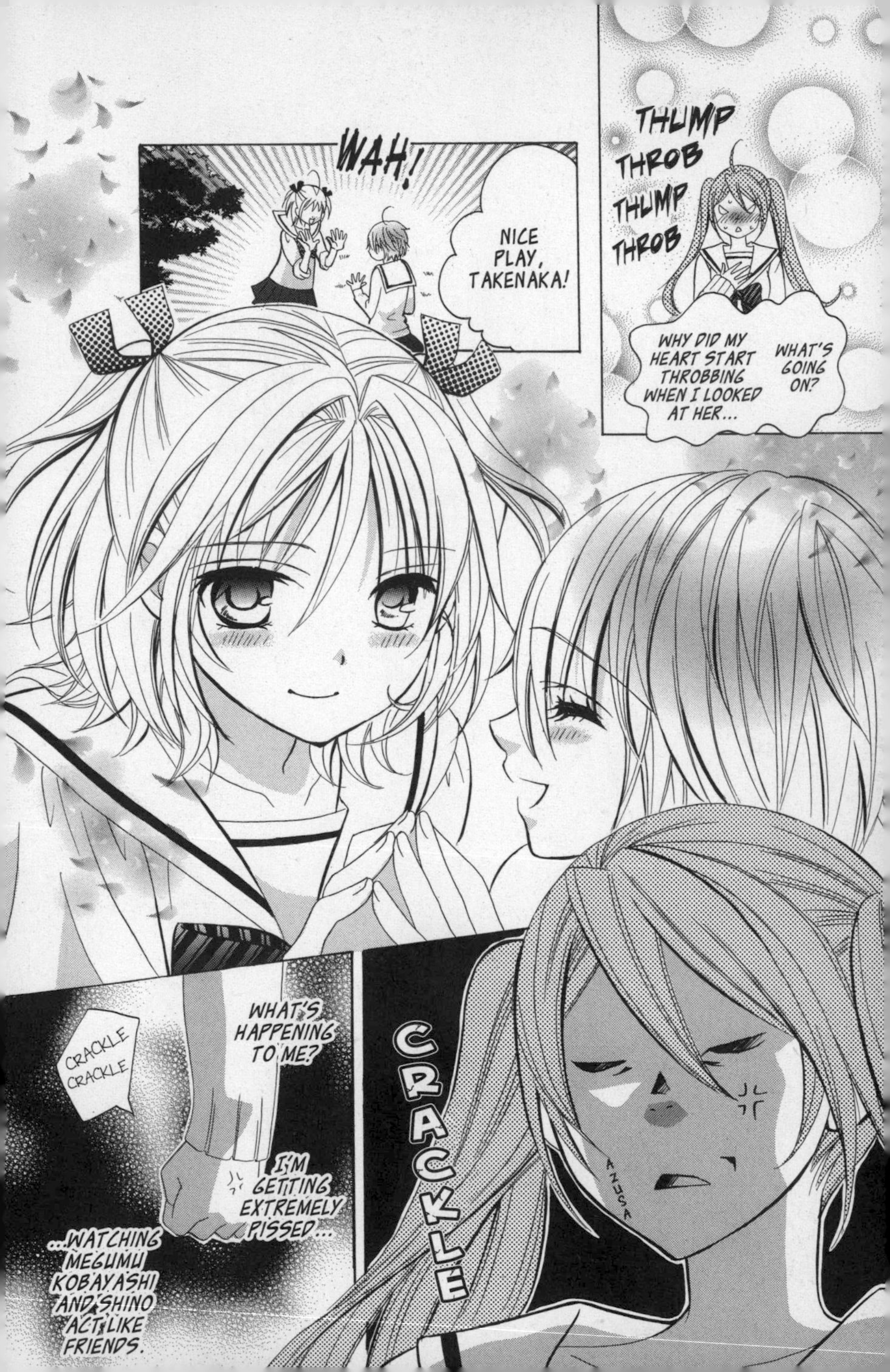
THUMP THROB THUMP THROB
WHAT'S GOING ON?
WHY DID MY HEART START THROBBING WHEN I LOOKED AT HER...
WAH!
NICE PLAY, TAKENAKA!
CRACKLE
AZUSA
WHAT'S HAPPENING TO ME?
CRACKLE CRACKLE
I'M GETTING EXTREMELY PISSED...
...WATCHING MEGUMU KOBAYASHI AND SHINO ACT LIKE FRIENDS.

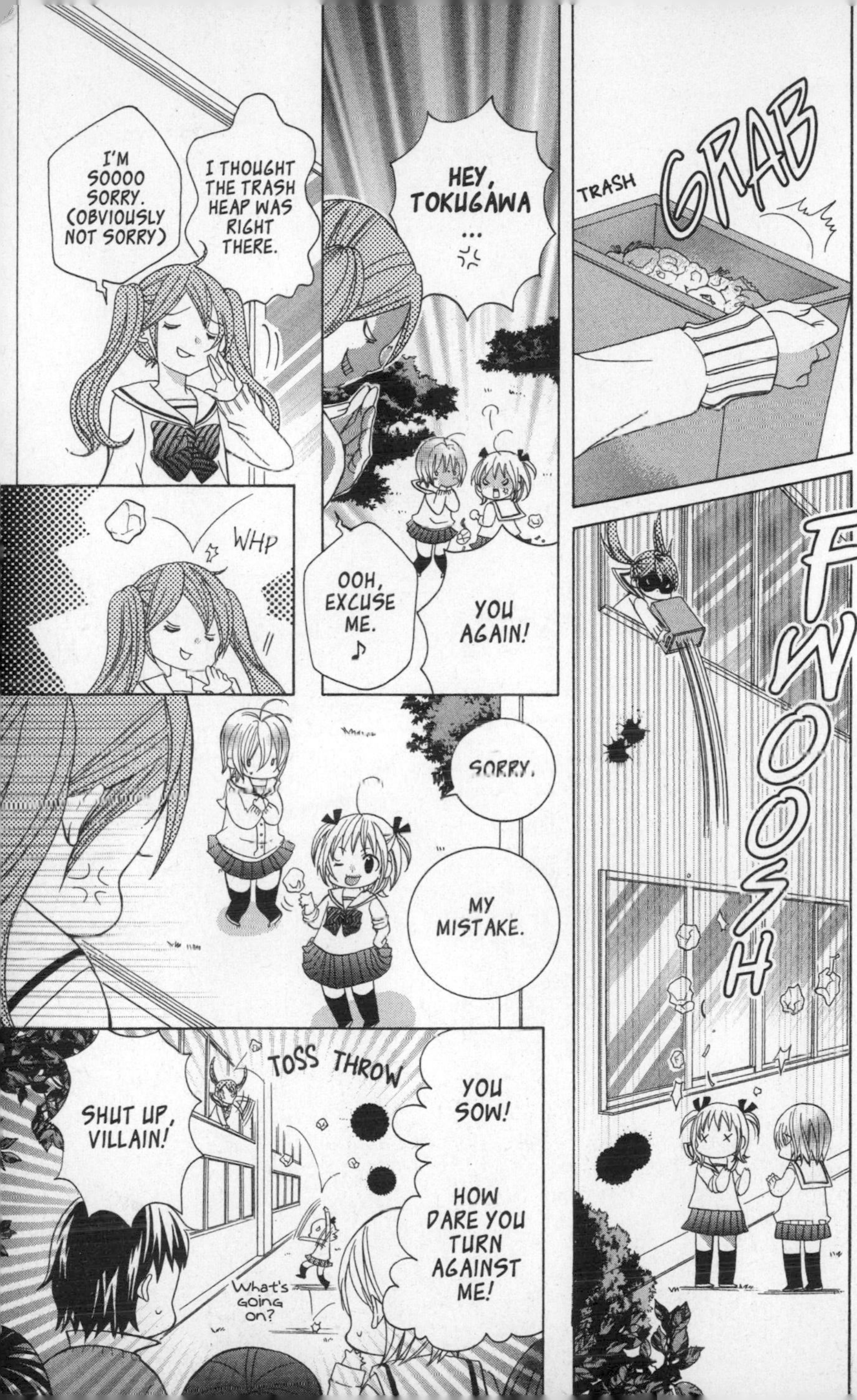
TRASH
GRAB
FWOOSH
HEY, TOKUGAWA ...
I THOUGHT THE TRASH HEAP WAS RIGHT THERE.
I'M SOOOO SORRY. (OBVIOUSLY NOT SORRY)
YOU AGAIN!
OOH, EXCUSE ME. ♪
WHP
SORRY.
MY MISTAKE.
YOU SOW!
HOW DARE YOU TURN AGAINST ME!
TOSS THROW
SHUT UP, VILLAIN!
What's going on?

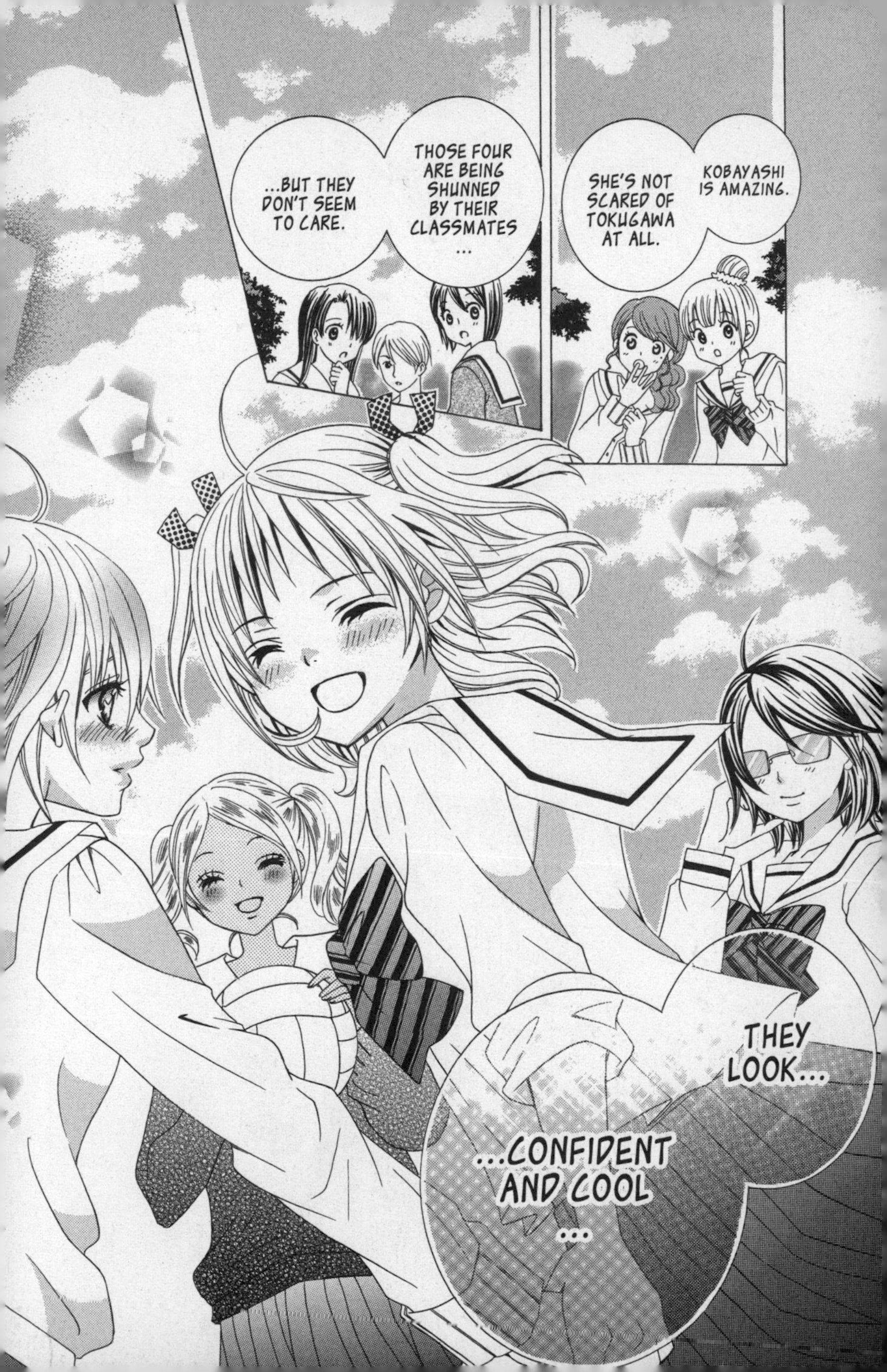
KOBAYASHI IS AMAZING.
SHE'S NOT SCARED OF TOKUGAWA AT ALL.
THOSE FOUR ARE BEING SHUNNED BY THEIR CLASSMATES ...
...BUT THEY DON'T SEEM TO CARE.
THEY LOOK...
...CONFIDENT AND COOL ...

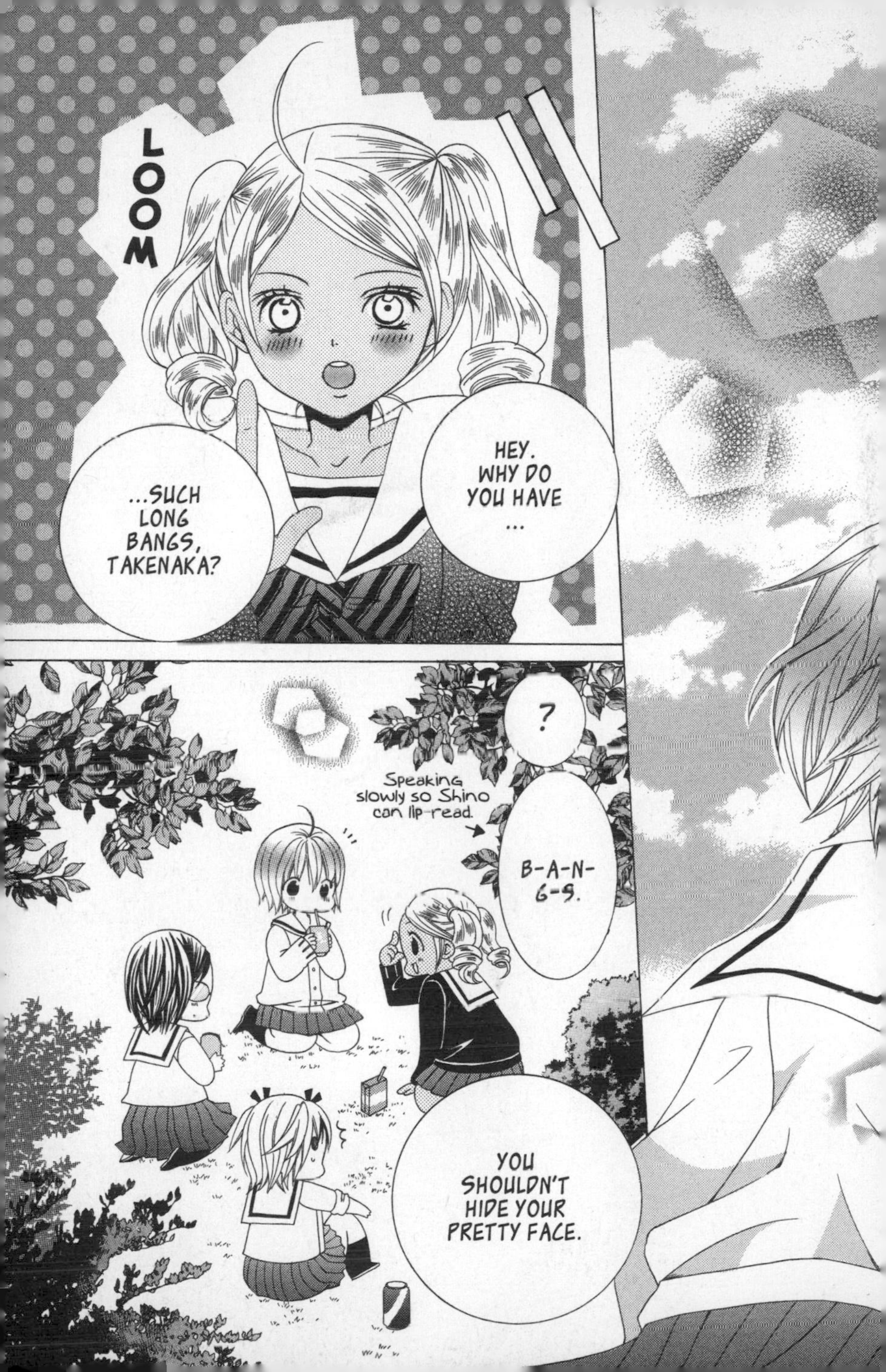
HEY. WHY DO YOU HAVE ...
...SUCH LONG BANGS, TAKENAKA?
LOOM
?
Speaking slowly so Shino can lip-read.
B-A-N-G-S.
YOU SHOULDN'T HIDE YOUR PRETTY FACE.

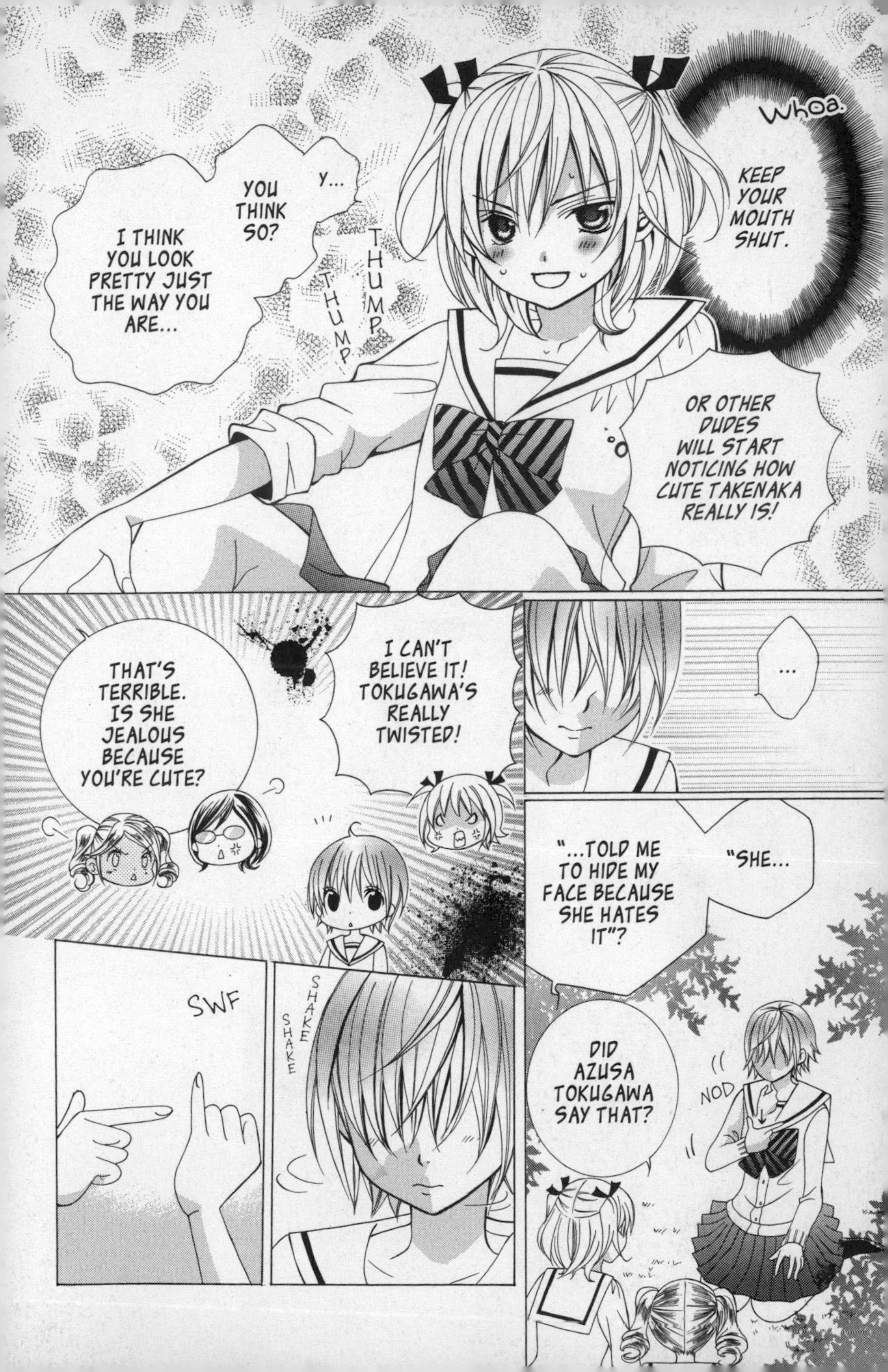

Whoa.
KEEP YOUR MOUTH SHUT.
OR OTHER DUDES WILL START NOTICING HOW CUTE TAKENAKA REALLY IS!
Y...
YOU THINK SO?
THUMP THUMP
I THINK YOU LOOK PRETTY JUST THE WAY YOU ARE...
...
"SHE...
"...TOLD ME TO HIDE MY FACE BECAUSE SHE HATES IT"?
NOD
DID AZUSA TOKUGAWA SAY THAT?
I CAN'T BELIEVE IT! TOKUGAWA'S REALLY TWISTED!
THAT'S TERRIBLE. IS SHE JEALOUS BECAUSE YOU'RE CUTE?
SHAKE SHAKE
SWF

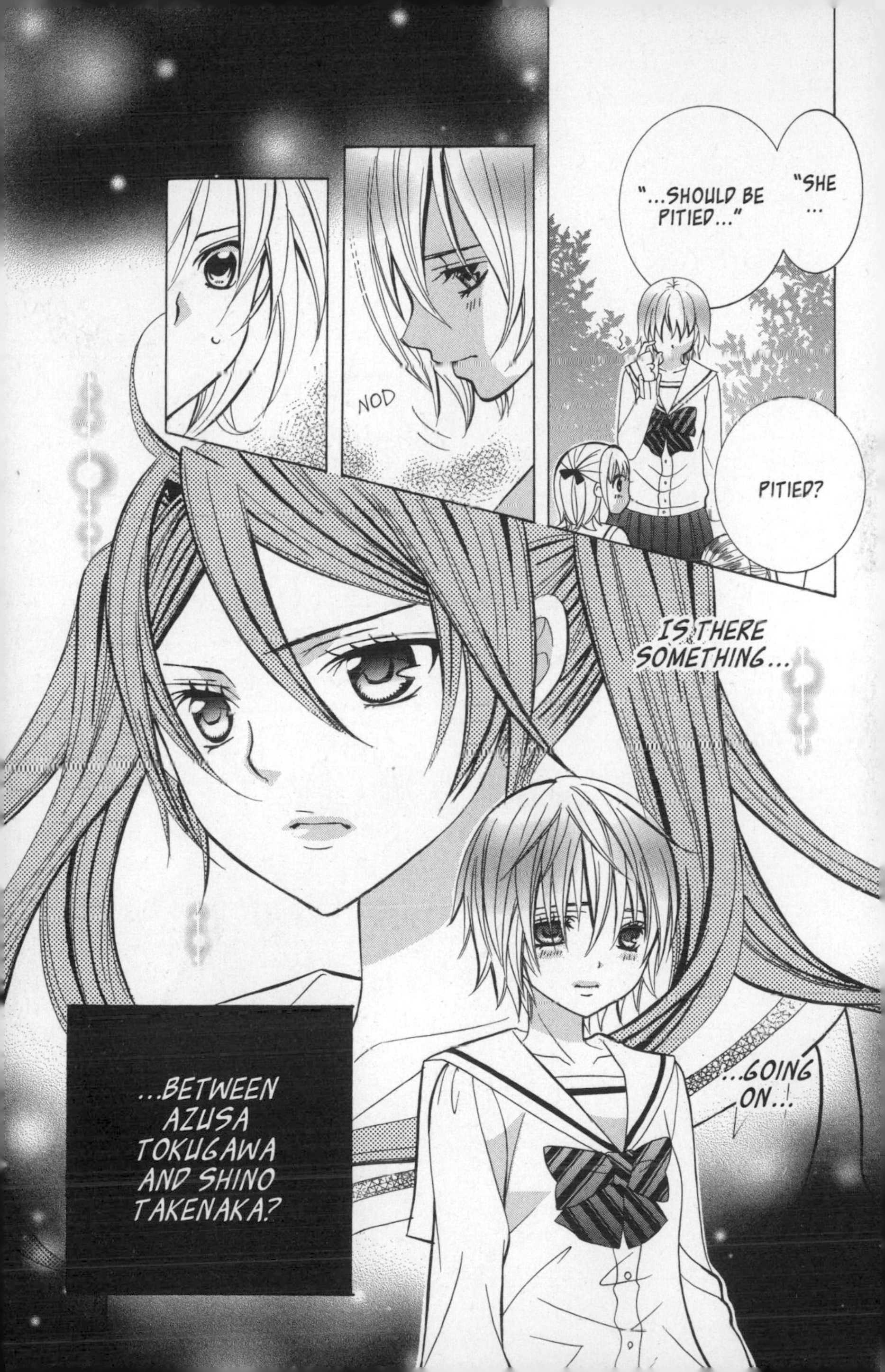
"SHE ...
"...SHOULD BE PITIED..."
PITIED?
NOD
IS THERE SOMETHING...
...GOING ON..!
...BETWEEN AZUSA TOKUGAWA AND SHINO TAKENAKA?

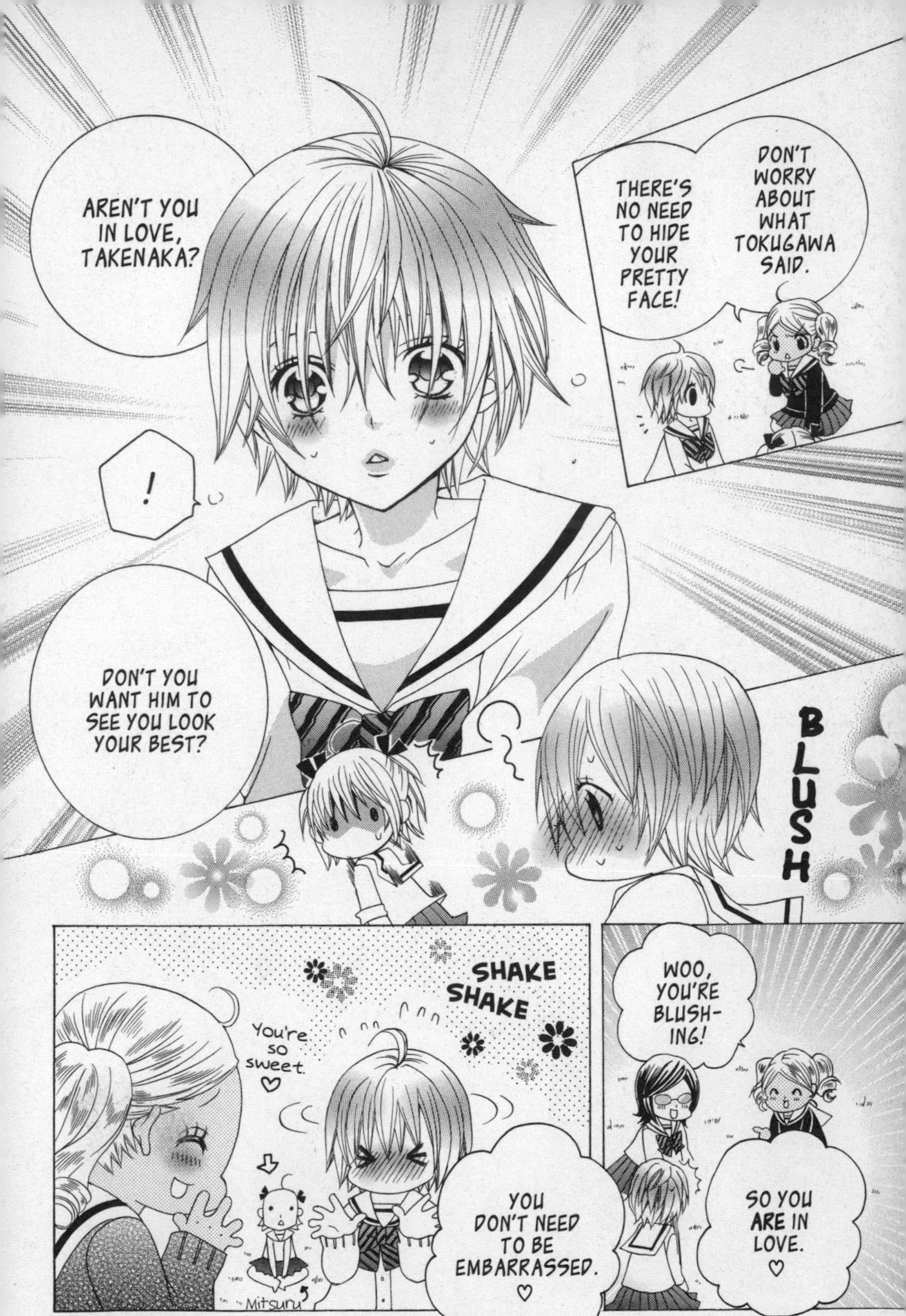
DON'T WORRY ABOUT WHAT TOKUGAWA SAID.
THERE'S NO NEED TO HIDE YOUR PRETTY FACE!
AREN'T YOU IN LOVE, TAKENAKA?
!
DON'T YOU WANT HIM TO SEE YOU LOOK YOUR BEST?
BLUSH
WOO, YOU'RE BLUSH-ING!
SO YOU ARE IN LOVE. ♡
SHAKE SHAKE
YOU DON'T NEED TO BE EMBARRASSED. ♡
You're so sweet. ♡
Mitsuru

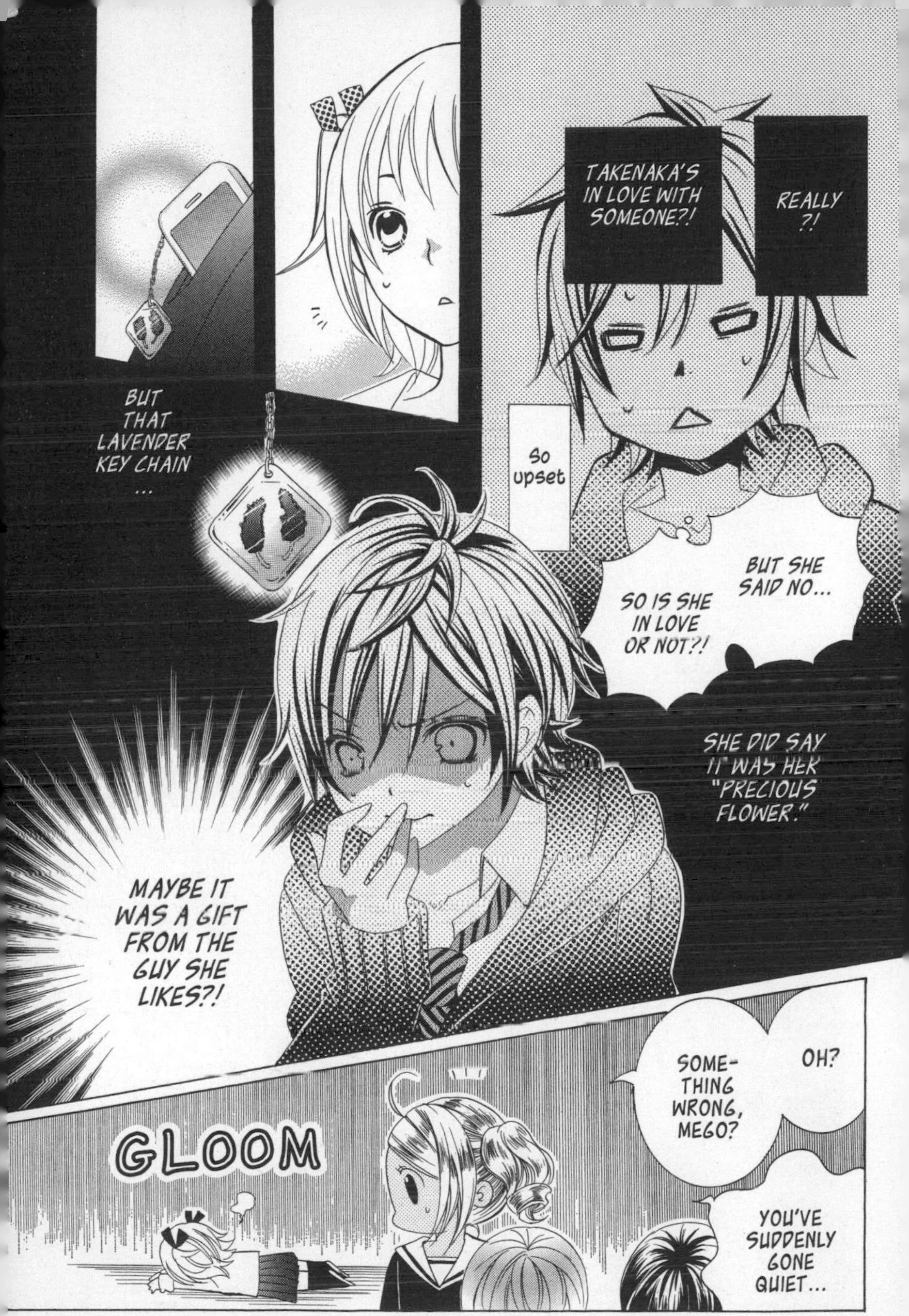
TAKENAKA'S IN LOVE WITH SOMEONE?!
REALLY ?!
So upset
BUT SHE SAID NO...
SO IS SHE IN LOVE OR NOT?!
BUT THAT LAVENDER KEY CHAIN ...
SHE DID SAY IT WAS HER "PRECIOUS FLOWER."
MAYBE IT WAS A GIFT FROM THE GUY SHE LIKES?!
OH?
SOME-THING WRONG, MEGO?
YOU'VE SUDDENLY GONE QUIET...
GLOOM

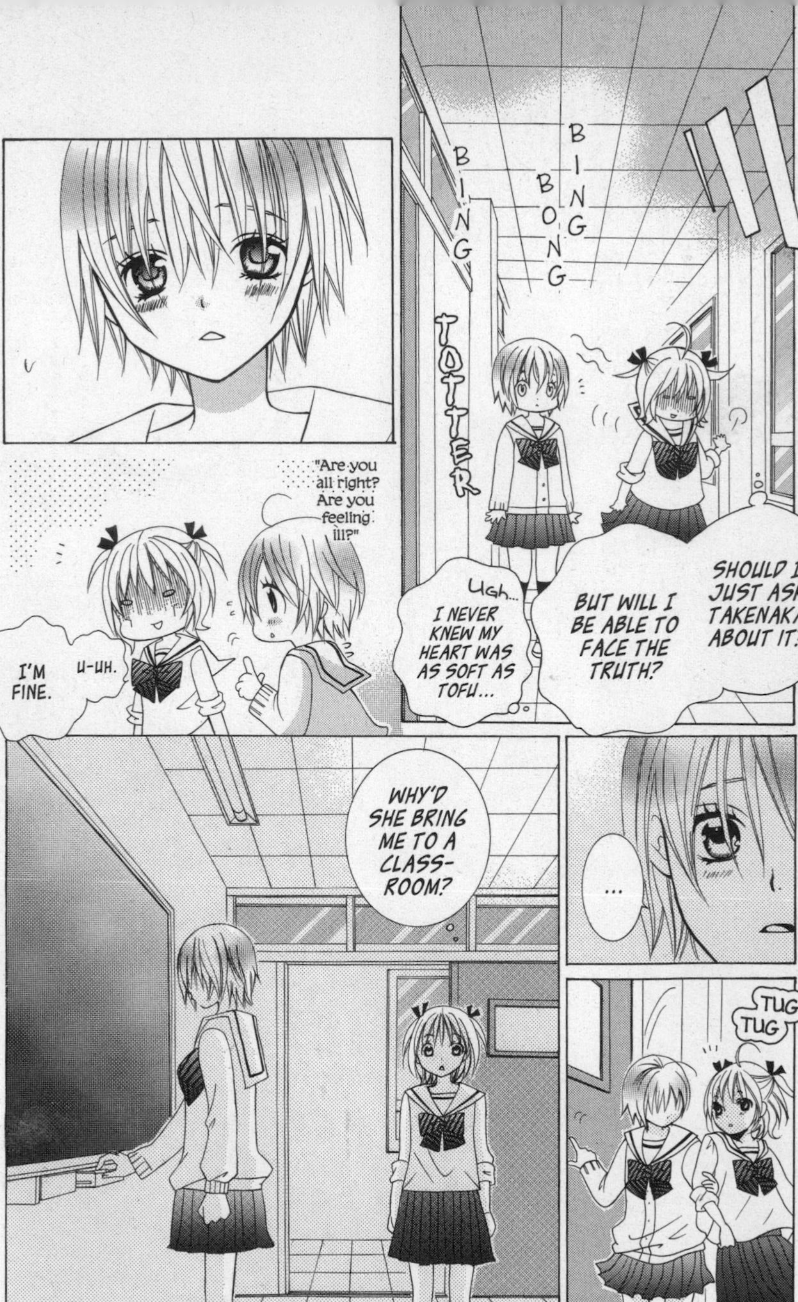
BING
BONG
BING
TOTTER
SHOULD I JUST ASK TAKENAKA ABOUT IT?
BUT WILL I BE ABLE TO FACE THE TRUTH?
UGH... I NEVER KNEW MY HEART WAS AS SOFT AS TOFU...
"Are you all right? Are you feeling ill?"
U-UH.
I'M FINE.
...
TUG TUG
WHY'D SHE BRING ME TO A CLASS-ROOM?

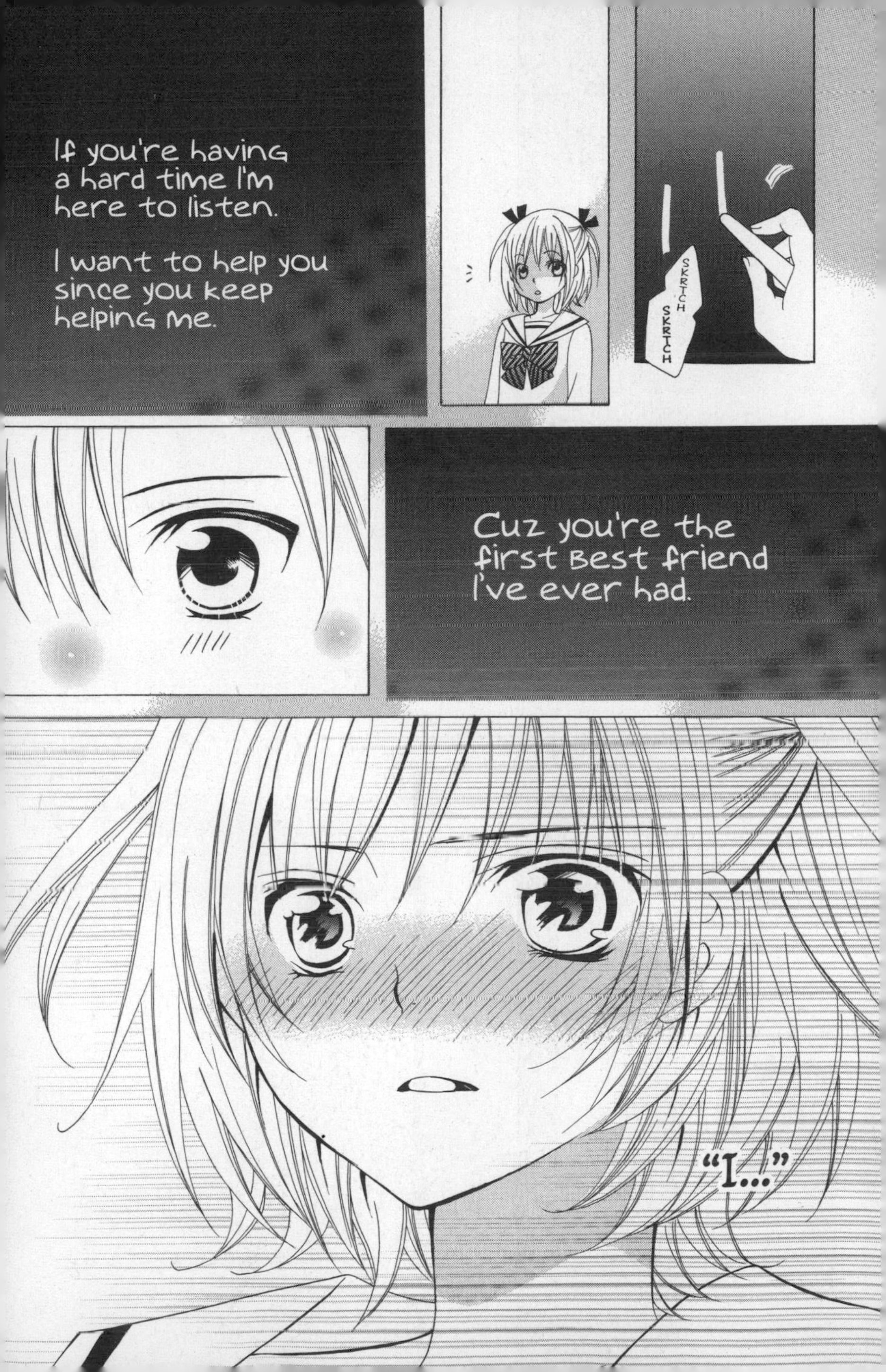
SKRTCH
SKRTCH
If you're having a hard time I'm here to listen.
I want to help you since you keep helping me.
Cuz you're the first best friend I've ever had.
"I..."

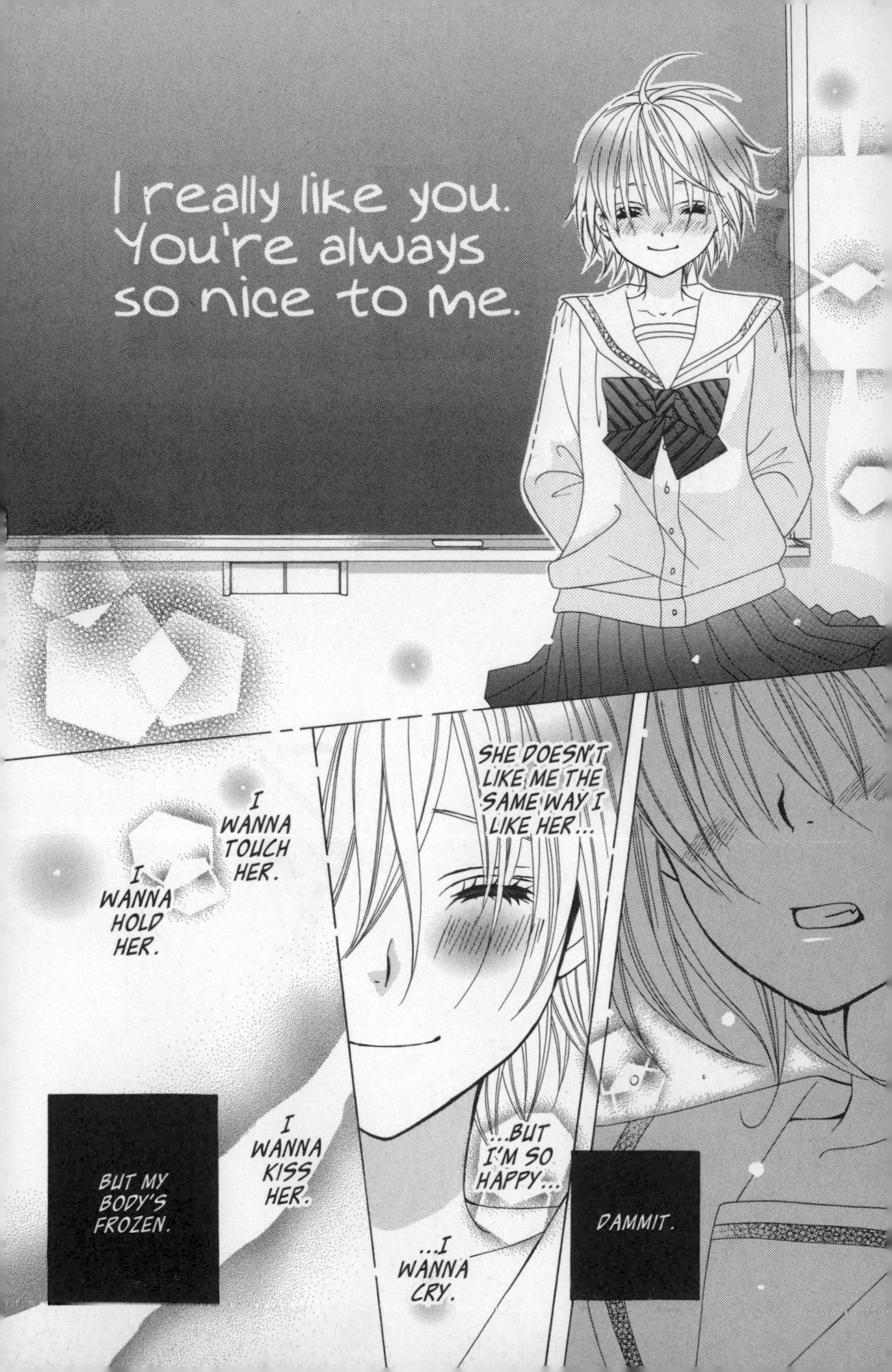
I really like you. You're always so nice to me.
SHE DOESN'T LIKE ME THE SAME WAY I LIKE HER...
...BUT I'M SO HAPPY...
DAMMIT.
I WANNA TOUCH HER.
I WANNA HOLD HER.
I WANNA KISS HER.
...I WANNA CRY.
BUT MY BODY'S FROZEN.

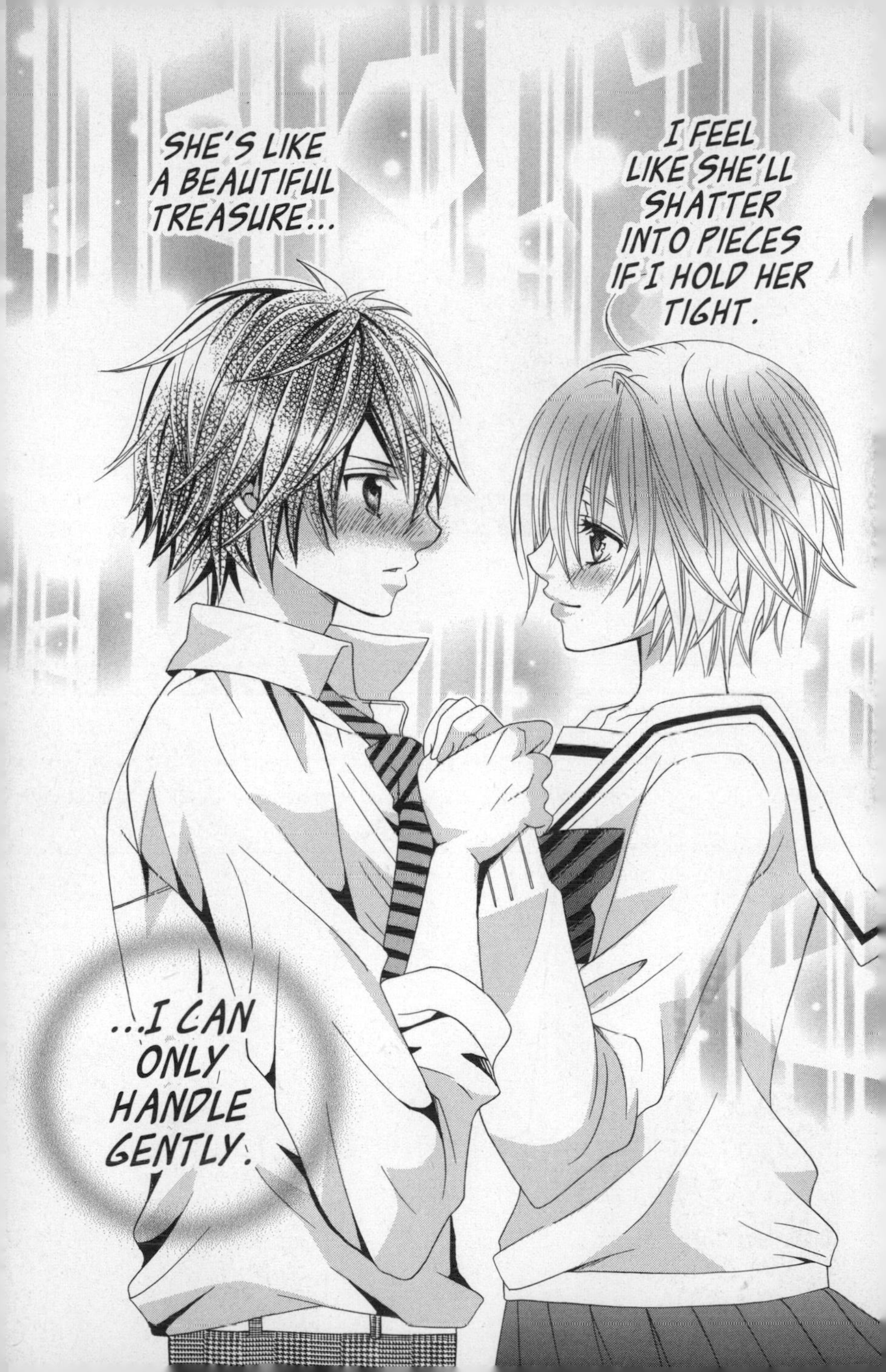
I FEEL LIKE SHE'LL SHATTER INTO PIECES IF I HOLD HER TIGHT.
SHE'S LIKE A BEAUTIFUL TREASURE...
...I CAN ONLY HANDLE GENTLY.

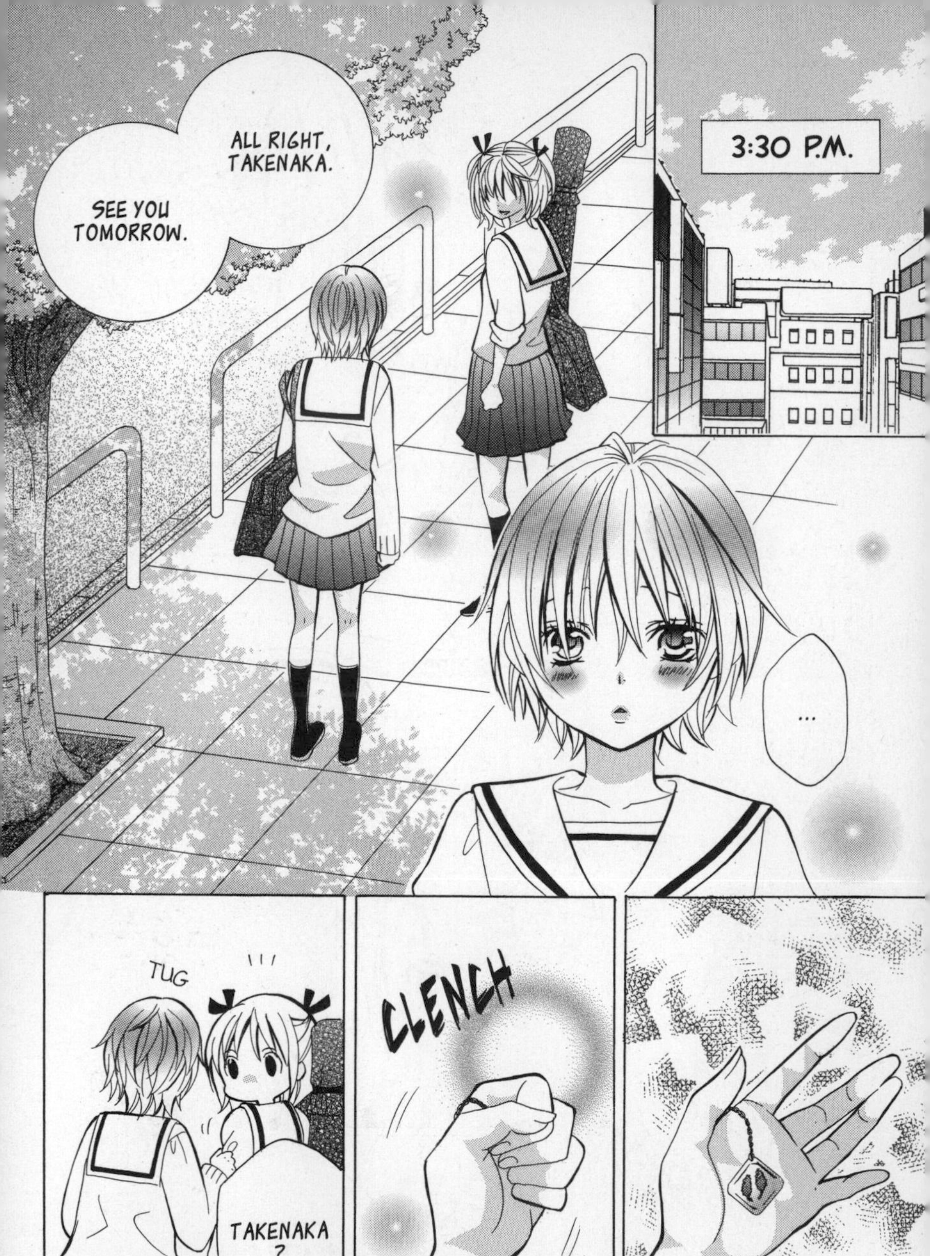

3:30 P.M.
ALL RIGHT, TAKENAKA.
SEE YOU TOMORROW.
...
CLENCH
TUG
!!!
TAKENAKA ?

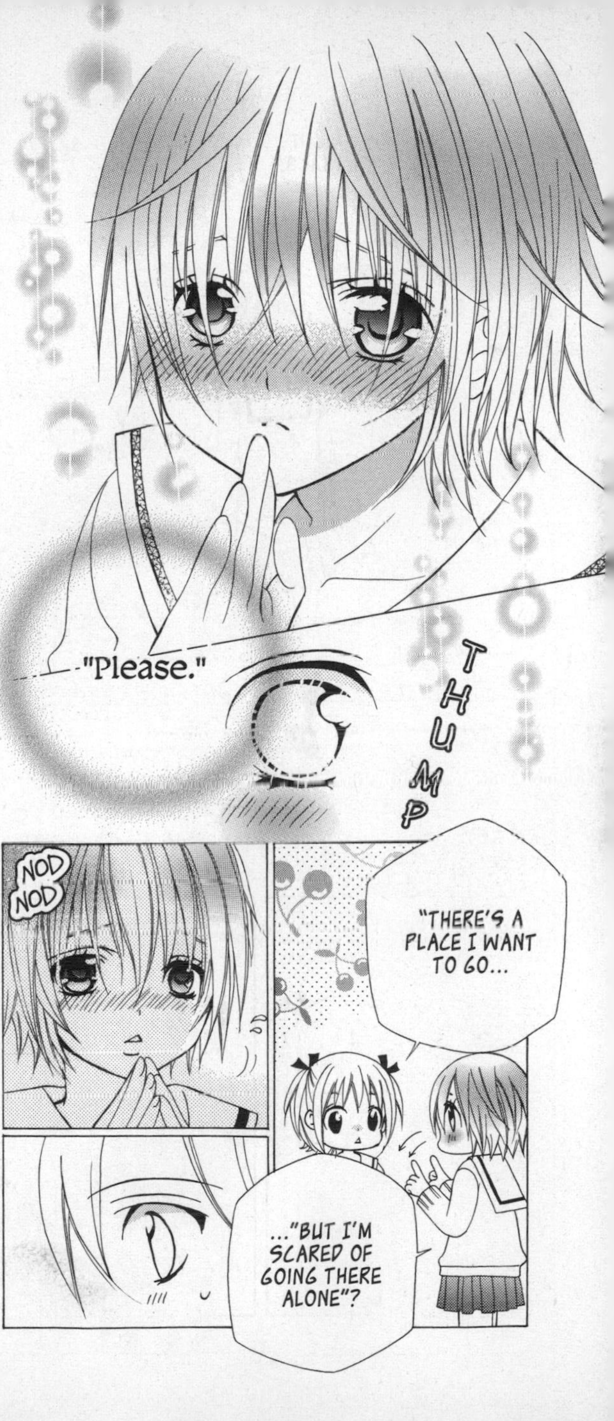
"Please."
THUMP
"THERE'S A PLACE I WANT TO GO...
..."BUT I'M SCARED OF GOING THERE ALONE"?
NOD NOD

SPECIAL THANKS

Yuka Ito-sama,
Rieko Hirai-sama,
Kayoko Takahashi-sama,
Kawasaki-sama,
Nagisa Sato Sensei.

Rei Nanase Sensei,
Arisu Fujishiro Sensei,
Mumi Mimura Sensei,
Masayo Nagata-sama,
Naochan-sama,
Asuka Sakura Sensei,
and many others.

Bookstore Dan Kinshicho Branch, Kinokuniya Shinjuku Branch, LIBRO Ikebukuro Branch, Kinokuniya Hankyu 32-Bangai Branch.

Sendai Hachimonjiya Bookstore, Books HOSHINO Kintetsu Pass'e Branch, Asahiya Tennnoji MiO Branch, Kurashiki Kikuya Bookstore.

Salesperson:
Mizusawa sama

Previous salesperson:
Hurvna-sama

Previous editor:
Nakata-sama

Current editor:
Shoji-sama

I also sincerely express my gratitude to everyone who picked up this volume.

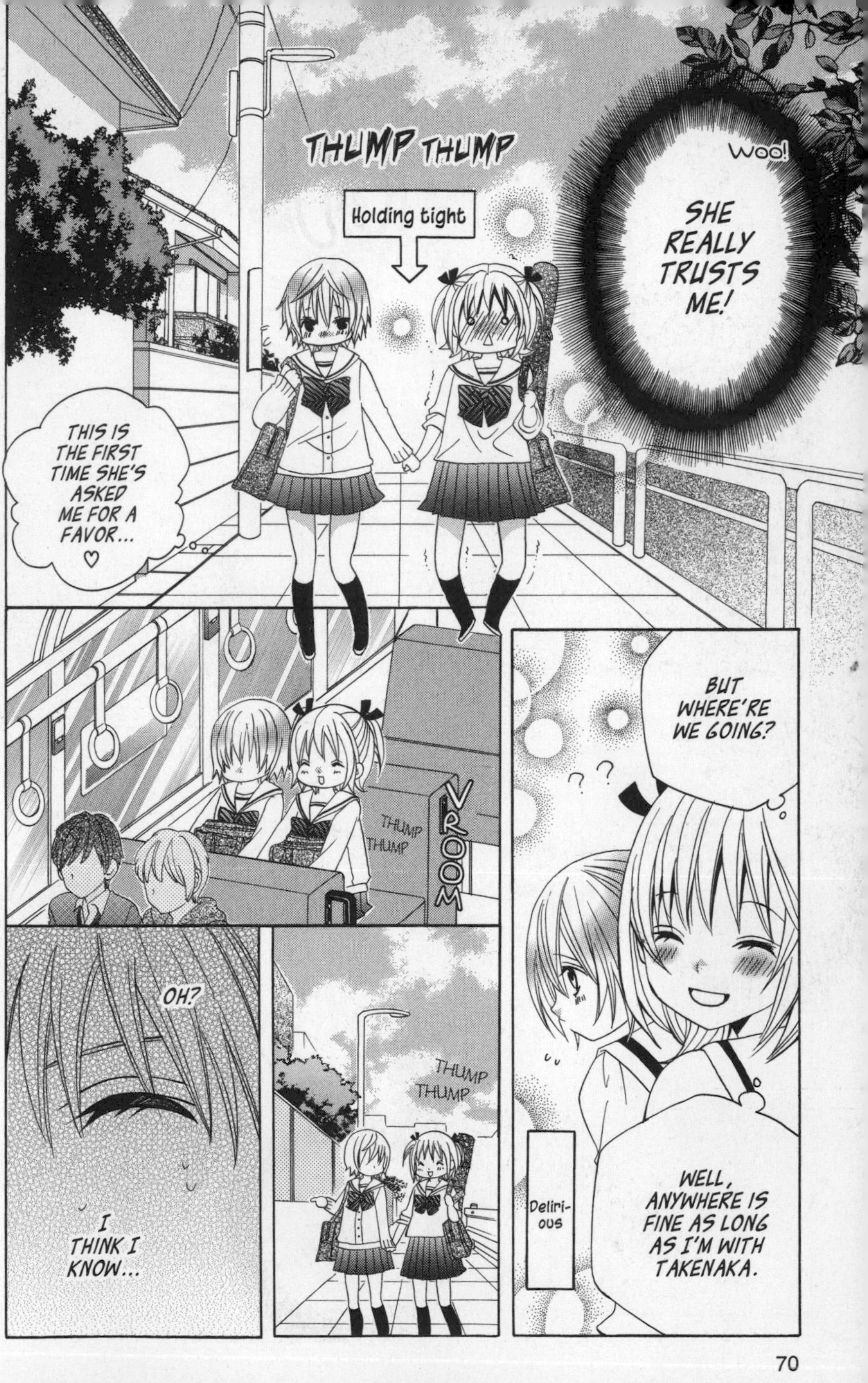
Woo!
SHE REALLY TRUSTS ME!
THUMP THUMP
Holding tight
THIS IS THE FIRST TIME SHE'S ASKED ME FOR A FAVOR... ♡
BUT WHERE'RE WE GOING?
??
WELL, ANYWHERE IS FINE AS LONG AS I'M WITH TAKENAKA.
Deliri-ous
VROOM
THUMP THUMP
THUMP THUMP
OH?
I THINK I KNOW...

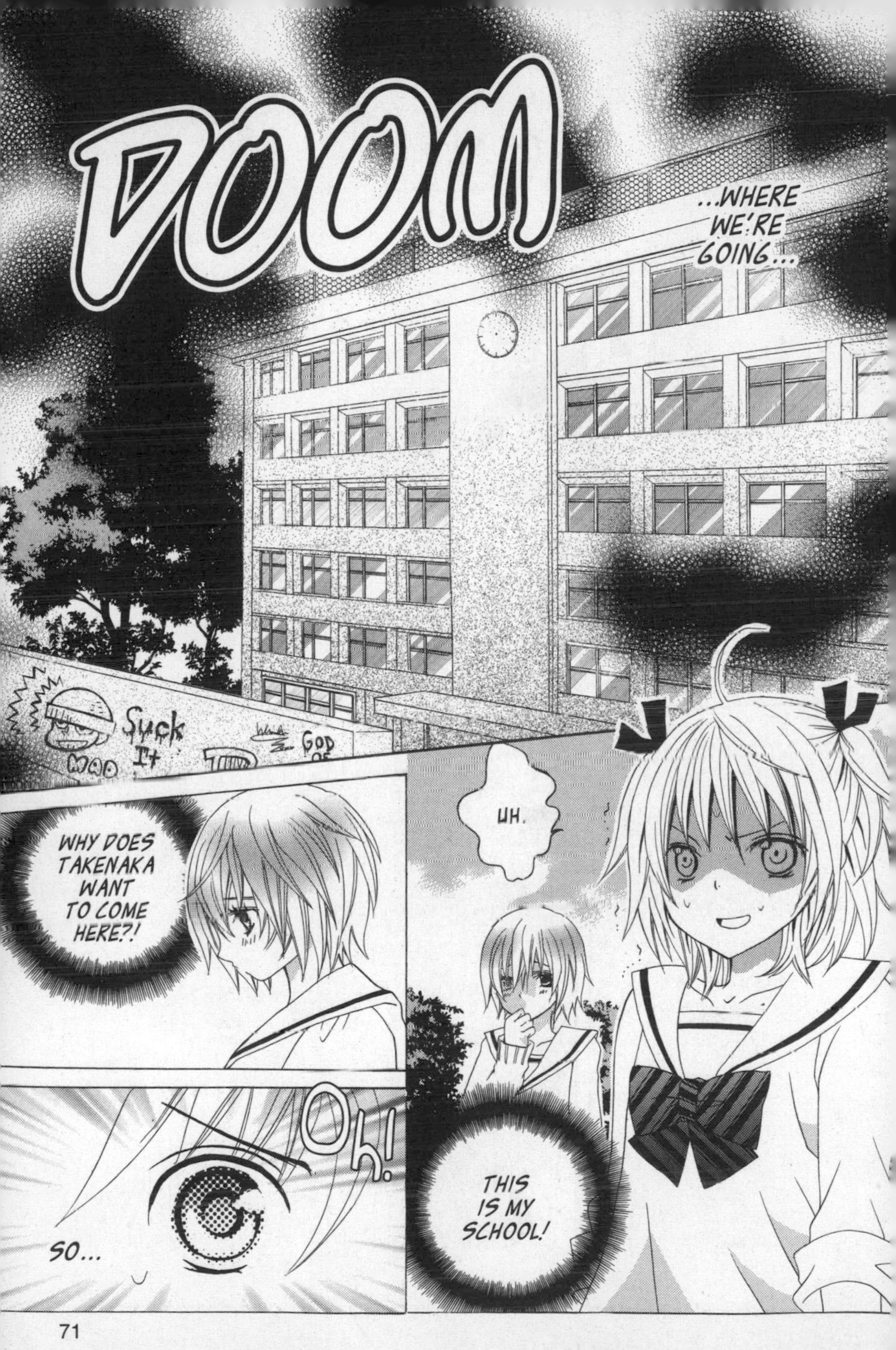
DOOM
...WHERE WE'RE GOING...
Suck It
UH.
THIS IS MY SCHOOL!
WHY DOES TAKENAKA WANT TO COME HERE?!
Oh!
SO...

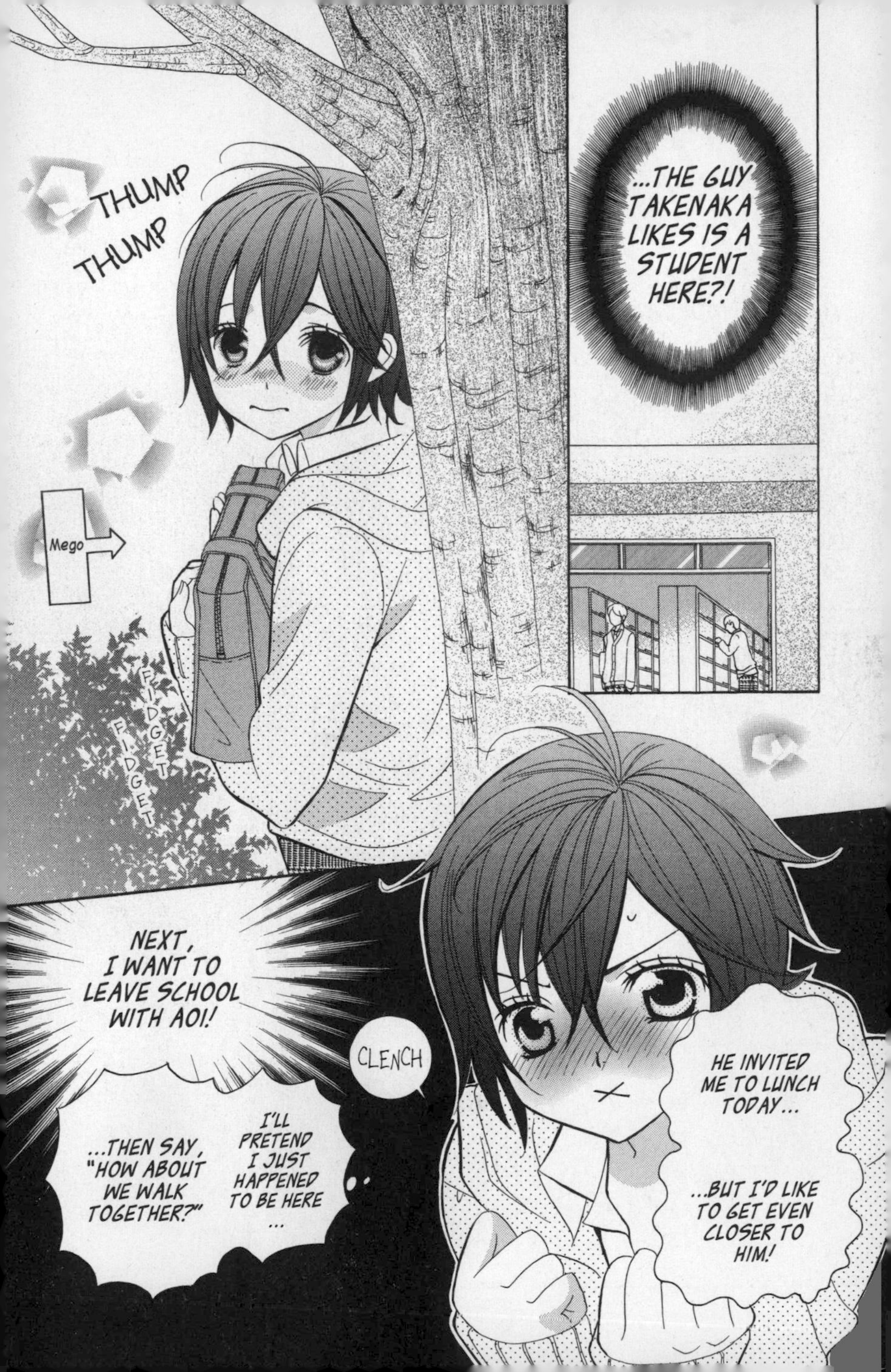
...THE GUY TAKENAKA LIKES IS A STUDENT HERE?!
THUMP
THUMP
Mego
FIDGET
FIDGET
HE INVITED ME TO LUNCH TODAY...
...BUT I'D LIKE TO GET EVEN CLOSER TO HIM!
CLENCH
NEXT, I WANT TO LEAVE SCHOOL WITH AOI!
I'LL PRETEND I JUST HAPPENED TO BE HERE...
...THEN SAY, "HOW ABOUT WE WALK TOGETHER?"

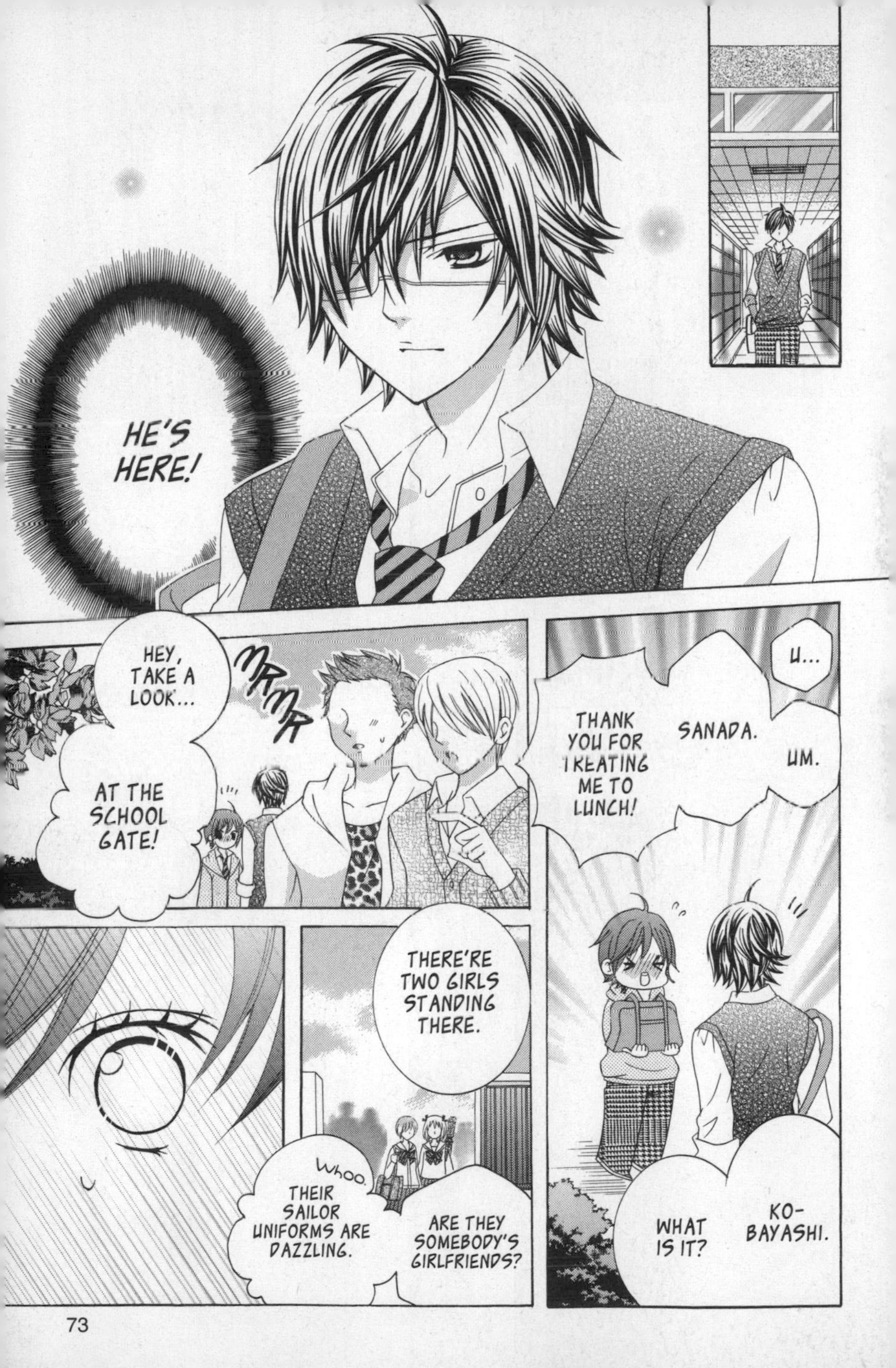

HE'S HERE!
U...
UM.
SANADA.
THANK YOU FOR TREATING ME TO LUNCH!
KO-BAYASHI.
WHAT IS IT?
HEY, TAKE A LOOK...
AT THE SCHOOL GATE!
MRMR
THERE'RE TWO GIRLS STANDING THERE.
ARE THEY SOMEBODY'S GIRLFRIENDS?
Whoo.
THEIR SAILOR UNIFORMS ARE DAZZLING.

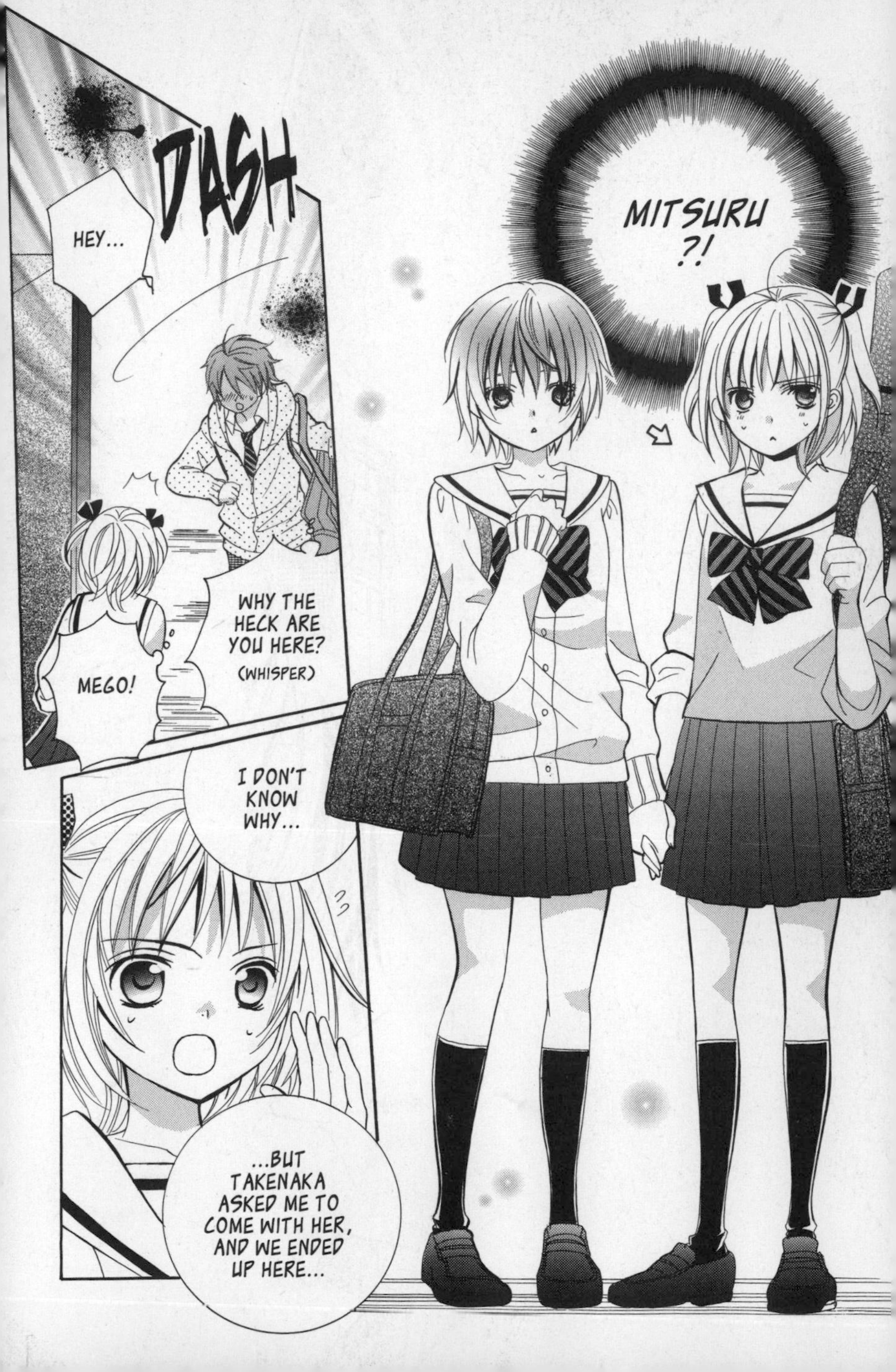
MITSURU ?!
DASH
HEY...
WHY THE HECK ARE YOU HERE?
(WHISPER)
MEGO!
I DON'T KNOW WHY...
...BUT TAKENAKA ASKED ME TO COME WITH HER, AND WE ENDED UP HERE...

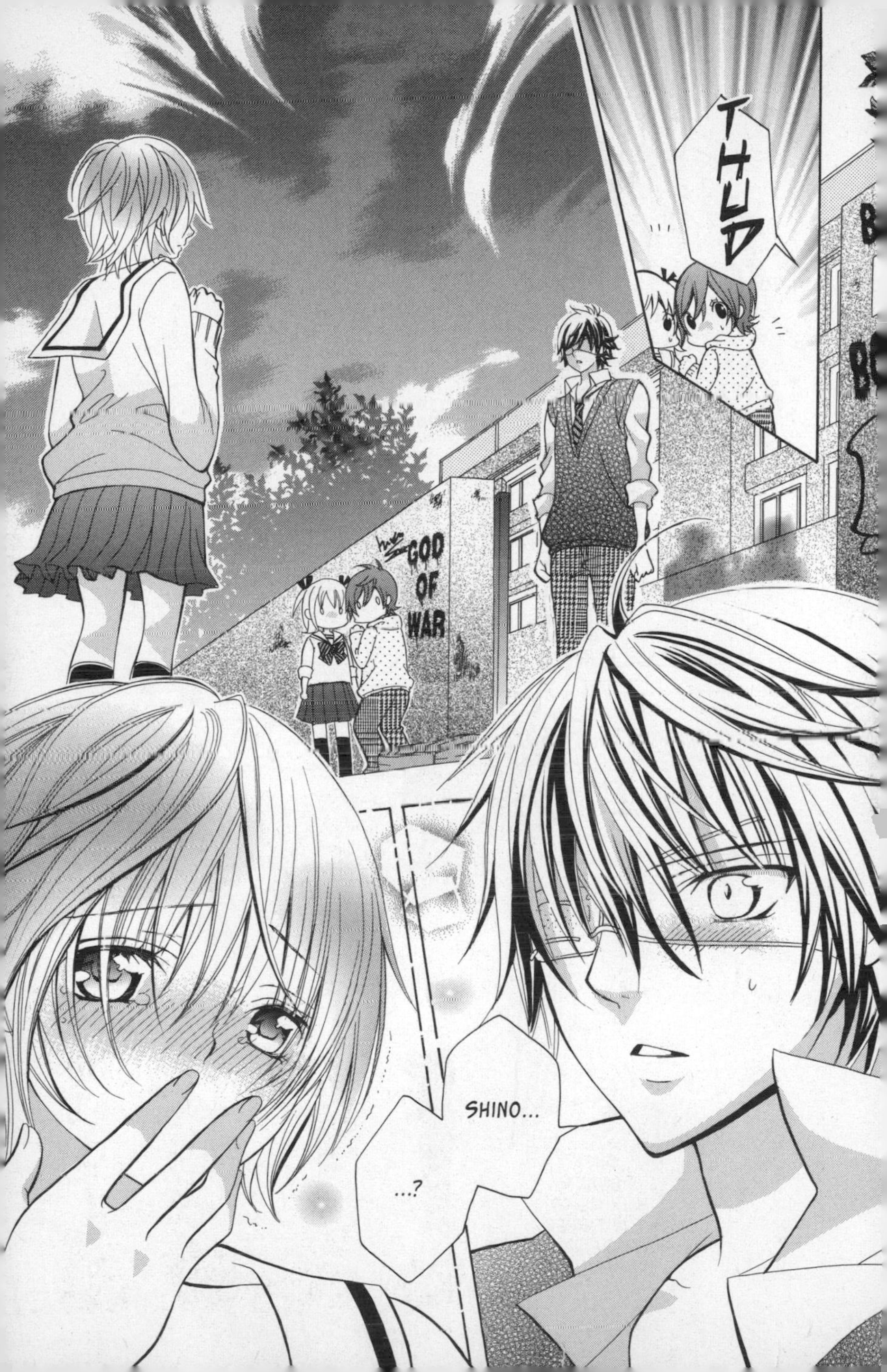
THUD
!!
GOD OF WAR
SHINO...
...?

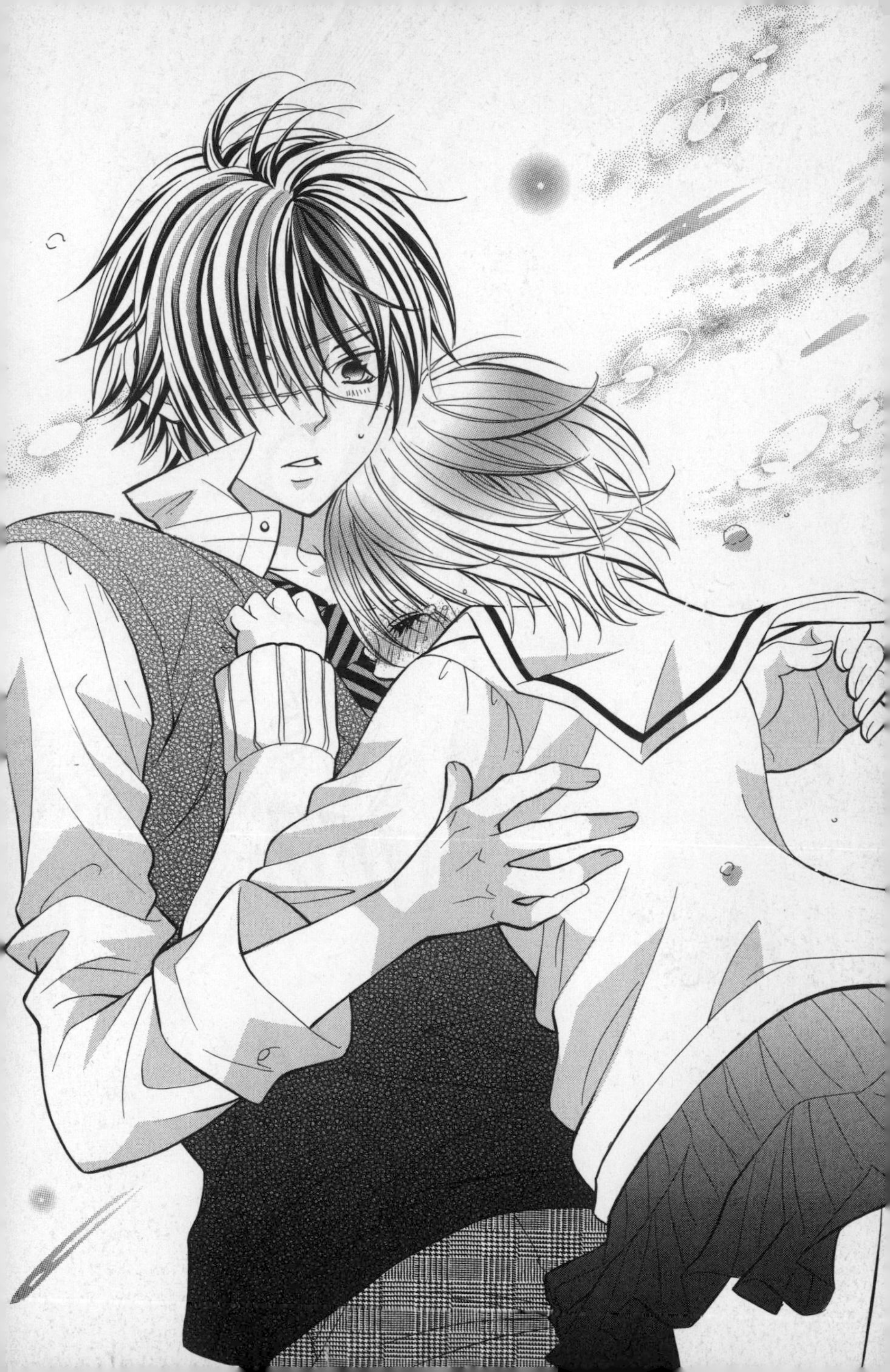

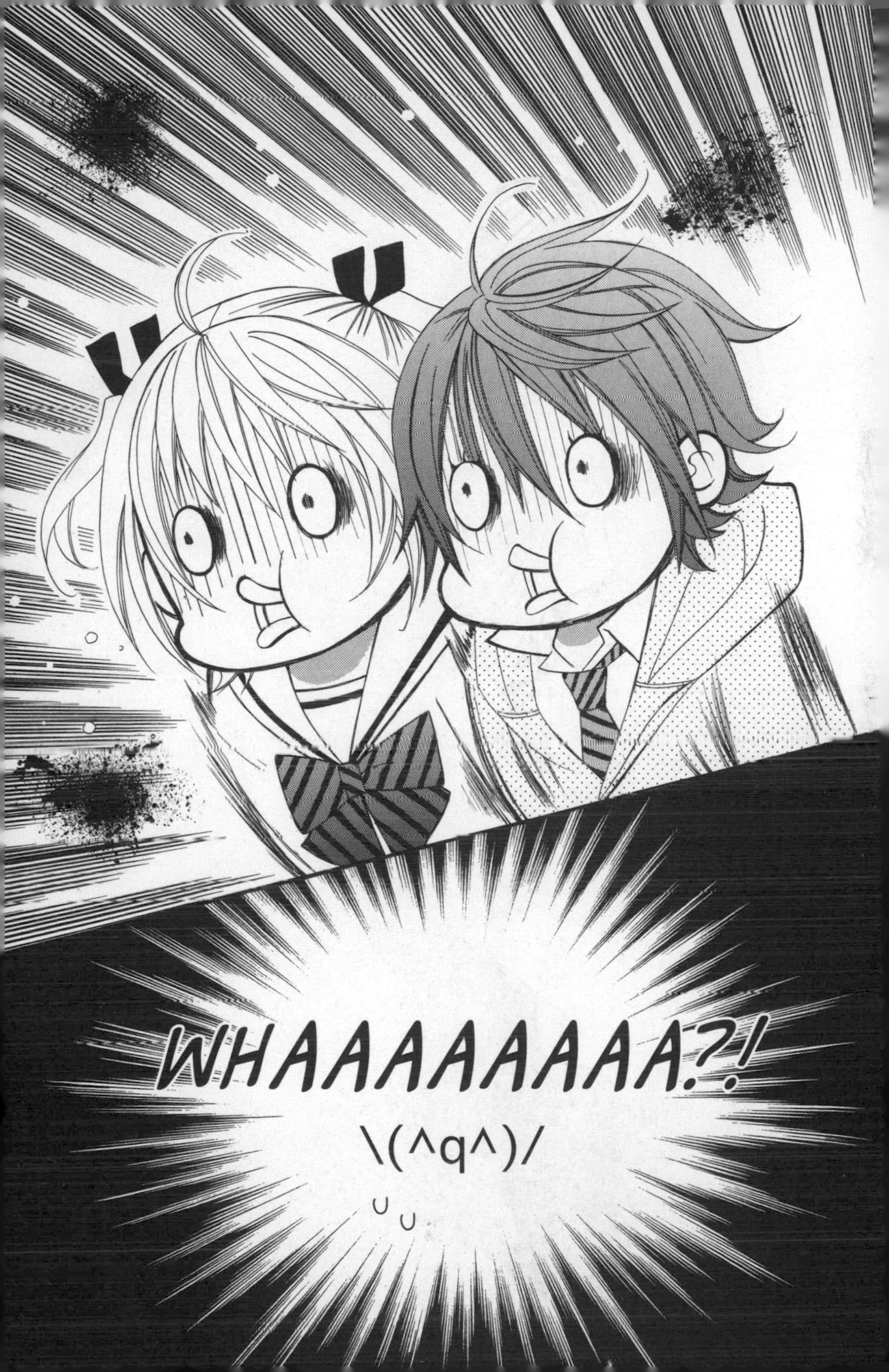
WHAAAAAAAAA?!
\(^q^)/

Chapter 8

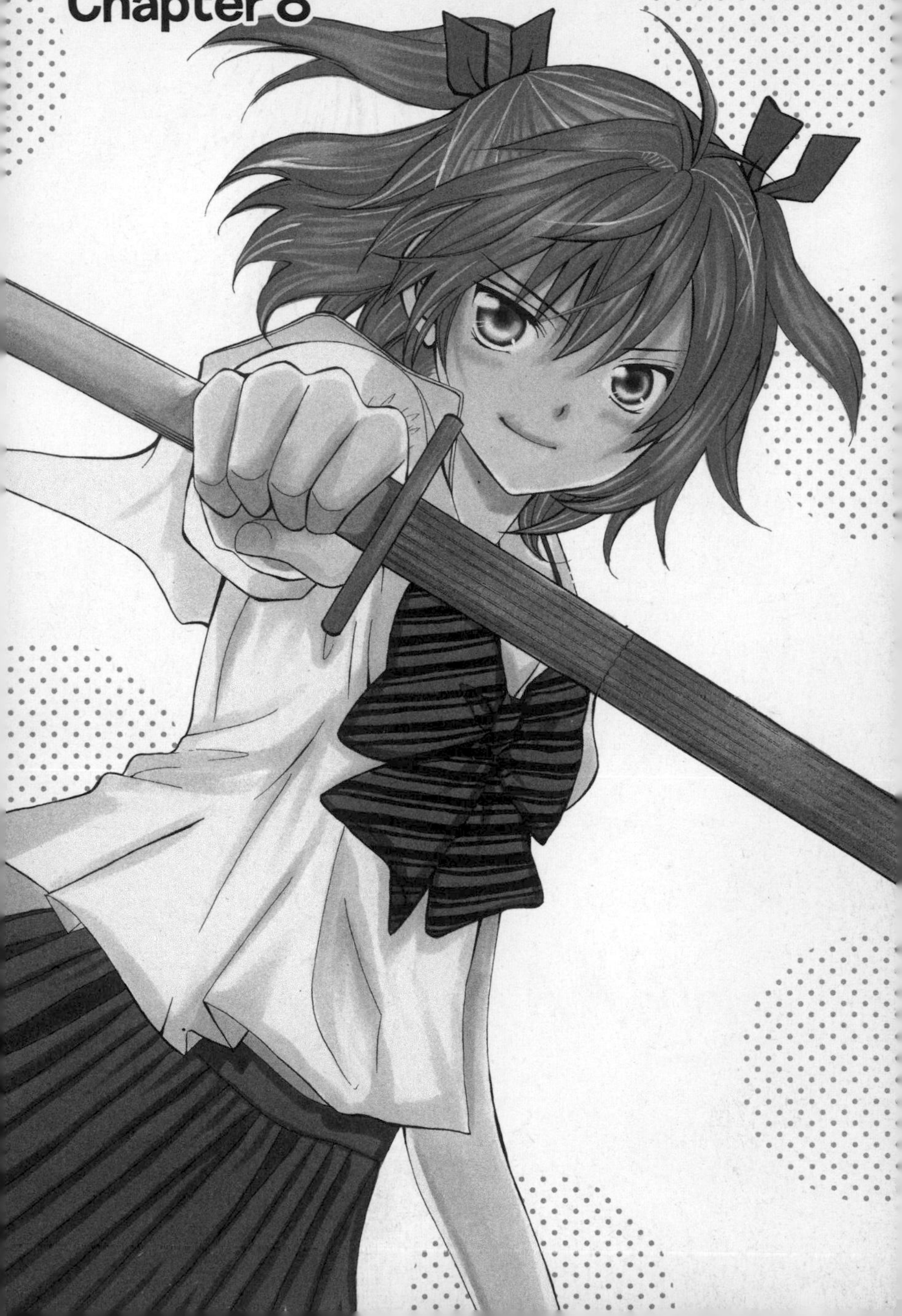

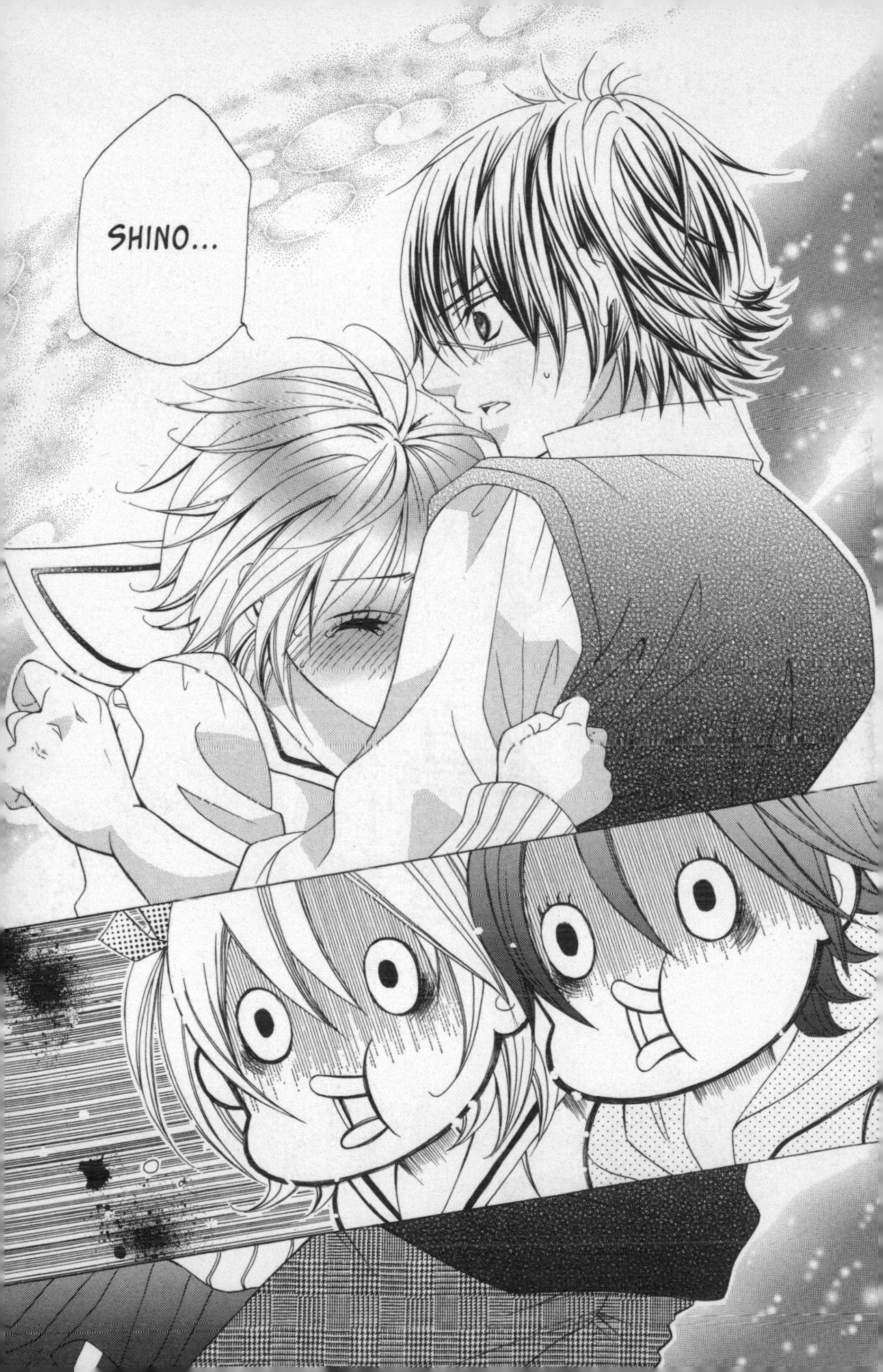
SHINO...

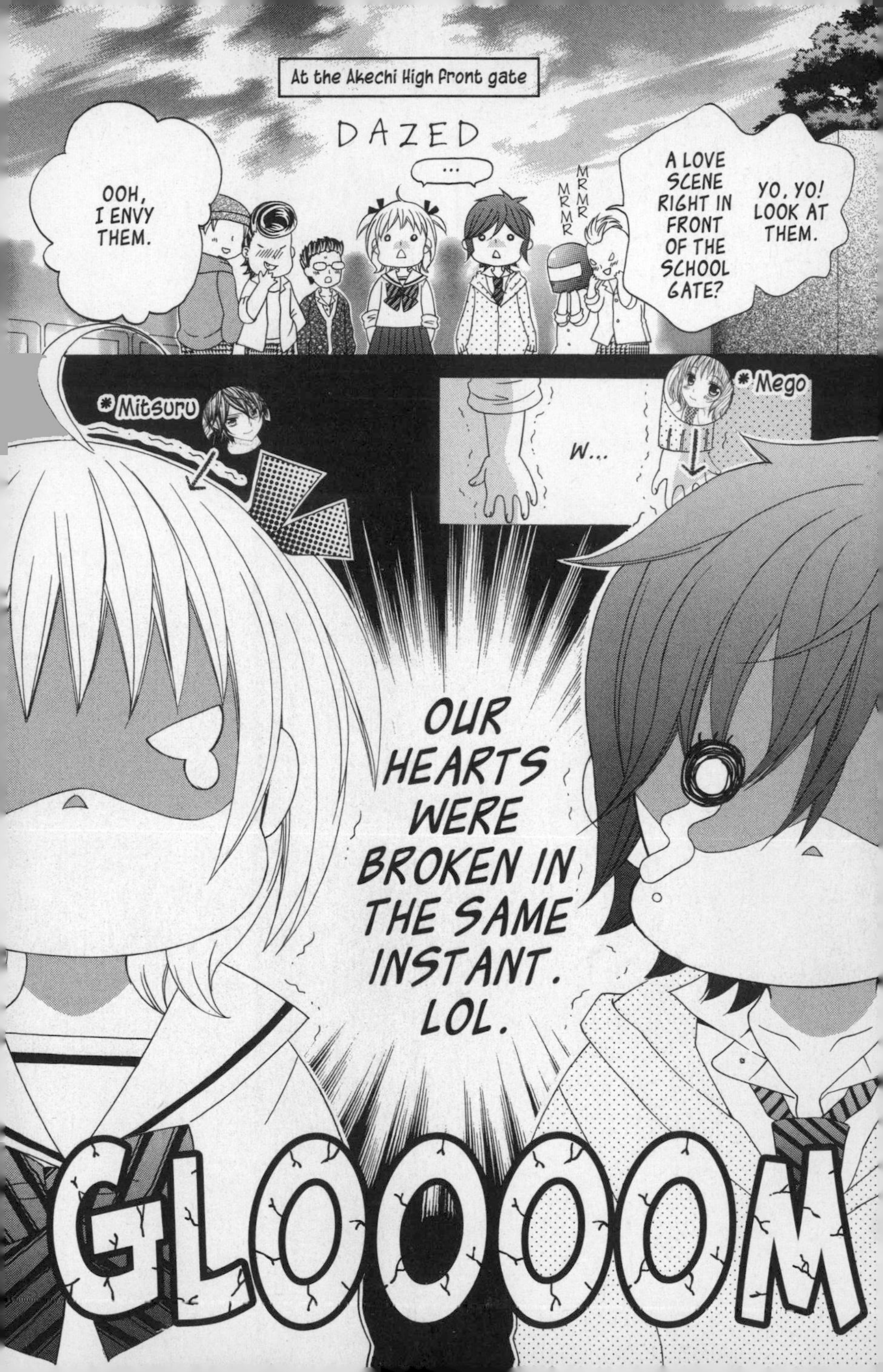
At the Akechi High front gate
YO, YO! LOOK AT THEM.
A LOVE SCENE RIGHT IN FRONT OF THE SCHOOL GATE?
MRMR MRMR
...
DAZED
OOH, I ENVY THEM.
* Mego
W...
* Mitsuru
OUR HEARTS WERE BROKEN IN THE SAME INSTANT. LOL.
GLOOOOM

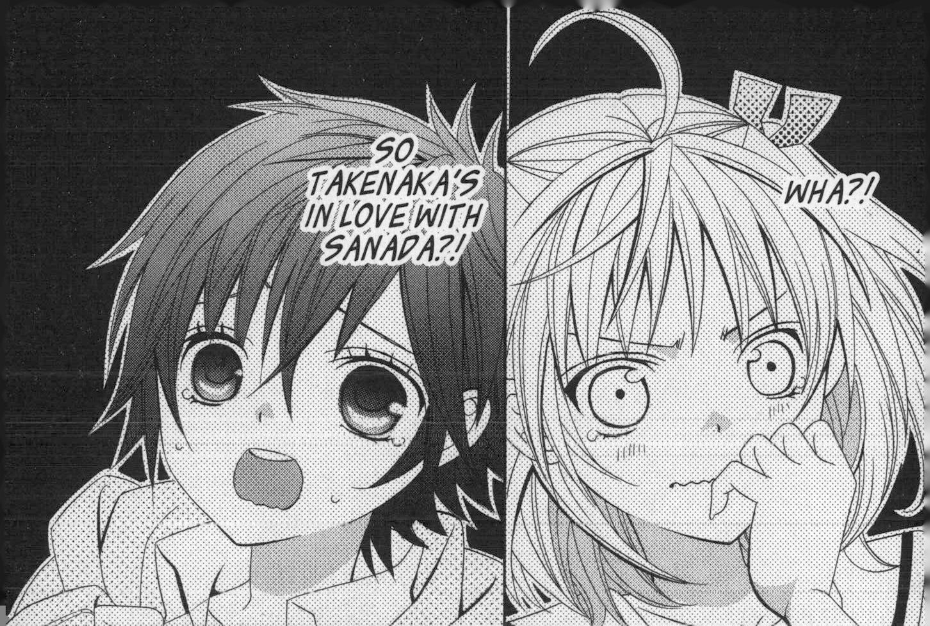
WHA?!
AOI CAN'T STAND WOMEN, BUT THEY'RE HOLDING EACH OTHER!
SO TAKENAKA'S IN LOVE WITH SANADA?!
SO TAKENAKA IS AN EXCEPTION?!

WHAT'S NEW.

I FEEL LONELY BECAUSE I DON'T HAVE ANY FRIENDS WHO ARE KIS-MY-FT2 OR SEXY ZONE FANS (I WANNA BE FRIENDS WITH SEXY ZONE FANGIRLS...), SO I'M TRYING TO CONVERT MY ASSISTANTS BY LENDING THEM DVDS. LOL.
I WENT TO KARAOKE ALONE THE OTHER DAY (I HADN'T GONE IN AGES) AND PASSIONATELY SANG THE KIS-MY-FT2 MEDLEY AND SEXY ZONE'S "SUKI SUGITE," "KAZE WO KITTE," "GAME" AND "TELEPORTATION" THREE TIMES EACH. (*SMILE*)

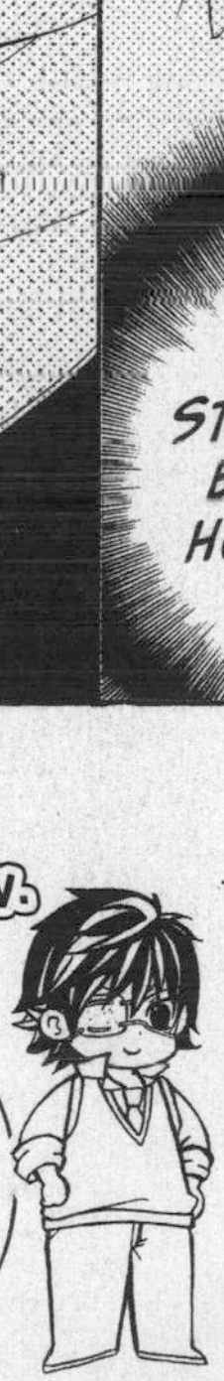

I'M NOW INTO THE *NAKUNA, HARACHAN*, *NOBUNAGA NO CHEF* AND *YAE NO SAKURA* TV DRAMAS!

NOWADAYS, I'M ROOTING FOR SEXY ZONE IN ADDITION TO KIS-MY-FT2. ♪ ♪

(SEXY ZONE MEMBERS ARE SO YOUNG, I FEEL LIKE I'M A NEIGHBORHOOD AUNTIE WHO'S ROOTING FOR THEM [*SMILE*])

"LOVEHOLIC SENPAI" (KENTO NAKAJIMA) IS TOO FUNNY! LOL (^0^)
I WANT TO WATCH A YANKI DRAMA FEATURING FUMA-KEN (KENTO NAKAJIMA AND FUMA KIKUCHI)!! (^0^)

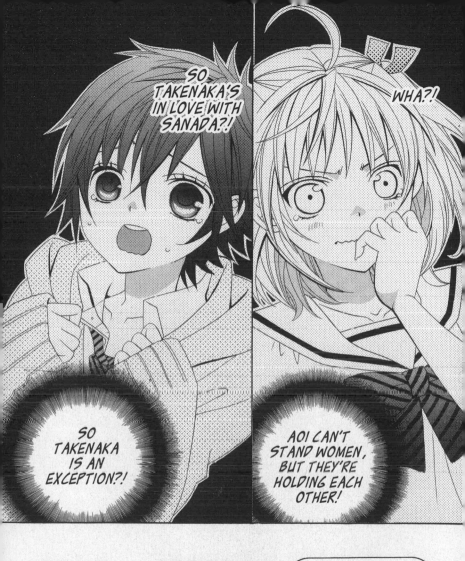

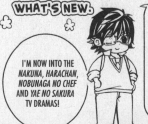

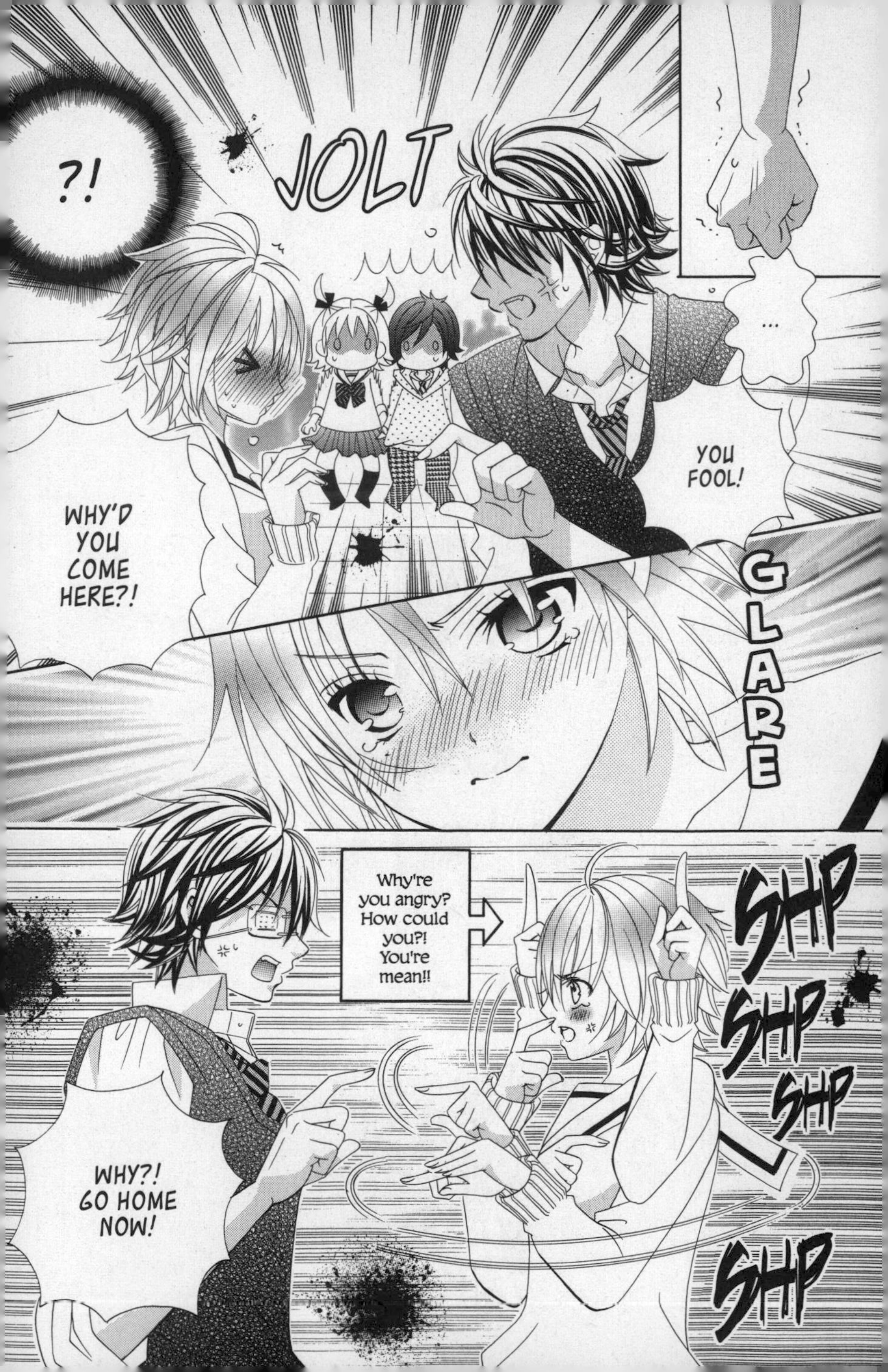
...
YOU FOOL!
JOLT
?!
WHY'D YOU COME HERE?!
GLARE
SHP SHP SHP SHP
SHP
Why're you angry? How could you?! You're mean!!
WHY?! GO HOME NOW!

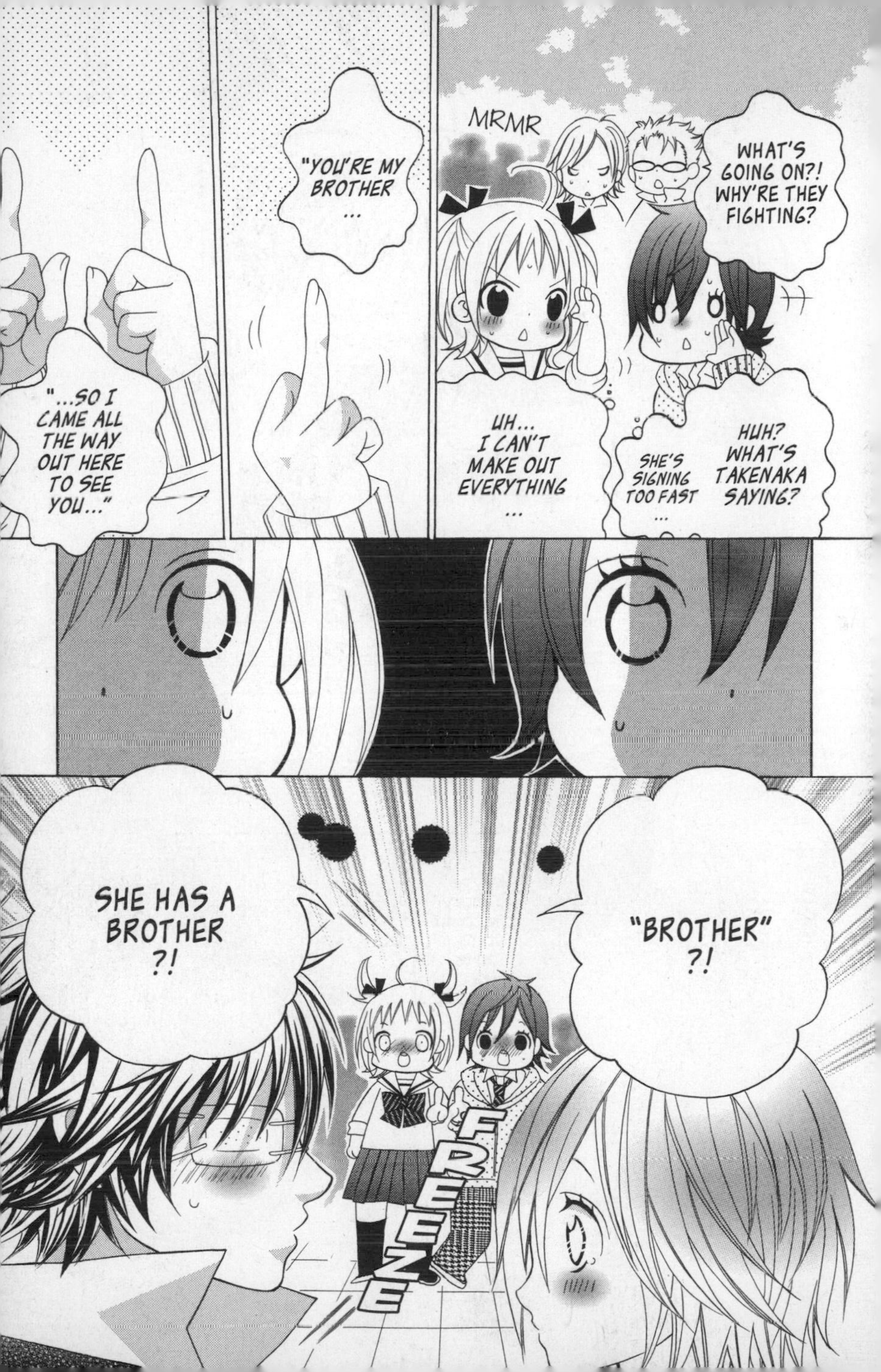
WHAT'S GOING ON?! WHY'RE THEY FIGHTING?
MRMR
HUH? WHAT'S TAKENAKA SAYING?
SHE'S SIGNING TOO FAST ...
UH... I CAN'T MAKE OUT EVERYTHING ...
"YOU'RE MY BROTHER ...
"...SO I CAME ALL THE WAY OUT HERE TO SEE YOU..."
"BROTHER" ?!
SHE HAS A BROTHER ?!
FREEZE

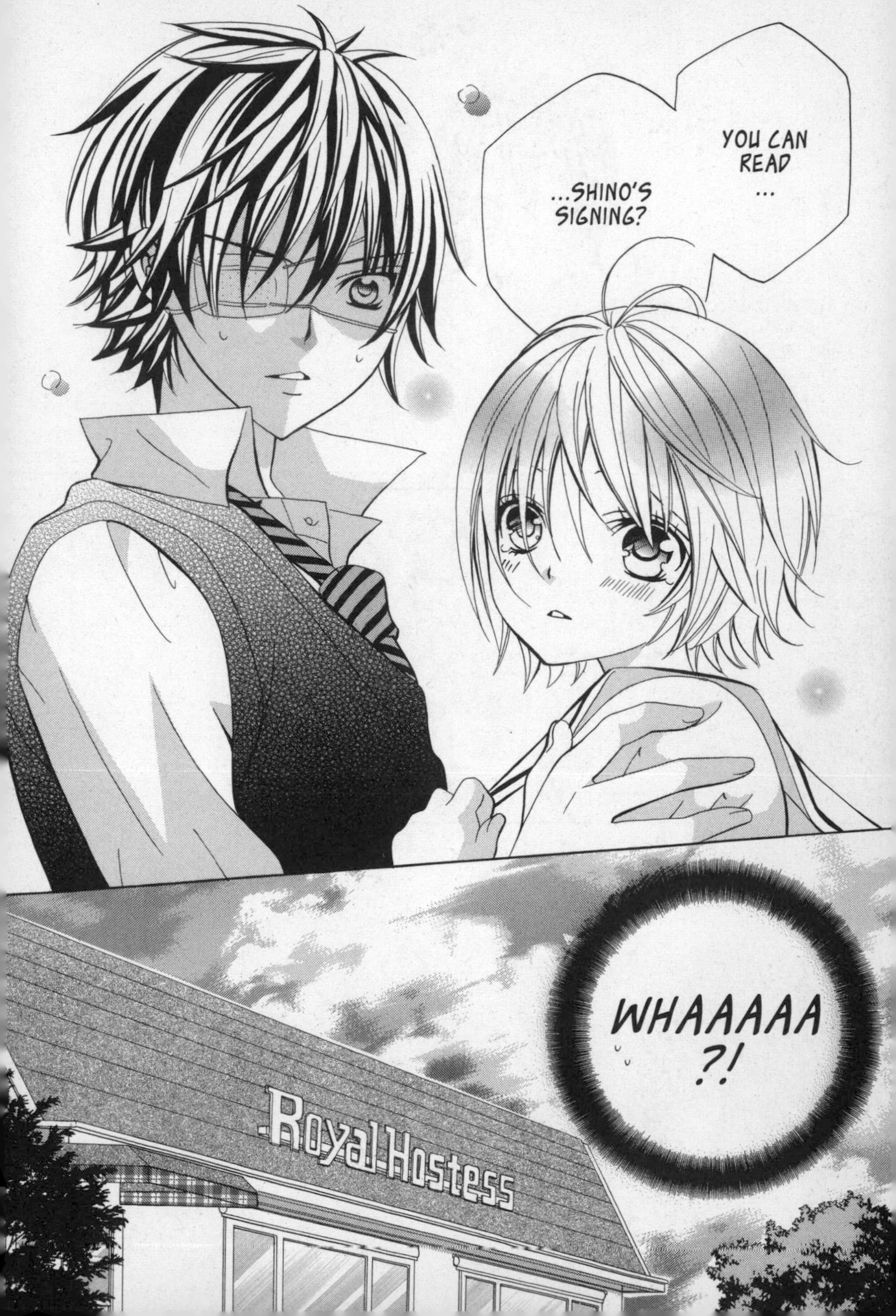
YOU CAN READ ...
...SHINO'S SIGNING?
Royal Hostess
WHAAAAA ?!

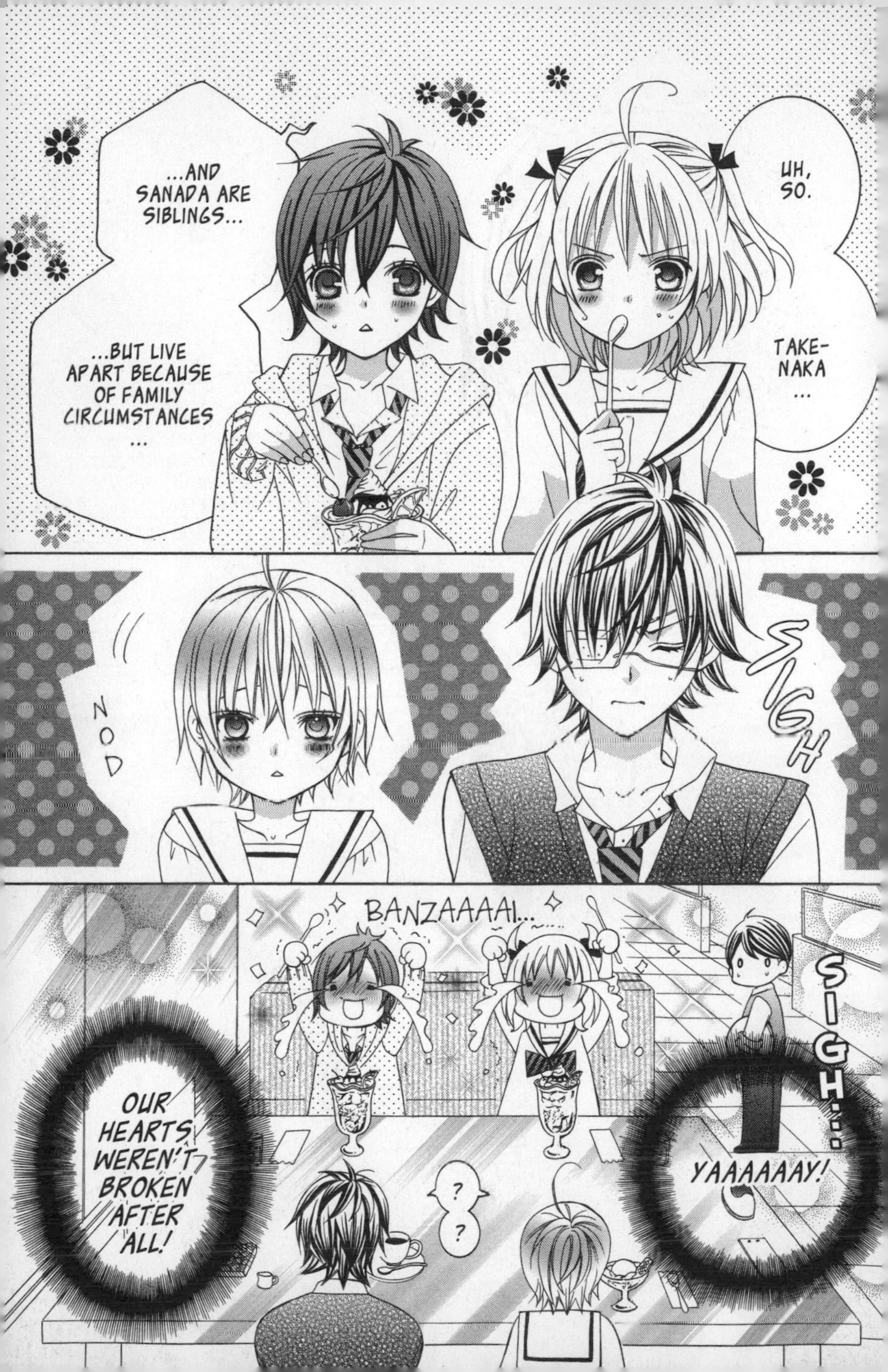
UH, SO.
TAKE-NAKA ...
...AND SANADA ARE SIBLINGS...
...BUT LIVE APART BECAUSE OF FAMILY CIRCUMSTANCES ...
SIGH
NOD
SIGH...
YAAAAAAY!
BANZAAAAI...
?
?
OUR HEARTS WEREN'T BROKEN AFTER ALL!

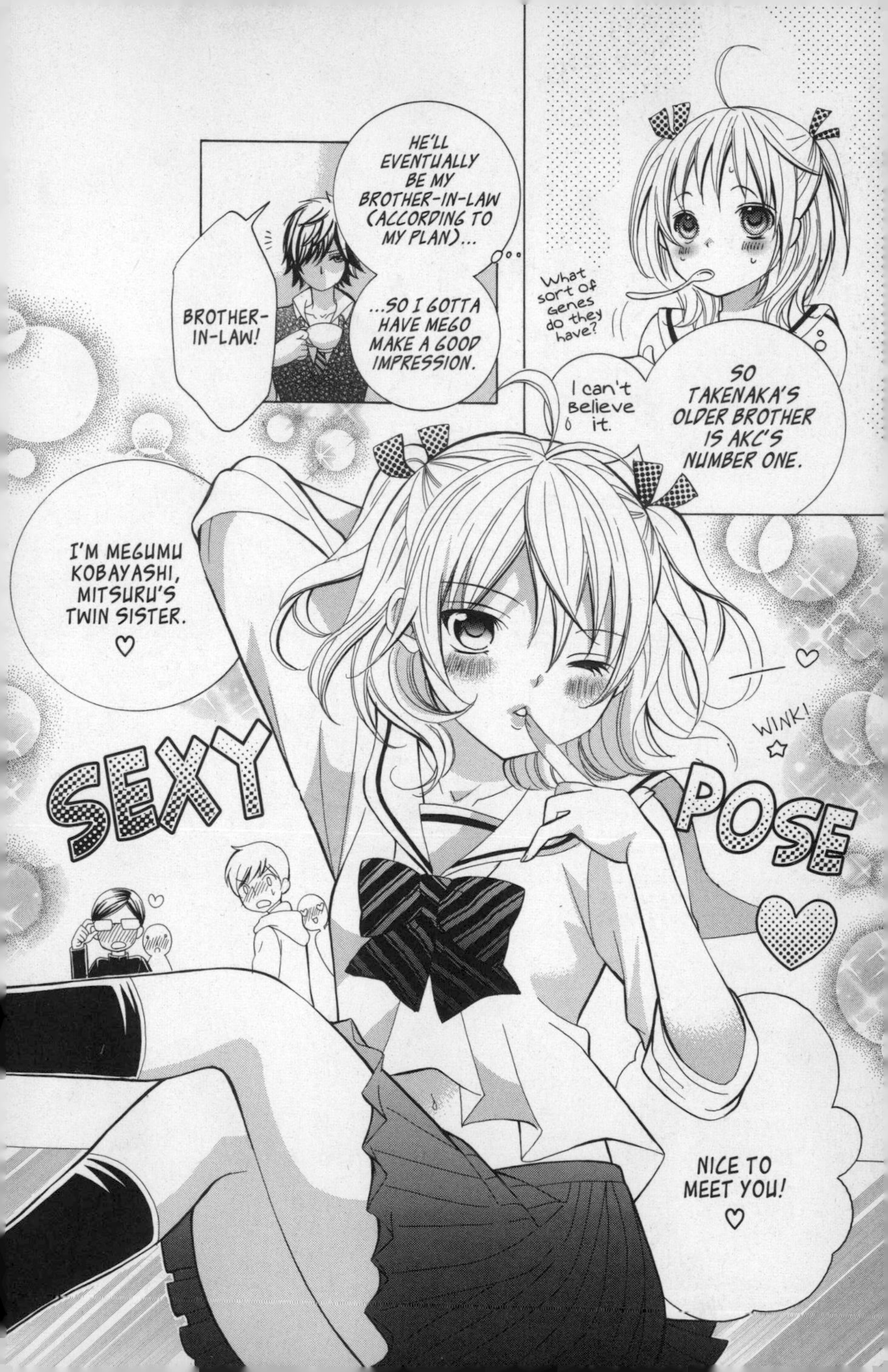

What sort of genes do they have?
SO TAKENAKA'S OLDER BROTHER IS AKC'S NUMBER ONE.
I can't believe it.
HE'LL EVENTUALLY BE MY BROTHER-IN-LAW (ACCORDING TO MY PLAN)...
...SO I GOTTA HAVE MEGO MAKE A GOOD IMPRESSION.
BROTHER-IN-LAW!
—♡
WINK!
I'M MEGUMU KOBAYASHI, MITSURU'S TWIN SISTER. ♡
SEXY POSE ♡
NICE TO MEET YOU! ♡

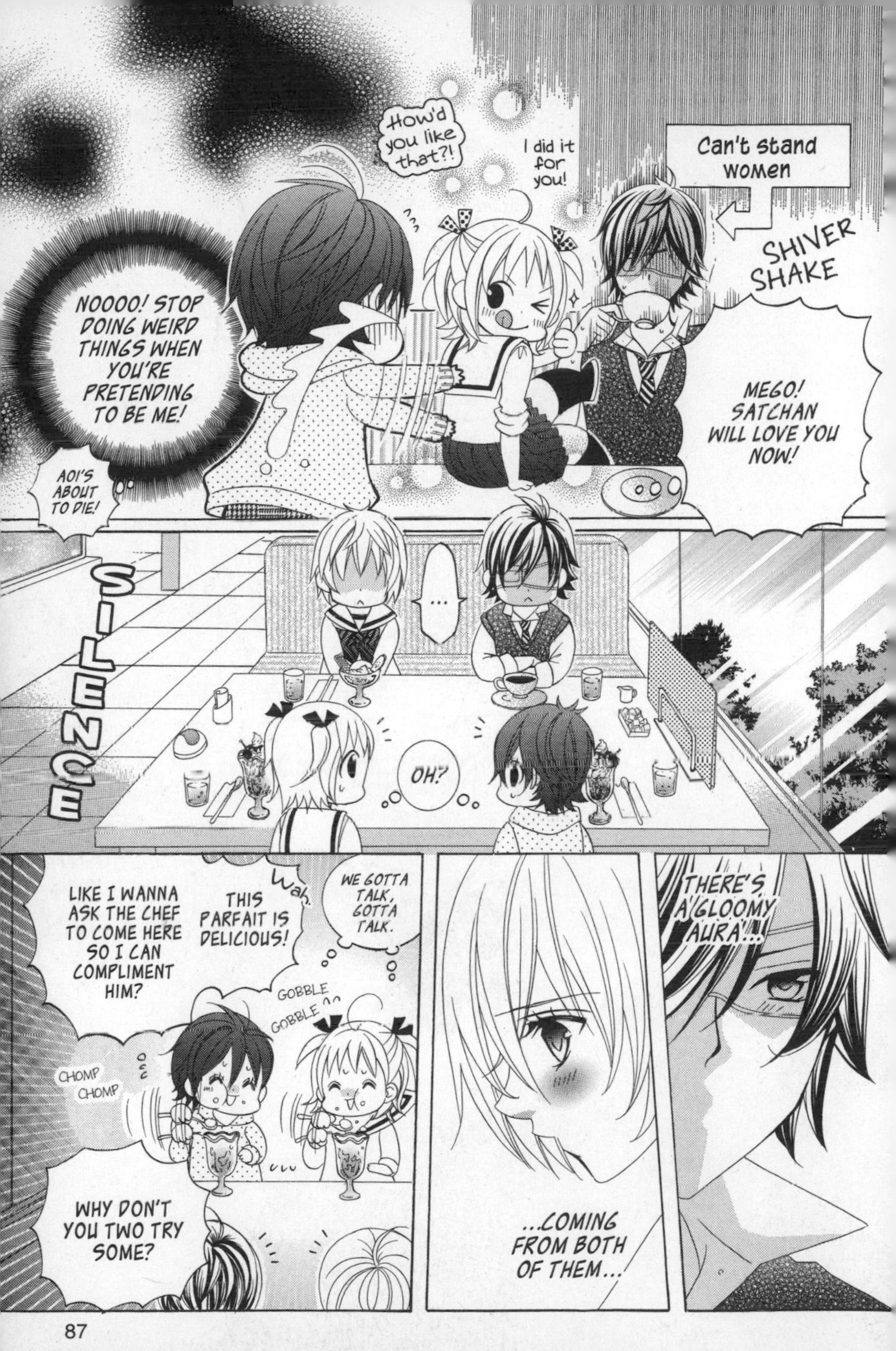
Can't stand women
SHIVER SHAKE
I did it for you!
How'd you like that?!
MEGO! SATCHAN WILL LOVE YOU NOW!
NOOOO! STOP DOING WEIRD THINGS WHEN YOU'RE PRETENDING TO BE ME!
AOI'S ABOUT TO DIE!
...
SILENCE
OH?
THERE'S A GLOOMY AURA...
...COMING FROM BOTH OF THEM...
WE GOTTA TALK, GOTTA TALK.
Wah
THIS PARFAIT IS DELICIOUS!
LIKE I WANNA ASK THE CHEF TO COME HERE SO I CAN COMPLIMENT HIM?
GOBBLE GOBBLE
CHOMP CHOMP
WHY DON'T YOU TWO TRY SOME?

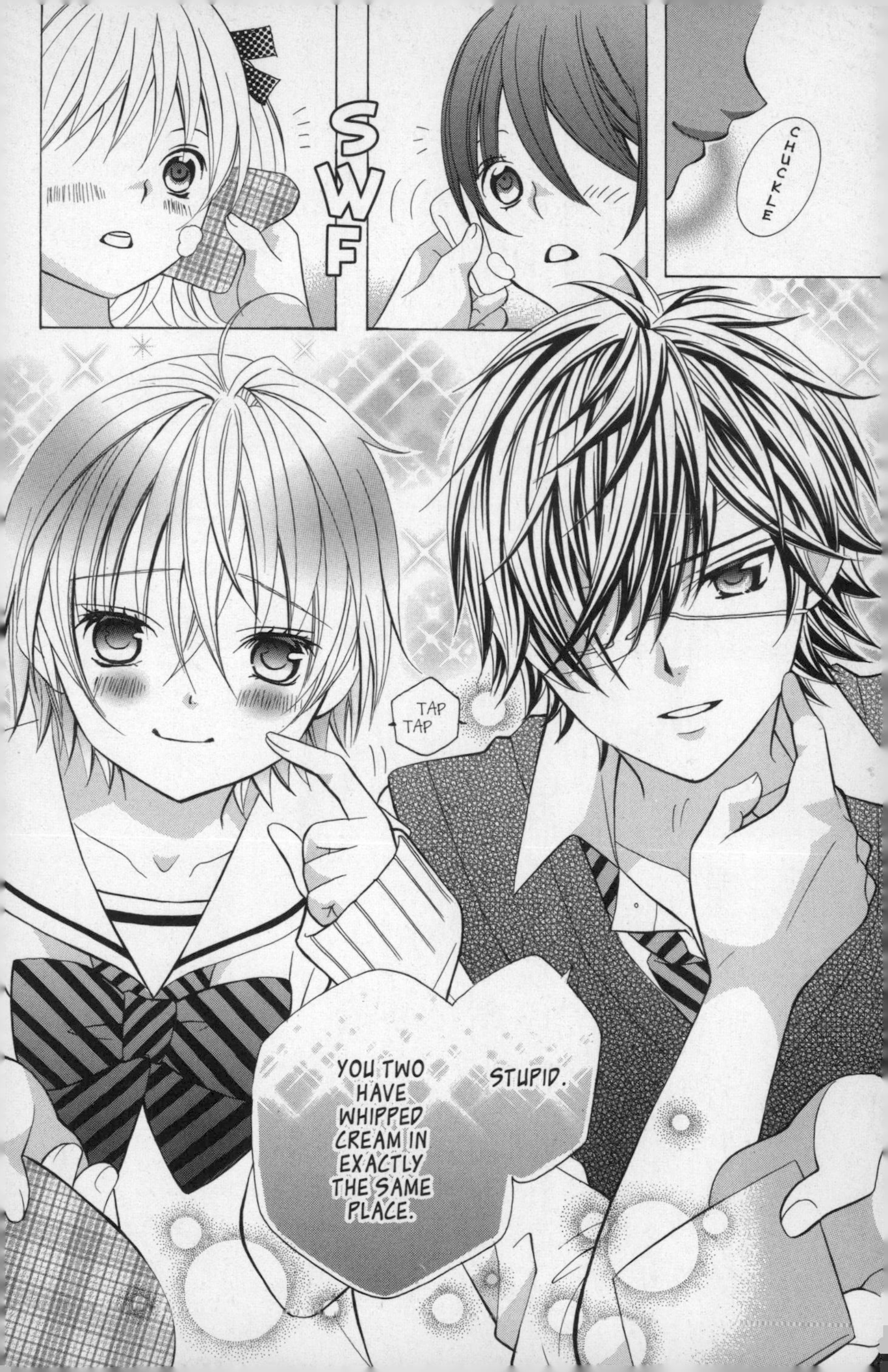
CHUCKLE
SWF
TAP TAP
STUPID.
YOU TWO HAVE WHIPPED CREAM IN EXACTLY THE SAME PLACE.

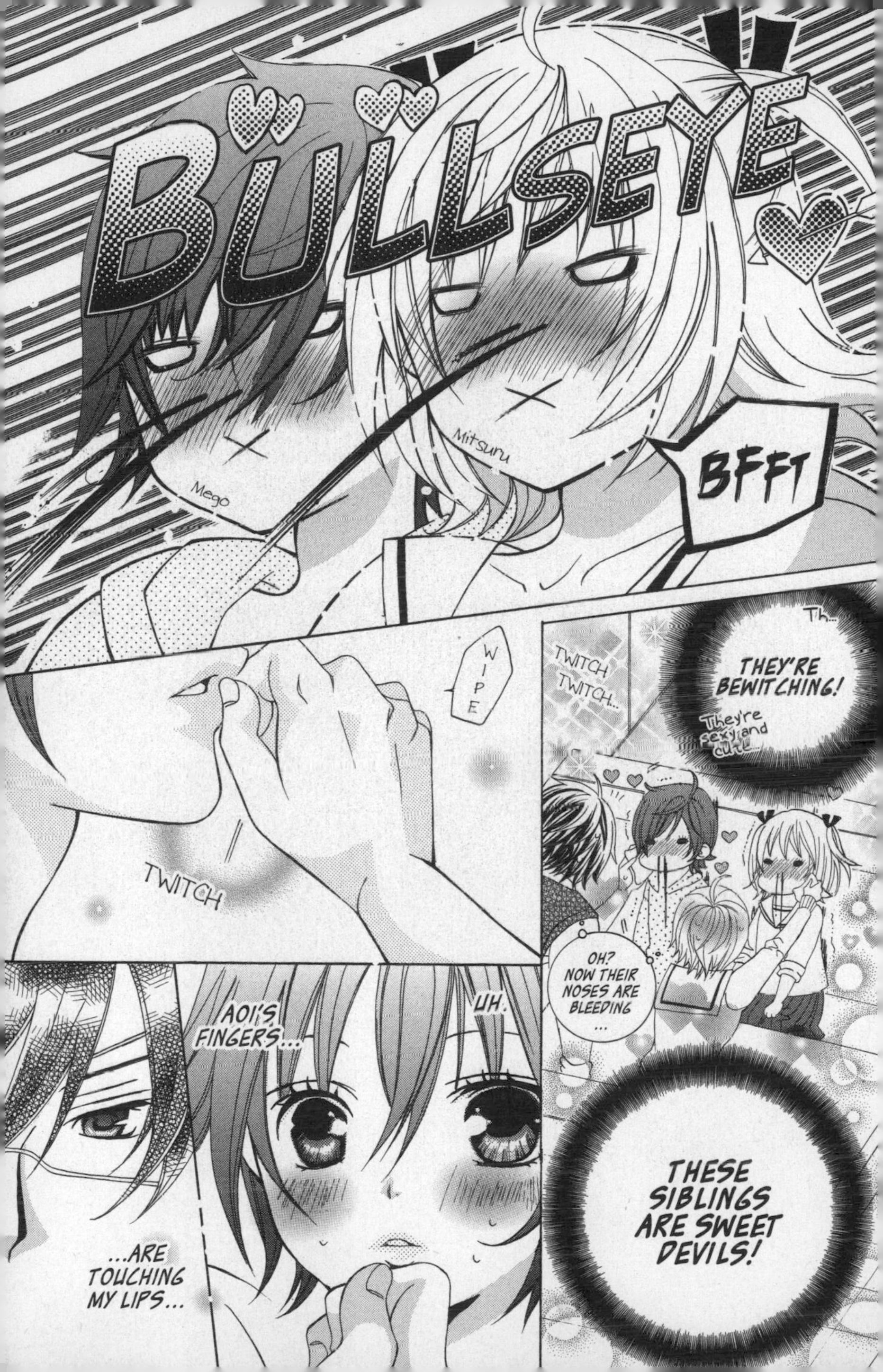
BULLSEYE
BFFT
Mitsuru
Mego
Th...
THEY'RE BEWITCHING!
They're sexy and cute...
TWITCH TWITCH...
OH? NOW THEIR NOSES ARE BLEEDING...
THESE SIBLINGS ARE SWEET DEVILS!
WIPE
TWITCH
UH.
AOI'S FINGERS...
...ARE TOUCHING MY LIPS...

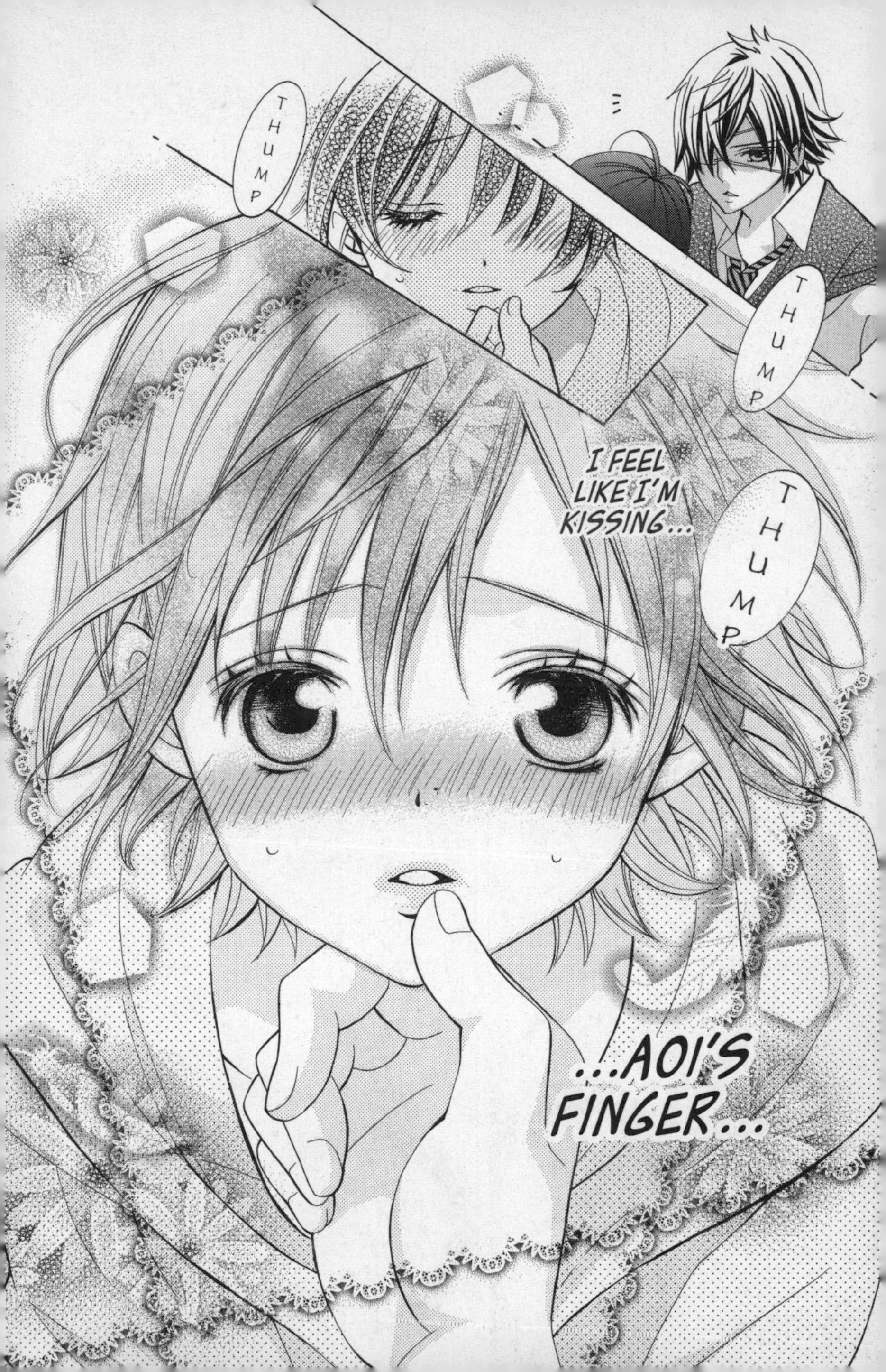
THUMP
THUMP
THUMP
I FEEL LIKE I'M KISSING...
...AOI'S FINGER...

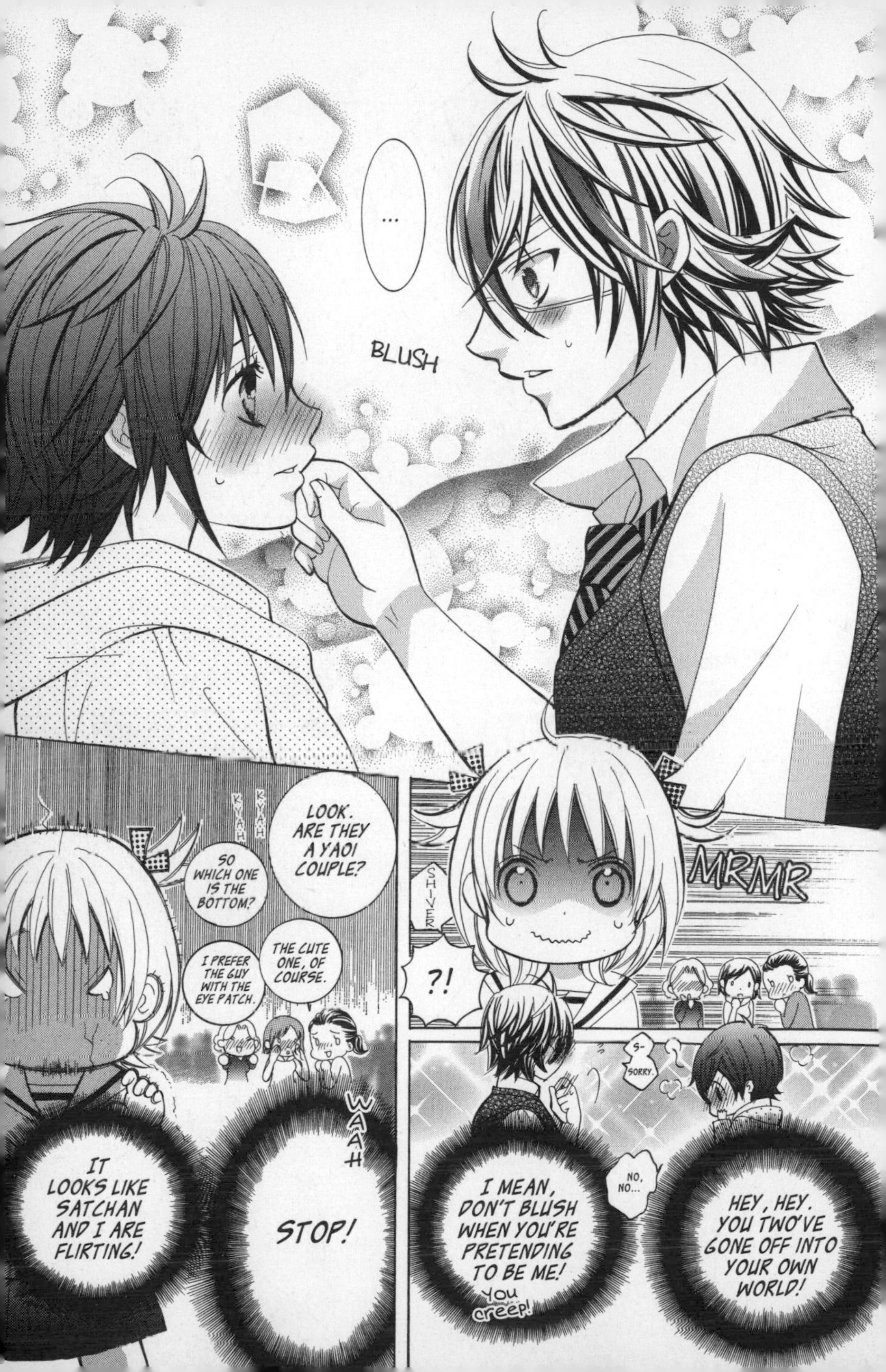
...
BLUSH
MRMR
SHIVER
?!
S-SORRY.
HEY, HEY. YOU TWO'VE GONE OFF INTO YOUR OWN WORLD!
NO, NO...
I MEAN, DON'T BLUSH WHEN YOU'RE PRETENDING TO BE ME!
YOU CREEP!
LOOK. ARE THEY A YAOI COUPLE?
KYAH KYAH
SO WHICH ONE IS THE BOTTOM?
THE CUTE ONE, OF COURSE.
I PREFER THE GUY WITH THE EYE PATCH.
WAAAH
STOP!
IT LOOKS LIKE SATCHAN AND I ARE FLIRTING!

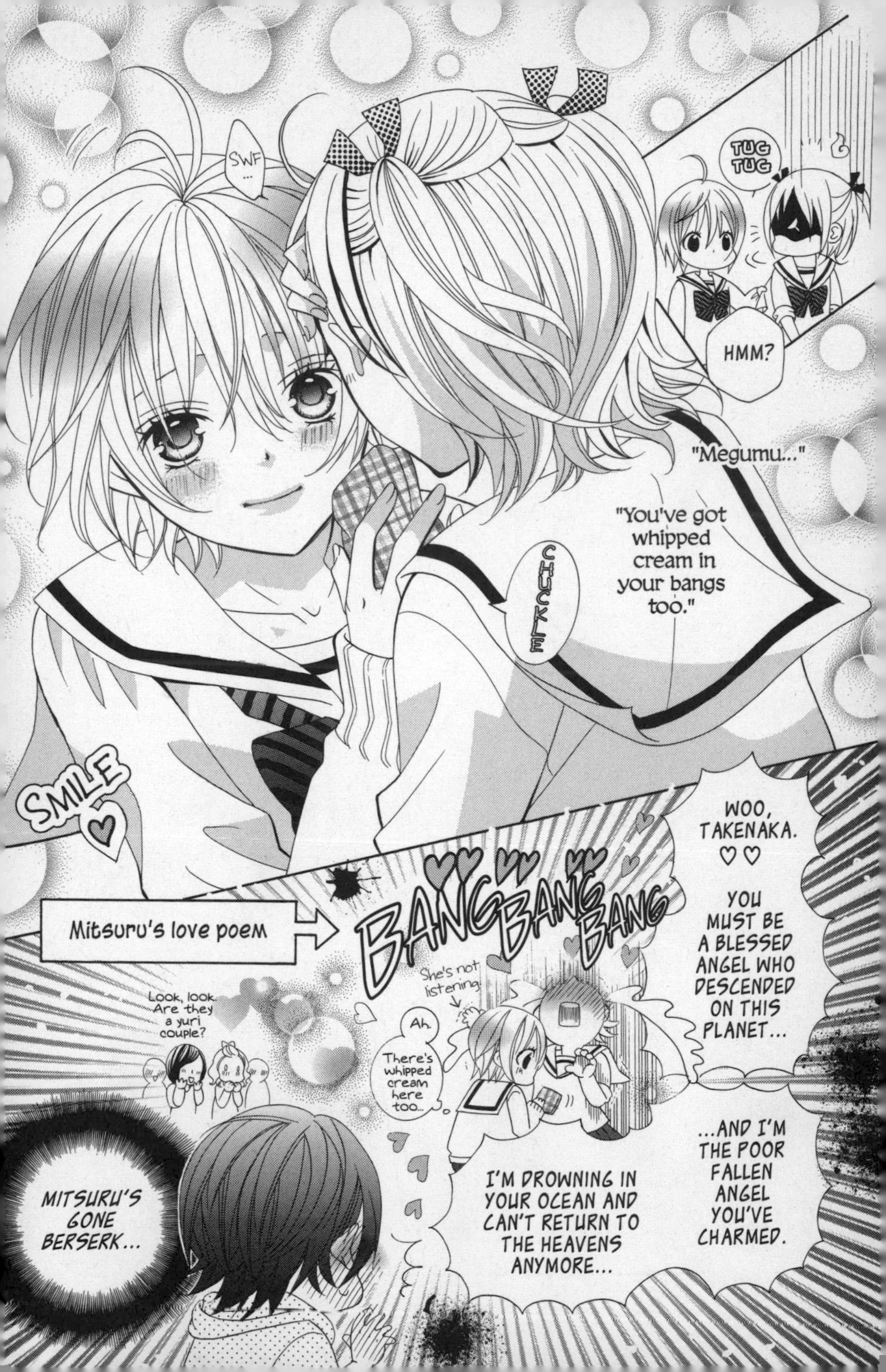
TUG TUG
HMM?
"Megumu..."
"You've got whipped cream in your bangs too."
CHUCKLE
SWF...
SMILE ♡
WOO, TAKENAKA. ♡ ♡
YOU MUST BE A BLESSED ANGEL WHO DESCENDED ON THIS PLANET...
...AND I'M THE POOR FALLEN ANGEL YOU'VE CHARMED.
I'M DROWNING IN YOUR OCEAN AND CAN'T RETURN TO THE HEAVENS ANYMORE...
BANG BANG BANG
Mitsuru's love poem
She's not listening.
Ah.
There's whipped cream here too...
Look, look. Are they a yuri couple?
MITSURU'S GONE BERSERK...

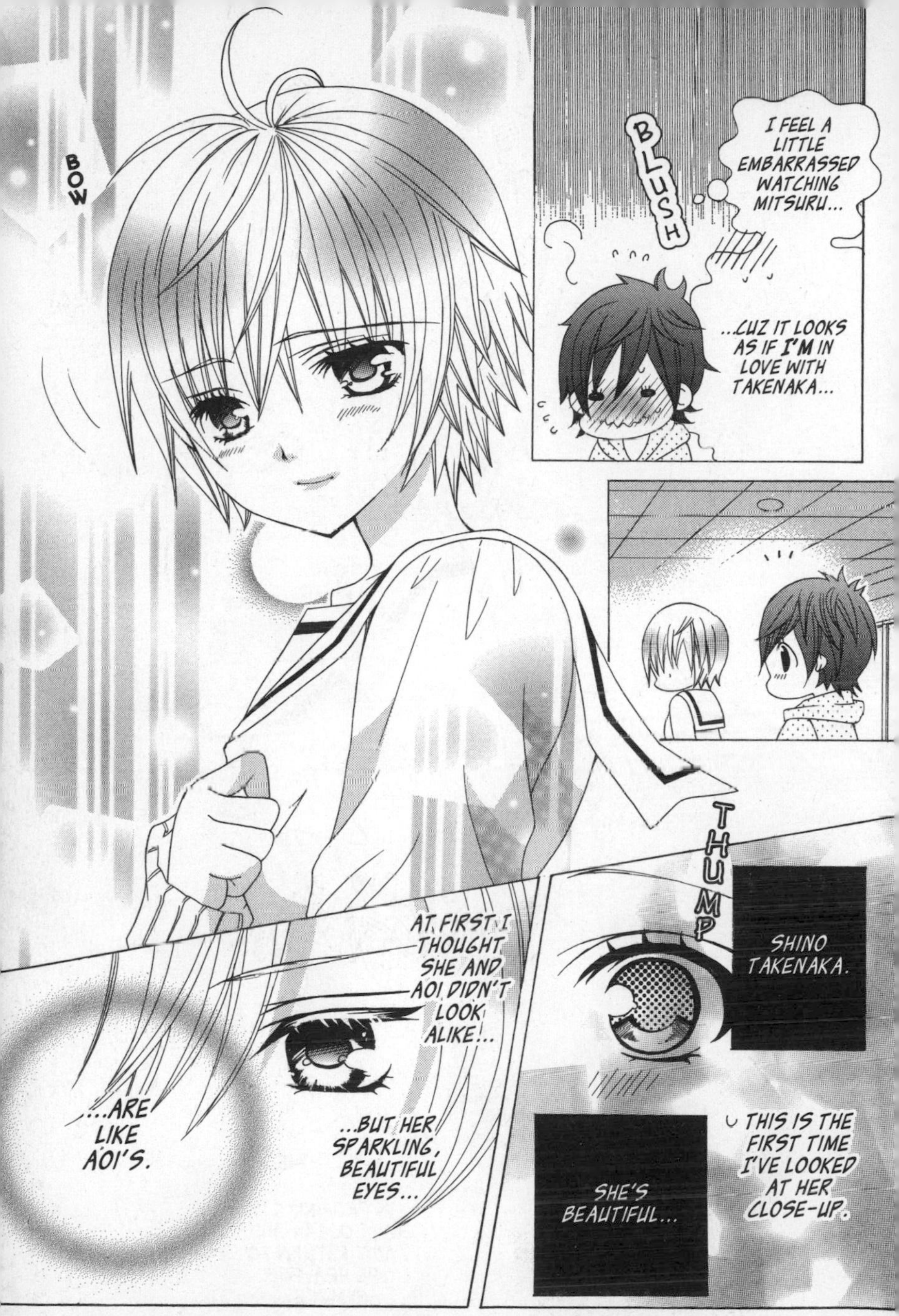
BLUSH
I FEEL A LITTLE EMBARRASSED WATCHING MITSURU...
...CUZ IT LOOKS AS IF I'M IN LOVE WITH TAKENAKA...
BOW
THUMP
SHINO TAKENAKA.
THIS IS THE FIRST TIME I'VE LOOKED AT HER CLOSE-UP.
SHE'S BEAUTIFUL...
AT FIRST I THOUGHT SHE AND AOI DIDN'T LOOK ALIKE...
...BUT HER SPARKLING, BEAUTIFUL EYES...
...ARE LIKE AOI'S.

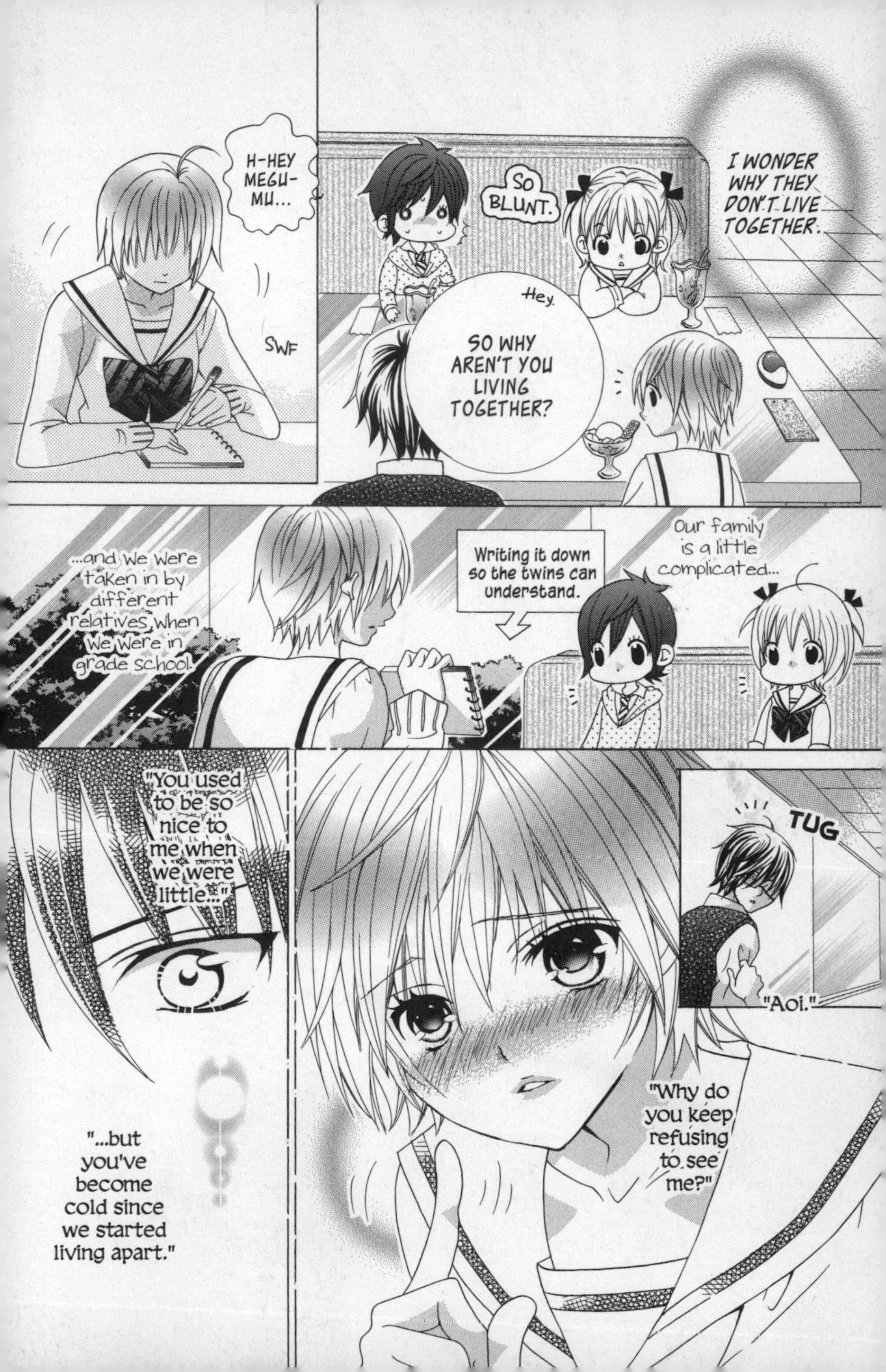
I WONDER WHY THEY DON'T LIVE TOGETHER.
SO BLUNT.
Hey.
SO WHY AREN'T YOU LIVING TOGETHER?
H-HEY MEGUMU...
SWF
Our family is a little complicated...
Writing it down so the twins can understand.
...and we were taken in by different relatives when we were in grade school.
TUG
"Aoi."
"Why do you keep refusing to see me?"
"You used to be so nice to me when we were little..."
"...but you've become cold since we started living apart."

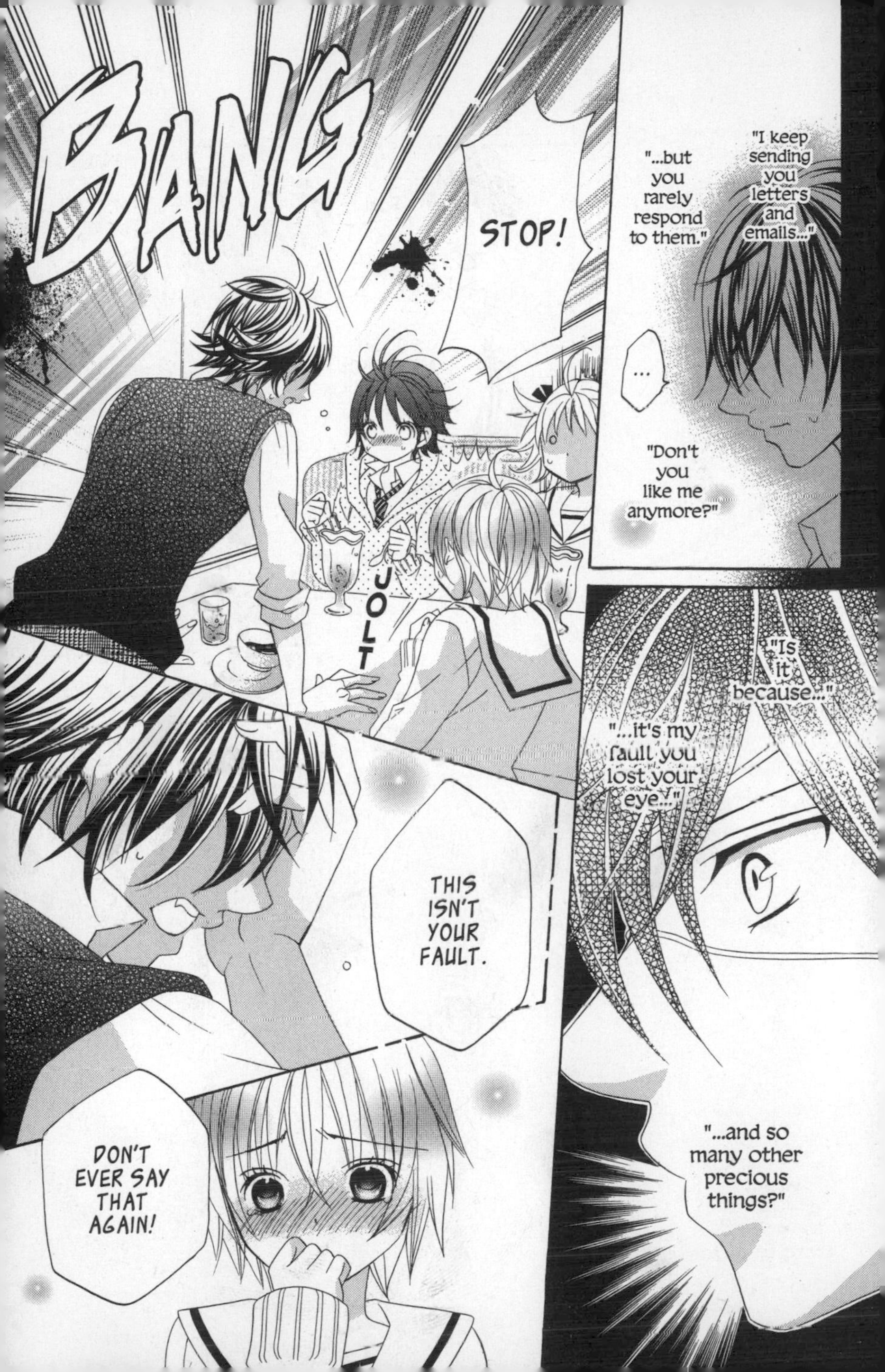
"I keep sending you letters and emails..."
"...but you rarely respond to them."
...
"Don't you like me anymore?"
BANG
STOP!
JOLT
"Is it because..."
"...it's my fault you lost your eye..."
"...and so many other precious things?"
THIS ISN'T YOUR FAULT.
DON'T EVER SAY THAT AGAIN!

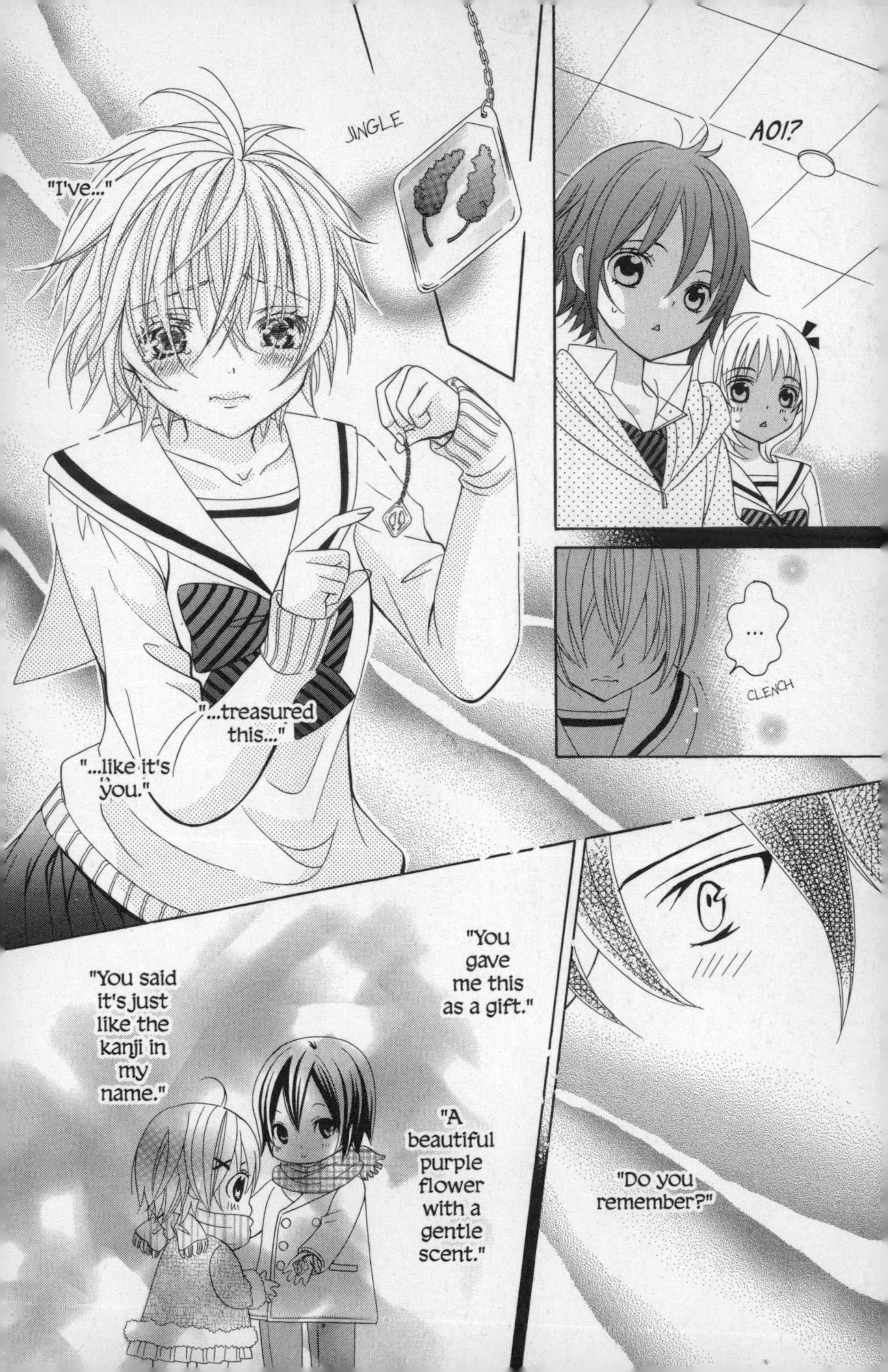
AOI!?
...
CLENCH
JINGLE
"I've..."
"...treasured this..."
"...like it's you."
"Do you remember?"
"You gave me this as a gift."
"You said it's just like the kanji in my name."
"A beautiful purple flower with a gentle scent."

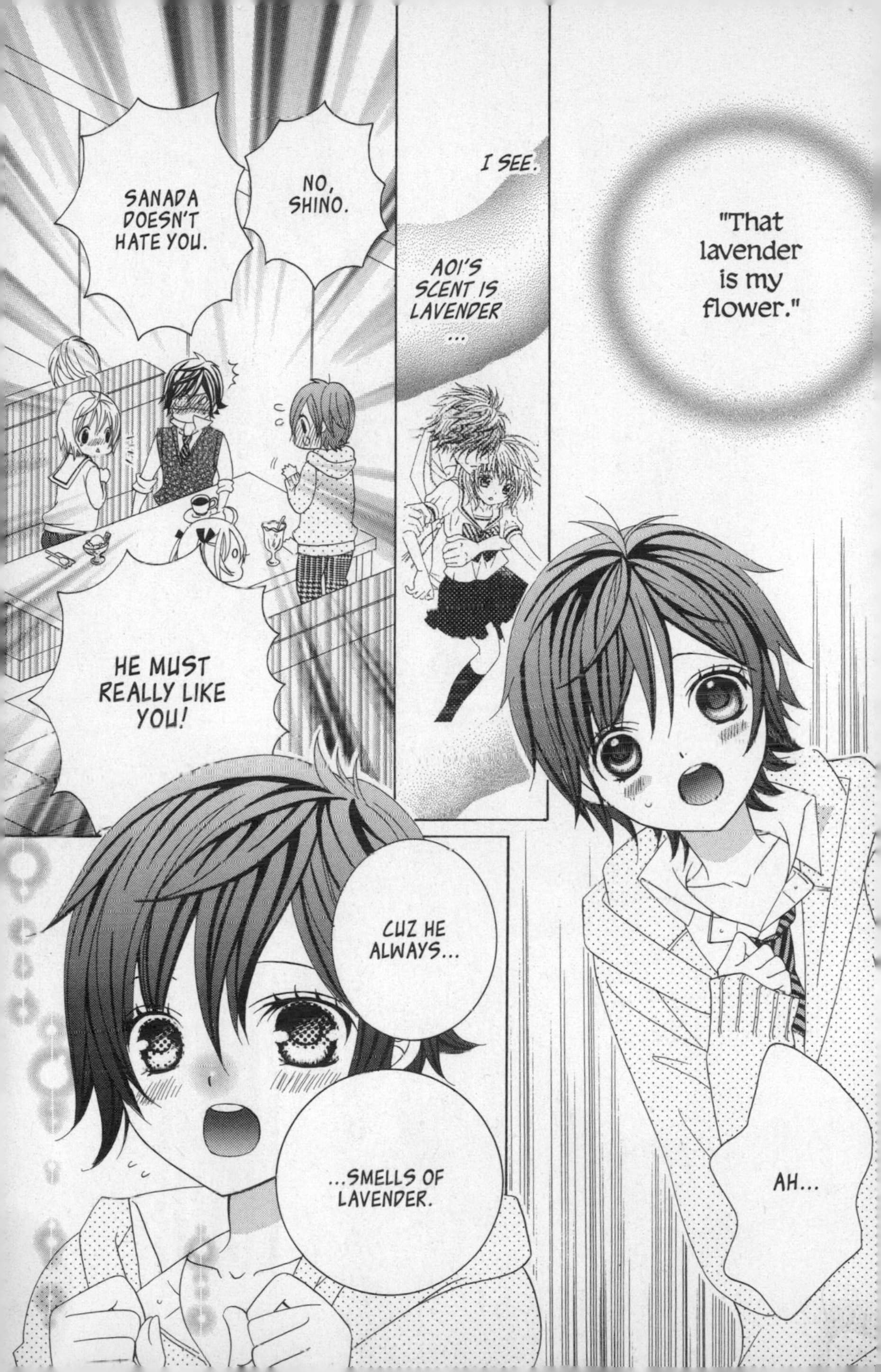
"That lavender is my flower."
AH...
I SEE.
AOI'S SCENT IS LAVENDER ...
NO, SHINO.
SANADA DOESN'T HATE YOU.
HE MUST REALLY LIKE YOU!
CUZ HE ALWAYS...
...SMELLS OF LAVENDER.

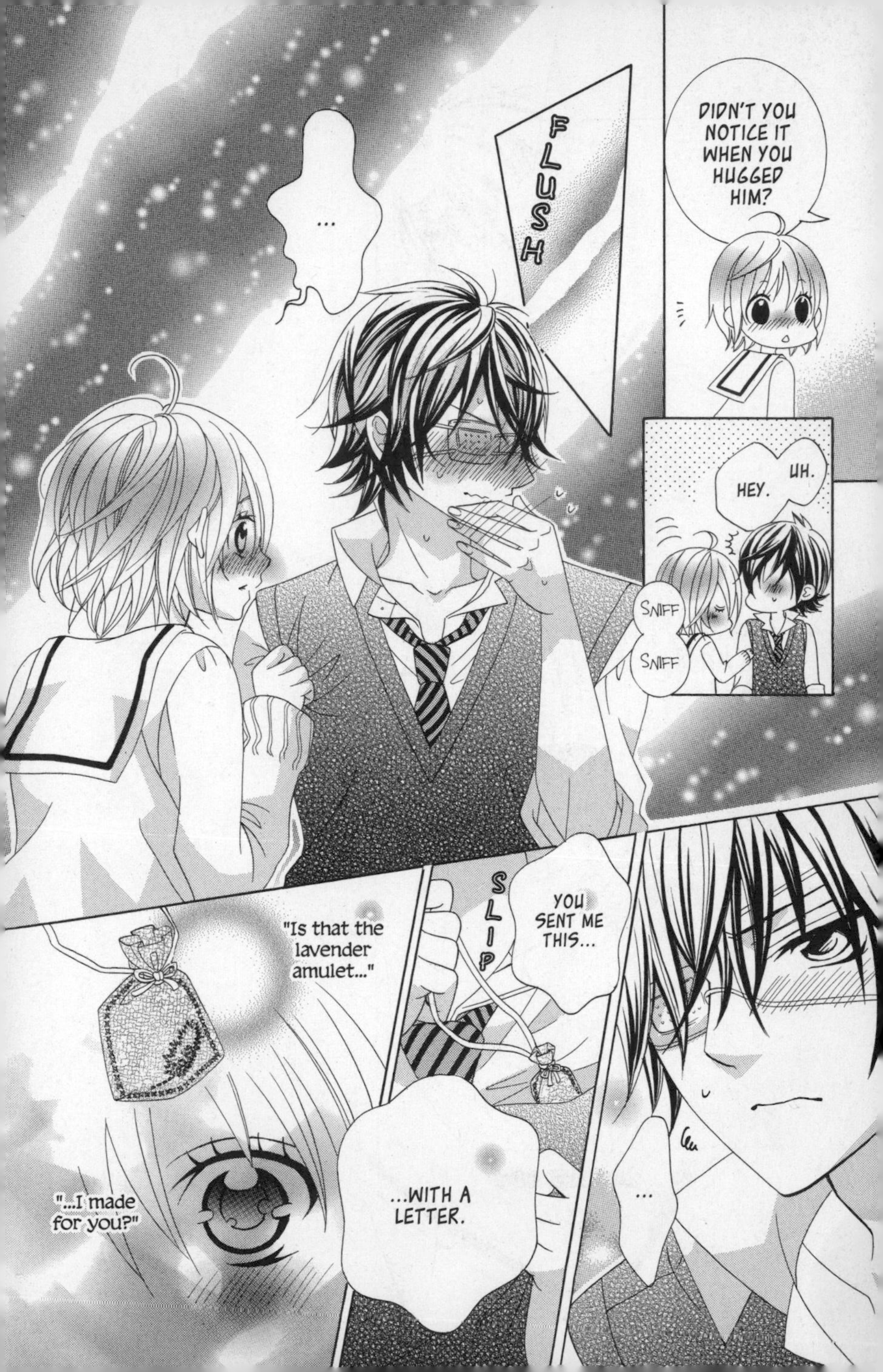
DIDN'T YOU NOTICE IT WHEN YOU HUGGED HIM?
UH.
HEY.
SNIFF
SNIFF
FLUSH
...
...
SLIP
YOU SENT ME THIS...
...WITH A LETTER.
"Is that the lavender amulet..."
"...I made for you?"

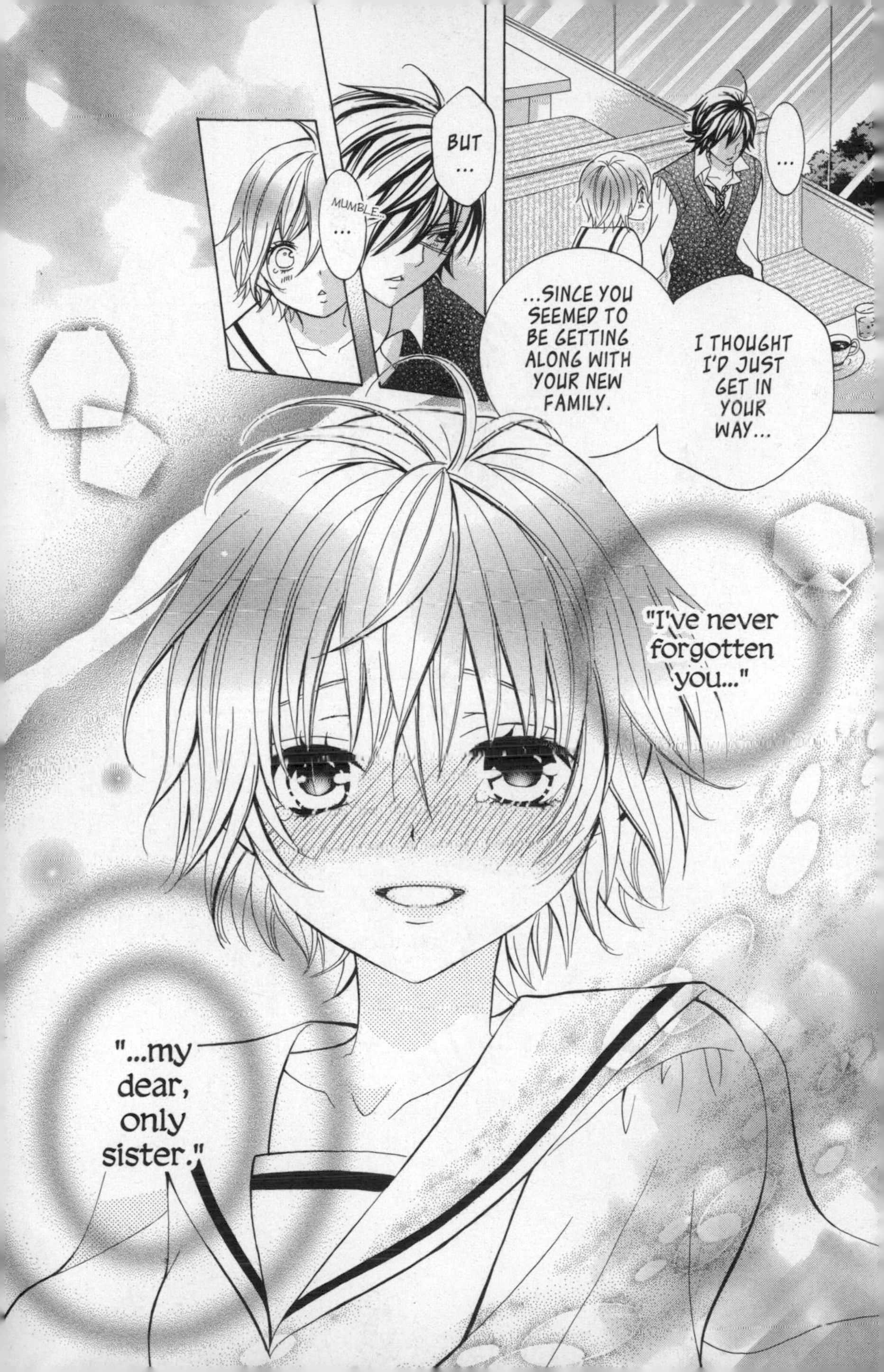
...
...SINCE YOU SEEMED TO BE GETTING ALONG WITH YOUR NEW FAMILY.
I THOUGHT I'D JUST GET IN YOUR WAY...
BUT ...
MUMBLE... ...
"I've never forgotten you..."
"...my dear, only sister."

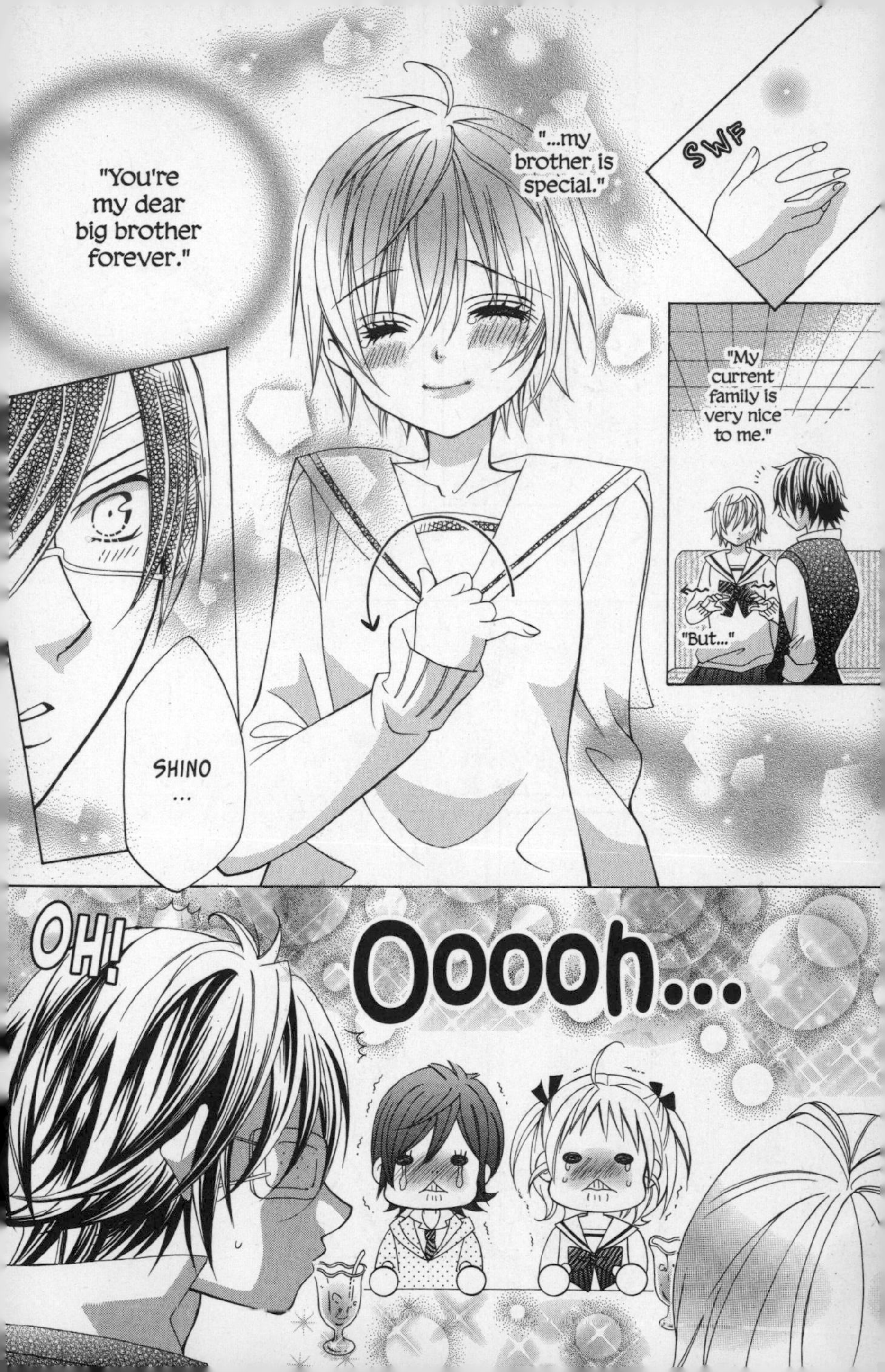
SWF
"My current family is very nice to me."
"But..."
"...my brother is special."
"You're my dear big brother forever."
SHINO ...
Ooooh...
OH!

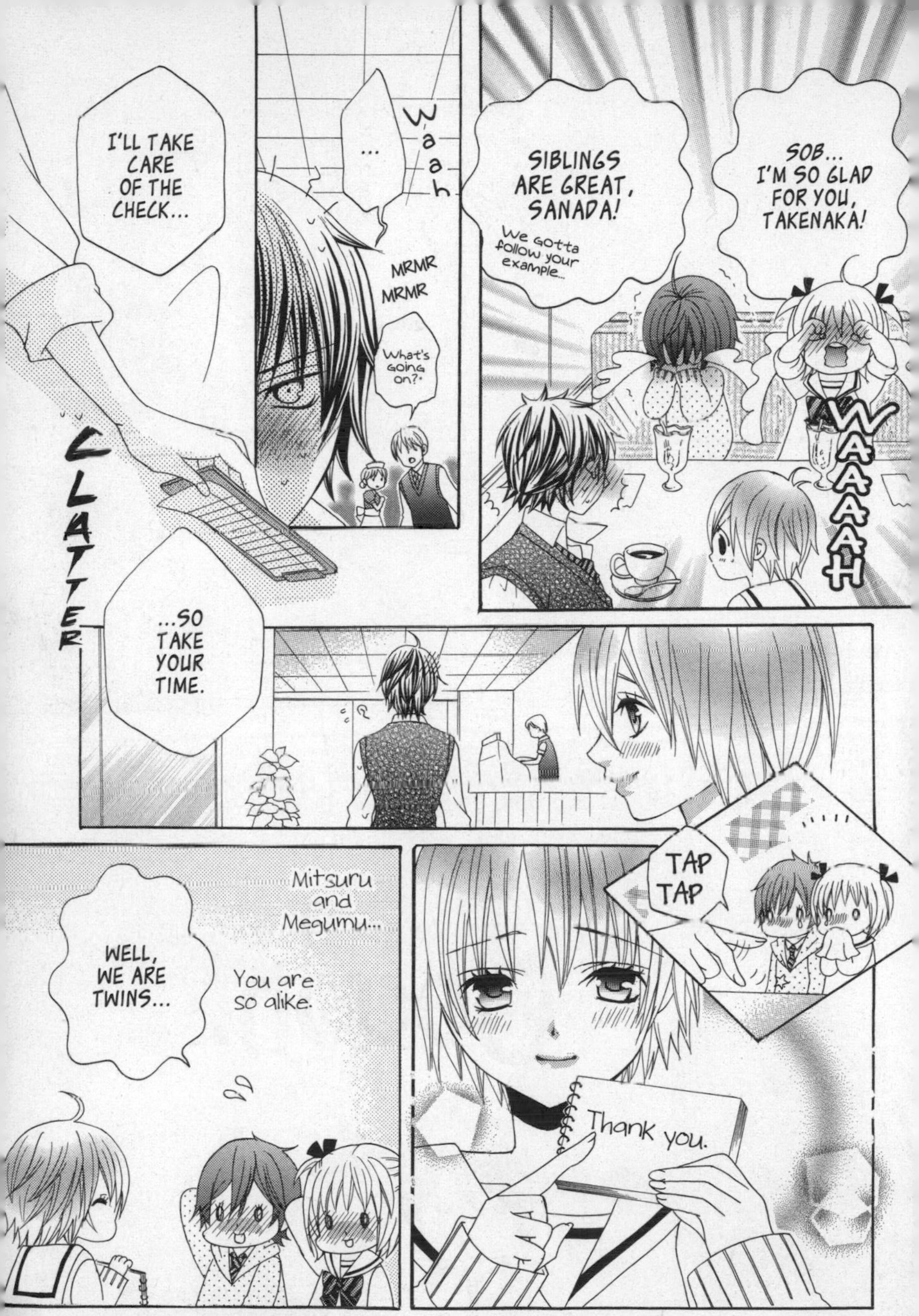
SOB... I'M SO GLAD FOR YOU, TAKENAKA!
SIBLINGS ARE GREAT, SANADA!
We gotta follow your example...
WAAAAAH
Waah
...
MRMR MRMR
What's going on?
I'LL TAKE CARE OF THE CHECK...
CLATTER
...SO TAKE YOUR TIME.
TAP TAP
Thank you.
Mitsuru and Megumu...
You are so alike.
WELL, WE ARE TWINS...

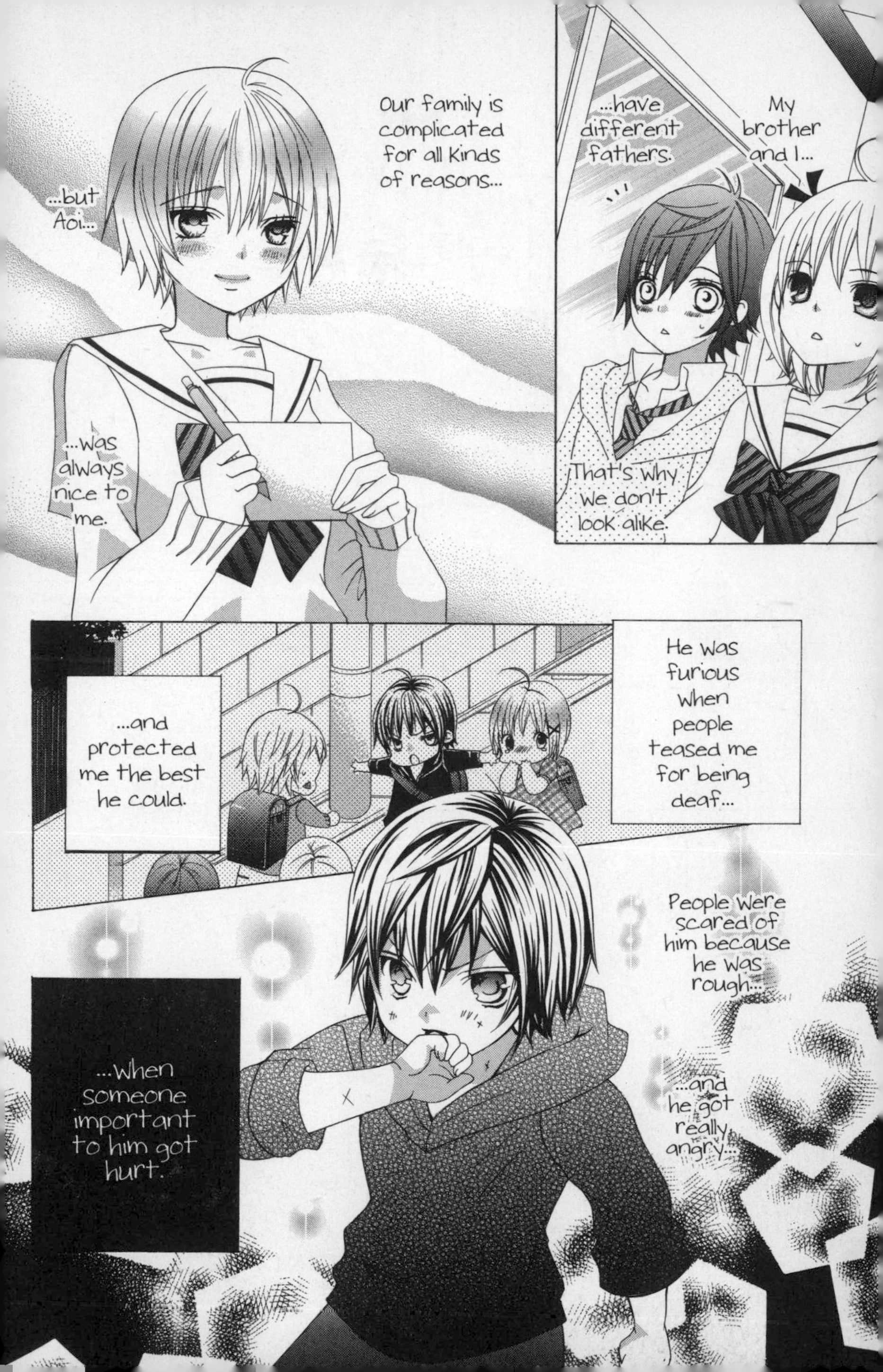
My brother and I...
...have different fathers.
That's why we don't look alike.
Our family is complicated for all kinds of reasons...
...but Aoi...
...was always nice to me.
He was furious when people teased me for being deaf...
...and protected me the best he could.
People were scared of him because he was rough...
...and he got really angry...
...when someone important to him got hurt.

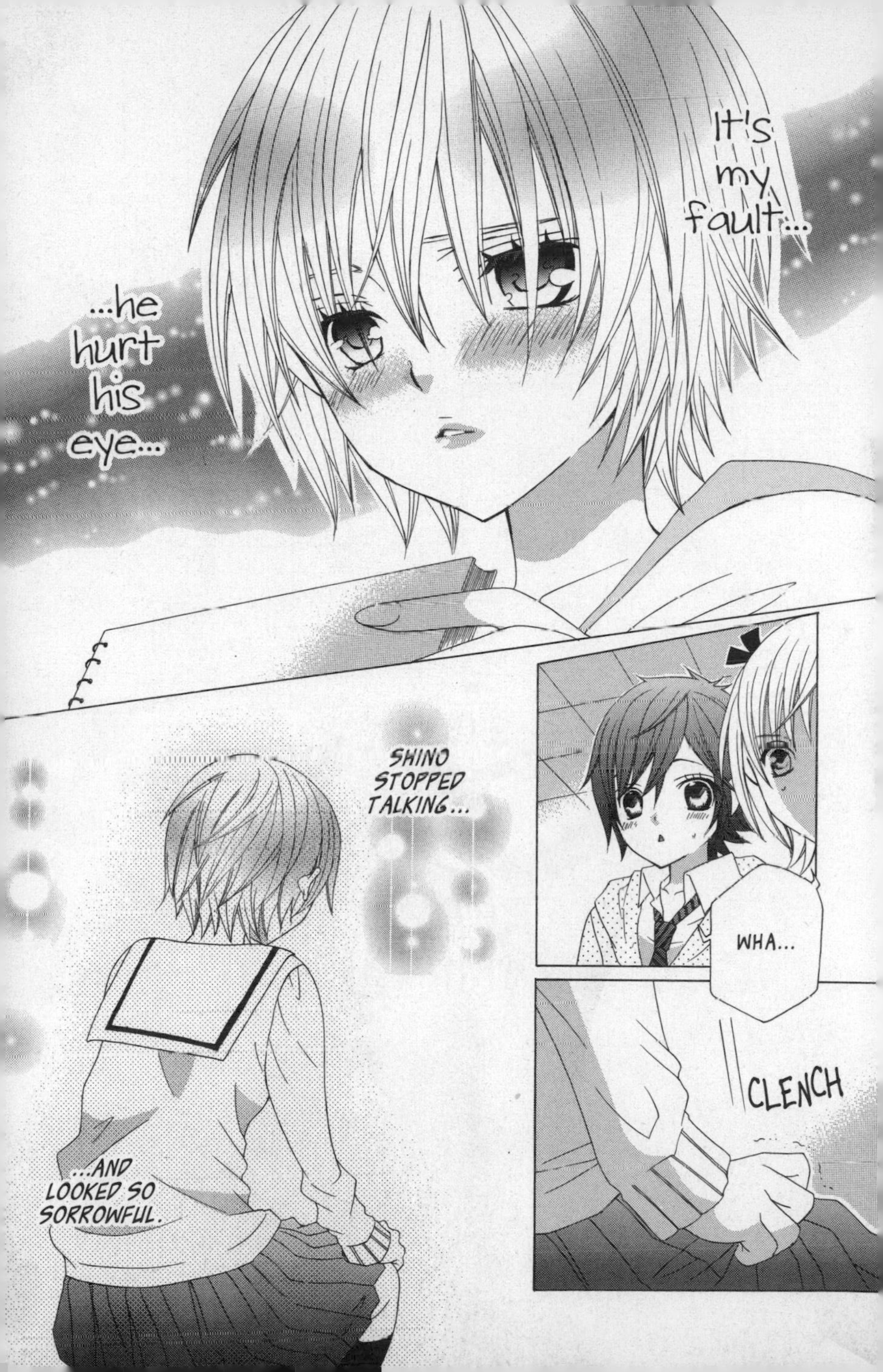
It's my fault...
...he hurt his eye...
WHA...
CLENCH
SHINO STOPPED TALKING...
...AND LOOKED SO SORROWFUL.

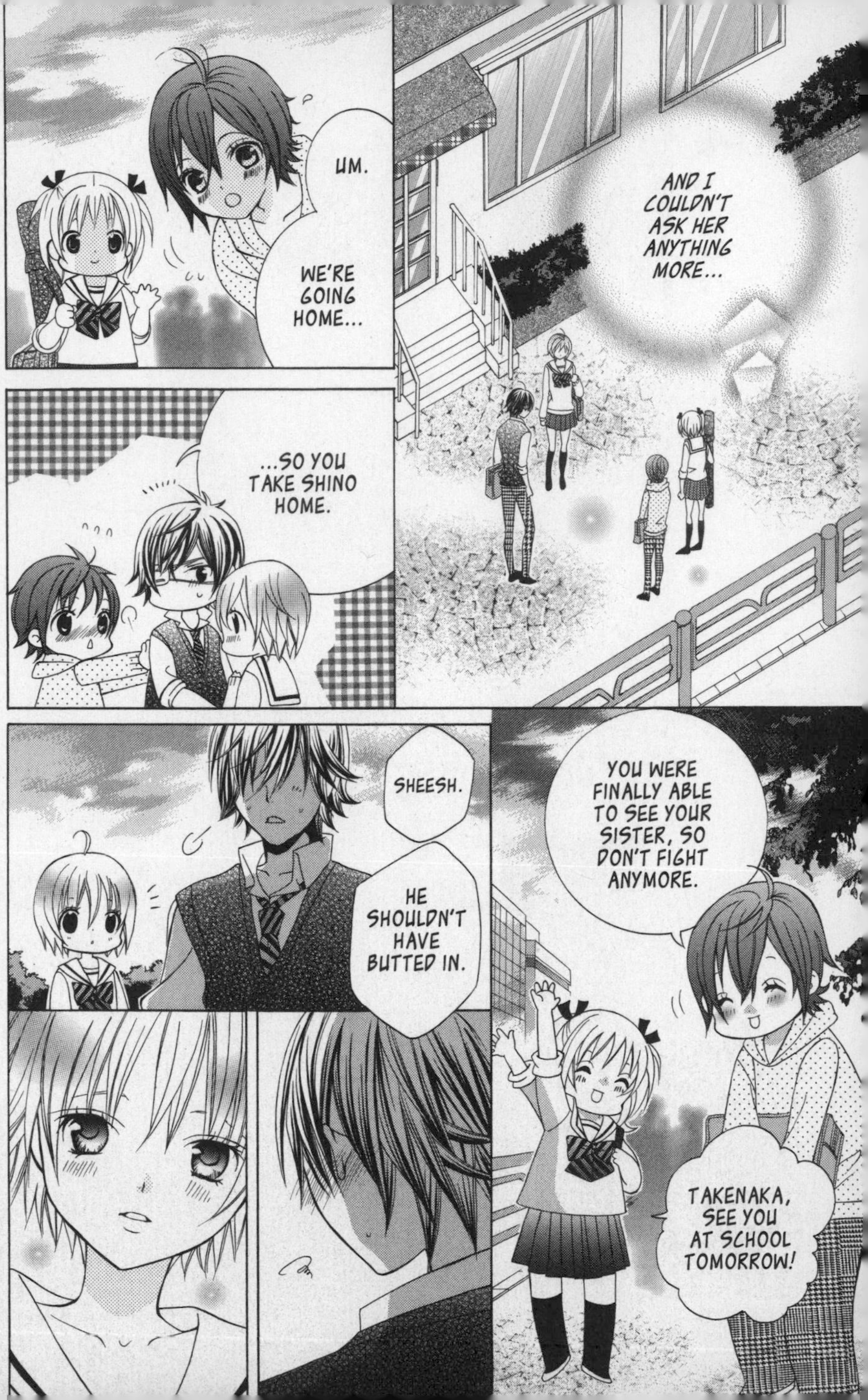
AND I COULDN'T ASK HER ANYTHING MORE...
UM.
WE'RE GOING HOME...
...SO YOU TAKE SHINO HOME.
YOU WERE FINALLY ABLE TO SEE YOUR SISTER, SO DON'T FIGHT ANYMORE.
TAKENAKA, SEE YOU AT SCHOOL TOMORROW!
SHEESH.
HE SHOULDN'T HAVE BUTTED IN.

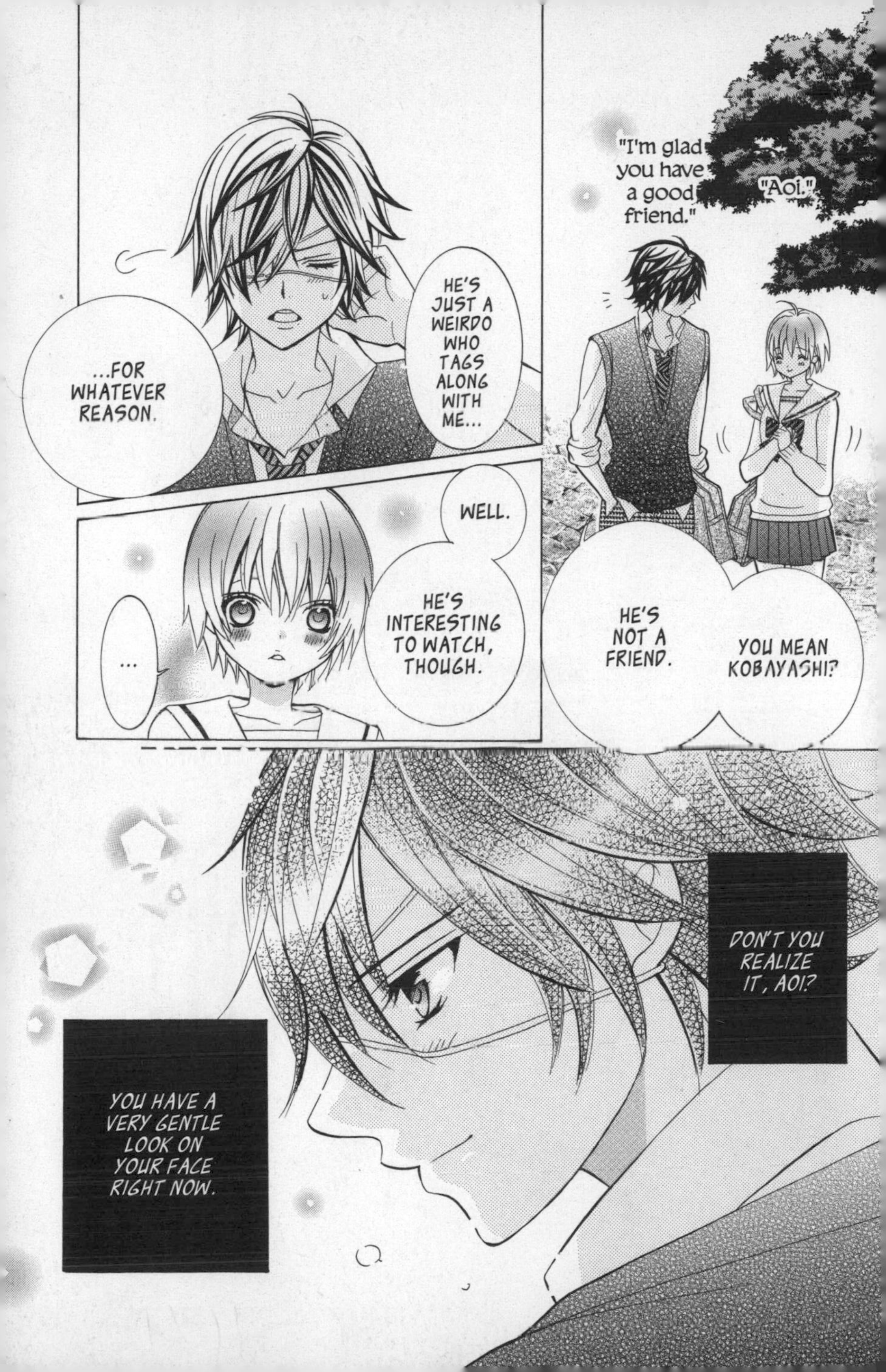
"Aoi."
"I'm glad you have a good friend."
YOU MEAN KOBAYASHI?
HE'S NOT A FRIEND.
HE'S JUST A WEIRDO WHO TAGS ALONG WITH ME...
...FOR WHATEVER REASON.
WELL.
HE'S INTERESTING TO WATCH, THOUGH.
...
DON'T YOU REALIZE IT, AOI?
YOU HAVE A VERY GENTLE LOOK ON YOUR FACE RIGHT NOW.

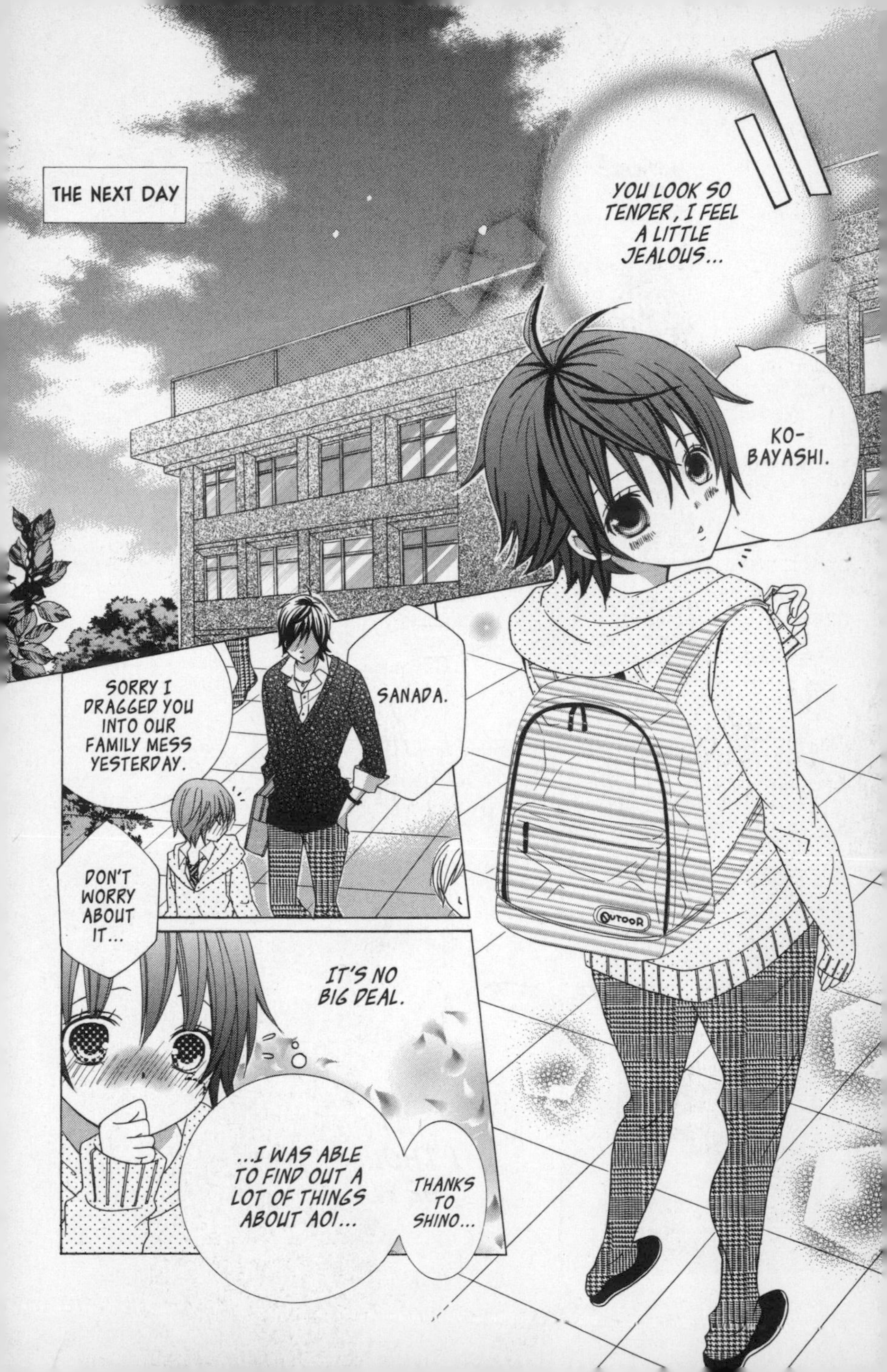

YOU LOOK SO TENDER, I FEEL A LITTLE JEALOUS...
THE NEXT DAY
KO-BAYASHI.
SANADA.
SORRY I DRAGGED YOU INTO OUR FAMILY MESS YESTERDAY.
DON'T WORRY ABOUT IT...
IT'S NO BIG DEAL.
THANKS TO SHINO...
...I WAS ABLE TO FIND OUT A LOT OF THINGS ABOUT AOI...

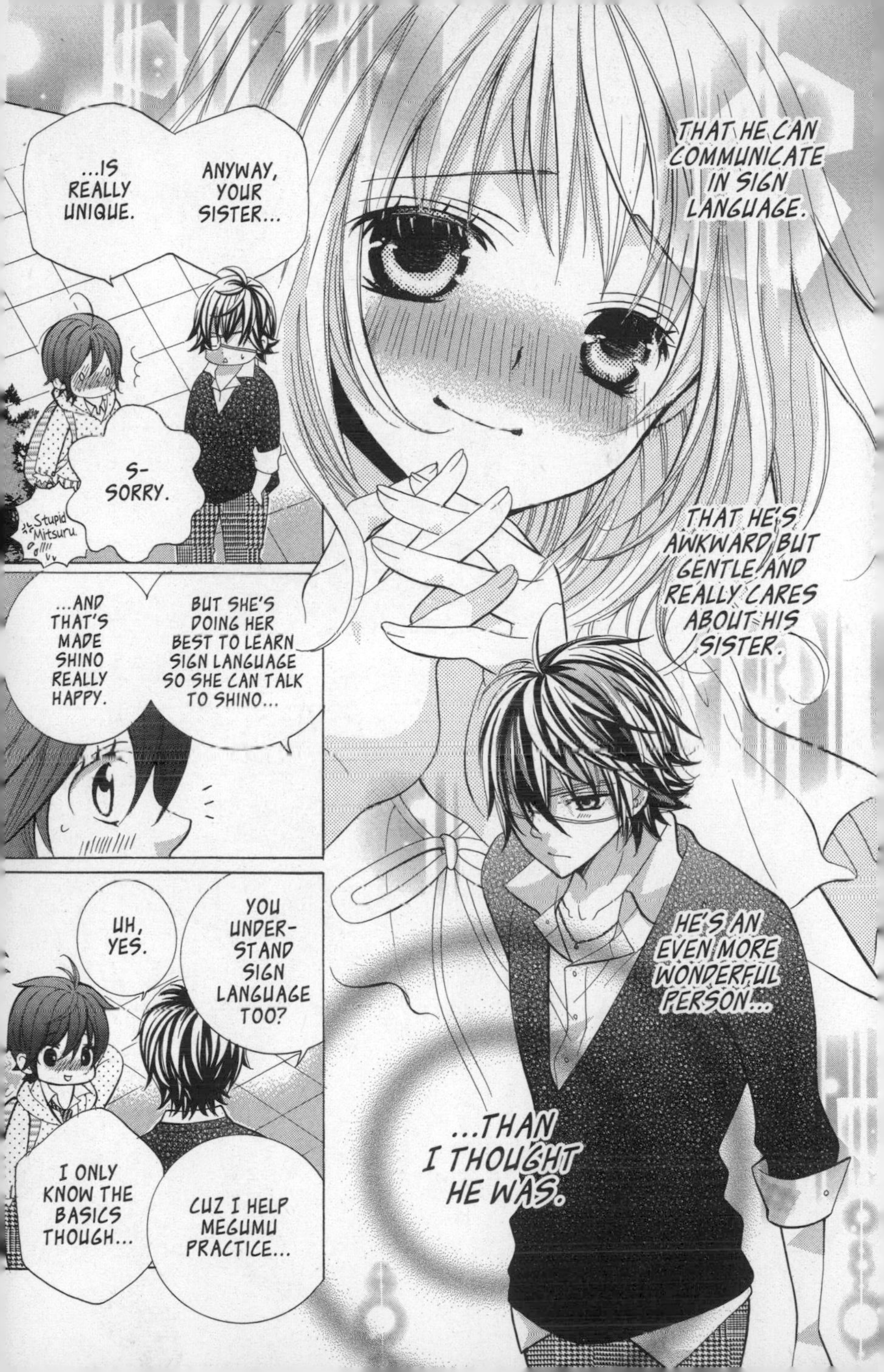
THAT HE CAN COMMUNICATE IN SIGN LANGUAGE.
THAT HE'S AWKWARD BUT GENTLE AND REALLY CARES ABOUT HIS SISTER.
HE'S AN EVEN MORE WONDERFUL PERSON...
...THAN I THOUGHT HE WAS.
ANYWAY, YOUR SISTER...
...IS REALLY UNIQUE.
S-SORRY.
Stupid Mitsuru.
BUT SHE'S DOING HER BEST TO LEARN SIGN LANGUAGE SO SHE CAN TALK TO SHINO...
...AND THAT'S MADE SHINO REALLY HAPPY.
YOU UNDER-STAND SIGN LANGUAGE TOO?
UH, YES.
CUZ I HELP MEGUMU PRACTICE...
I ONLY KNOW THE BASICS THOUGH...

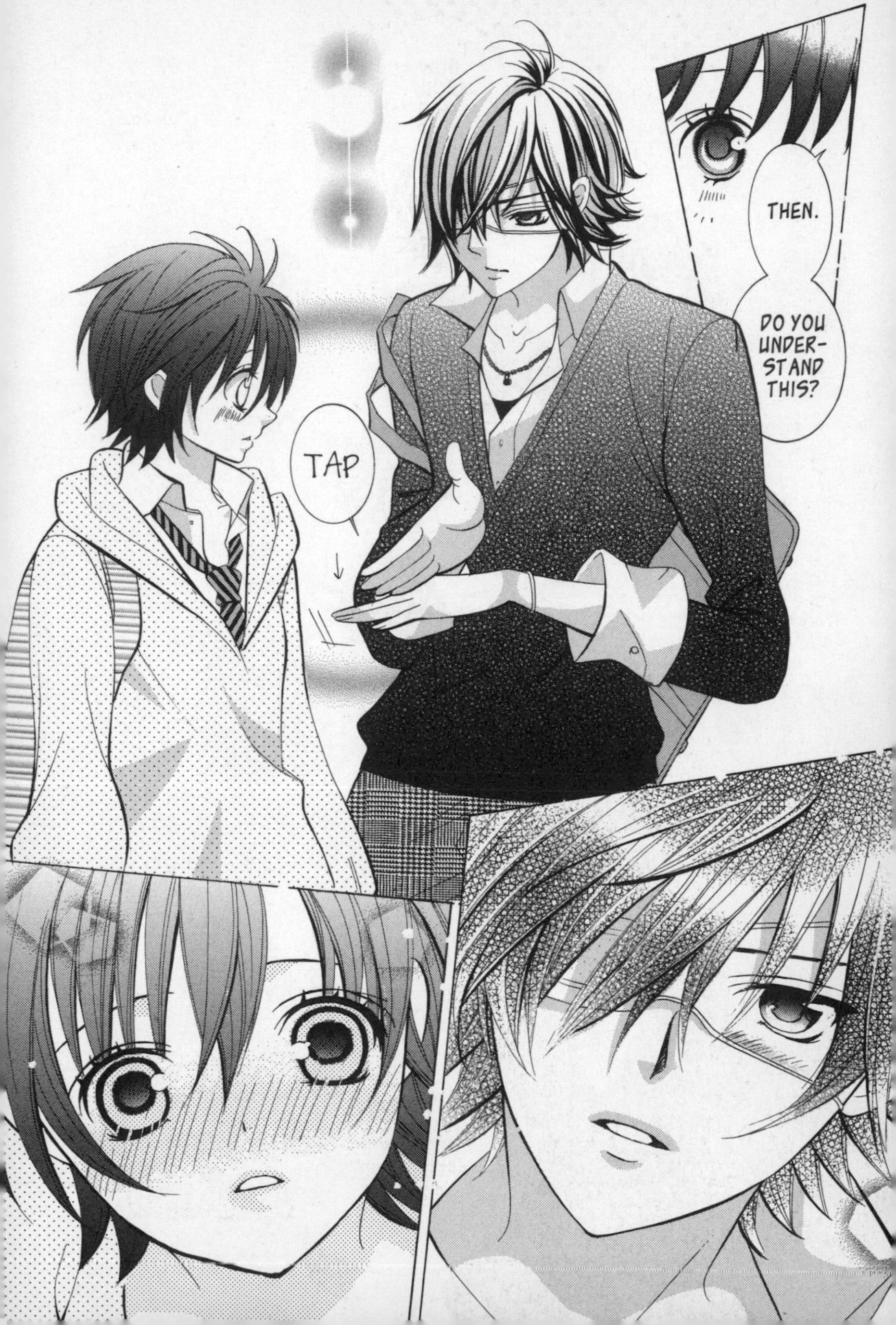
THEN.
DO YOU UNDER-STAND THIS?
TAP

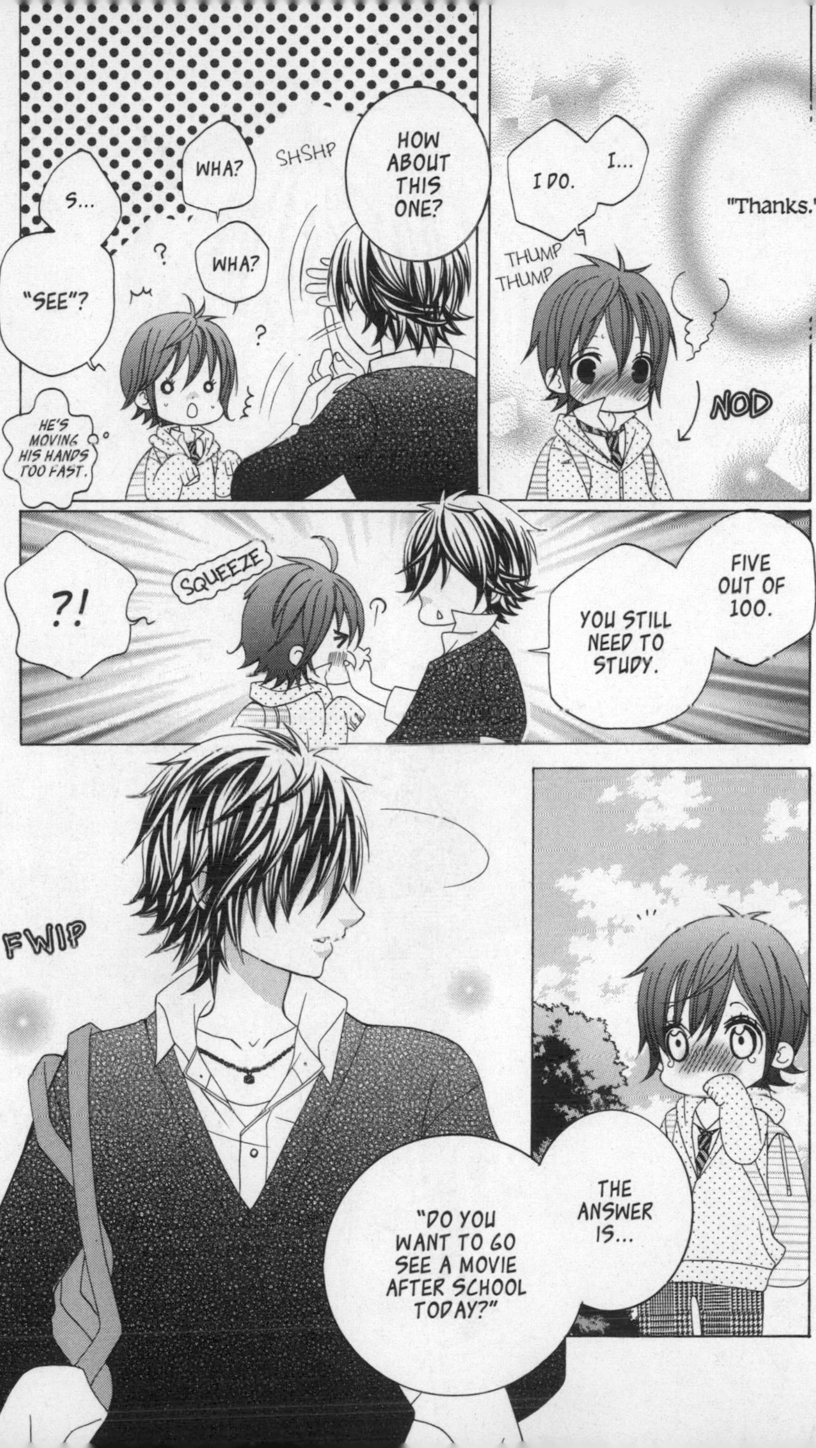
"Thanks."
I...
I DO.
THUMP THUMP
NOD
HOW ABOUT THIS ONE?
SHSHP
WHA?
WHA?
S...
"SEE"?
HE'S MOVING HIS HANDS TOO FAST.
FIVE OUT OF 100.
YOU STILL NEED TO STUDY.
SQUEEZE
?!
THE ANSWER IS...
"DO YOU WANT TO GO SEE A MOVIE AFTER SCHOOL TODAY?"
FWIP

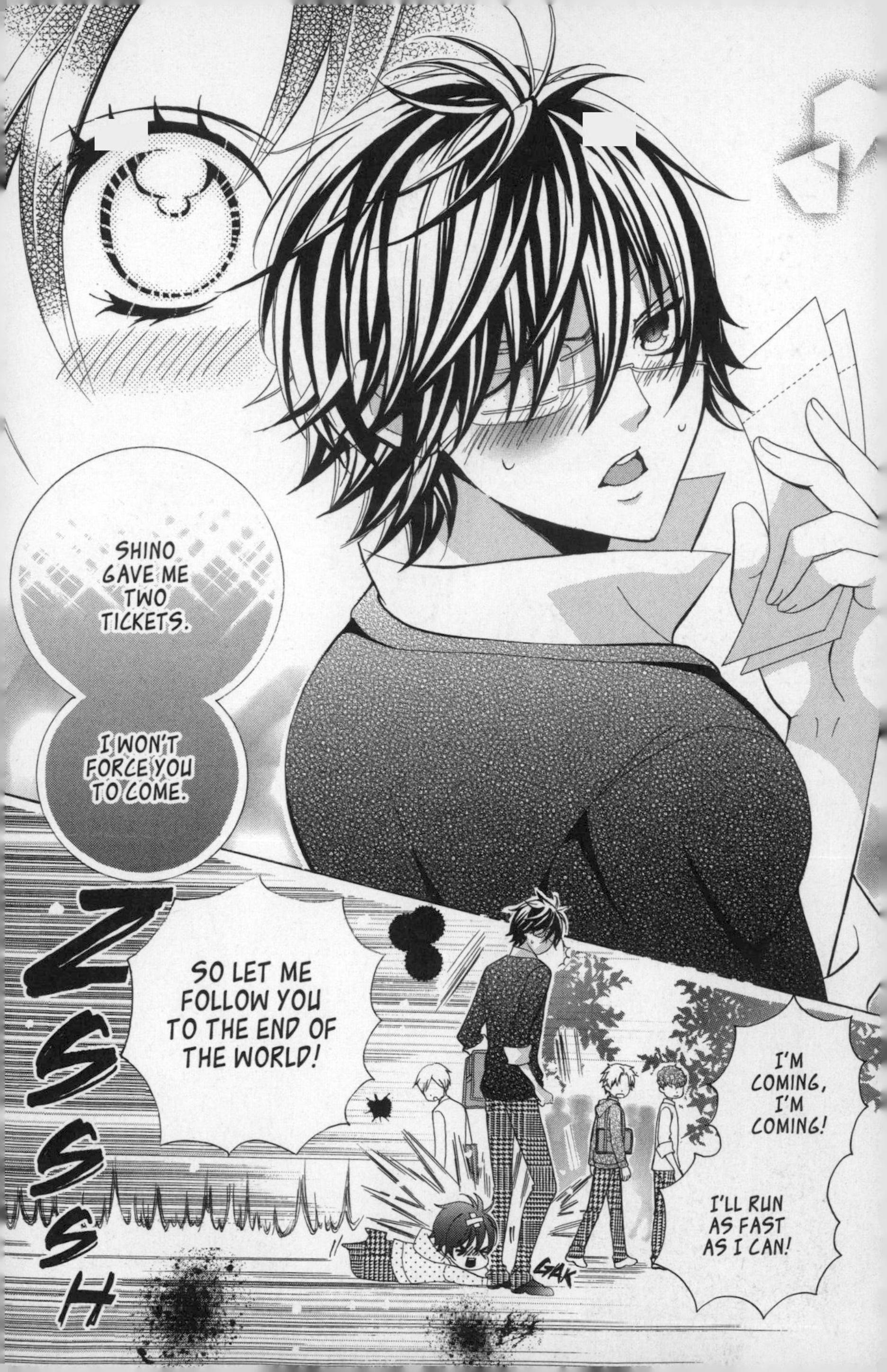
SHINO GAVE ME TWO TICKETS.
I WON'T FORCE YOU TO COME.
I'M COMING, I'M COMING!
I'LL RUN AS FAST AS I CAN!
GAK
SO LET ME FOLLOW YOU TO THE END OF THE WORLD!
ZSSSH

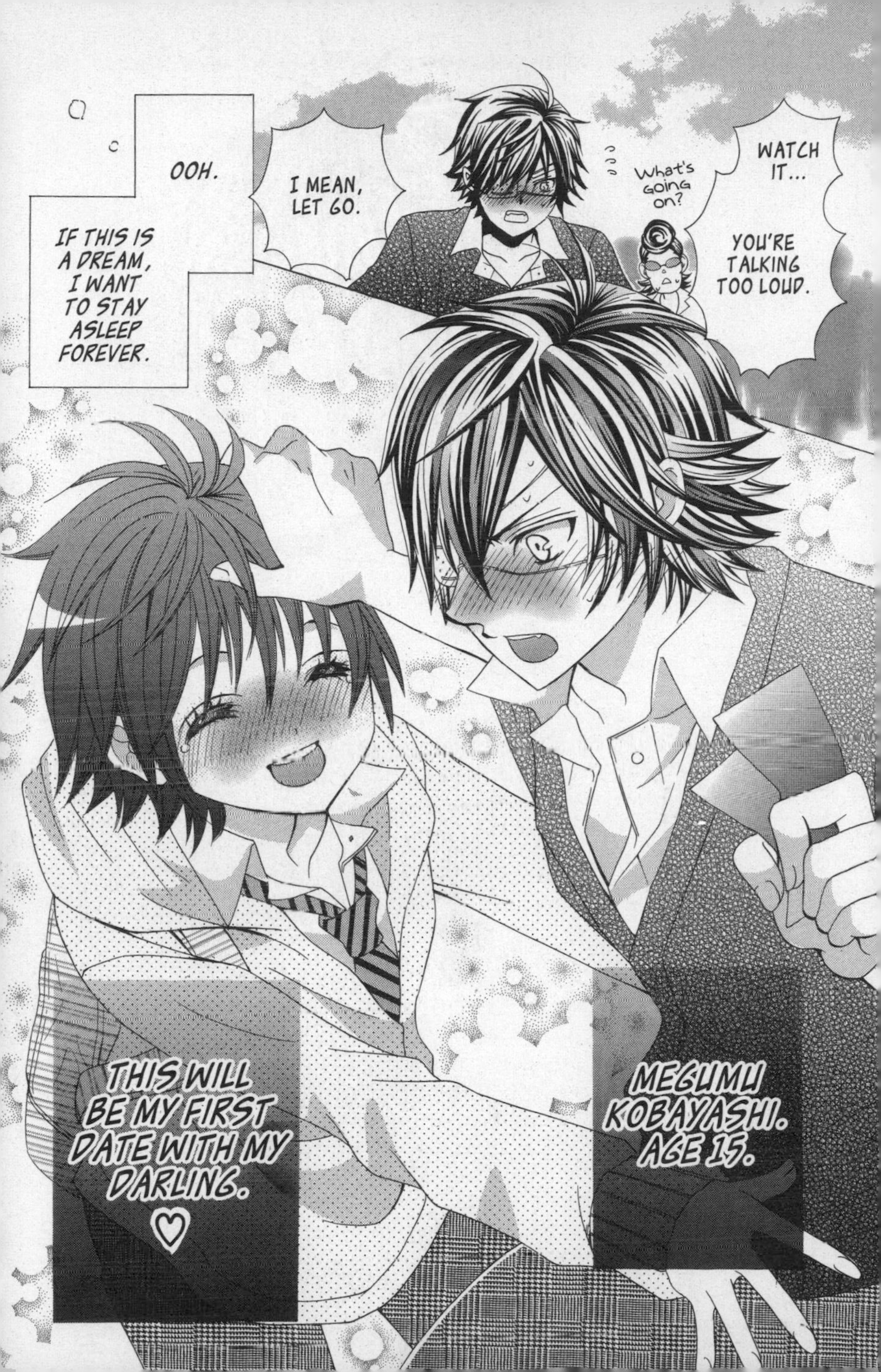
WATCH IT...
YOU'RE TALKING TOO LOUD.
What's going on?
I MEAN, LET GO.
OOH.
IF THIS IS A DREAM, I WANT TO STAY ASLEEP FOREVER.
MEGUMU KOBAYASHI. AGE 15.
THIS WILL BE MY FIRST DATE WITH MY DARLING. ♡

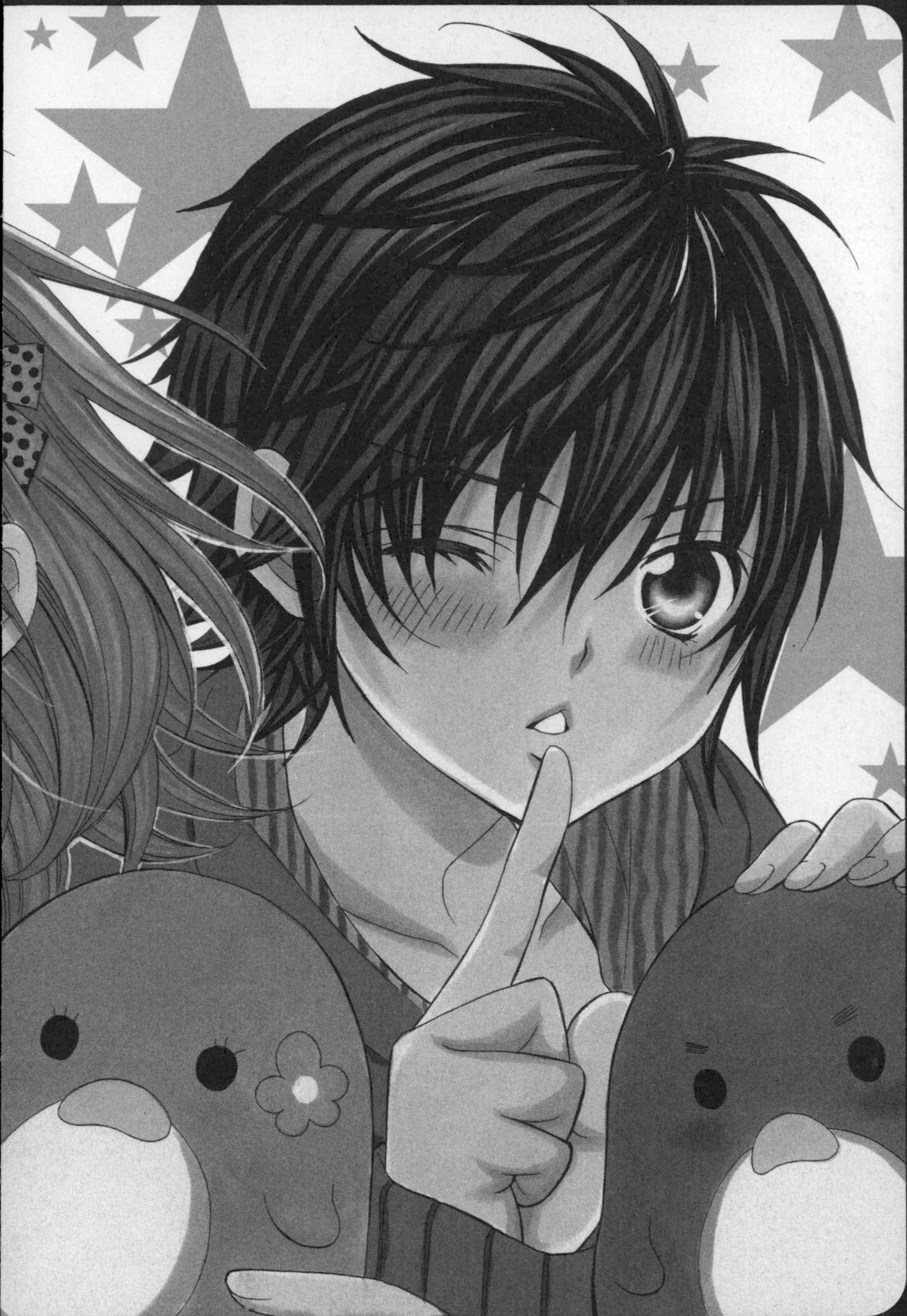

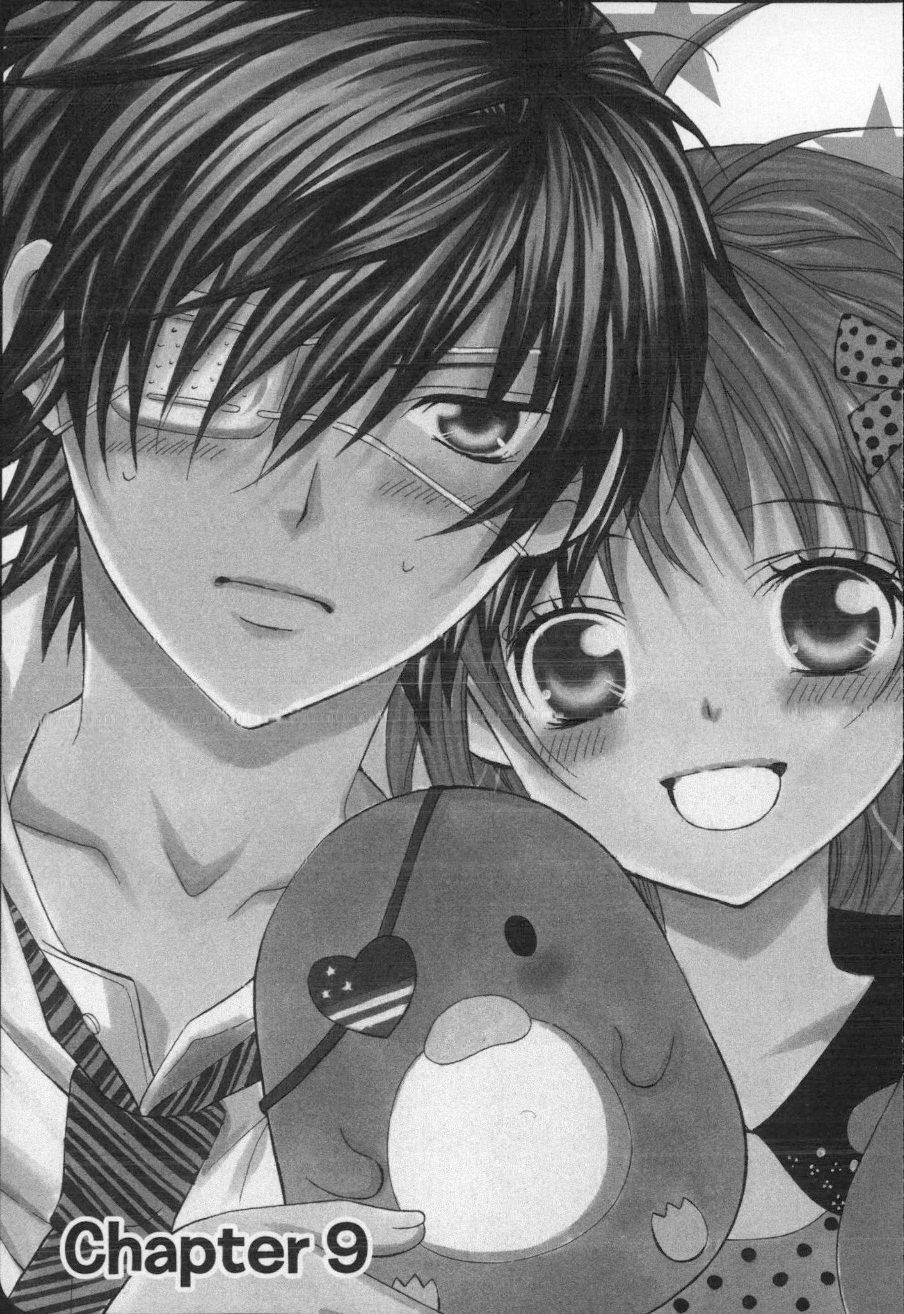
Chapter 9

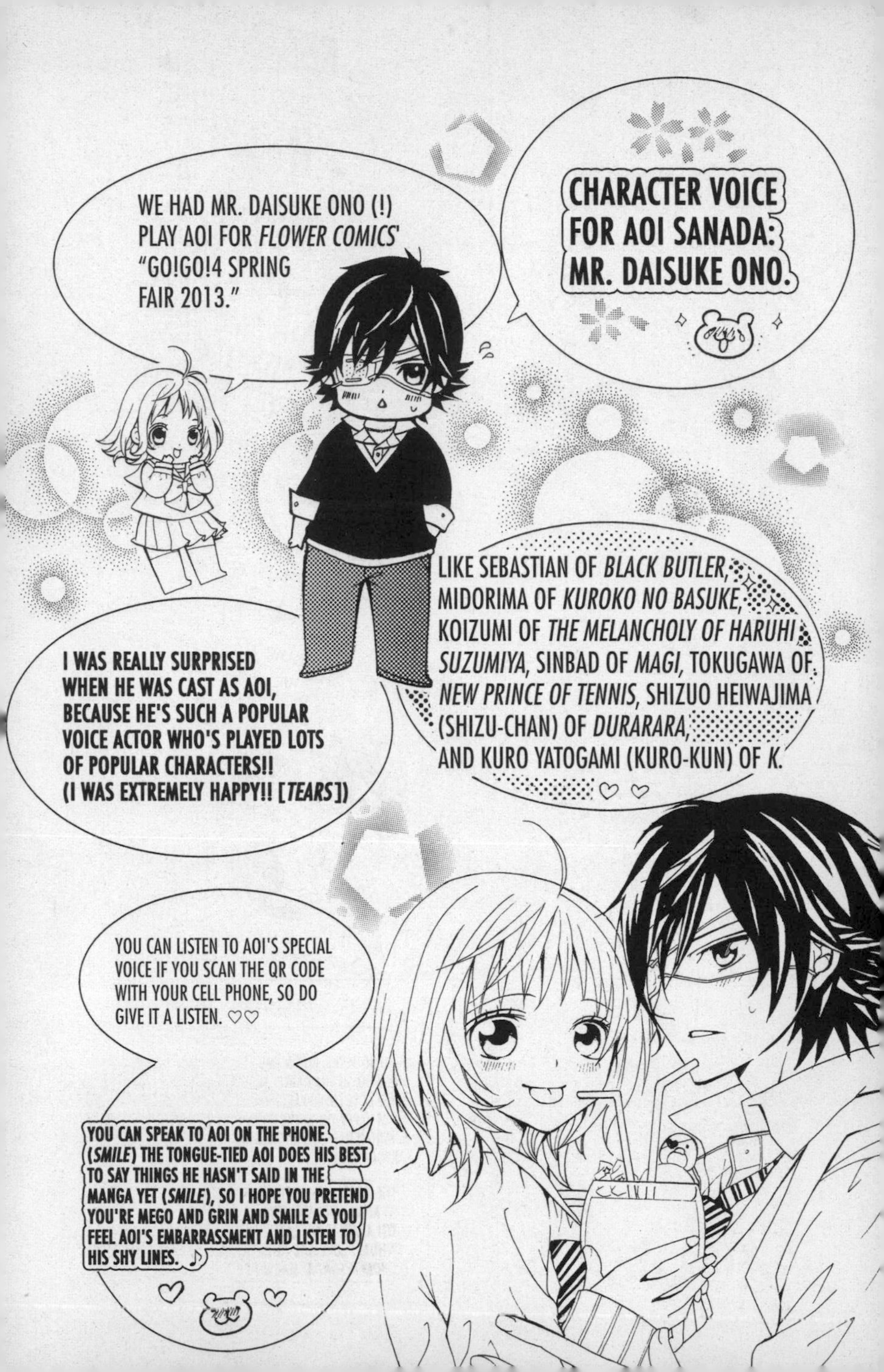
CHARACTER VOICE FOR AOI SANADA: MR. DAISUKE ONO.
WE HAD MR. DAISUKE ONO (!) PLAY AOI FOR *FLOWER COMICS*' "GO!GO!4 SPRING FAIR 2013."
LIKE SEBASTIAN OF *BLACK BUTLER*, MIDORIMA OF *KUROKO NO BASUKE*, KOIZUMI OF *THE MELANCHOLY OF HARUHI SUZUMIYA*, SINBAD OF *MAGI*, TOKUGAWA OF *NEW PRINCE OF TENNIS*, SHIZUO HEIWAJIMA (SHIZU-CHAN) OF *DURARARA*, AND KURO YATOGAMI (KURO-KUN) OF *K*. ♡ ♡
I WAS REALLY SURPRISED WHEN HE WAS CAST AS AOI, BECAUSE HE'S SUCH A POPULAR VOICE ACTOR WHO'S PLAYED LOTS OF POPULAR CHARACTERS!! (I WAS EXTREMELY HAPPY!! [*TEARS*])
YOU CAN LISTEN TO AOI'S SPECIAL VOICE IF YOU SCAN THE QR CODE WITH YOUR CELL PHONE, SO DO GIVE IT A LISTEN. ♡♡
YOU CAN SPEAK TO AOI ON THE PHONE. (*SMILE*) THE TONGUE-TIED AOI DOES HIS BEST TO SAY THINGS HE HASN'T SAID IN THE MANGA YET (*SMILE*), SO I HOPE YOU PRETEND YOU'RE MEGO AND GRIN AND SMILE AS YOU FEEL AOI'S EMBARRASSMENT AND LISTEN TO HIS SHY LINES. ♪

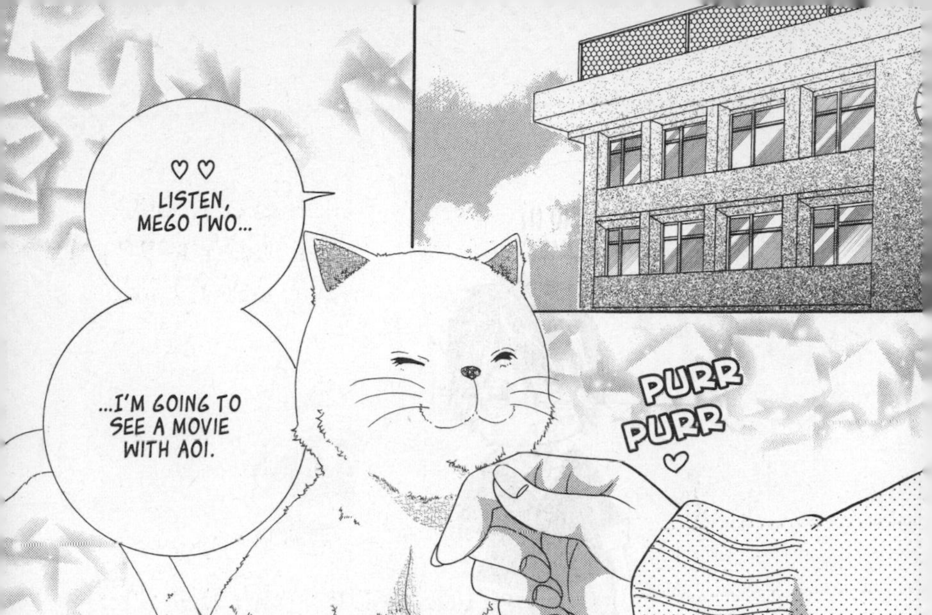
♡ ♡ LISTEN, MEGO TWO...
...I'M GOING TO SEE A MOVIE WITH AOI.
PURR PURR ♡
Backyard
HEY. SO THIS IS...
SQUIRM
WRIGGLE
Yeah, yeah. Great.
...WHAT PEOPLE CALL A "DATE," RIGHT?
No fair, Mego.
Play with us too.
UH.
HEY, EVERYONE.
DON'T WIGGLE SO MUCH. OR...

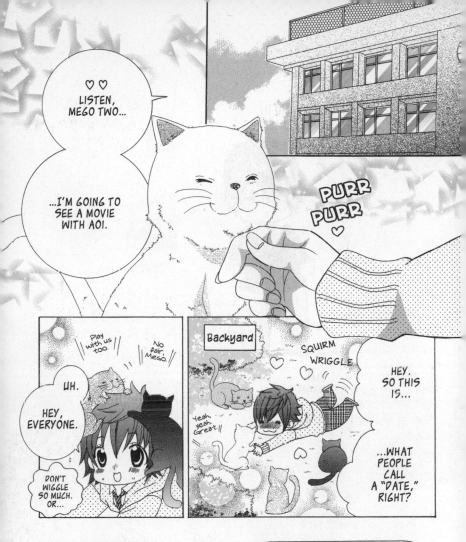

MANGA AND ANIME

I DREW SOMETHING FOR THE *INAZUMA ELEVEN GO! OFFICIAL ANTHOLOGY*, WHICH WILL BE ON SALE IN APRIL!!

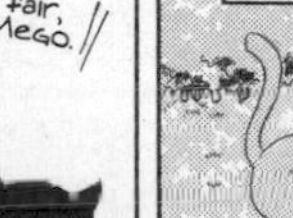

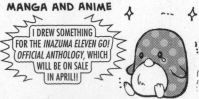

I REALLY LOVE *INAZUMA ELEVEN*, SO I WAS SO HAPPY THEY ASKED ME TO BE IN THIS ANTHOLOGY!! (*TEARS*)
I WENT TO SEE THE *INAZUMA ELEVEN GO VS. DANBALL SENKI W* MOVIE DURING NEW YEAR'S AND CRIED SO MUCH...!
I WAS VERY MOVED!!

I FIND BOTH THE *JOJO* ANIME AND THE *IXION SAGA DT* ANIME SO, SO ENJOYABLE...!! I LOVE *IXION SAGA*'S EREC-SAMA! (*SMILE*) I'VE LOVED PARTS 1 AND 2 OF *JOJO* SINCE I WAS LITTLE, SO I'M HAPPY THE ANIME COVERS BOTH PARTS. (*TEARS*) I LOVE JONATHAN IN PART 1 AND CAESAR IN PART 2. I'M A FAN OF KAKYOIN IN PART 3. LOL.

THE *ARATA: THE LEGEND* ANIME WILL BEGIN AIRING IN APRIL, AND I'M VERY MUCH LOOKING FORWARD TO IT!! *ARATA* IS THE LATEST MANGA BY YUU WATASE SENSEI, WHOM I LOVE AND RESPECT, AND THE MANGA RUNS IN *SHONEN SUNDAY* MAGAZINE.

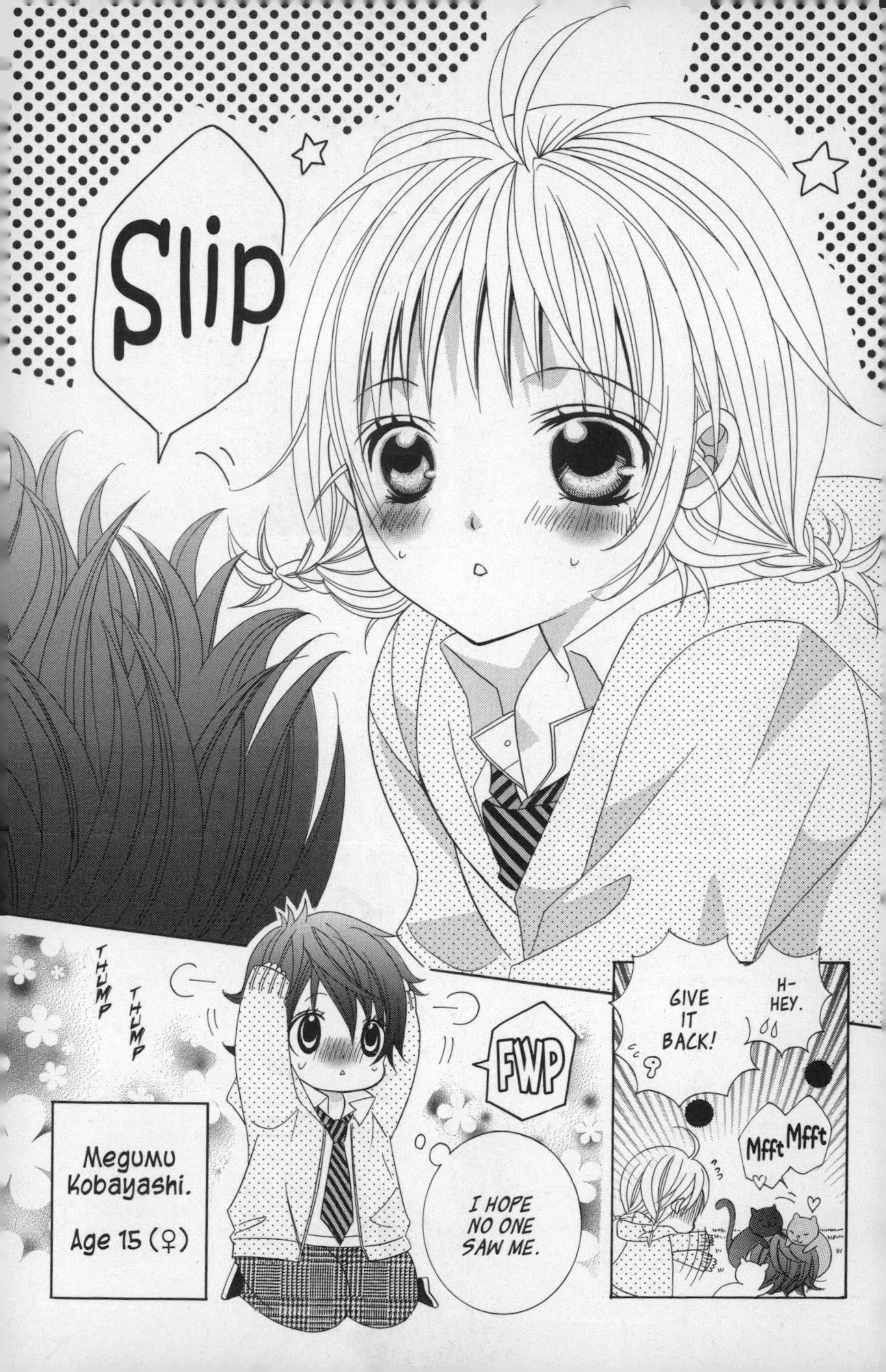
Slip
H-HEY.
GIVE IT BACK!
Mfft Mfft
FWP
I HOPE NO ONE SAW ME.
THUMP THUMP
Megumu Kobayashi.
Age 15 (♀)

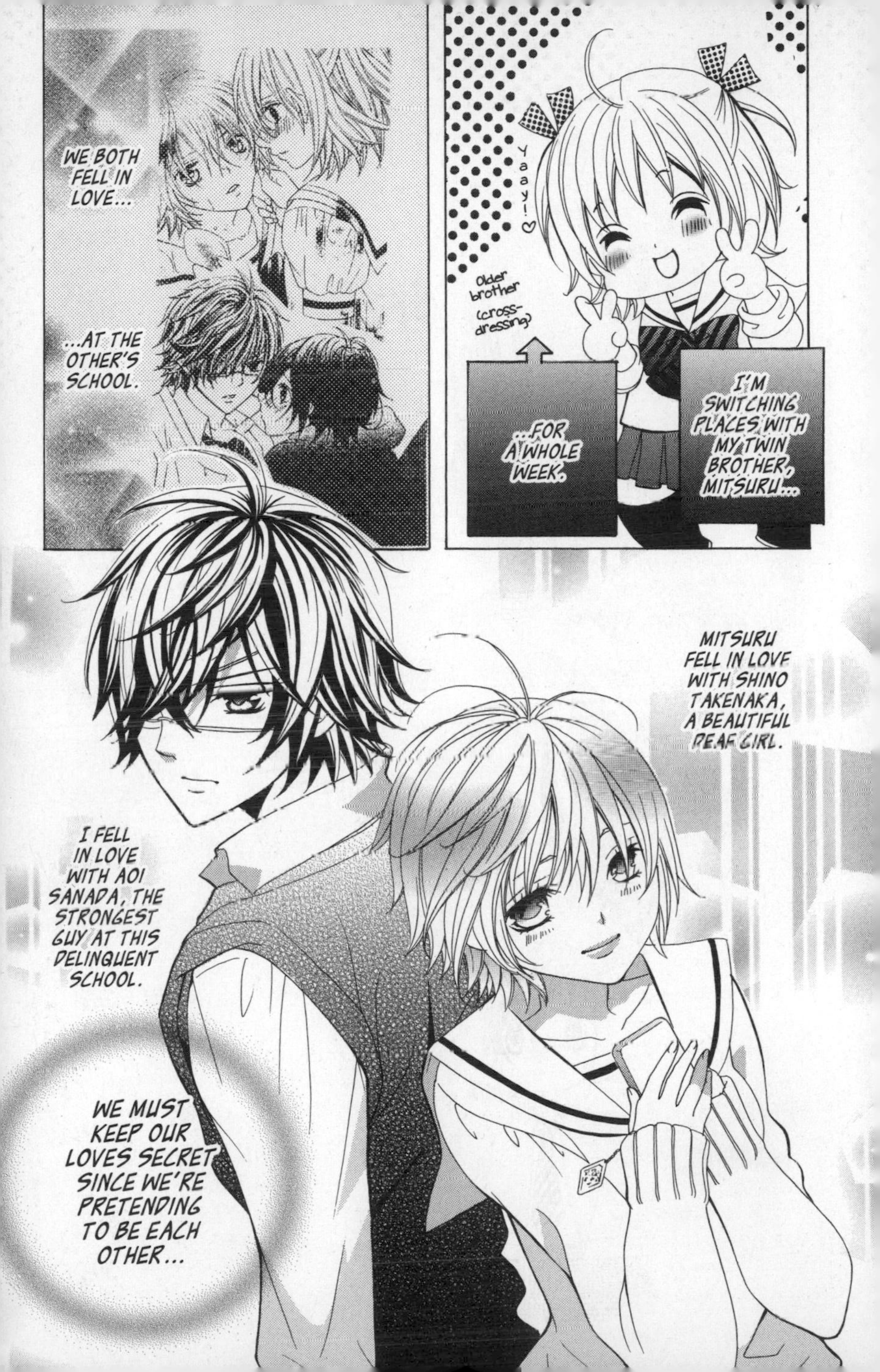
Yaaay! ♡
Older brother (cross-dressing)
I'M SWITCHING PLACES WITH MY TWIN BROTHER, MITSURU...
...FOR A WHOLE WEEK.
WE BOTH FELL IN LOVE...
...AT THE OTHER'S SCHOOL.
MITSURU FELL IN LOVE WITH SHINO TAKENAKA, A BEAUTIFUL DEAF GIRL.
I FELL IN LOVE WITH AOI SANADA, THE STRONGEST GUY AT THIS DELINQUENT SCHOOL.
WE MUST KEEP OUR LOVES SECRET SINCE WE'RE PRETENDING TO BE EACH OTHER...

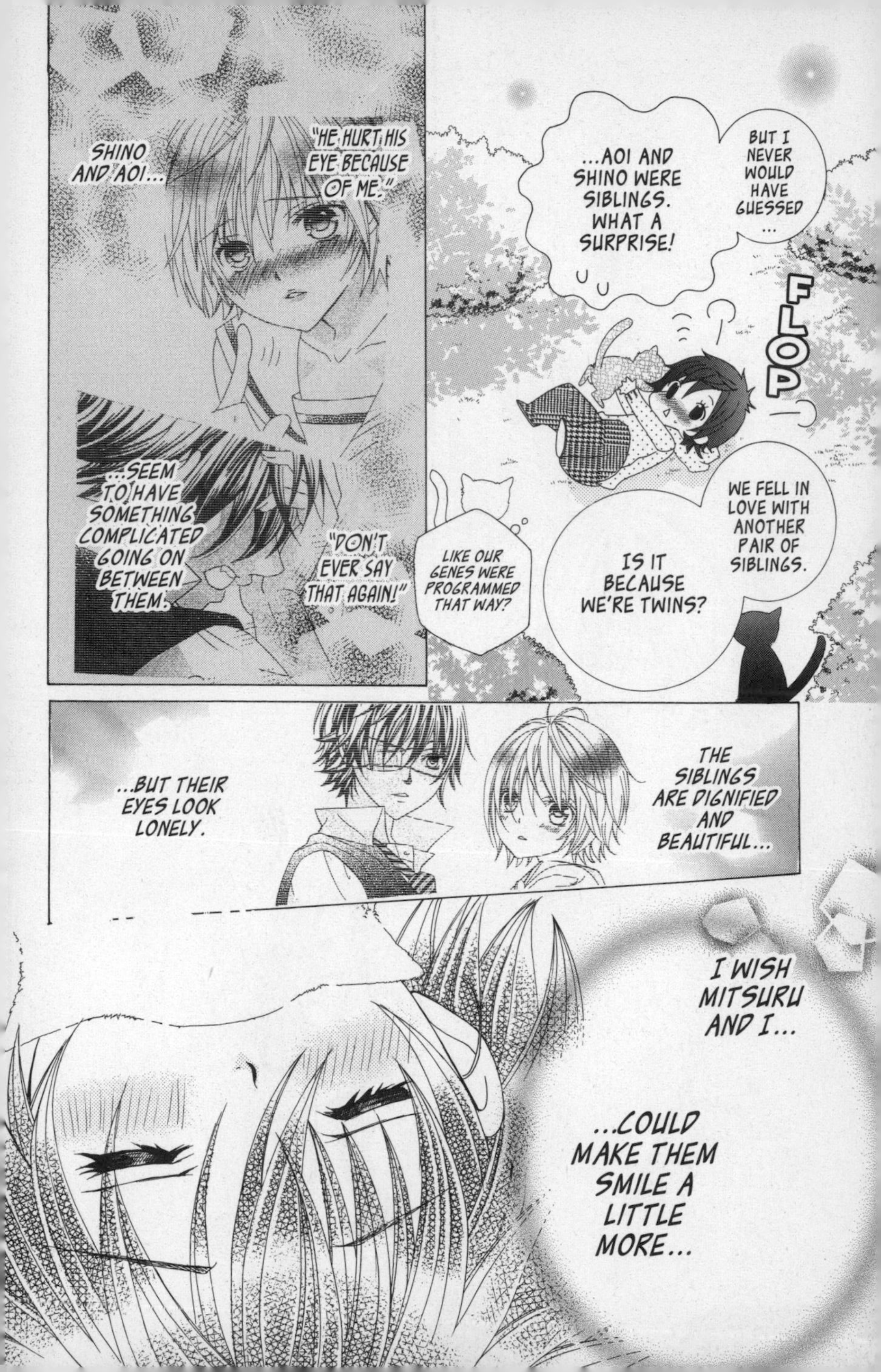
BUT I NEVER WOULD HAVE GUESSED...
...AOI AND SHINO WERE SIBLINGS. WHAT A SURPRISE!
FLOP
WE FELL IN LOVE WITH ANOTHER PAIR OF SIBLINGS.
IS IT BECAUSE WE'RE TWINS?
LIKE OUR GENES WERE PROGRAMMED THAT WAY?
"HE HURT HIS EYE BECAUSE OF ME."
SHINO AND AOI...
"DON'T EVER SAY THAT AGAIN!"
...SEEM TO HAVE SOMETHING COMPLICATED GOING ON BETWEEN THEM.
THE SIBLINGS ARE DIGNIFIED AND BEAUTIFUL...
...BUT THEIR EYES LOOK LONELY.
I WISH MITSURU AND I...
...COULD MAKE THEM SMILE A LITTLE MORE...

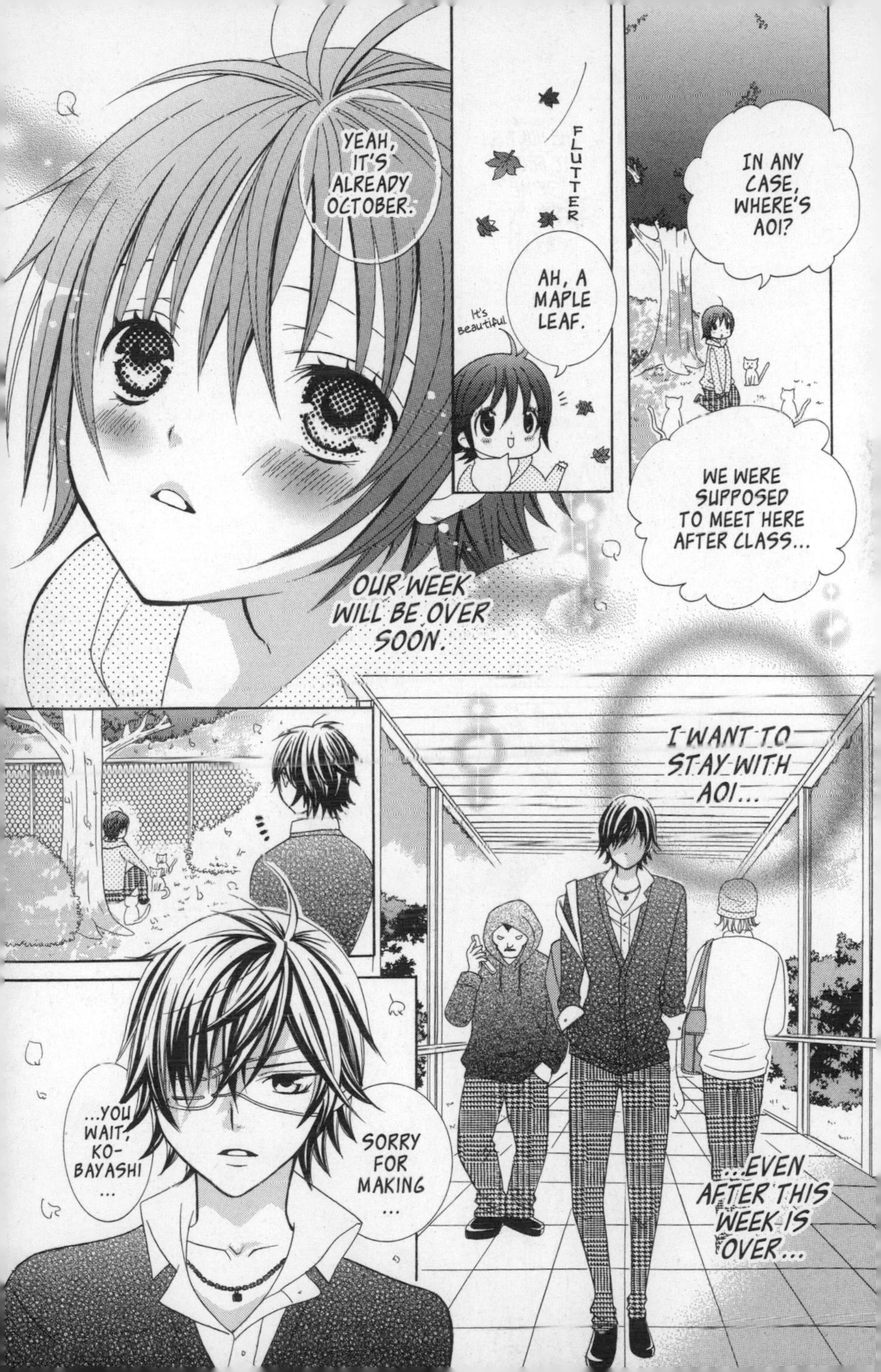
IN ANY CASE, WHERE'S AOI?
WE WERE SUPPOSED TO MEET HERE AFTER CLASS...
FLUTTER
AH, A MAPLE LEAF.
It's beautiful.
YEAH, IT'S ALREADY OCTOBER.
OUR WEEK WILL BE OVER SOON.
I WANT TO STAY WITH AOI...
...EVEN AFTER THIS WEEK IS OVER...
SORRY FOR MAKING ...
...YOU WAIT, KO-BAYASHI ...

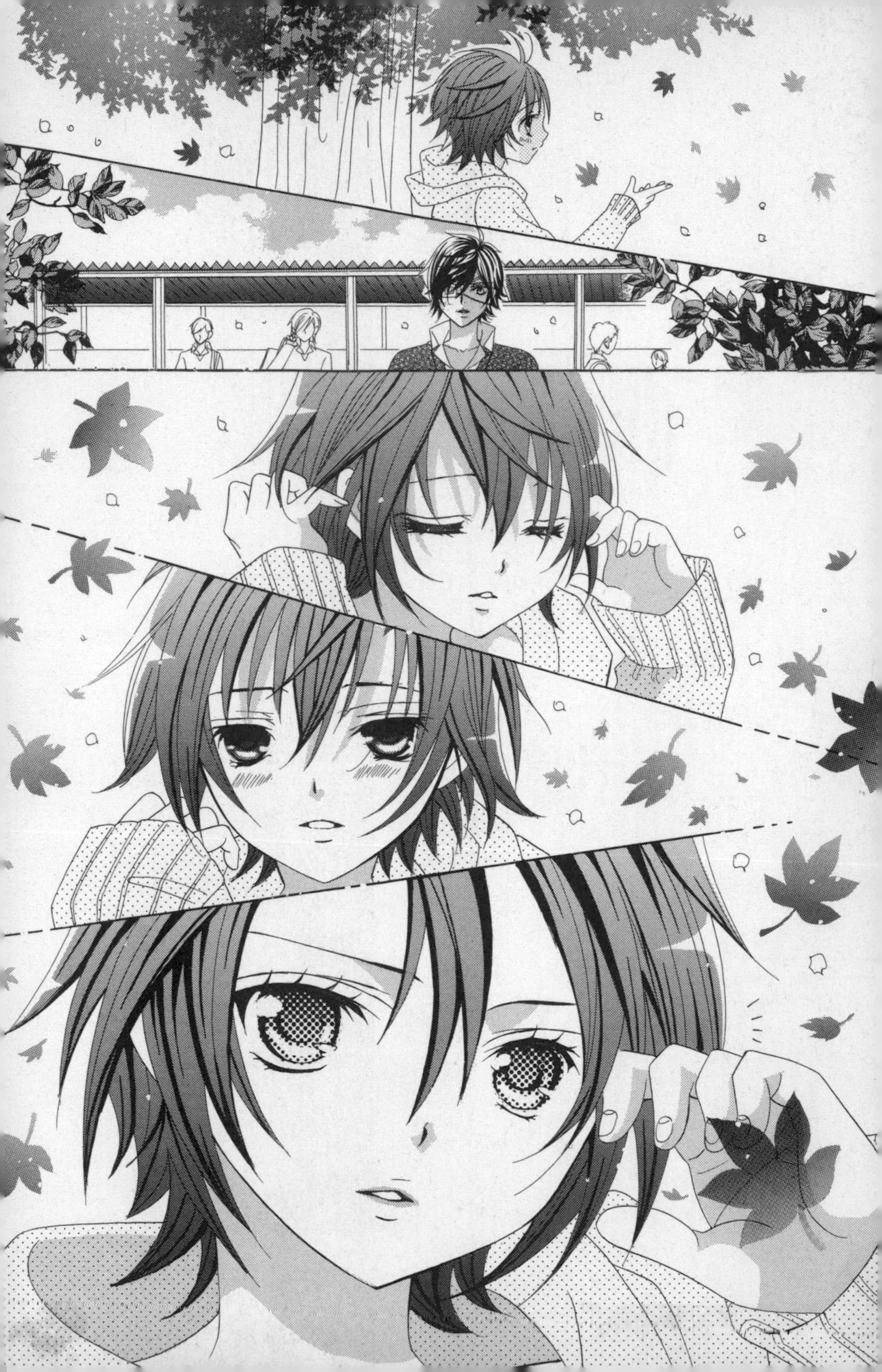

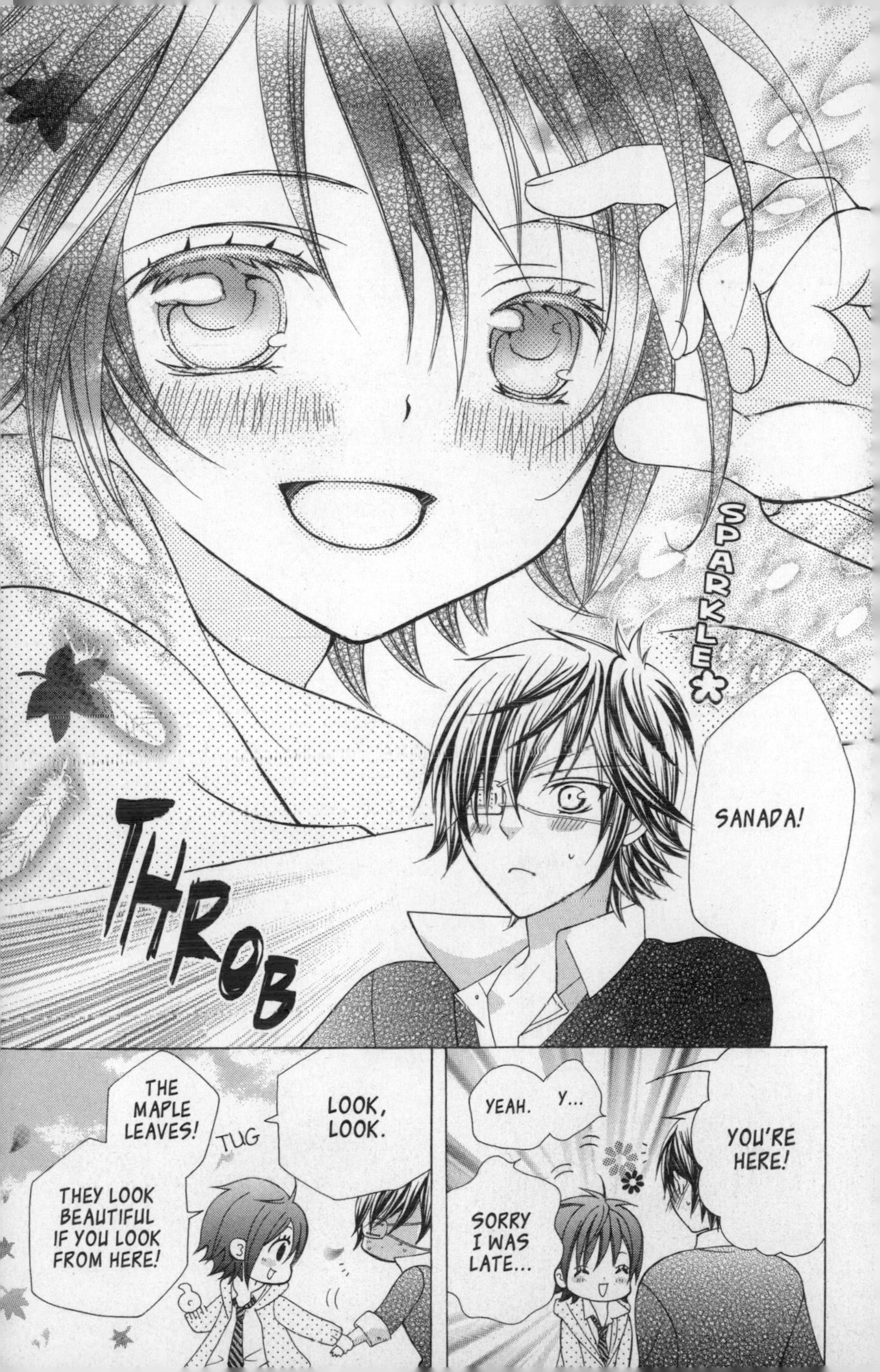
SPARKLE*
SANADA!
THROB
YOU'RE HERE!
Y...
YEAH.
SORRY I WAS LATE...
LOOK, LOOK.
TUG
THE MAPLE LEAVES!
THEY LOOK BEAUTIFUL IF YOU LOOK FROM HERE!

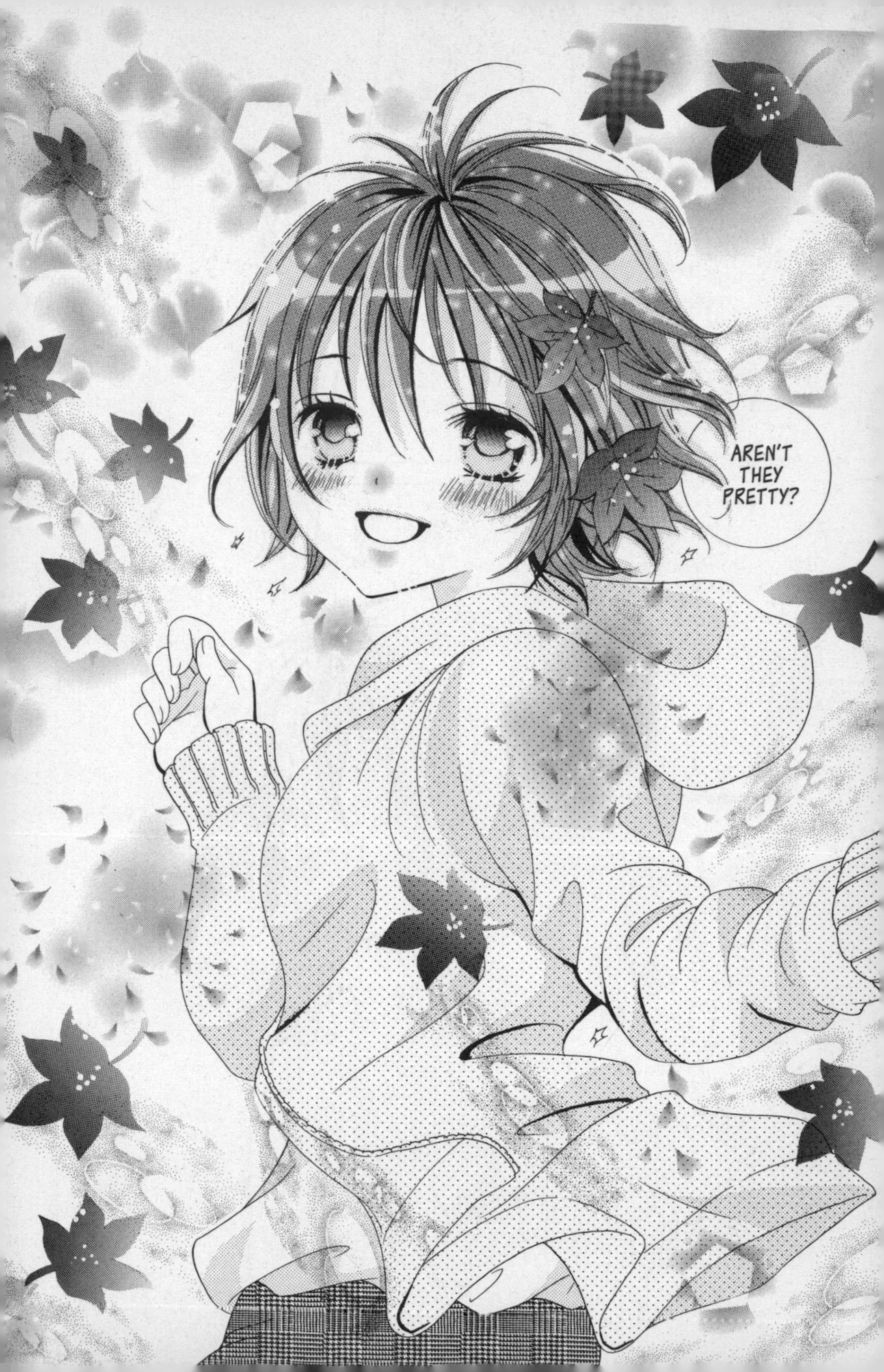
AREN'T THEY PRETTY?

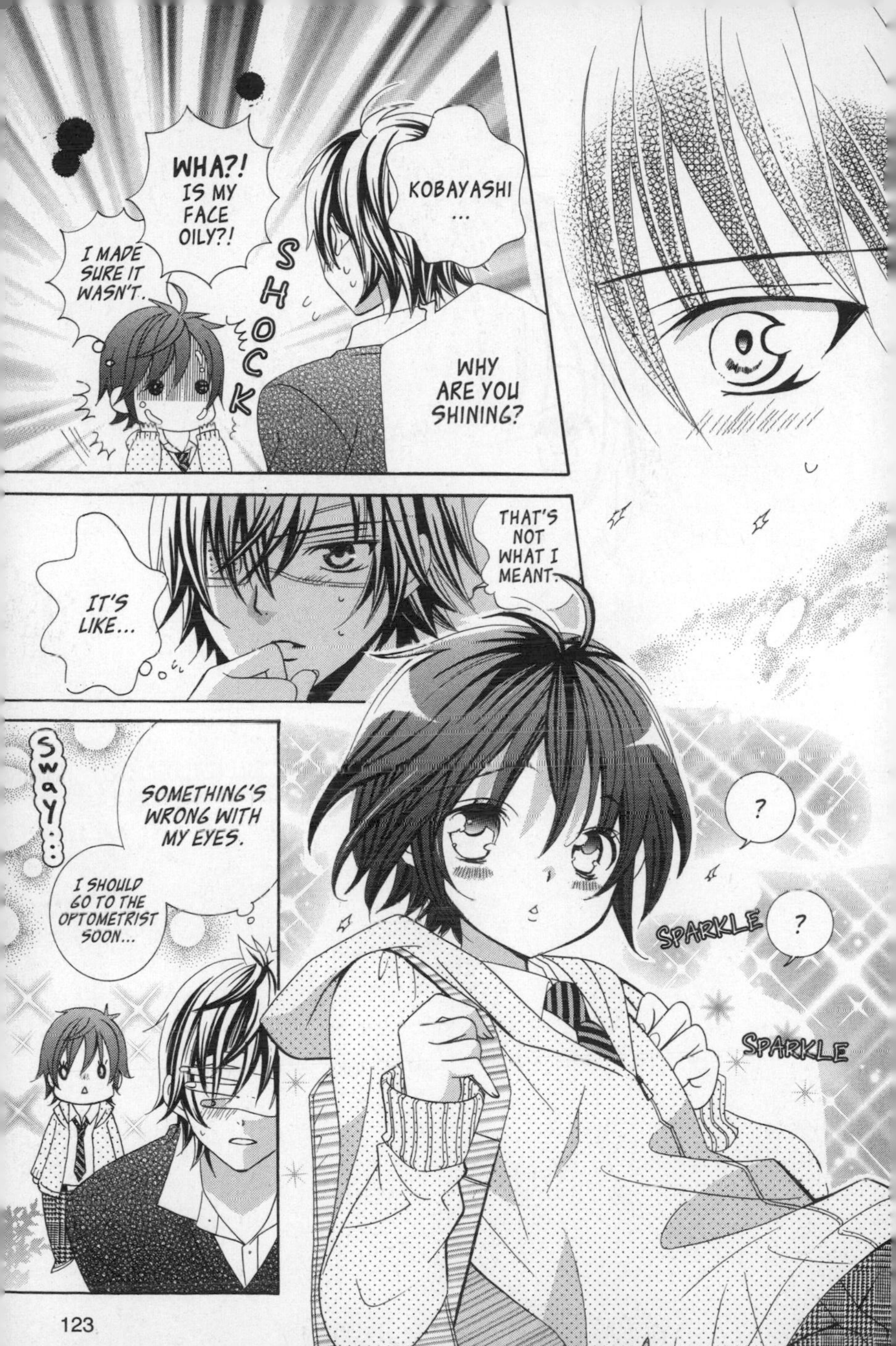
KOBAYASHI ...
WHY ARE YOU SHINING?
SHOCK
WHA?! IS MY FACE OILY?!
I MADE SURE IT WASN'T.
THAT'S NOT WHAT I MEANT.
IT'S LIKE...
?
SPARKLE
?
SPARKLE
SOMETHING'S WRONG WITH MY EYES.
I SHOULD GO TO THE OPTOMETRIST SOON...
Sway...

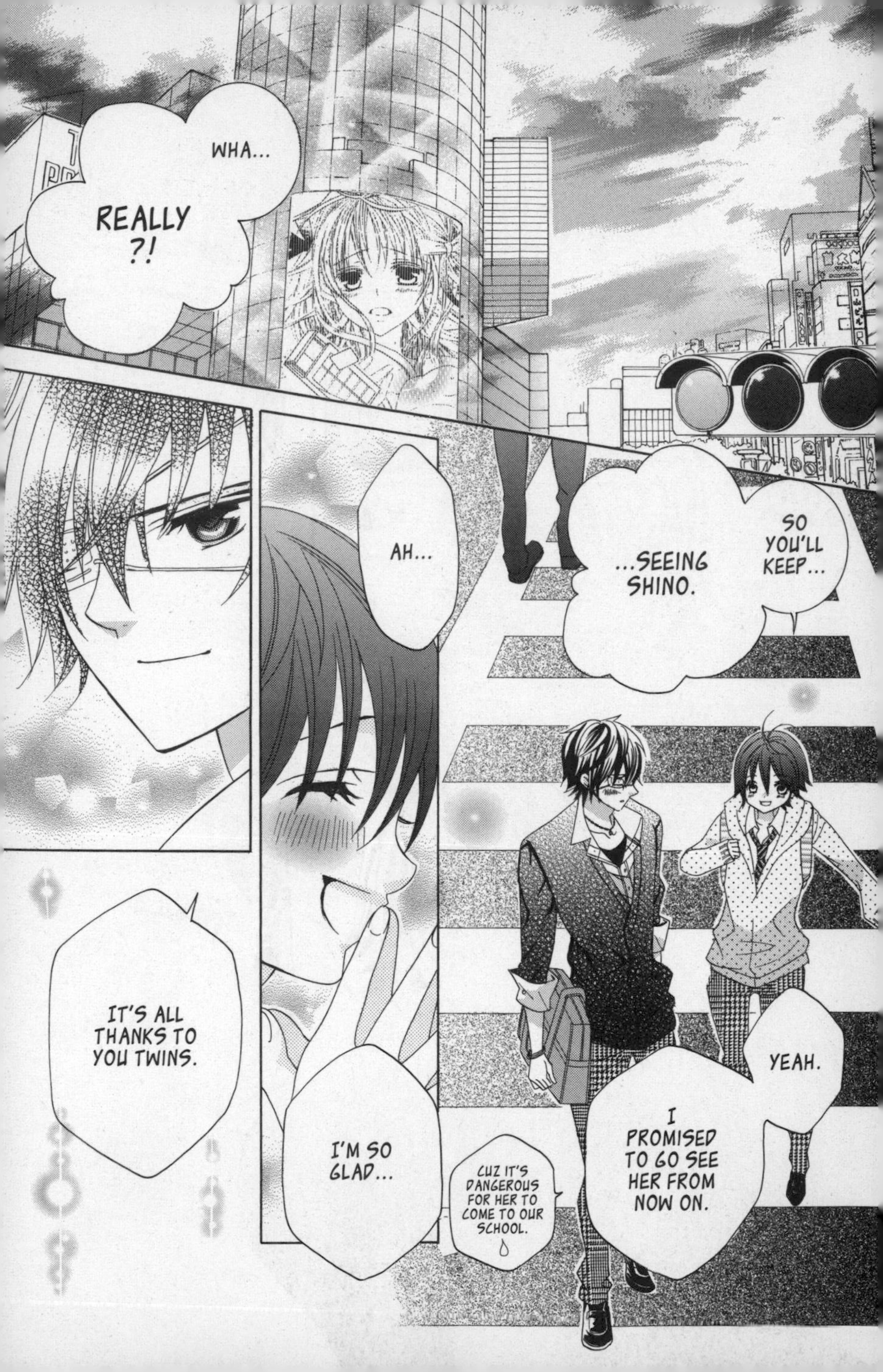
WHA...
REALLY ?!
SO YOU'LL KEEP...
...SEEING SHINO.
YEAH.
I PROMISED TO GO SEE HER FROM NOW ON.
CUZ IT'S DANGEROUS FOR HER TO COME TO OUR SCHOOL.
AH...
I'M SO GLAD...
IT'S ALL THANKS TO YOU TWINS.

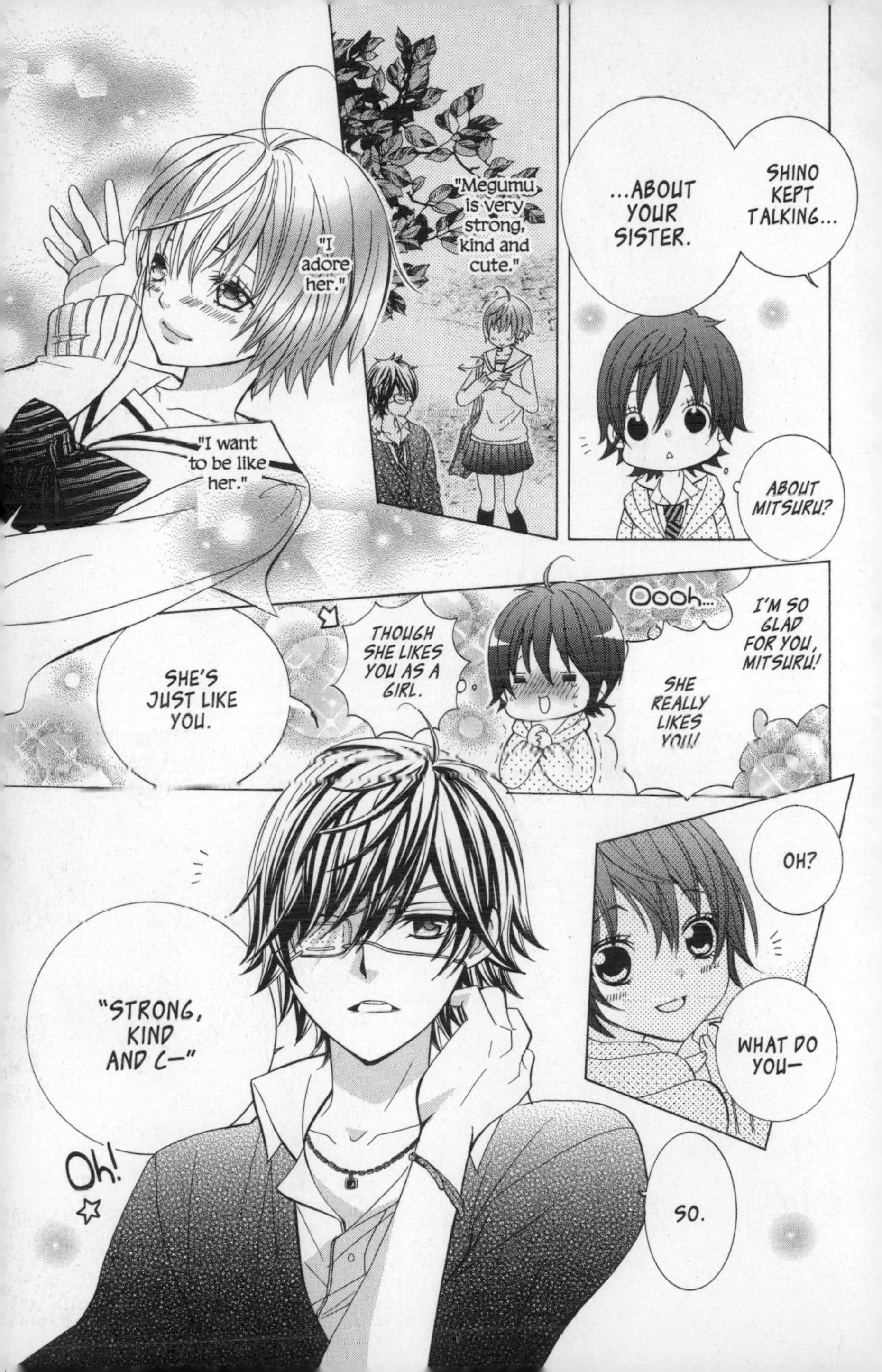
SHINO KEPT TALKING...
...ABOUT YOUR SISTER.
ABOUT MITSURU?
"Megumu is very strong, kind and cute."
"I adore her."
"I want to be like her."
I'M SO GLAD FOR YOU, MITSURU!
Oooh...
SHE REALLY LIKES YOU!
THOUGH SHE LIKES YOU AS A GIRL.
SHE'S JUST LIKE YOU.
OH?
WHAT DO YOU—
SO.
"STRONG, KIND AND C—"
Oh!

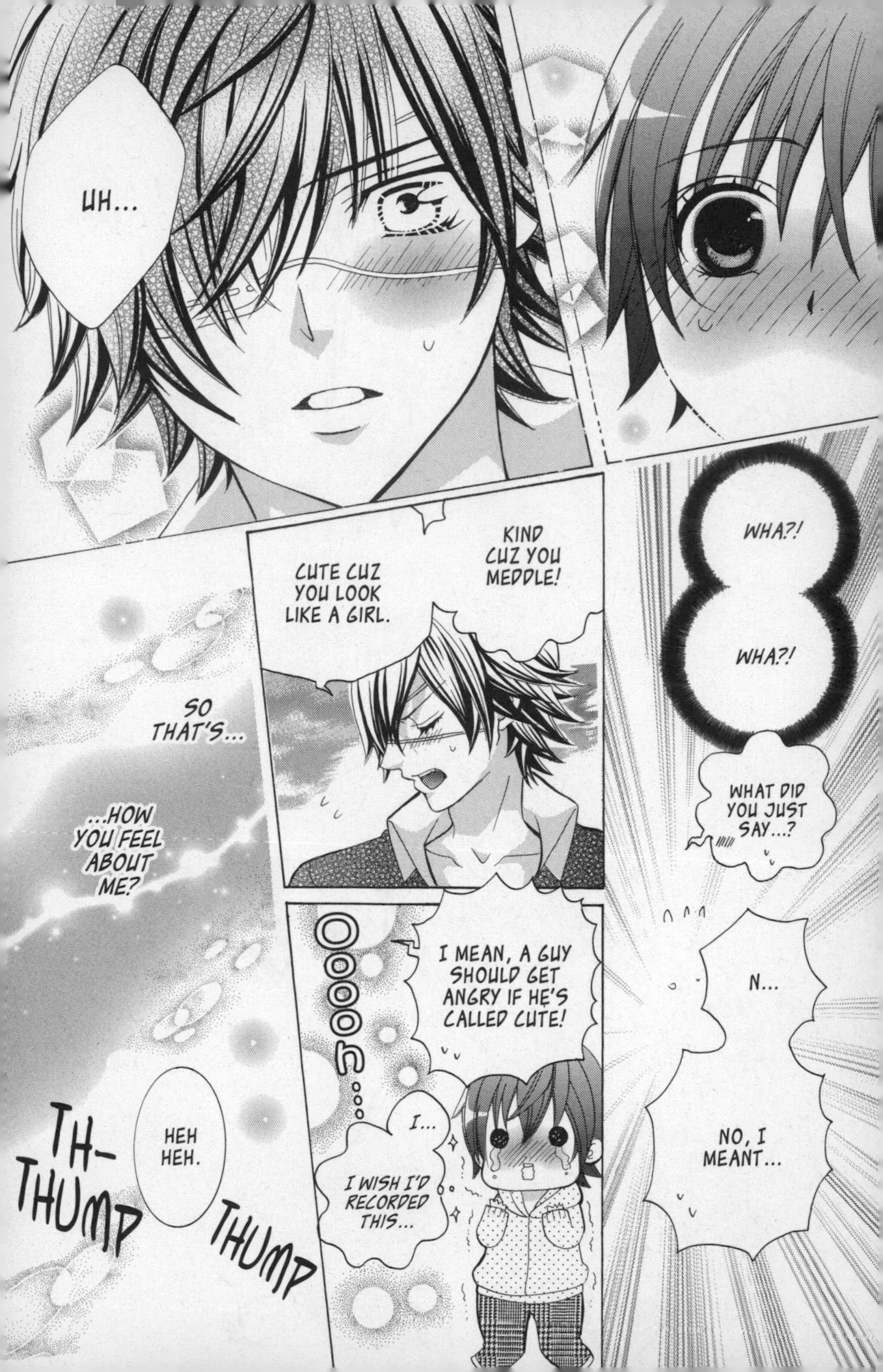
UH...
WHA?!
WHA?!
WHAT DID YOU JUST SAY...?
N...
NO, I MEANT...
KIND CUZ YOU MEDDLE!
CUTE CUZ YOU LOOK LIKE A GIRL.
I MEAN, A GUY SHOULD GET ANGRY IF HE'S CALLED CUTE!
Ooooh...
I...
I WISH I'D RECORDED THIS...
SO THAT'S...
...HOW YOU FEEL ABOUT ME?
HEH HEH.
TH-THUMP
THUMP

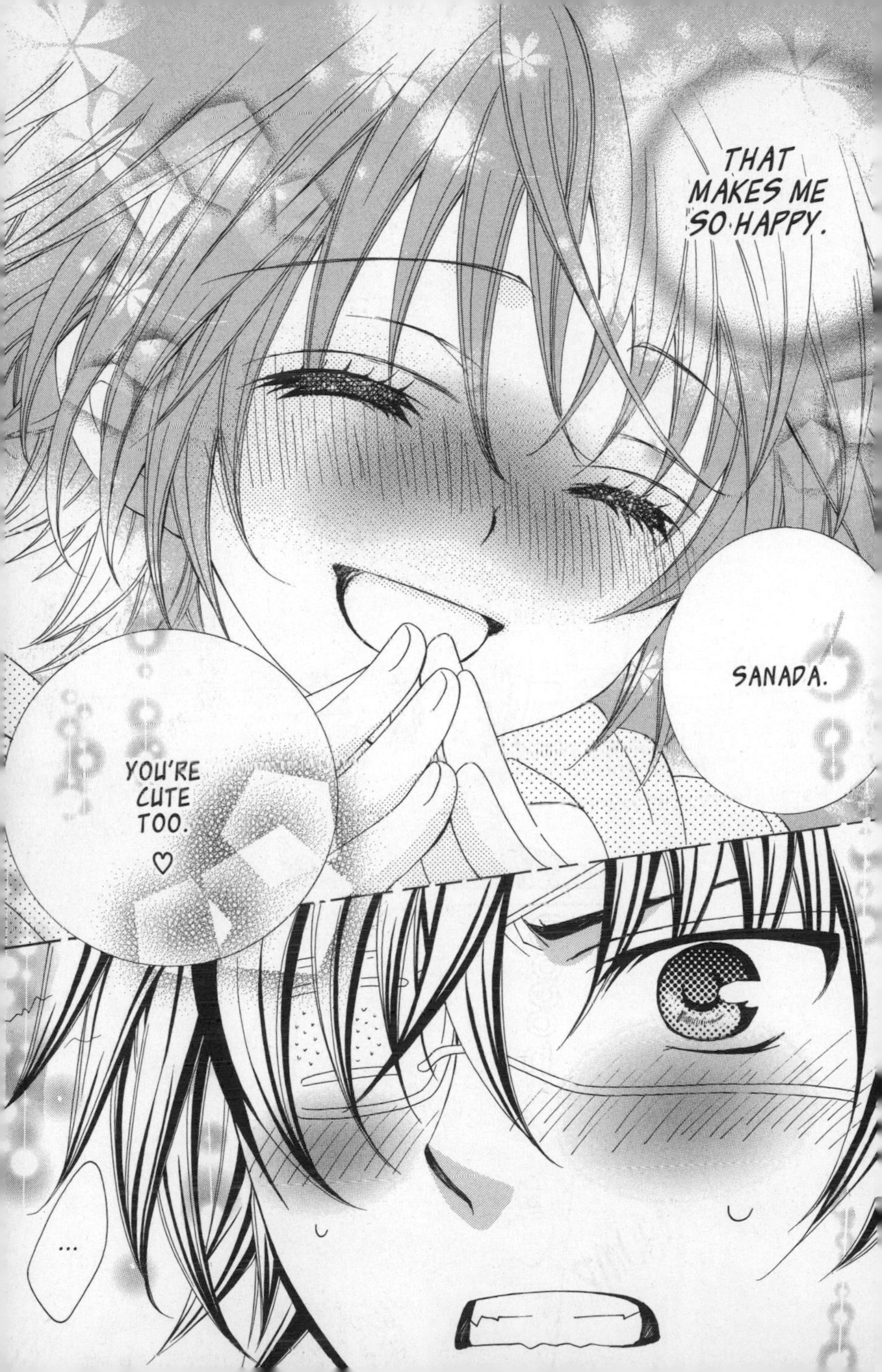
THAT MAKES ME SO HAPPY.
SANADA.
YOU'RE CUTE TOO. ♡
...

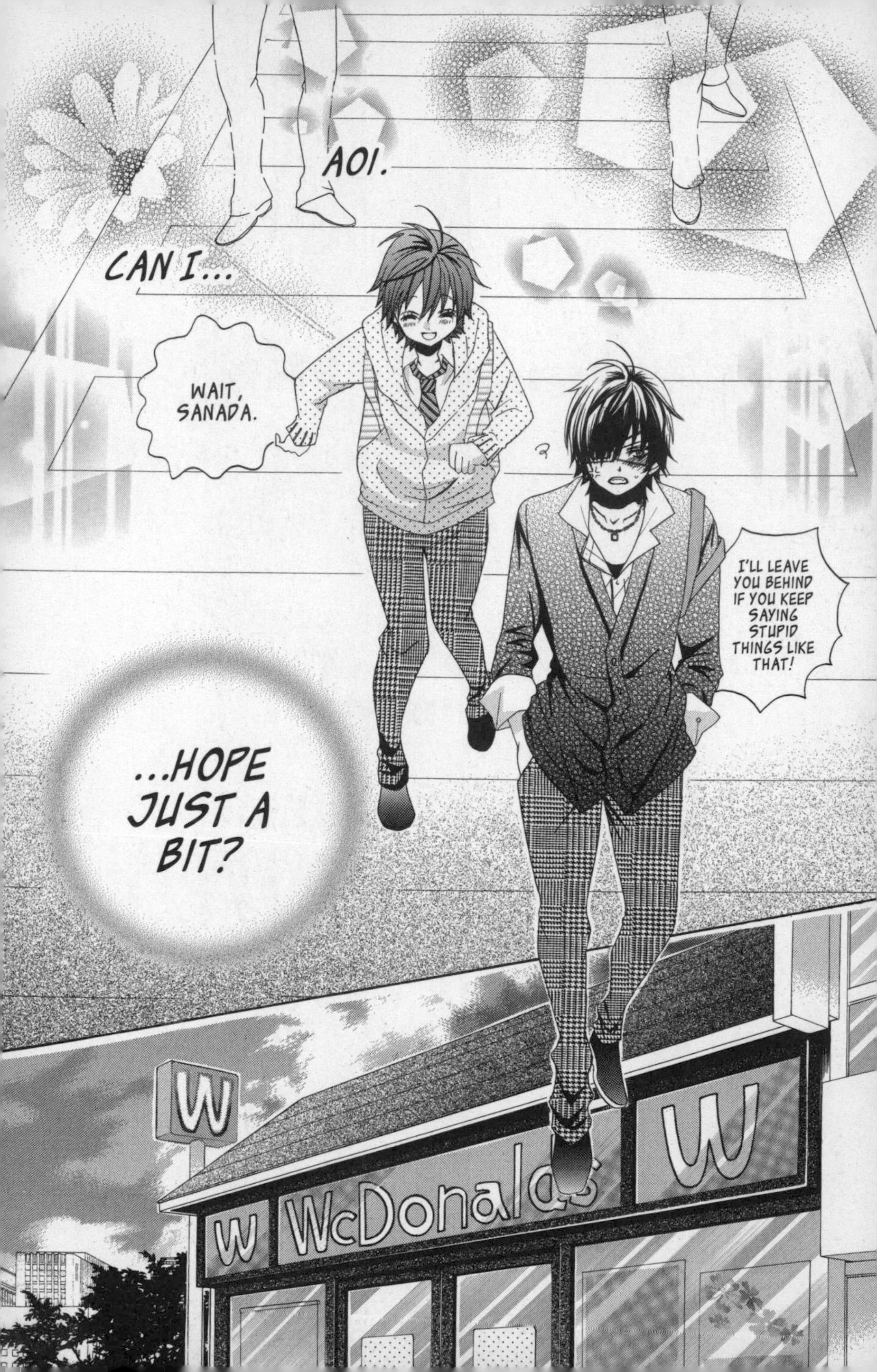
AOI.
CAN I...
WAIT, SANADA.
I'LL LEAVE YOU BEHIND IF YOU KEEP SAYING STUPID THINGS LIKE THAT!
...HOPE JUST A BIT?

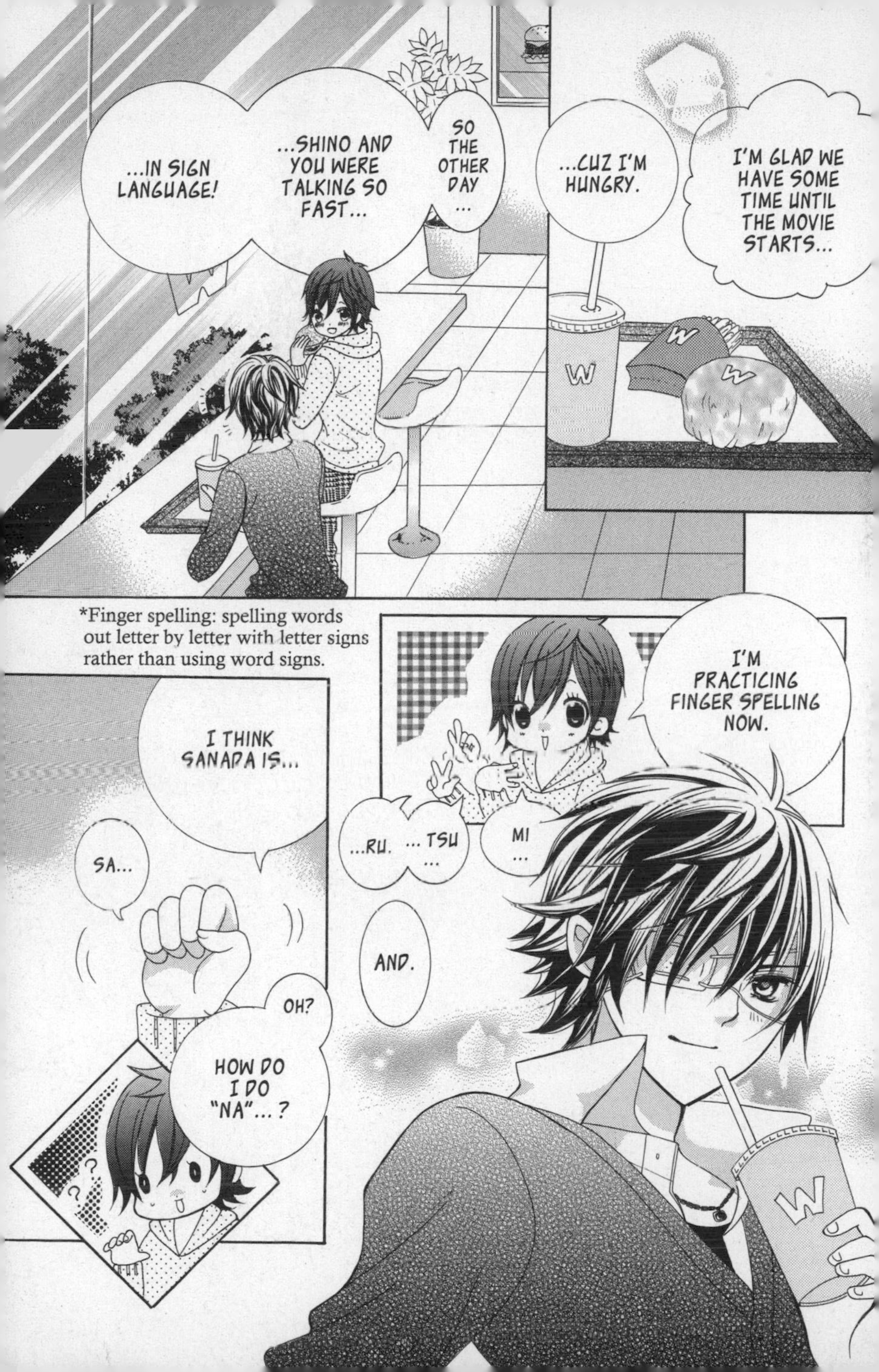
I'M GLAD WE HAVE SOME TIME UNTIL THE MOVIE STARTS...
...CUZ I'M HUNGRY.
SO THE OTHER DAY...
...SHINO AND YOU WERE TALKING SO FAST...
...IN SIGN LANGUAGE!
I'M PRACTICING FINGER SPELLING NOW.
MI...
...TSU...
...RU.
AND.
I THINK SANADA IS...
SA...
OH?
HOW DO I DO "NA"...?
*Finger spelling: spelling words out letter by letter with letter signs rather than using word signs.

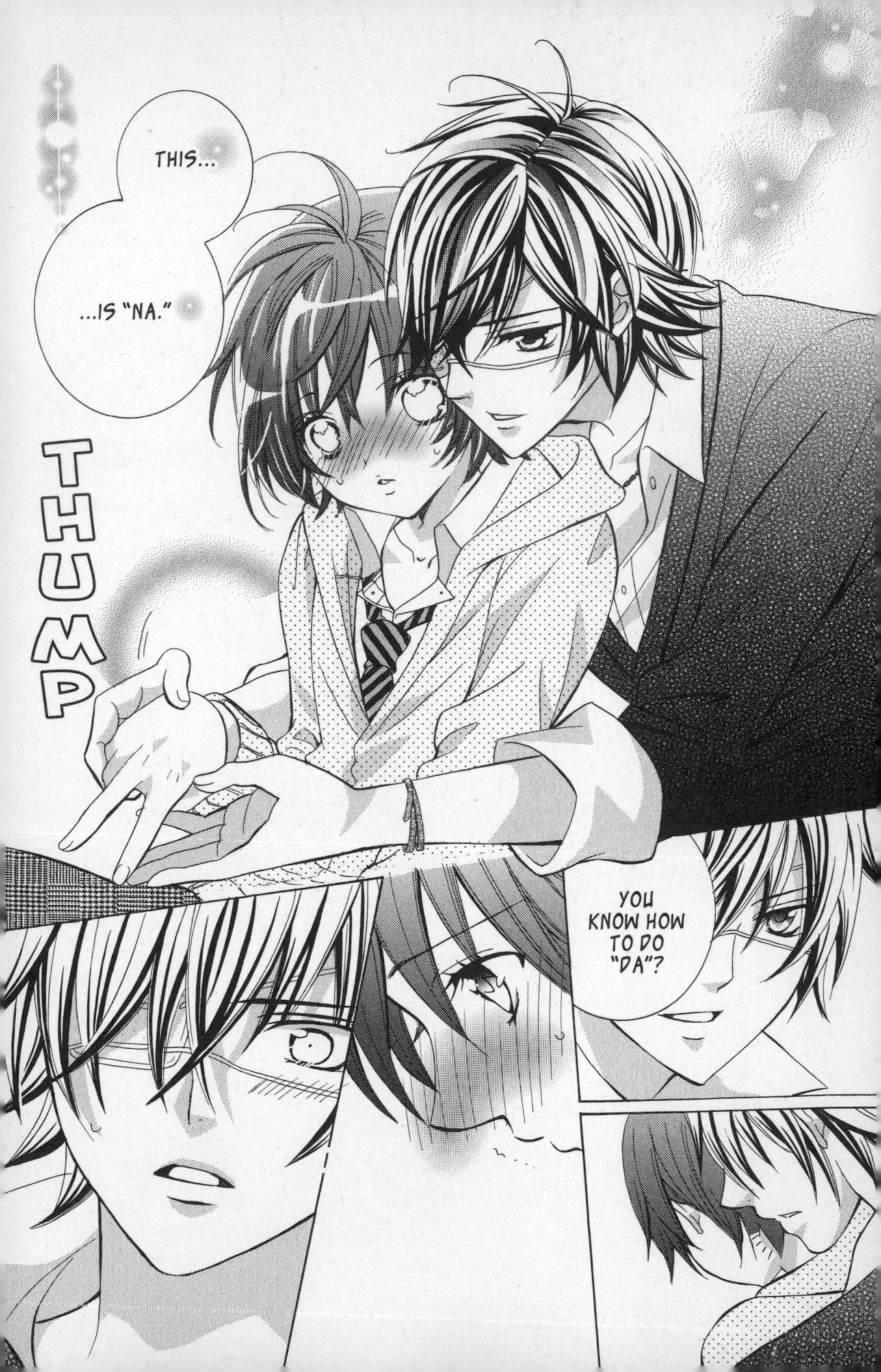
THIS...
...IS "NA."
THUMP
YOU KNOW HOW TO DO "DA"?

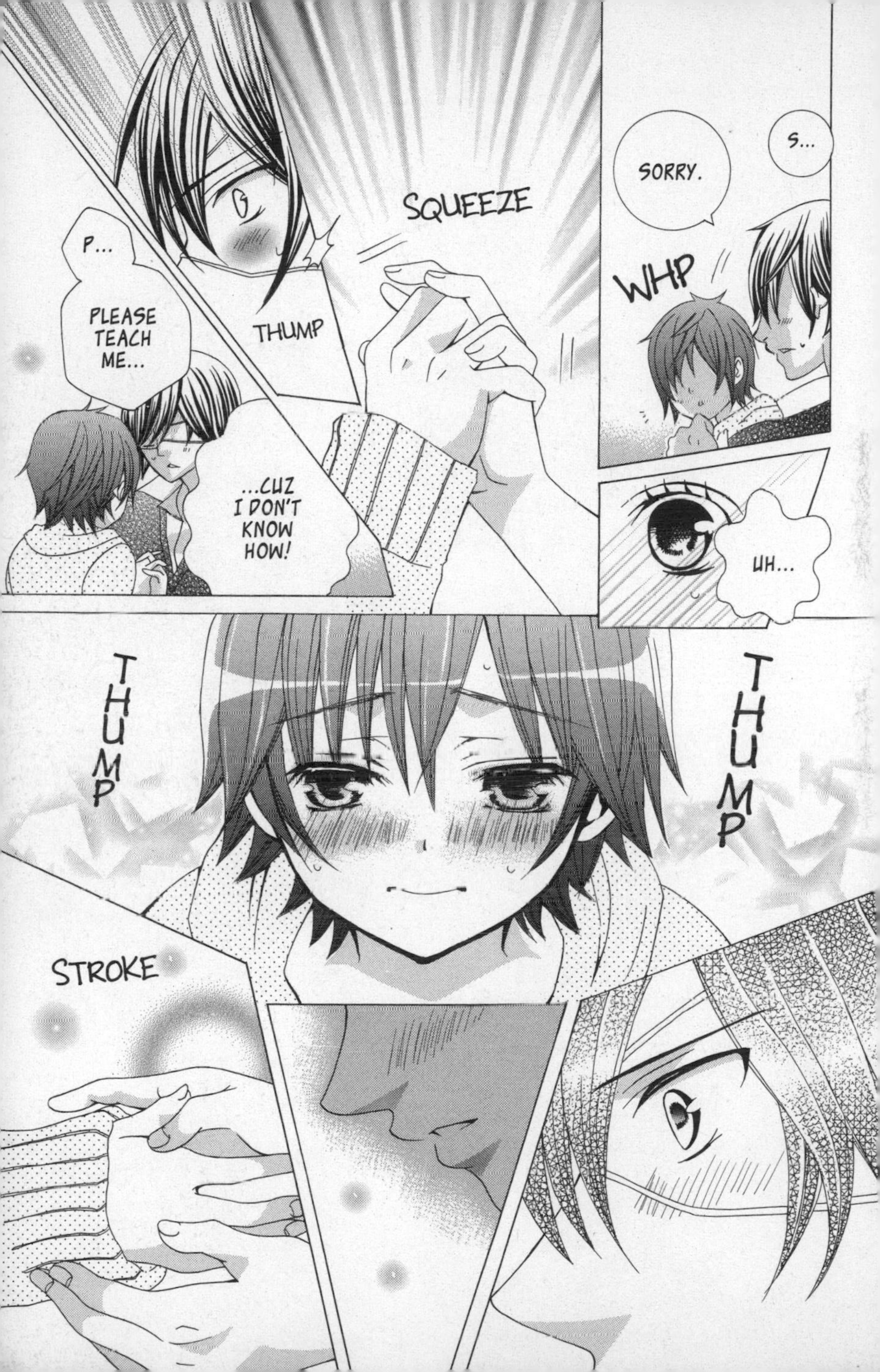
S...
SORRY.
WHP
UH...
SQUEEZE
P...
PLEASE TEACH ME...
THUMP
...CUZ I DON'T KNOW HOW!
THUMP
THUMP
STROKE

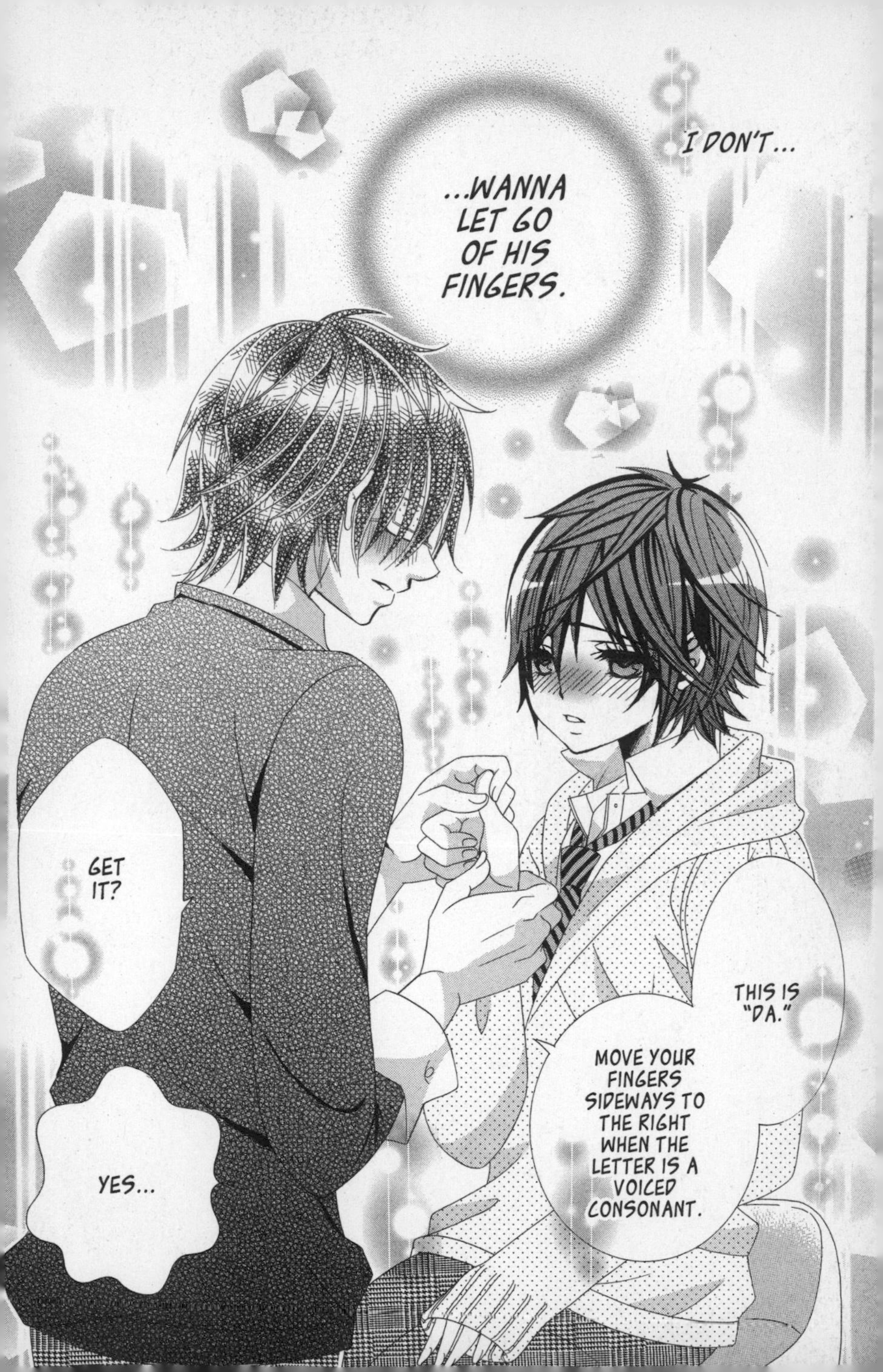
I DON'T...
...WANNA LET GO OF HIS FINGERS.
THIS IS "DA."
MOVE YOUR FINGERS SIDEWAYS TO THE RIGHT WHEN THE LETTER IS A VOICED CONSONANT.
GET IT?
YES...

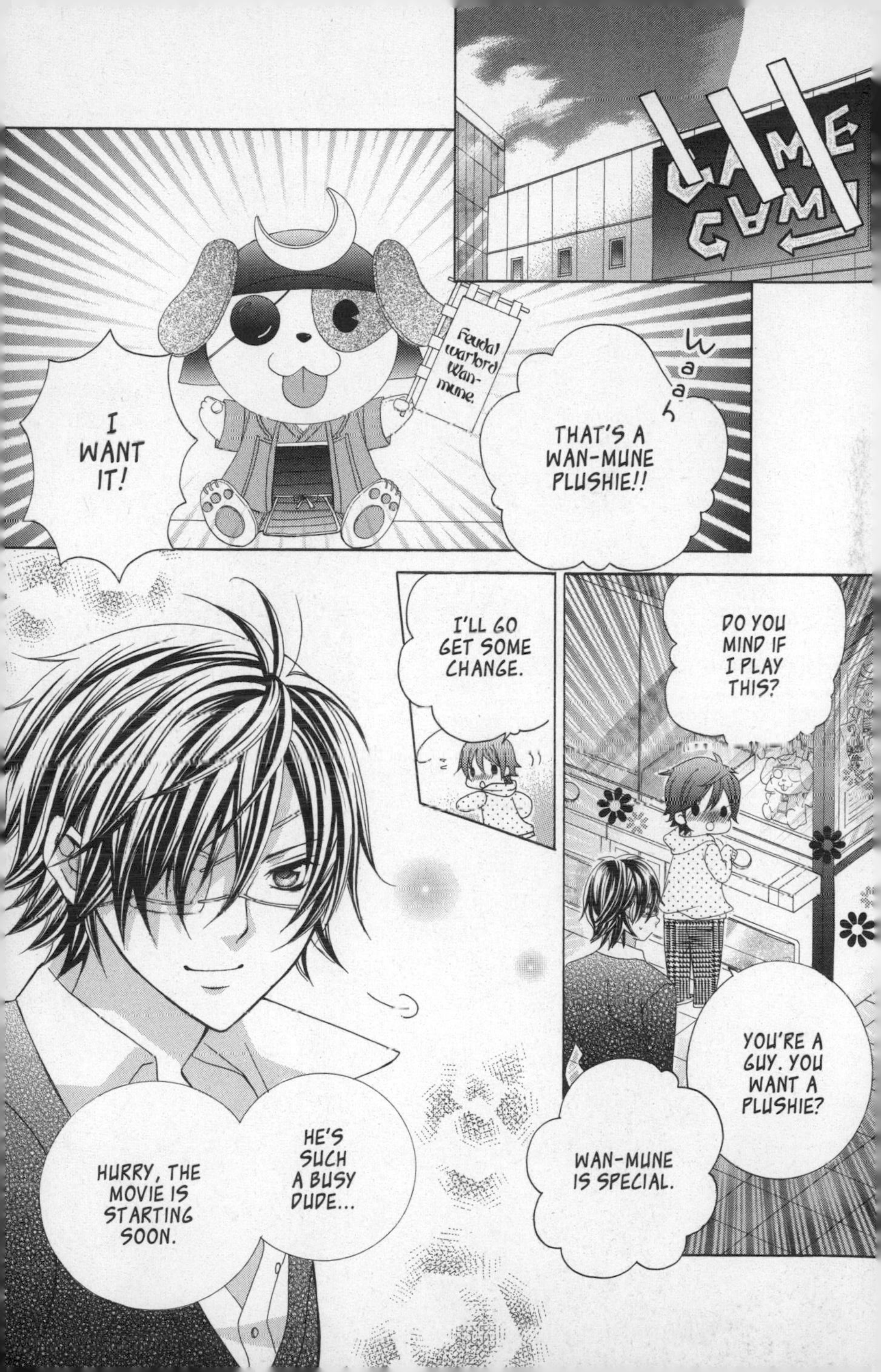
GAME
Waah
THAT'S A WAN-MUNE PLUSHIE!!
Feudal warlord Wan-mune.
I WANT IT!
DO YOU MIND IF I PLAY THIS?
YOU'RE A GUY. YOU WANT A PLUSHIE?
WAN-MUNE IS SPECIAL.
I'LL GO GET SOME CHANGE.
HE'S SUCH A BUSY DUDE...
HURRY, THE MOVIE IS STARTING SOON.

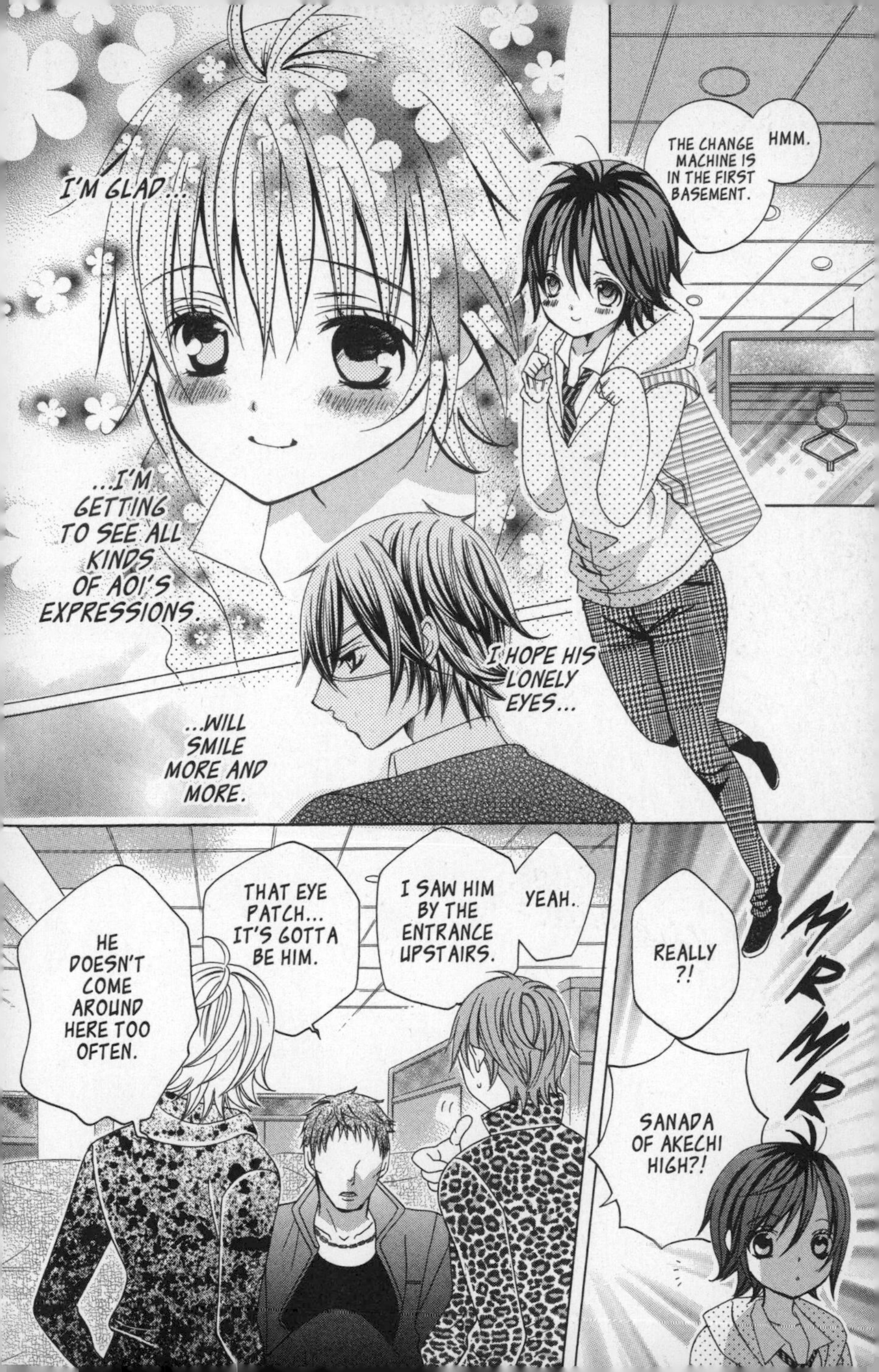
HMM.
THE CHANGE MACHINE IS IN THE FIRST BASEMENT.
I'M GLAD...
...I'M GETTING TO SEE ALL KINDS OF AOI'S EXPRESSIONS.
I HOPE HIS LONELY EYES...
...WILL SMILE MORE AND MORE.
MRMR
REALLY?!
SANADA OF AKECHI HIGH?!
YEAH.
I SAW HIM BY THE ENTRANCE UPSTAIRS.
THAT EYE PATCH... IT'S GOTTA BE HIM.
HE DOESN'T COME AROUND HERE TOO OFTEN.

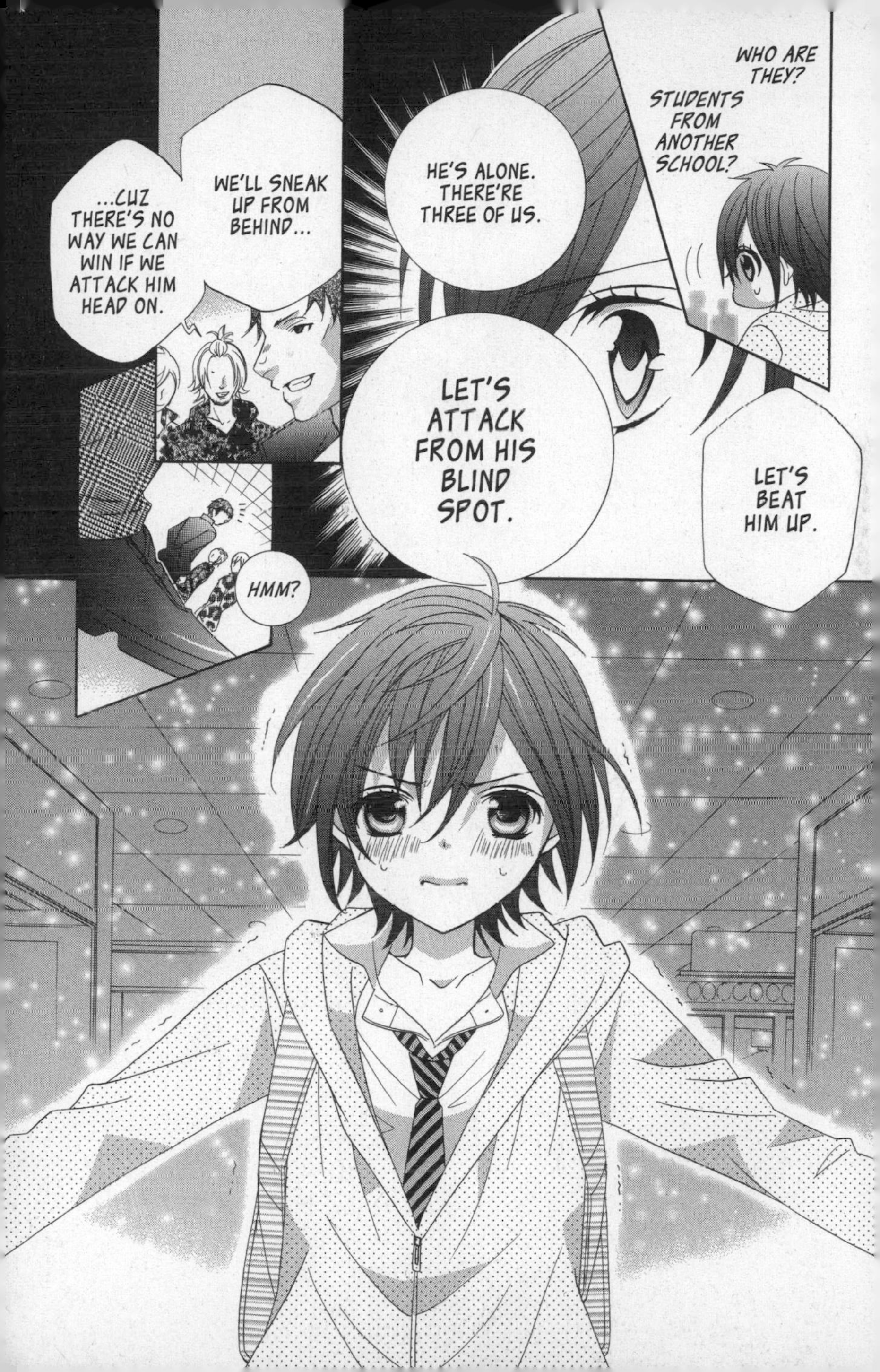
WHO ARE THEY?
STUDENTS FROM ANOTHER SCHOOL?
HE'S ALONE. THERE'RE THREE OF US.
LET'S BEAT HIM UP.
LET'S ATTACK FROM HIS BLIND SPOT.
WE'LL SNEAK UP FROM BEHIND...
...CUZ THERE'S NO WAY WE CAN WIN IF WE ATTACK HIM HEAD ON.
HMM?

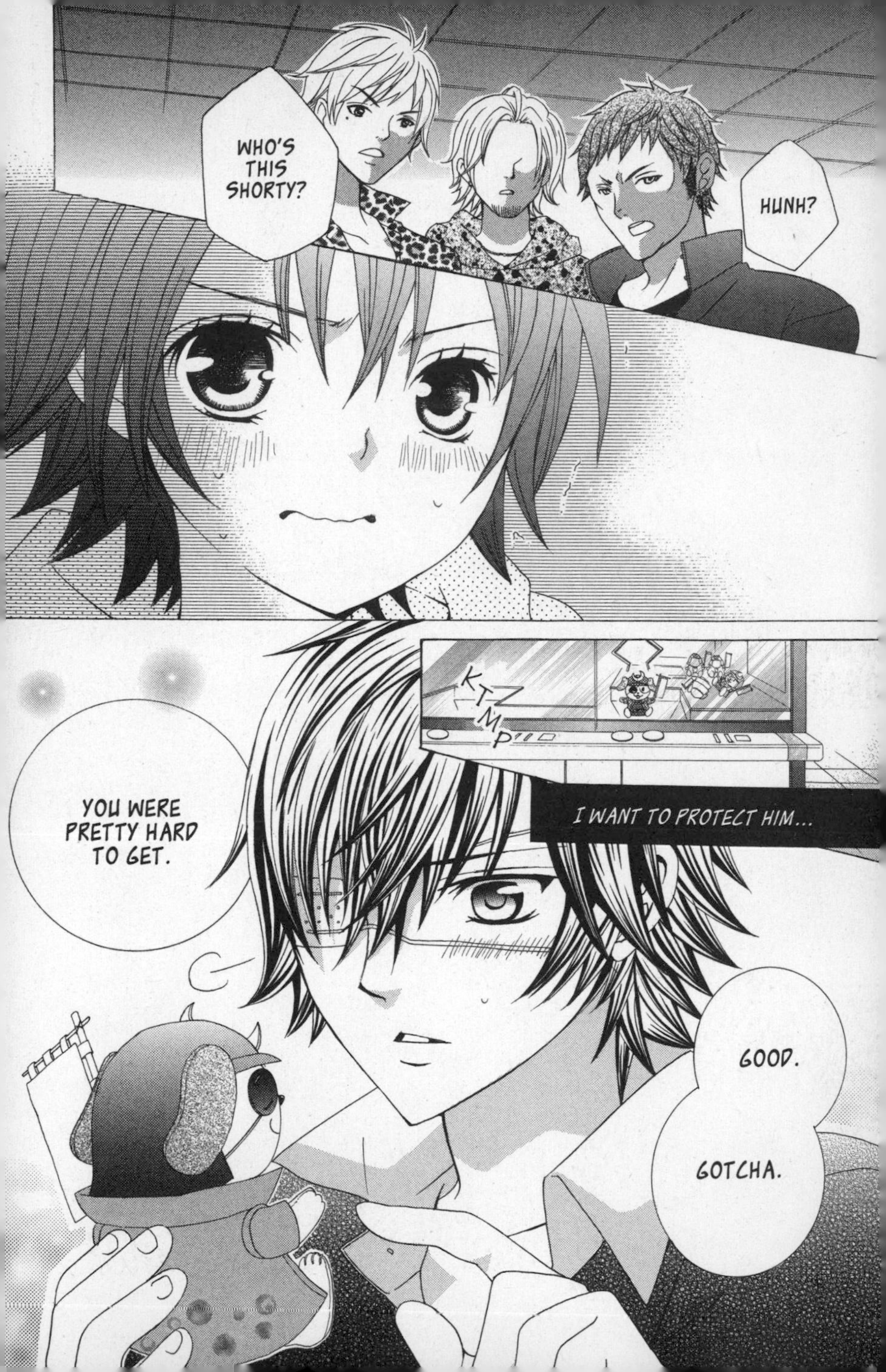
HUNH?
WHO'S THIS SHORTY?
I WANT TO PROTECT HIM...
YOU WERE PRETTY HARD TO GET.
GOOD.
GOTCHA.

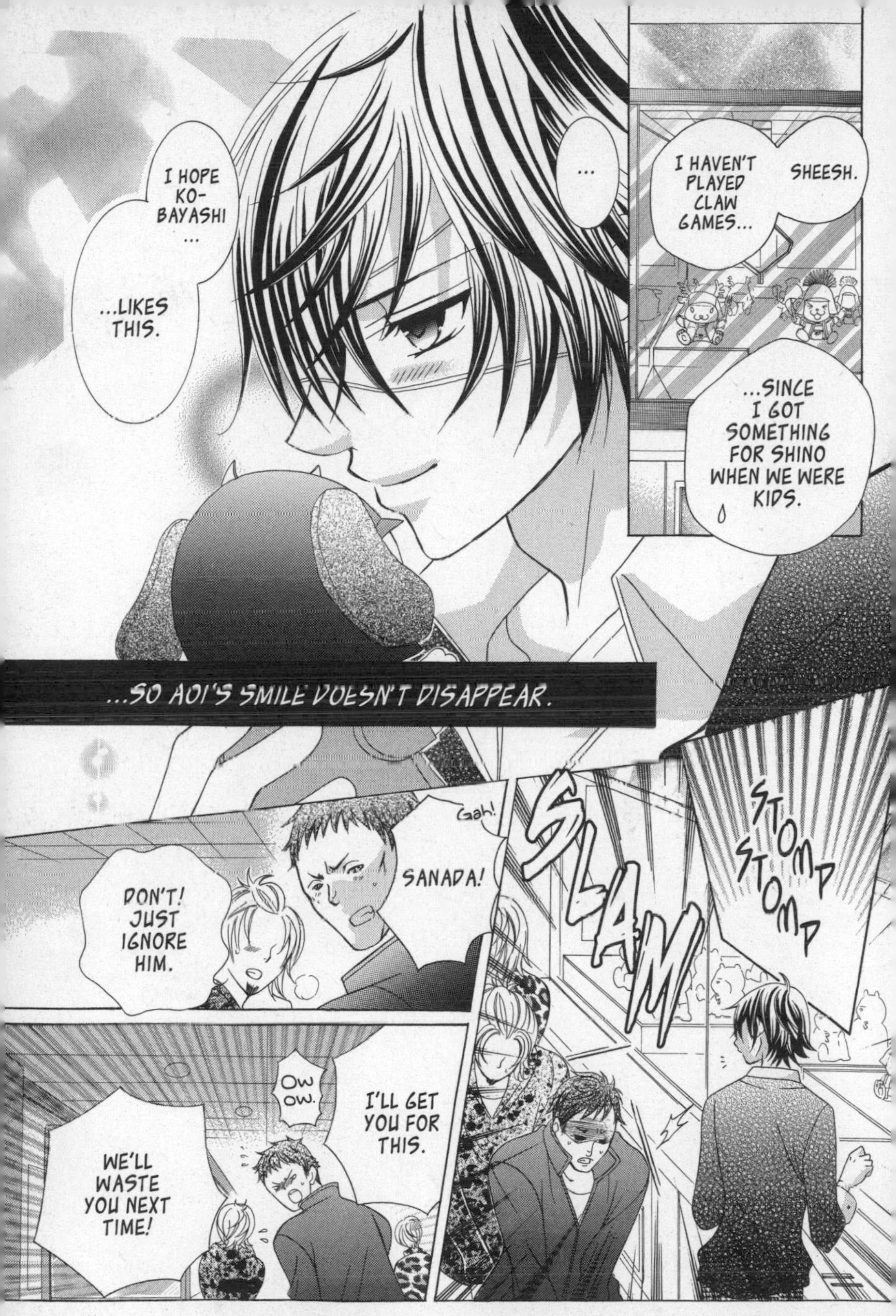
SHEESH.
I HAVEN'T PLAYED CLAW GAMES...
...SINCE I GOT SOMETHING FOR SHINO WHEN WE WERE KIDS.
...
I HOPE KO-BAYASHI ...
...LIKES THIS.
...SO AOI'S SMILE DOESN'T DISAPPEAR.
STOMP STOMP
SLAM
Gah!
SANADA!
DON'T! JUST IGNORE HIM.
I'LL GET YOU FOR THIS.
Ow ow.
WE'LL WASTE YOU NEXT TIME!

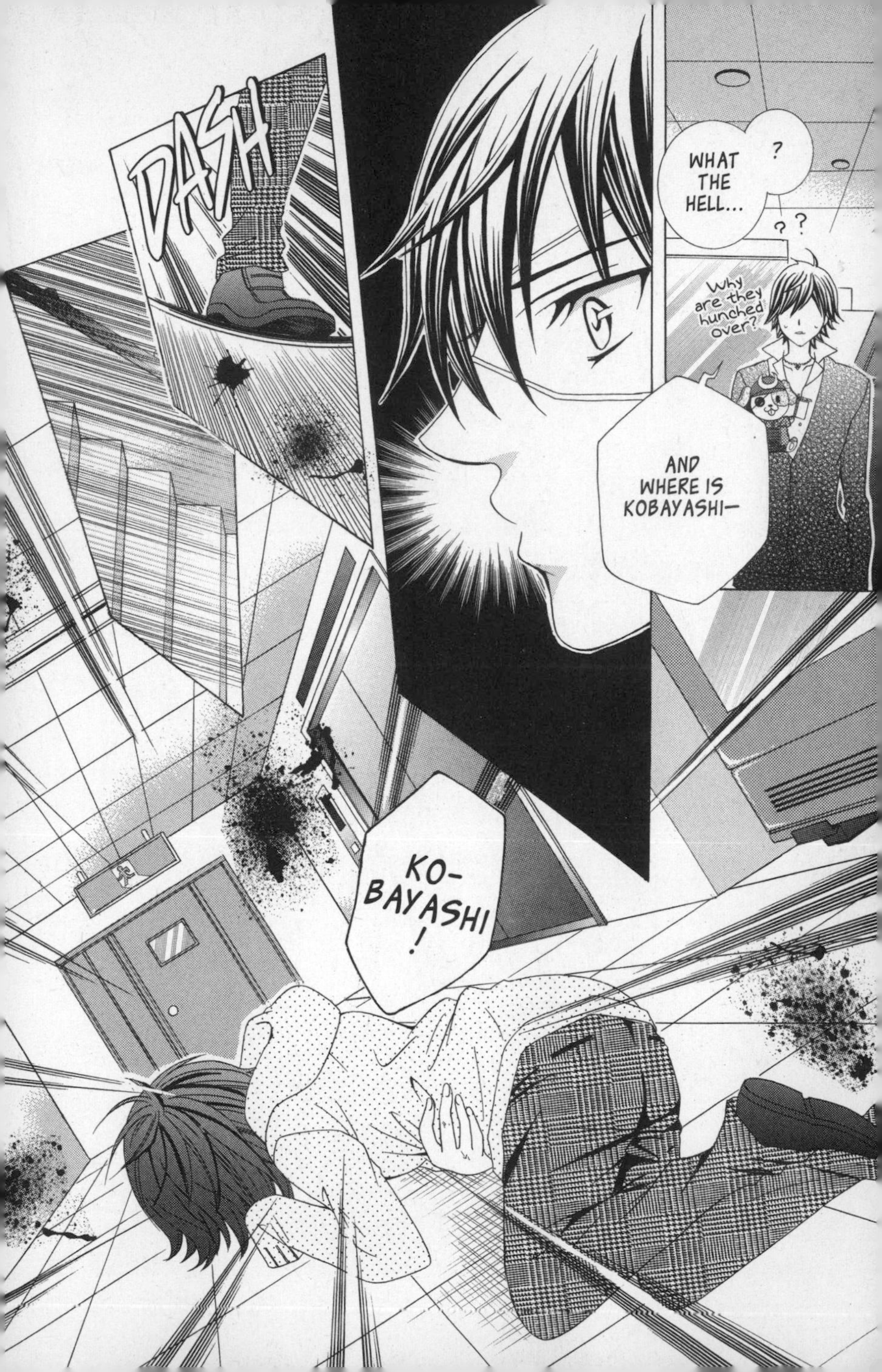
WHAT THE HELL...
?
? ?
Why are they hunched over?
AND WHERE IS KOBAYASHI—
DASH
KO-BAYASHI!

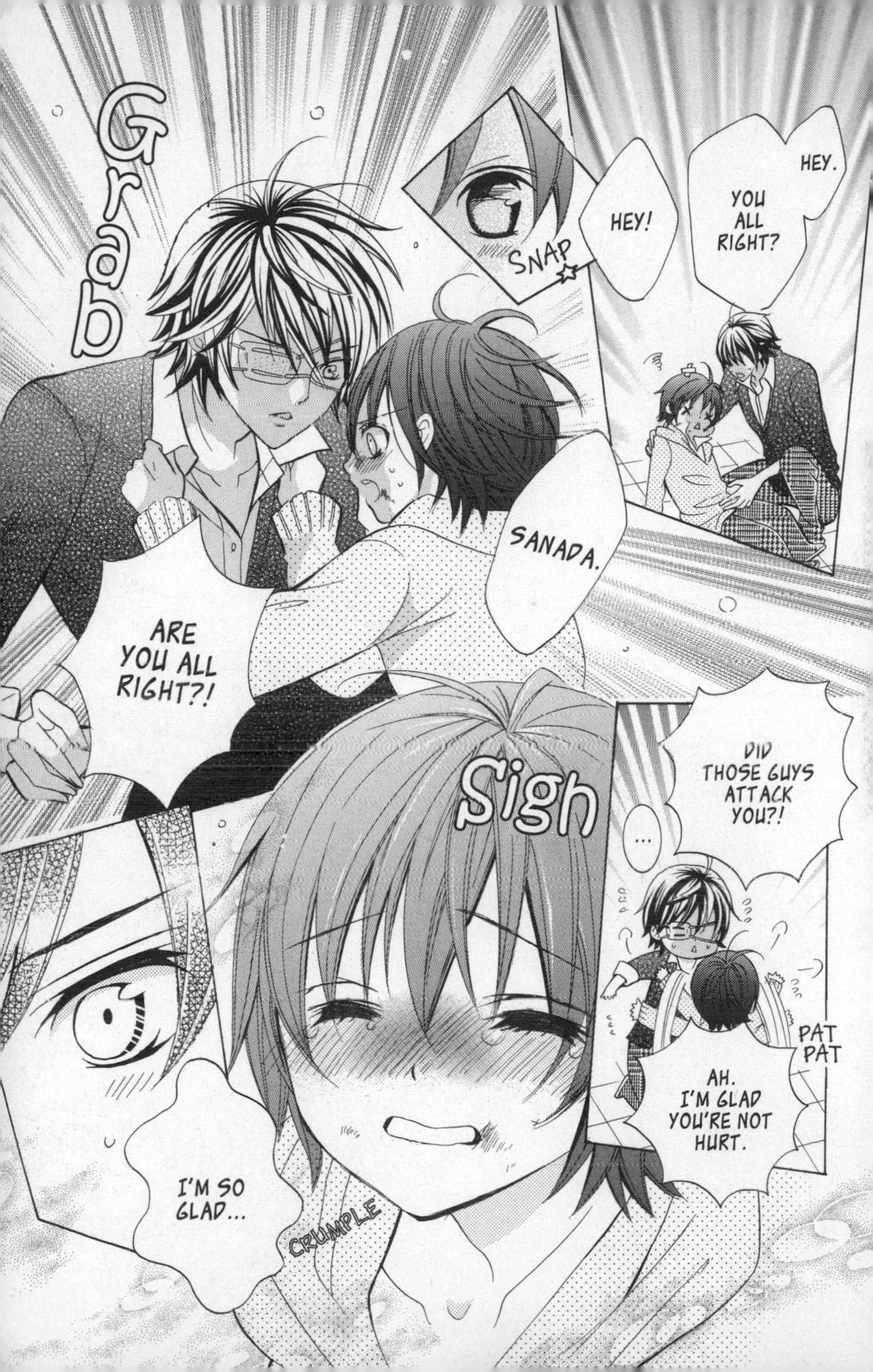
HEY.
YOU ALL RIGHT?
HEY!
SNAP
Grab
SANADA.
ARE YOU ALL RIGHT?!
DID THOSE GUYS ATTACK YOU?!
...
PAT PAT
AH. I'M GLAD YOU'RE NOT HURT.
Sigh
I'M SO GLAD...
CRUMPLE

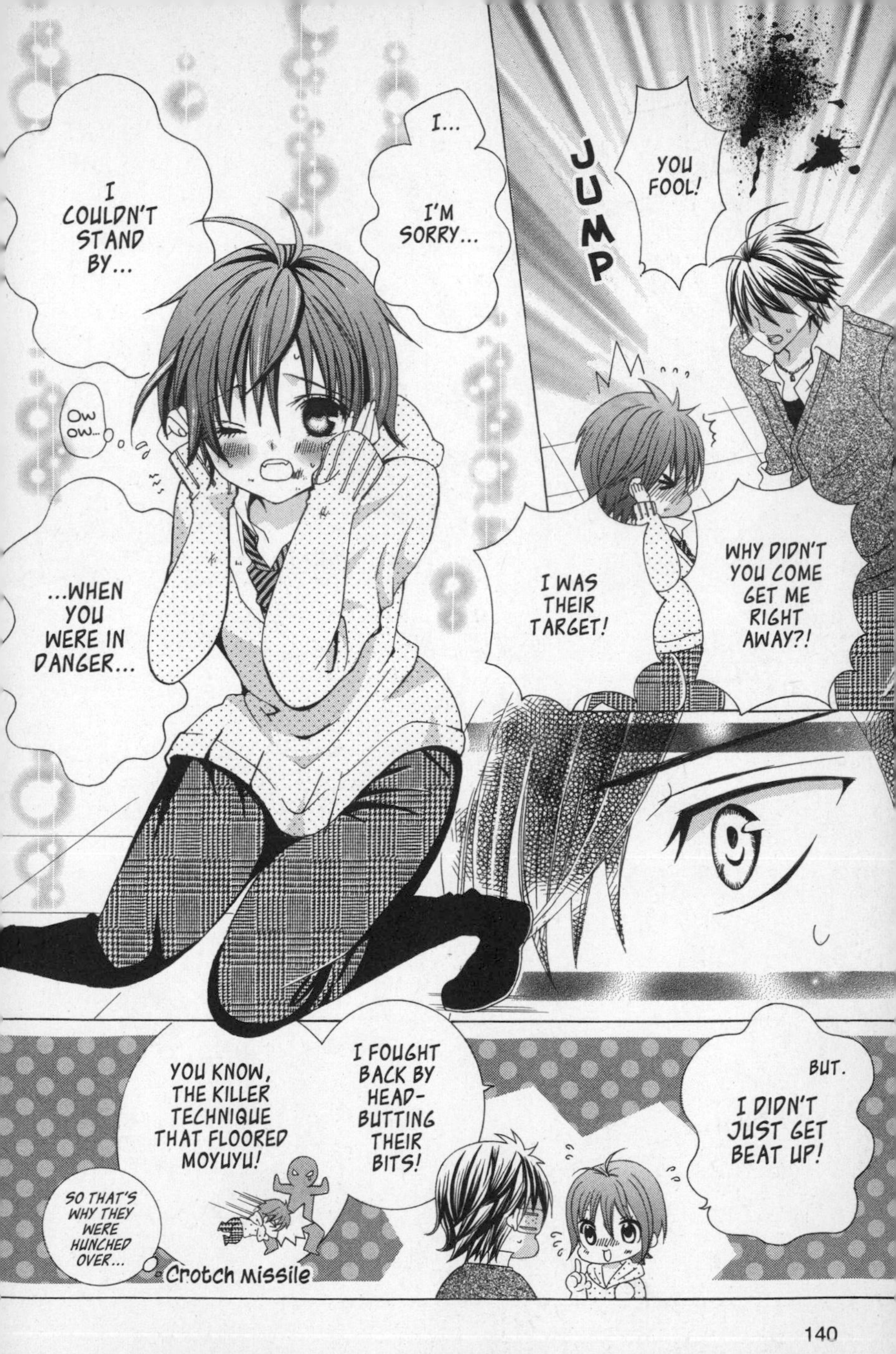
JUMP
YOU FOOL!
WHY DIDN'T YOU COME GET ME RIGHT AWAY?!
I WAS THEIR TARGET!
I...
I'M SORRY...
I COULDN'T STAND BY...
OW OW...
...WHEN YOU WERE IN DANGER...
BUT.
I DIDN'T JUST GET BEAT UP!
I FOUGHT BACK BY HEAD-BUTTING THEIR BITS!
YOU KNOW, THE KILLER TECHNIQUE THAT FLOORED MOYUYU!
SO THAT'S WHY THEY WERE HUNCHED OVER...
Crotch Missile

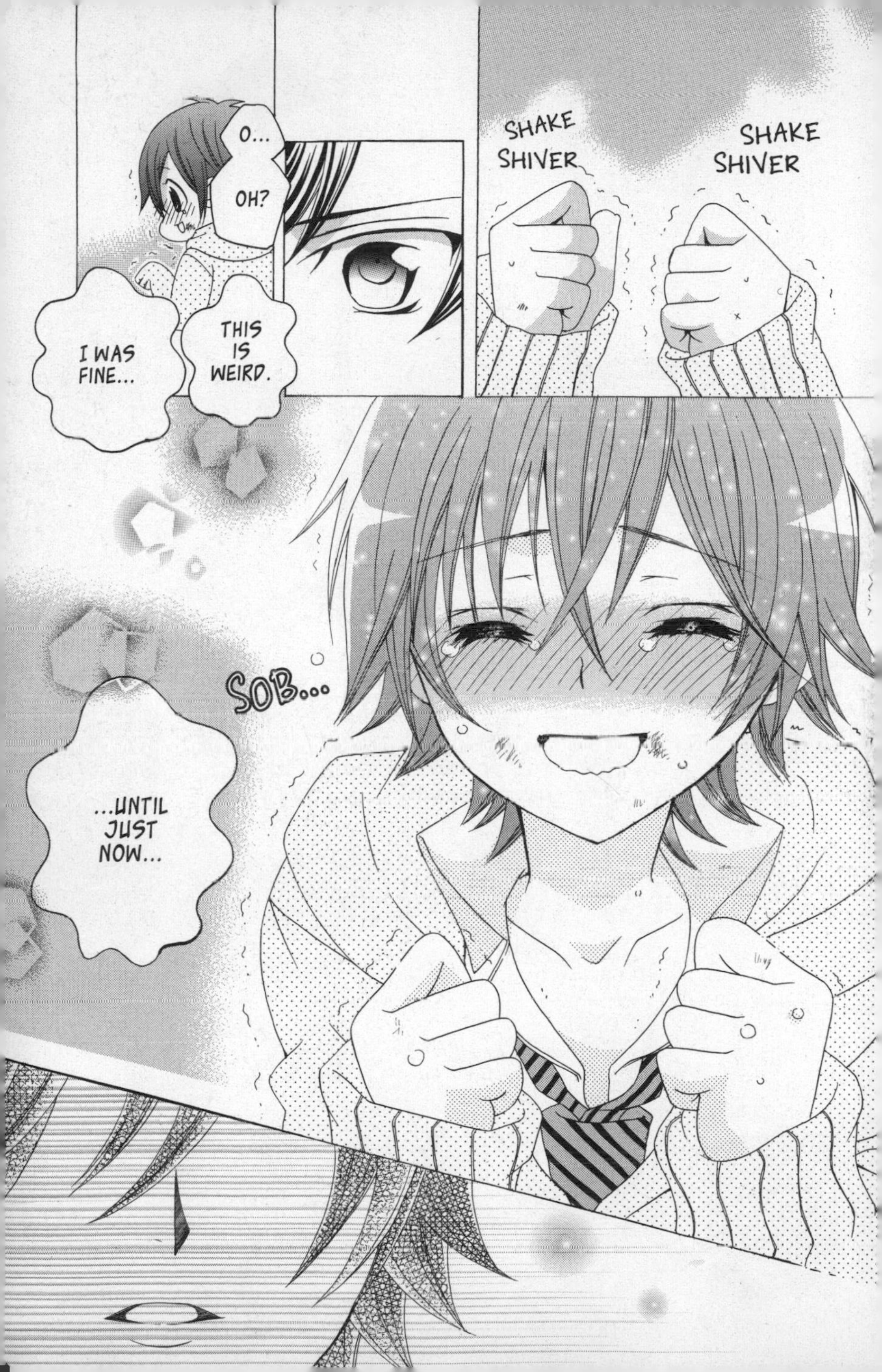
SHAKE SHIVER
SHAKE SHIVER
O... OH?
THIS IS WEIRD.
I WAS FINE...
SOB...
...UNTIL JUST NOW...

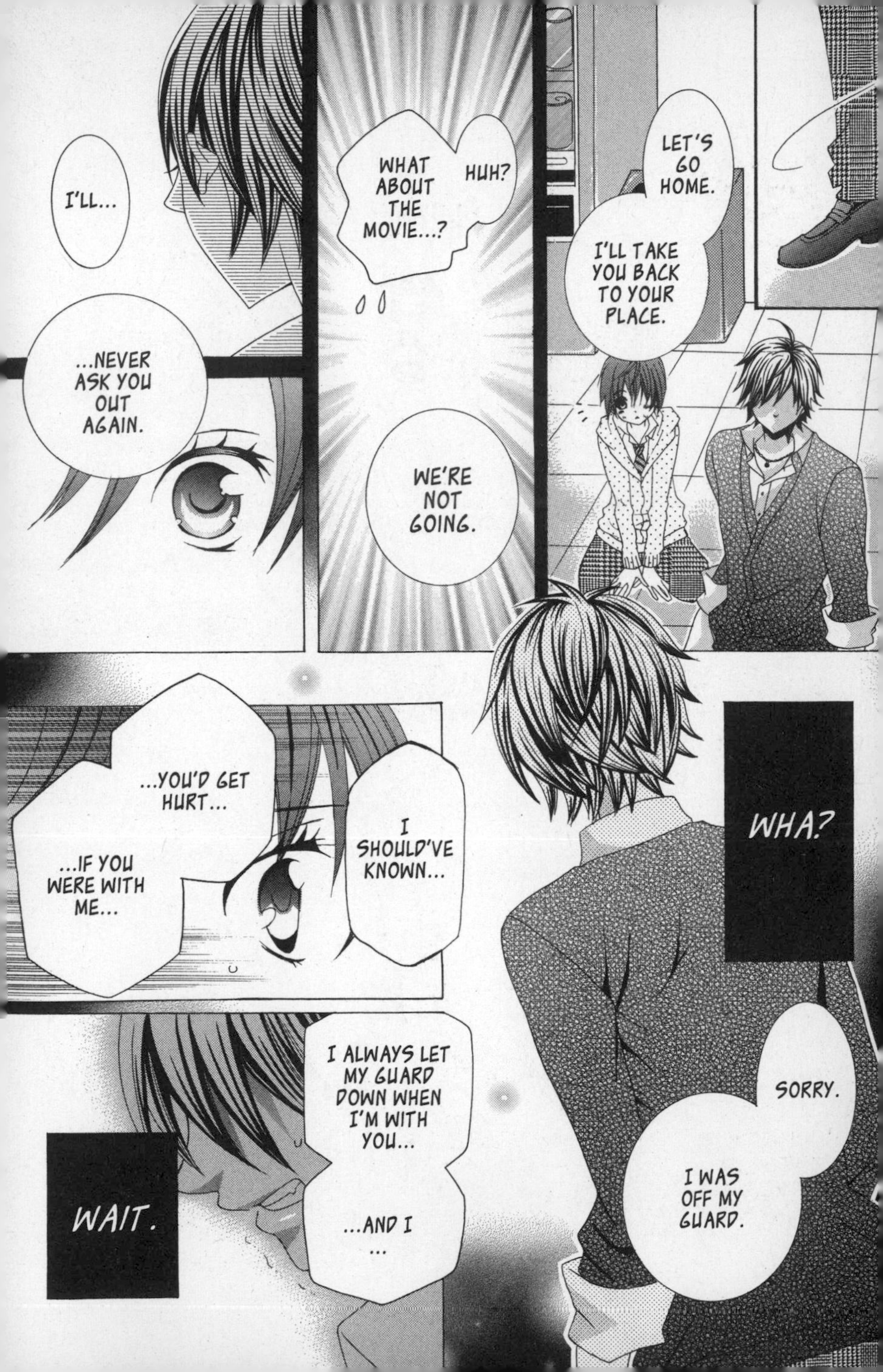
LET'S GO HOME.
I'LL TAKE YOU BACK TO YOUR PLACE.
HUH?
WHAT ABOUT THE MOVIE...?
WE'RE NOT GOING.
I'LL...
...NEVER ASK YOU OUT AGAIN.
WHA?
SORRY.
I WAS OFF MY GUARD.
I SHOULD'VE KNOWN...
...YOU'D GET HURT...
...IF YOU WERE WITH ME...
I ALWAYS LET MY GUARD DOWN WHEN I'M WITH YOU...
...AND I ...
WAIT.

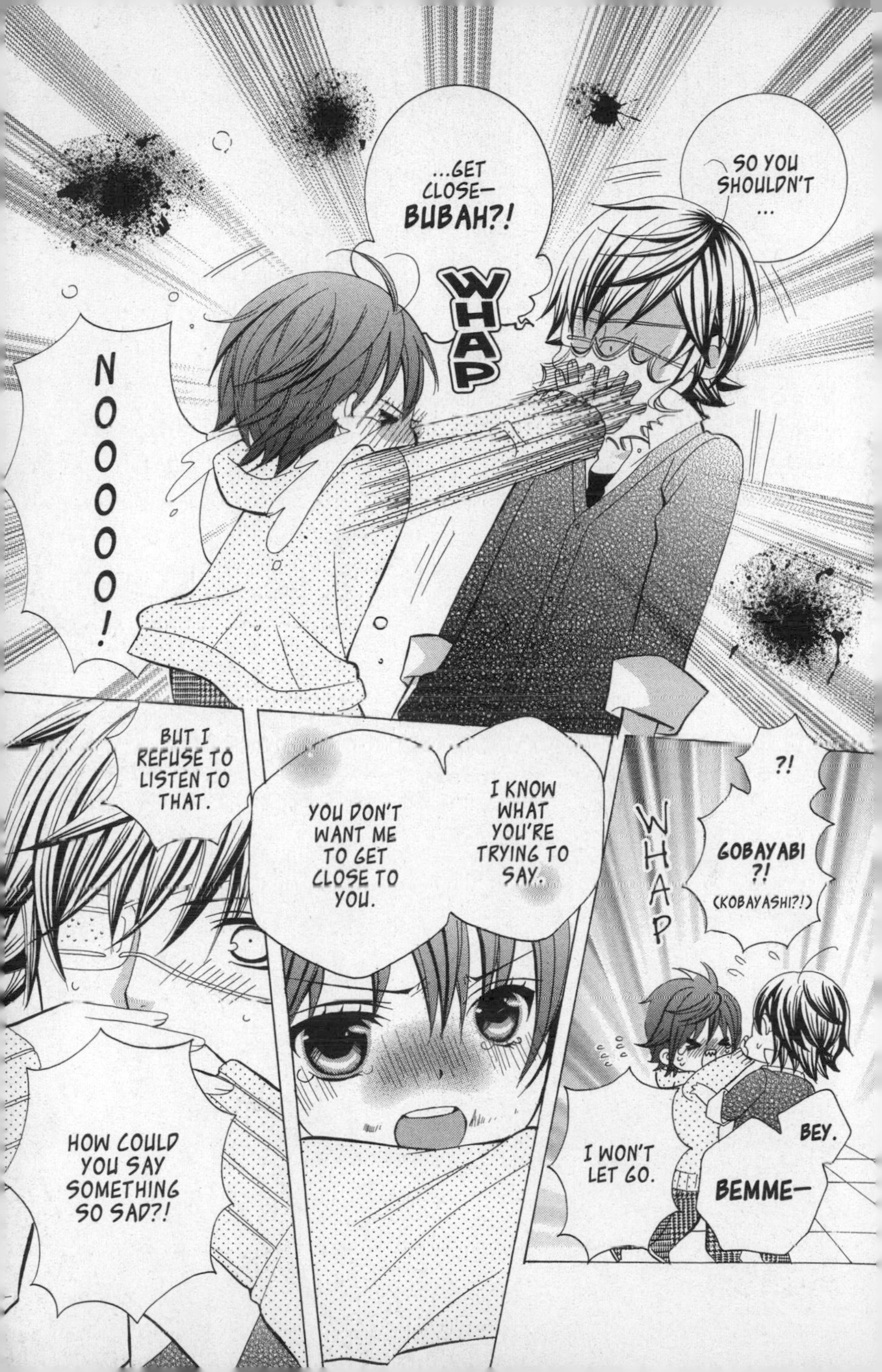
SO YOU SHOULDN'T ...
...GET CLOSE— BUBAH?!
WHAP
NOOOOOO!
?!
WHAP
GOBAYABI?!
(KOBAYASHI?!)
BEY.
BEMME—
I WON'T LET GO.
I KNOW WHAT YOU'RE TRYING TO SAY.
YOU DON'T WANT ME TO GET CLOSE TO YOU.
BUT I REFUSE TO LISTEN TO THAT.
HOW COULD YOU SAY SOMETHING SO SAD?!

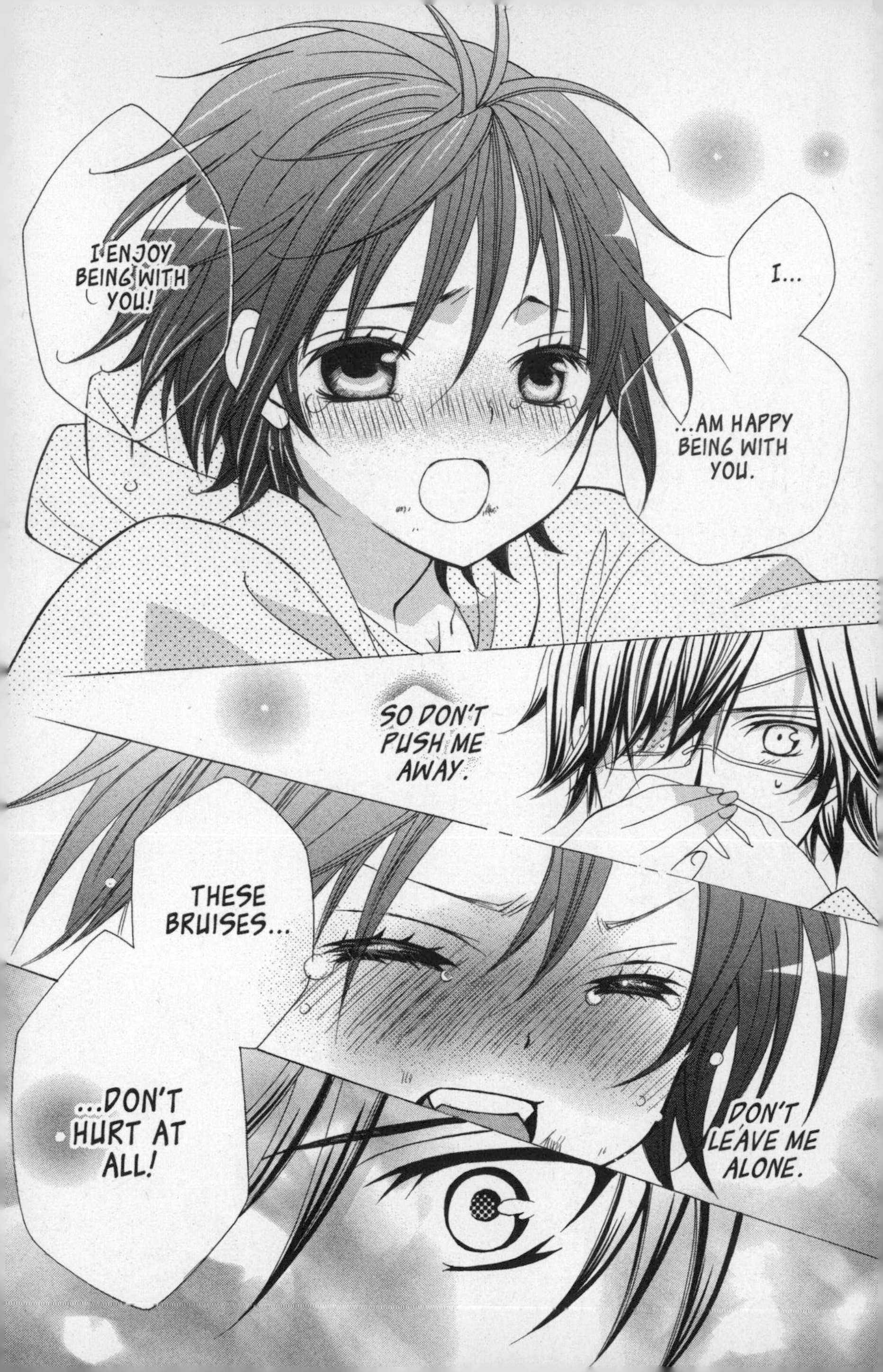
I...
...AM HAPPY BEING WITH YOU.
I ENJOY BEING WITH YOU!
SO DON'T PUSH ME AWAY.
DON'T LEAVE ME ALONE.
THESE BRUISES...
...DON'T HURT AT ALL!

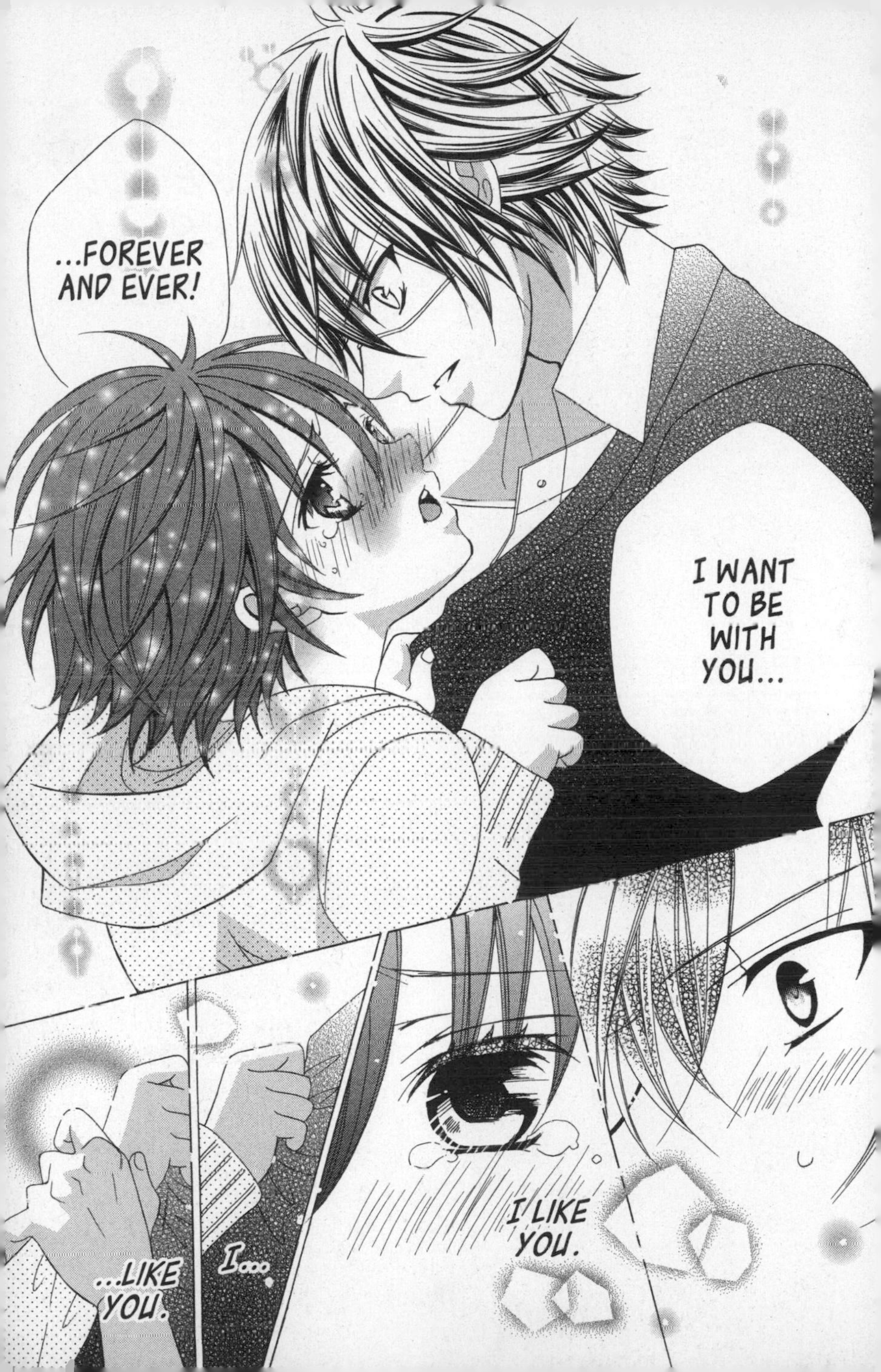
I WANT TO BE WITH YOU...
...FOREVER AND EVER!
I LIKE YOU.
I...
...LIKE YOU.

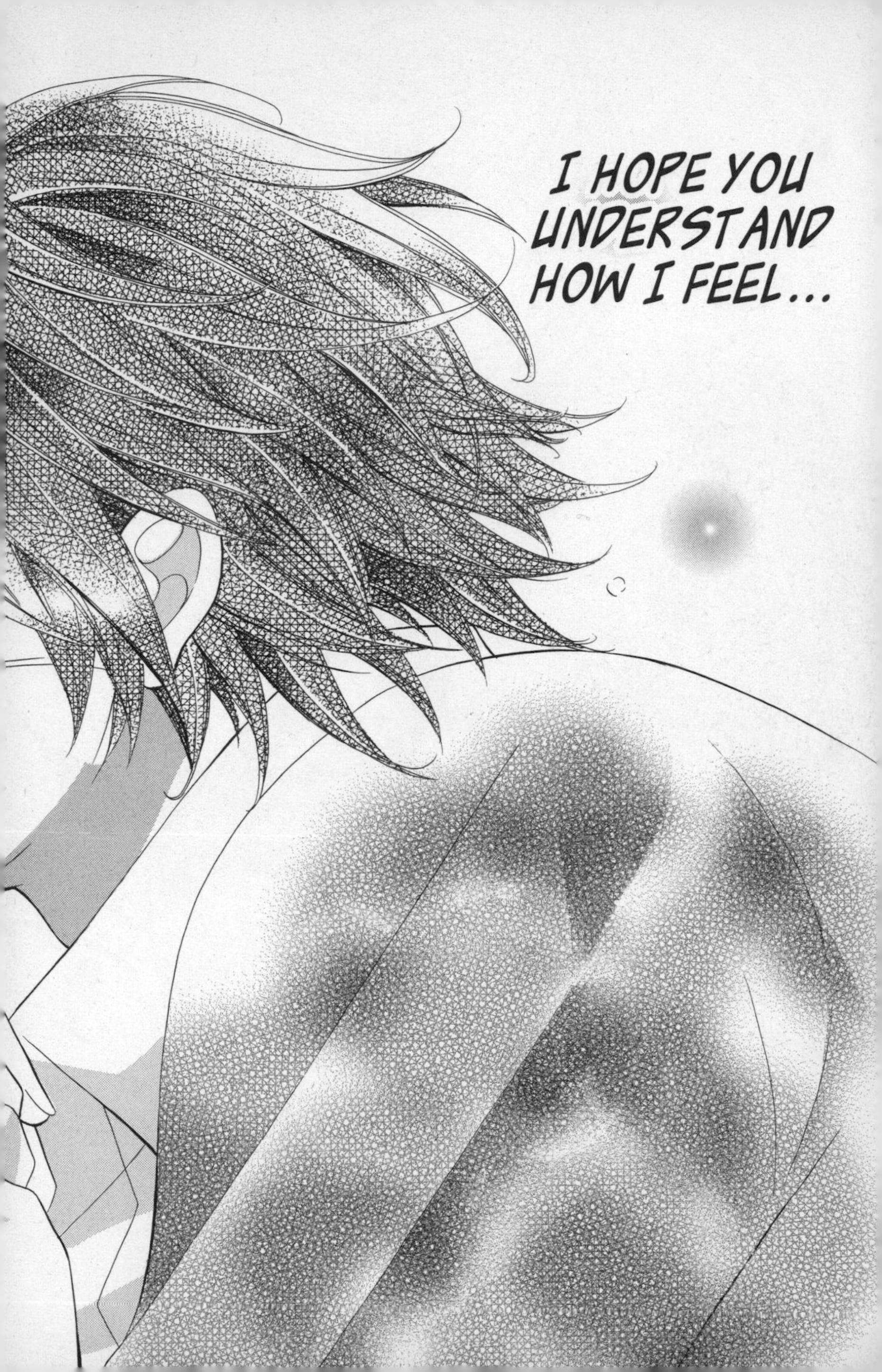
I HOPE YOU UNDERSTAND HOW I FEEL...

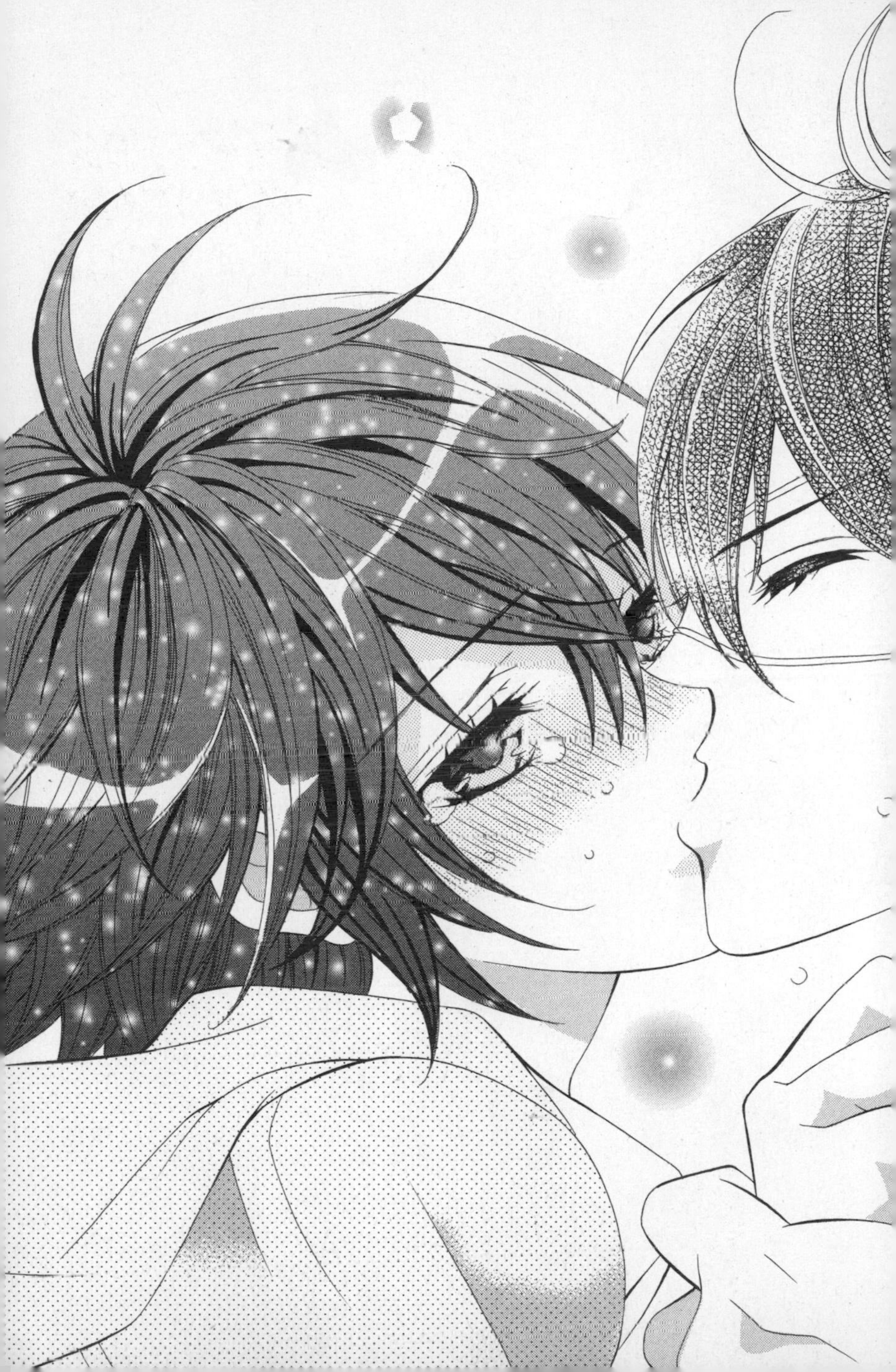

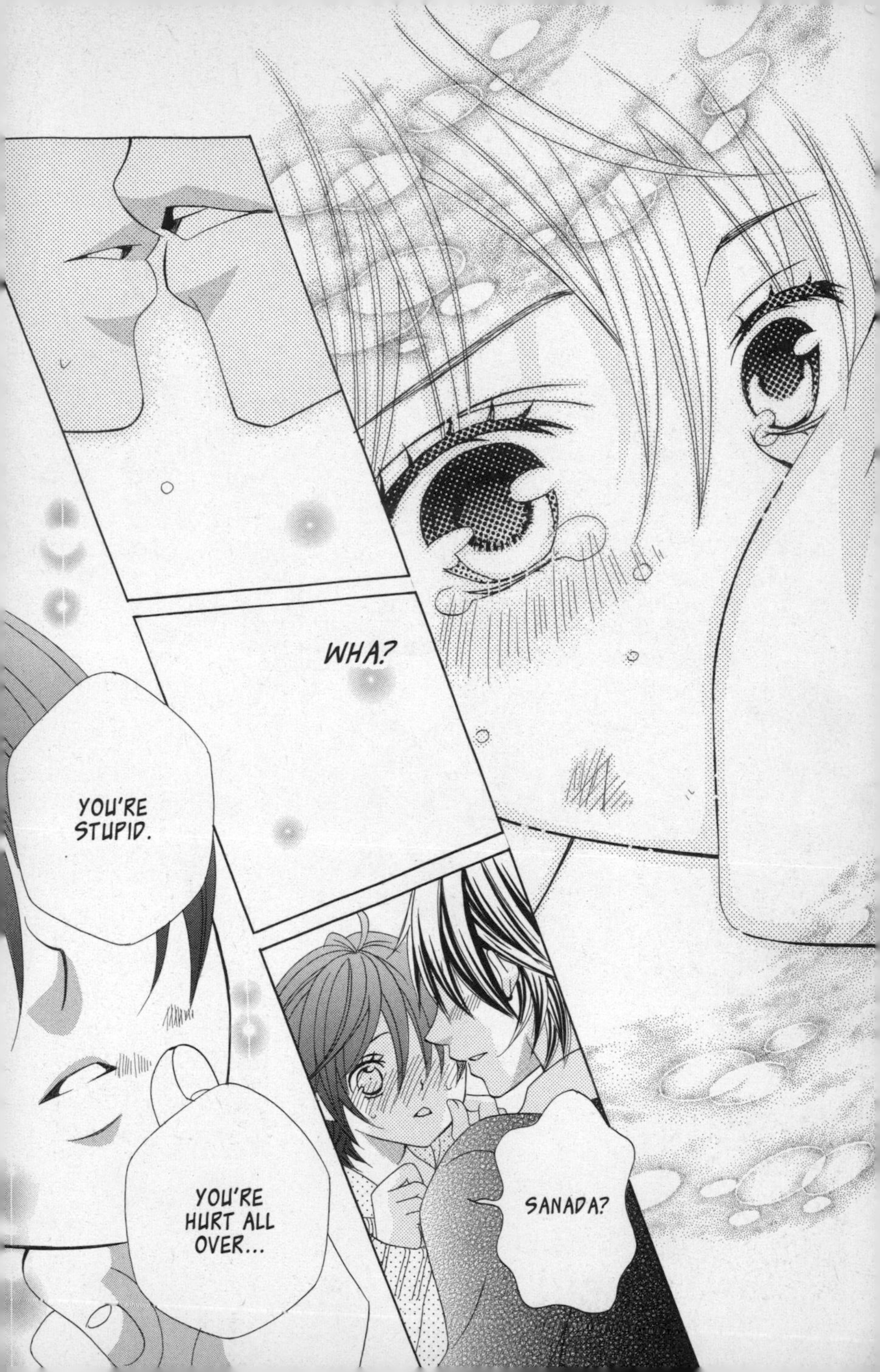
WHA?
SANADA?
YOU'RE STUPID.
YOU'RE HURT ALL OVER...

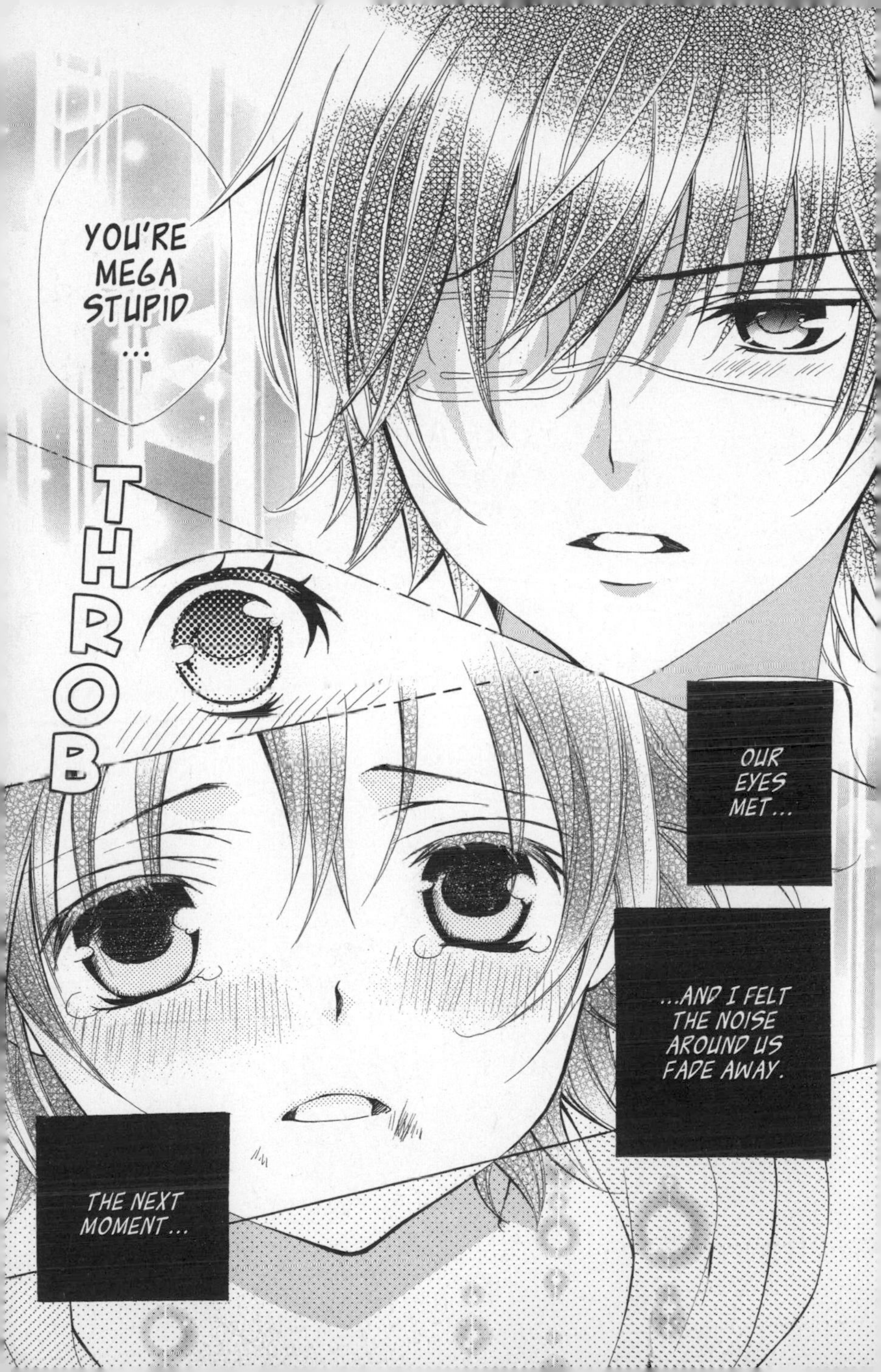
YOU'RE MEGA STUPID ...
THROB
OUR EYES MET...
...AND I FELT THE NOISE AROUND US FADE AWAY.
THE NEXT MOMENT...

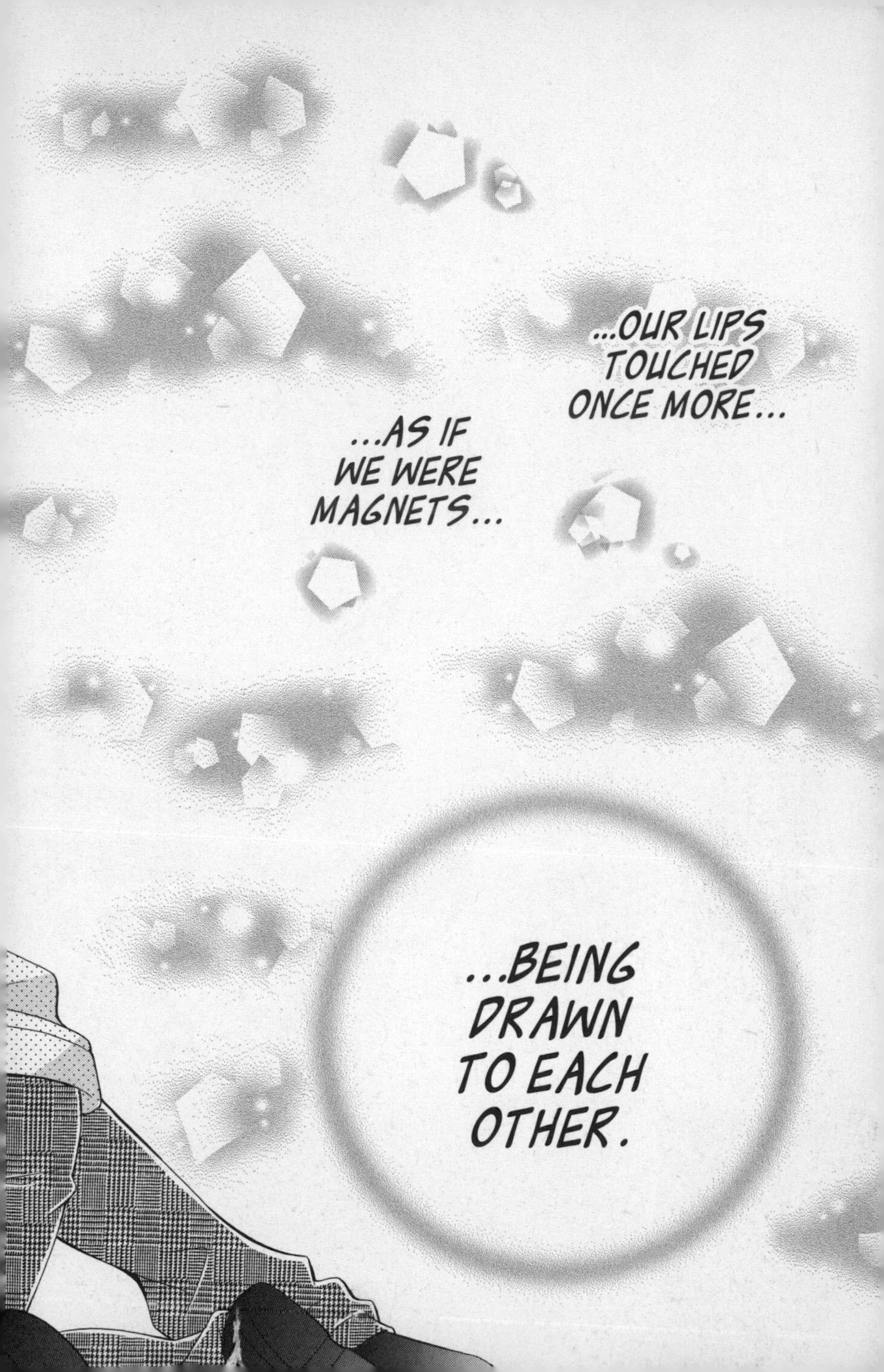
...OUR LIPS TOUCHED ONCE MORE...
...AS IF WE WERE MAGNETS...
...BEING DRAWN TO EACH OTHER.

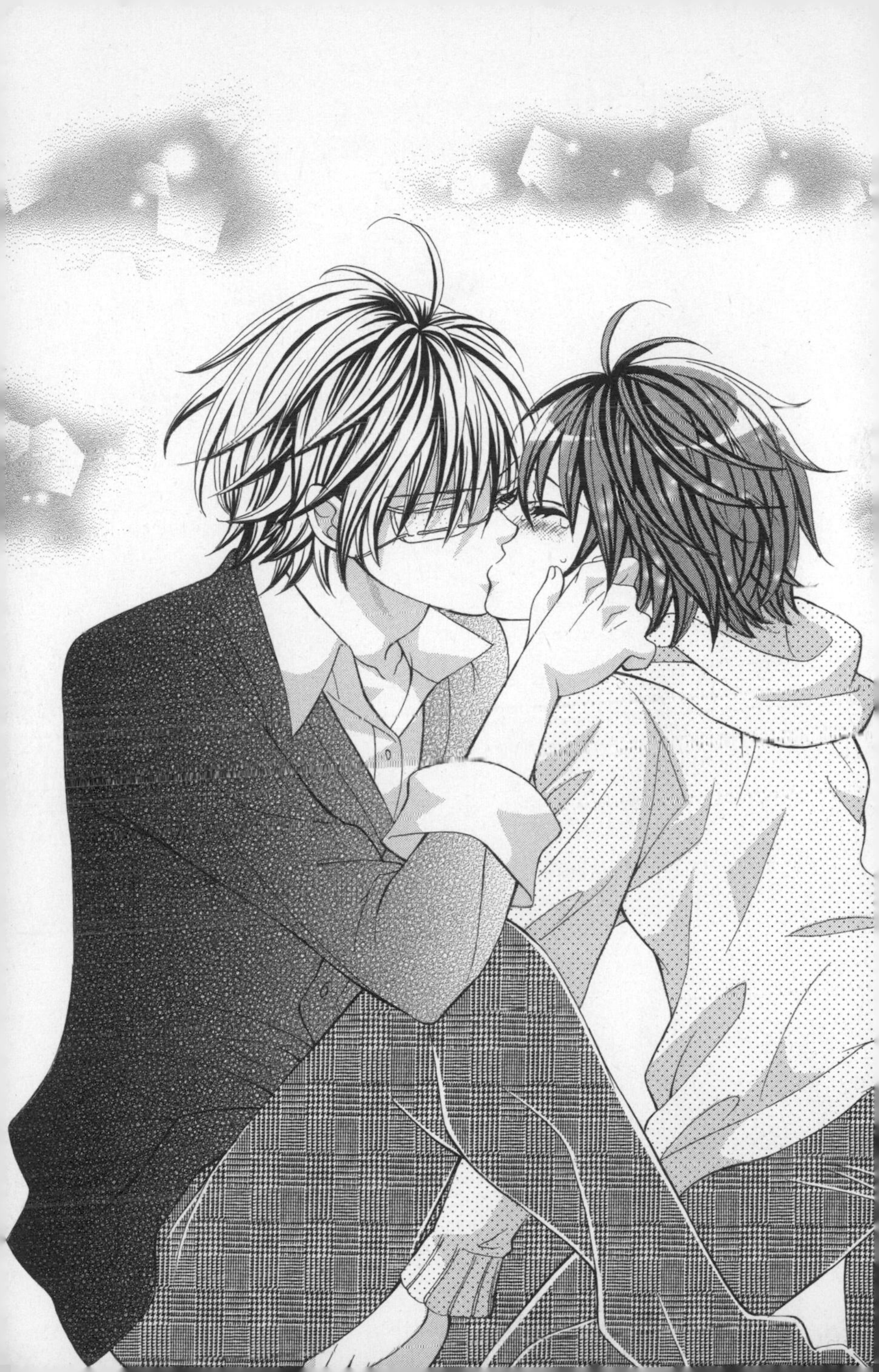

Chapter 10

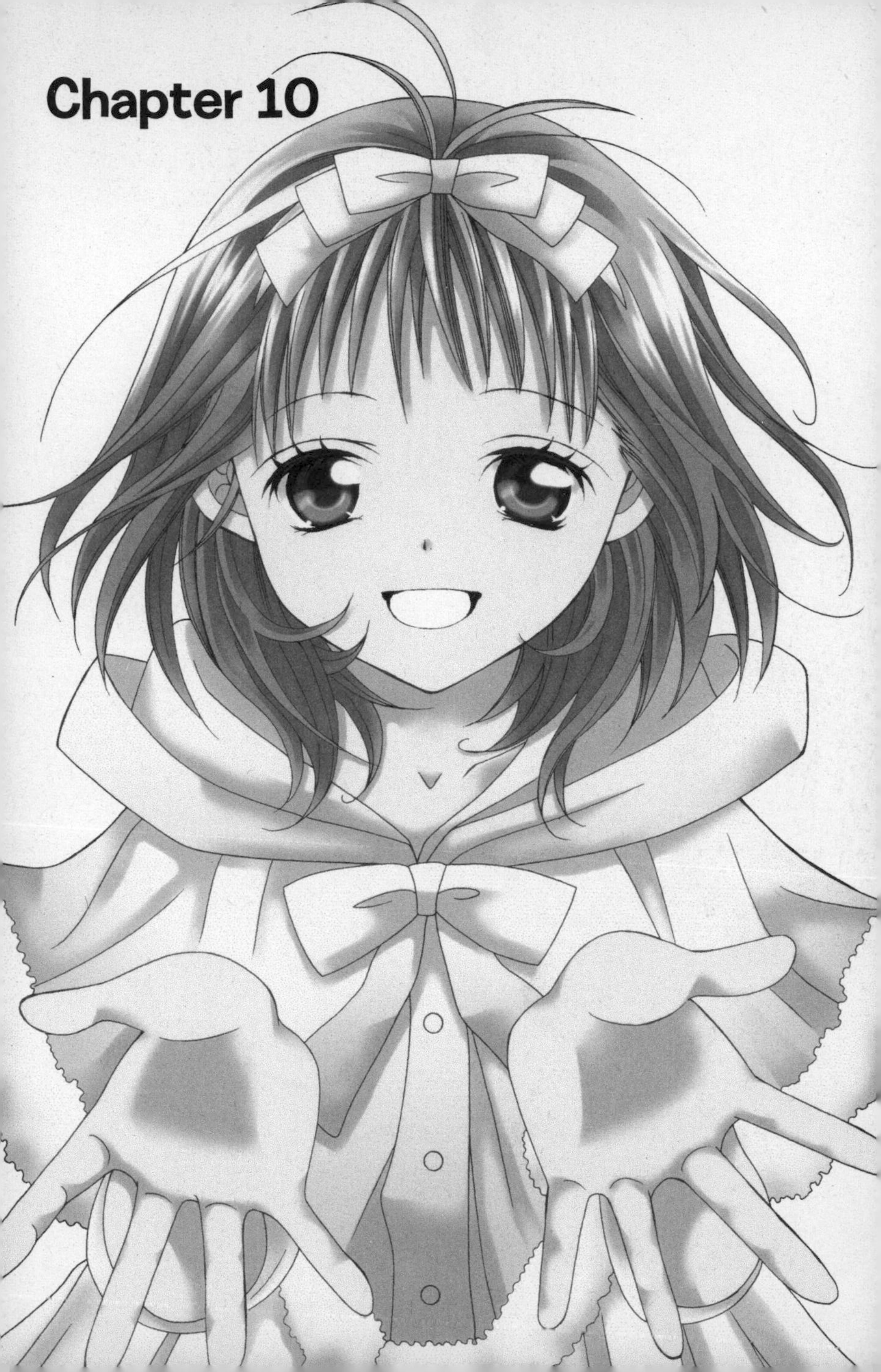

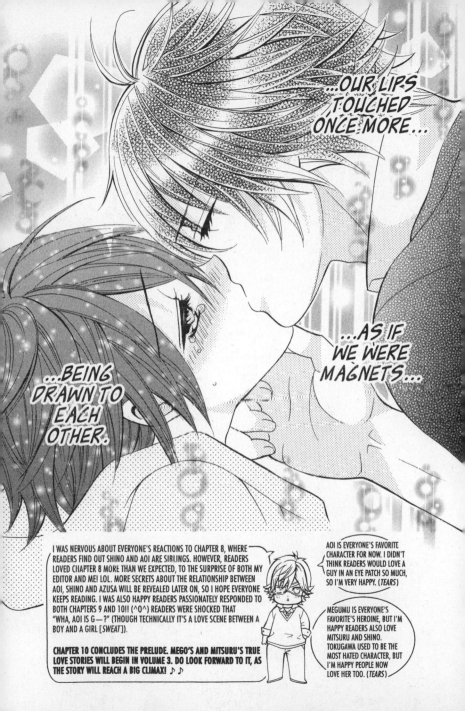

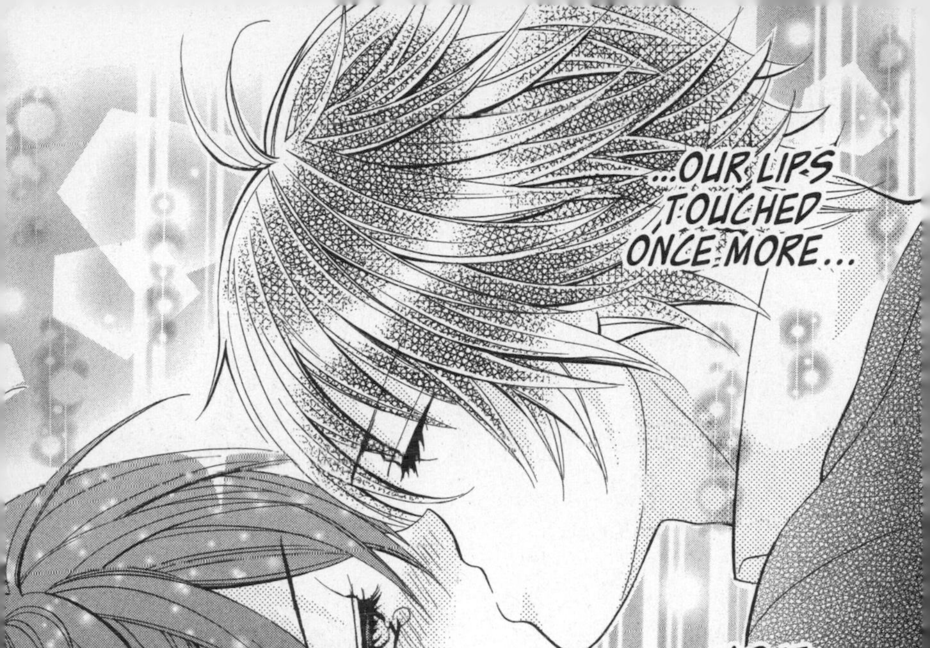
...OUR LIPS TOUCHED ONCE MORE...
...AS IF WE WERE MAGNETS...
...BEING DRAWN TO EACH OTHER.

I WAS NERVOUS ABOUT EVERYONE'S REACTIONS TO CHAPTER 8, WHERE READERS FIND OUT SHINO AND AOI ARE SIBLINGS. HOWEVER, READERS LOVED CHAPTER 8 MORE THAN WE EXPECTED, TO THE SURPRISE OF BOTH MY EDITOR AND ME! LOL. MORE SECRETS ABOUT THE RELATIONSHIP BETWEEN AOI, SHINO AND AZUSA WILL BE REVEALED LATER ON, SO I HOPE EVERYONE KEEPS READING. I WAS ALSO HAPPY READERS PASSIONATELY RESPONDED TO BOTH CHAPTERS 9 AND 10!! (^0^) READERS WERE SHOCKED THAT "WHA, AOI IS G—?" (THOUGH TECHNICALLY IT'S A LOVE SCENE BETWEEN A BOY AND A GIRL [*SWEAT*]).

CHAPTER 10 CONCLUDES THE PRELUDE. MEGO'S AND MITSURU'S TRUE LOVE STORIES WILL BEGIN IN VOLUME 3. DO LOOK FORWARD TO IT, AS THE STORY WILL REACH A BIG CLIMAX! ♪♪

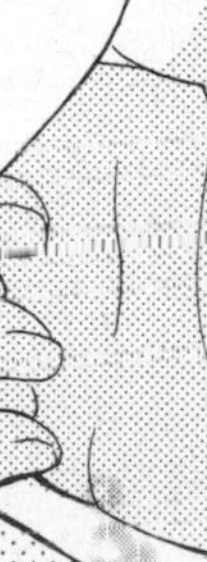

AOI IS EVERYONE'S FAVORITE CHARACTER FOR NOW. I DIDN'T THINK READERS WOULD LOVE A GUY IN AN EYE PATCH SO MUCH, SO I'M VERY HAPPY. (*TEARS*)

MEGUMU IS EVERYONE'S FAVORITE'S HEROINE, BUT I'M HAPPY READERS ALSO LOVE MITSURU AND SHINO. TOKUGAWA USED TO BE THE MOST HATED CHARACTER, BUT I'M HAPPY PEOPLE NOW LOVE HER TOO. (*TEARS*)

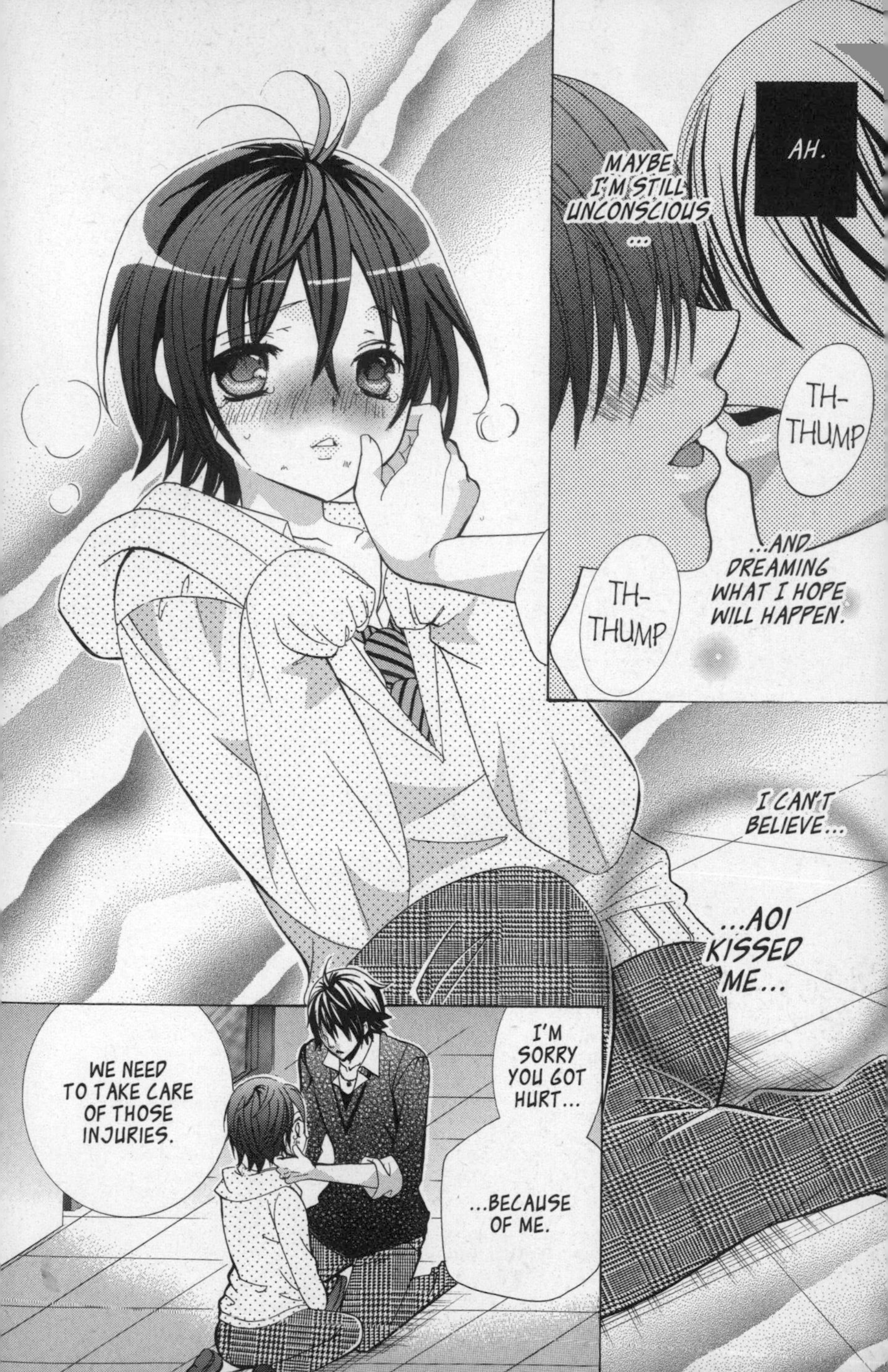
AH.
MAYBE I'M STILL UNCONSCIOUS ...
TH-THUMP
TH-THUMP
...AND DREAMING WHAT I HOPE WILL HAPPEN.
I CAN'T BELIEVE...
...AOI KISSED ME...
I'M SORRY YOU GOT HURT...
...BECAUSE OF ME.
WE NEED TO TAKE CARE OF THOSE INJURIES.

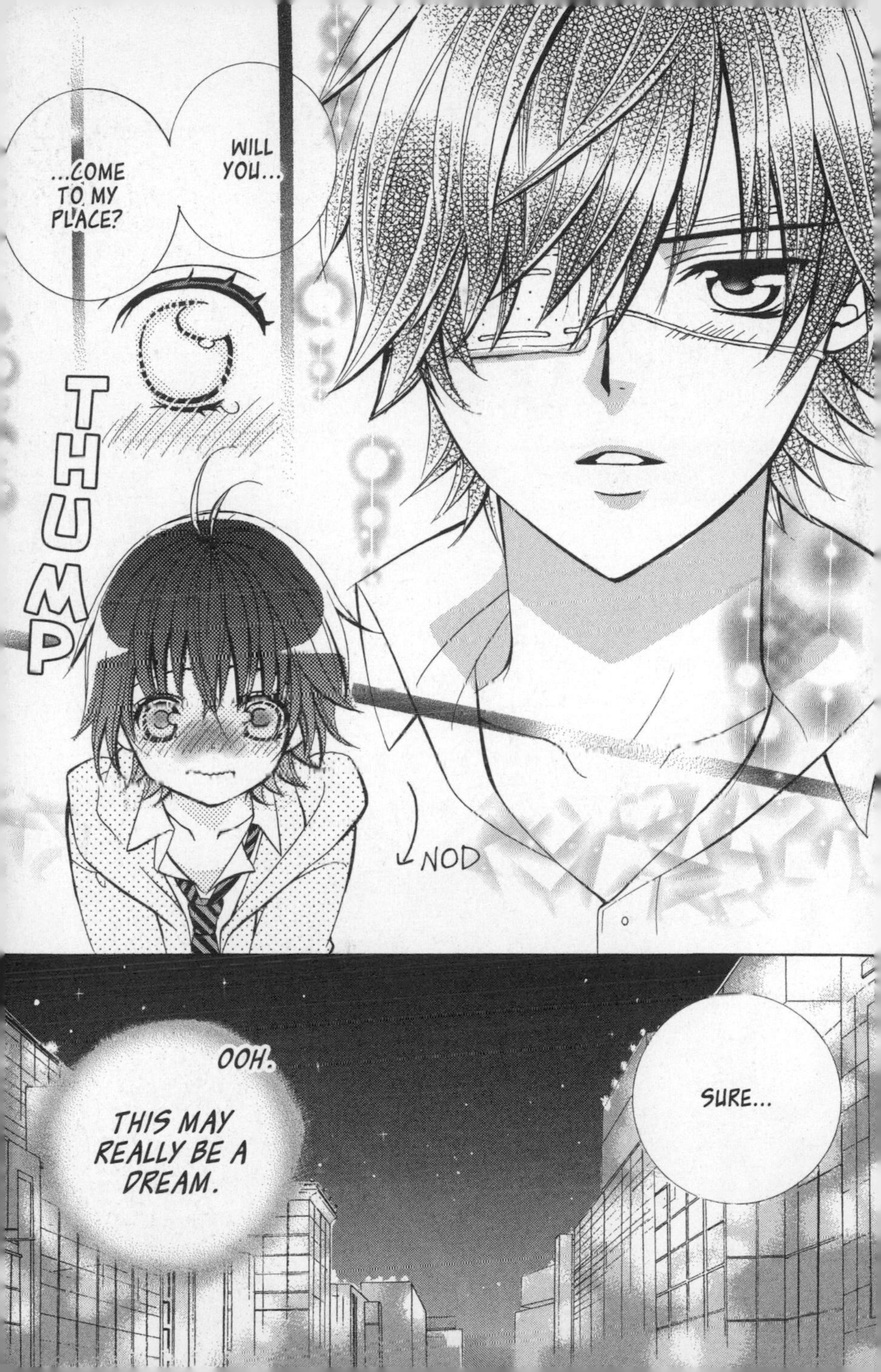
WILL YOU...
...COME TO MY PLACE?
THUMP
NOD
SURE...
OOH.
THIS MAY REALLY BE A DREAM.

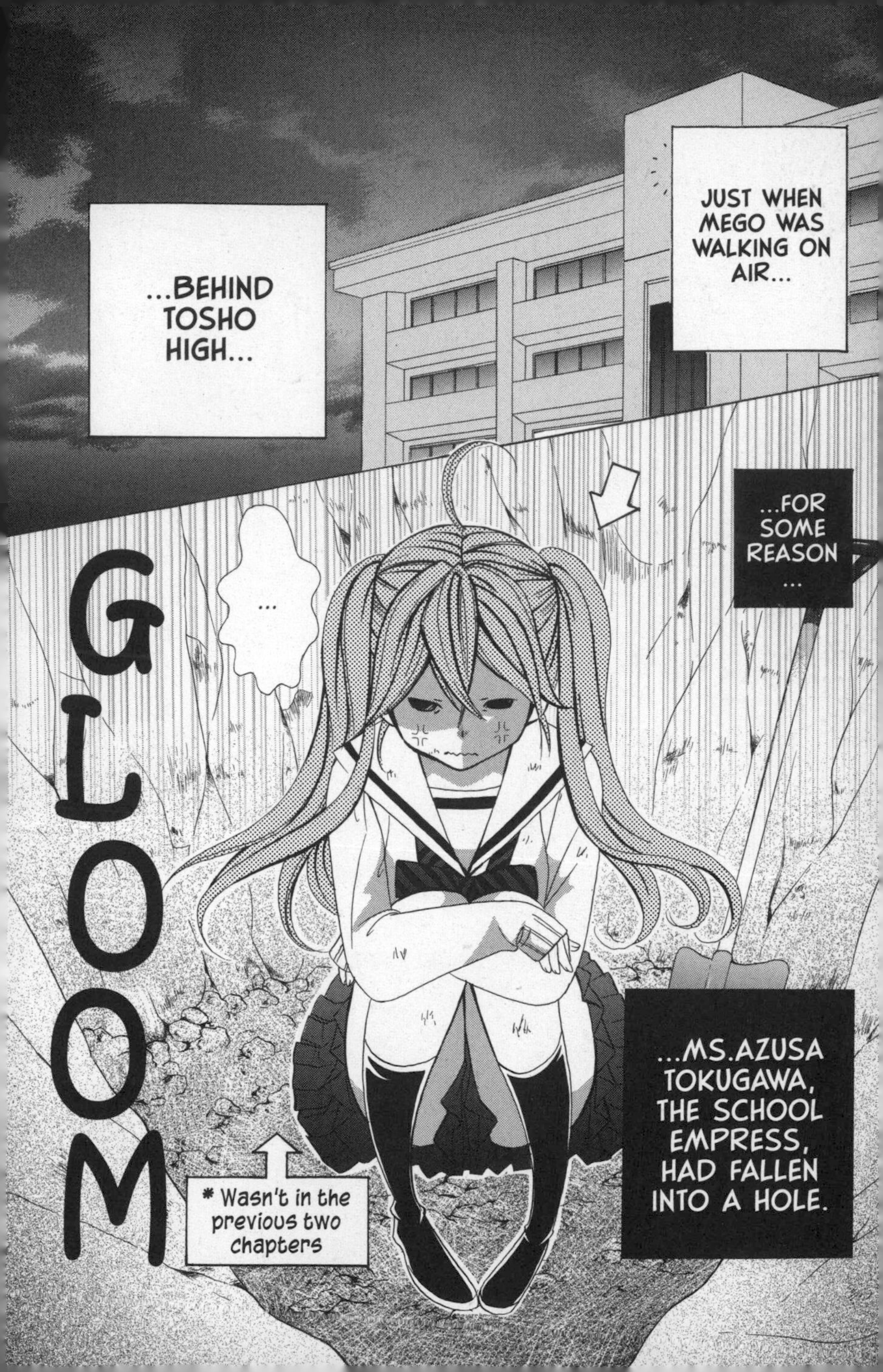
JUST WHEN MEGO WAS WALKING ON AIR...
...BEHIND TOSHO HIGH...
...FOR SOME REASON...
...
GLOOM
...MS.AZUSA TOKUGAWA, THE SCHOOL EMPRESS, HAD FALLEN INTO A HOLE.
* Wasn't in the previous two chapters

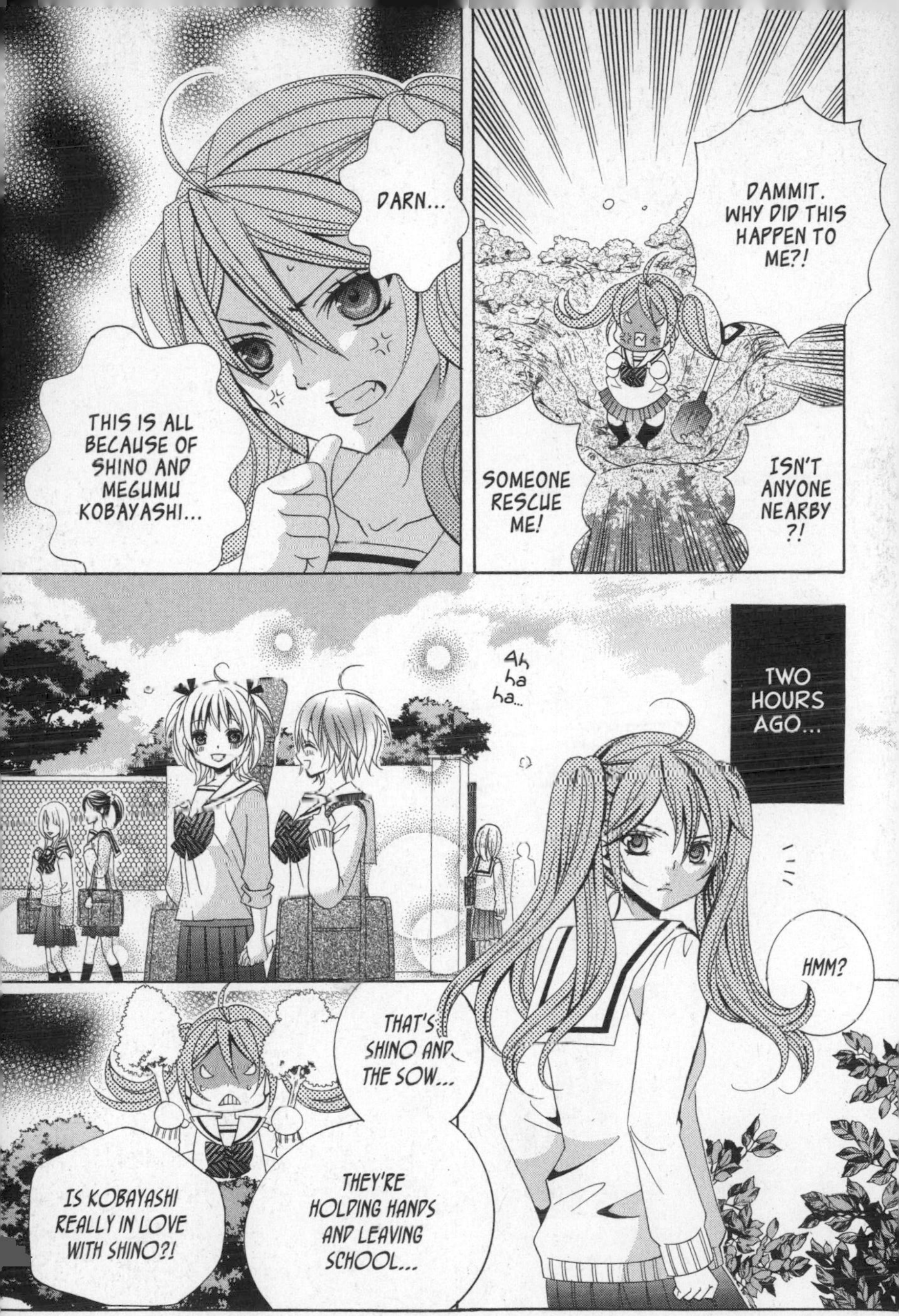
DAMMIT. WHY DID THIS HAPPEN TO ME?!
ISN'T ANYONE NEARBY?!
SOMEONE RESCUE ME!
DARN...
THIS IS ALL BECAUSE OF SHINO AND MEGUMU KOBAYASHI...
TWO HOURS AGO...
Ah ha ha...
HMM?
THAT'S SHINO AND THE SOW...
THEY'RE HOLDING HANDS AND LEAVING SCHOOL...
IS KOBAYASHI REALLY IN LOVE WITH SHINO?!

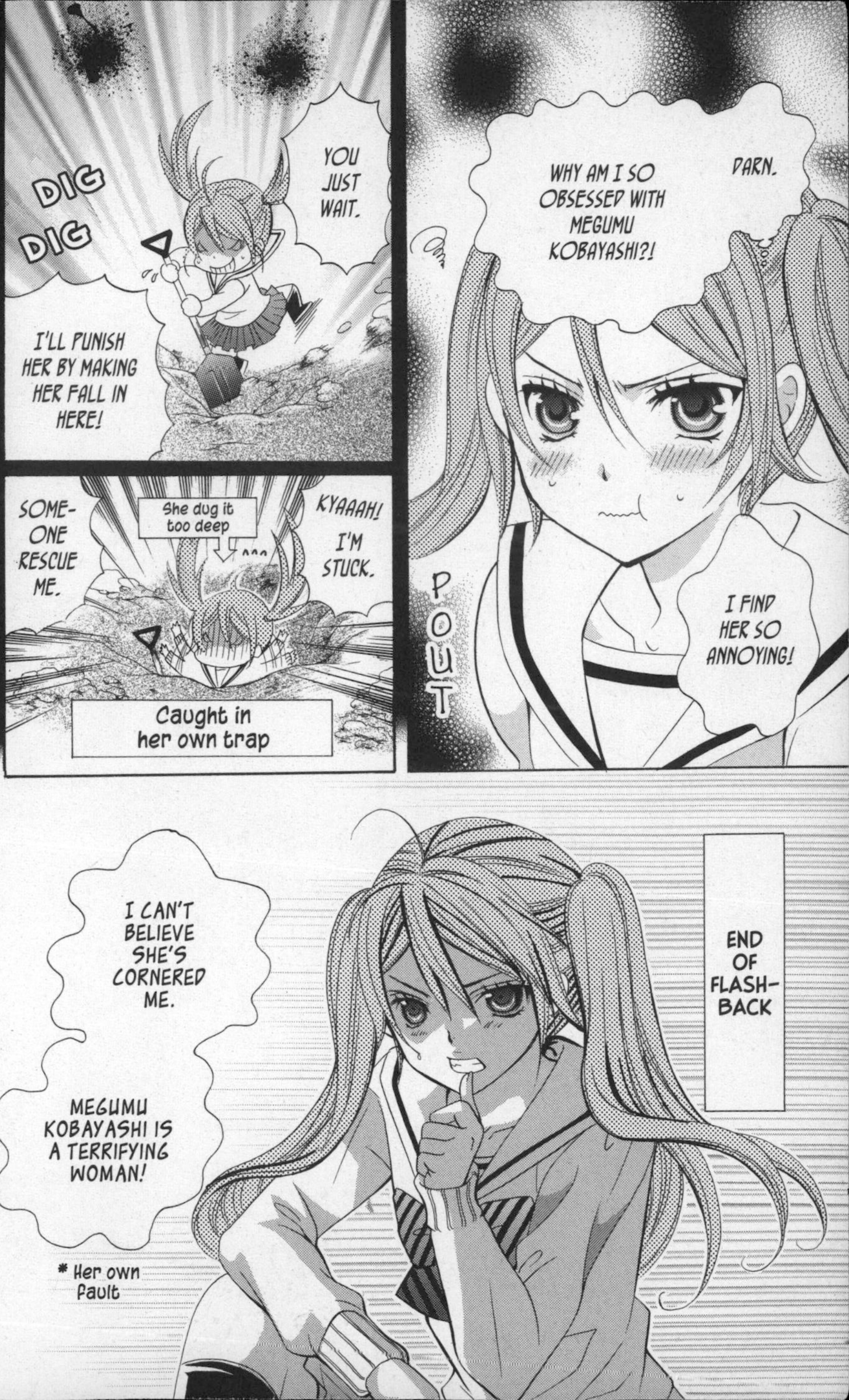
DARN.
WHY AM I SO OBSESSED WITH MEGUMU KOBAYASHI?!
POUT
I FIND HER SO ANNOYING!
YOU JUST WAIT.
DIG DIG
I'LL PUNISH HER BY MAKING HER FALL IN HERE!
KYAAAH!
I'M STUCK.
She dug it too deep
SOME-ONE RESCUE ME.
Caught in her own trap
END OF FLASH-BACK
I CAN'T BELIEVE SHE'S CORNERED ME.
MEGUMU KOBAYASHI IS A TERRIFYING WOMAN!
* Her own fault

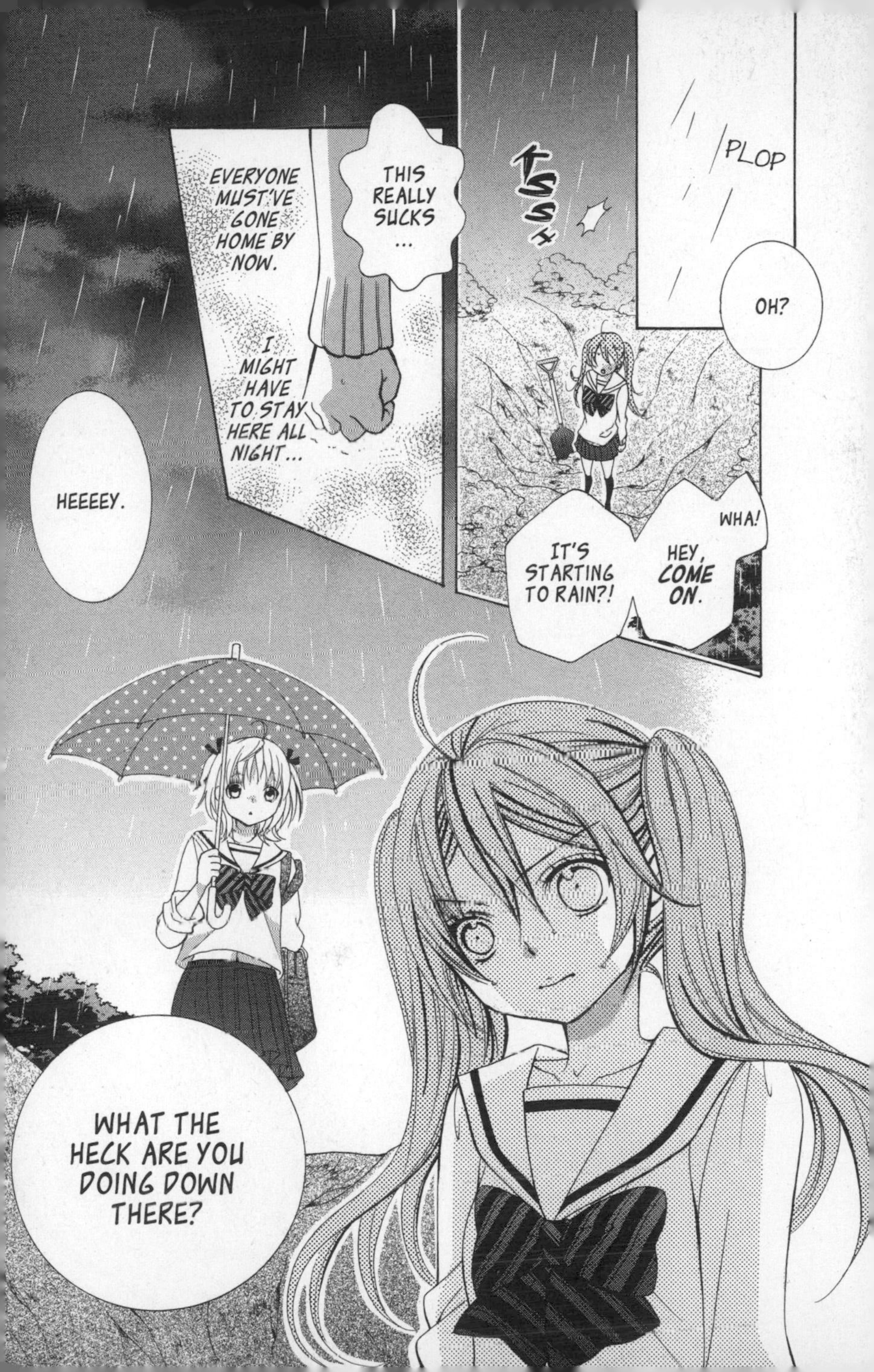
PLOP
OH?
TSSH
WHA!
HEY, COME ON.
IT'S STARTING TO RAIN?!
THIS REALLY SUCKS...
EVERYONE MUST'VE GONE HOME BY NOW.
I MIGHT HAVE TO STAY HERE ALL NIGHT...
HEEEEY.
WHAT THE HECK ARE YOU DOING DOWN THERE?

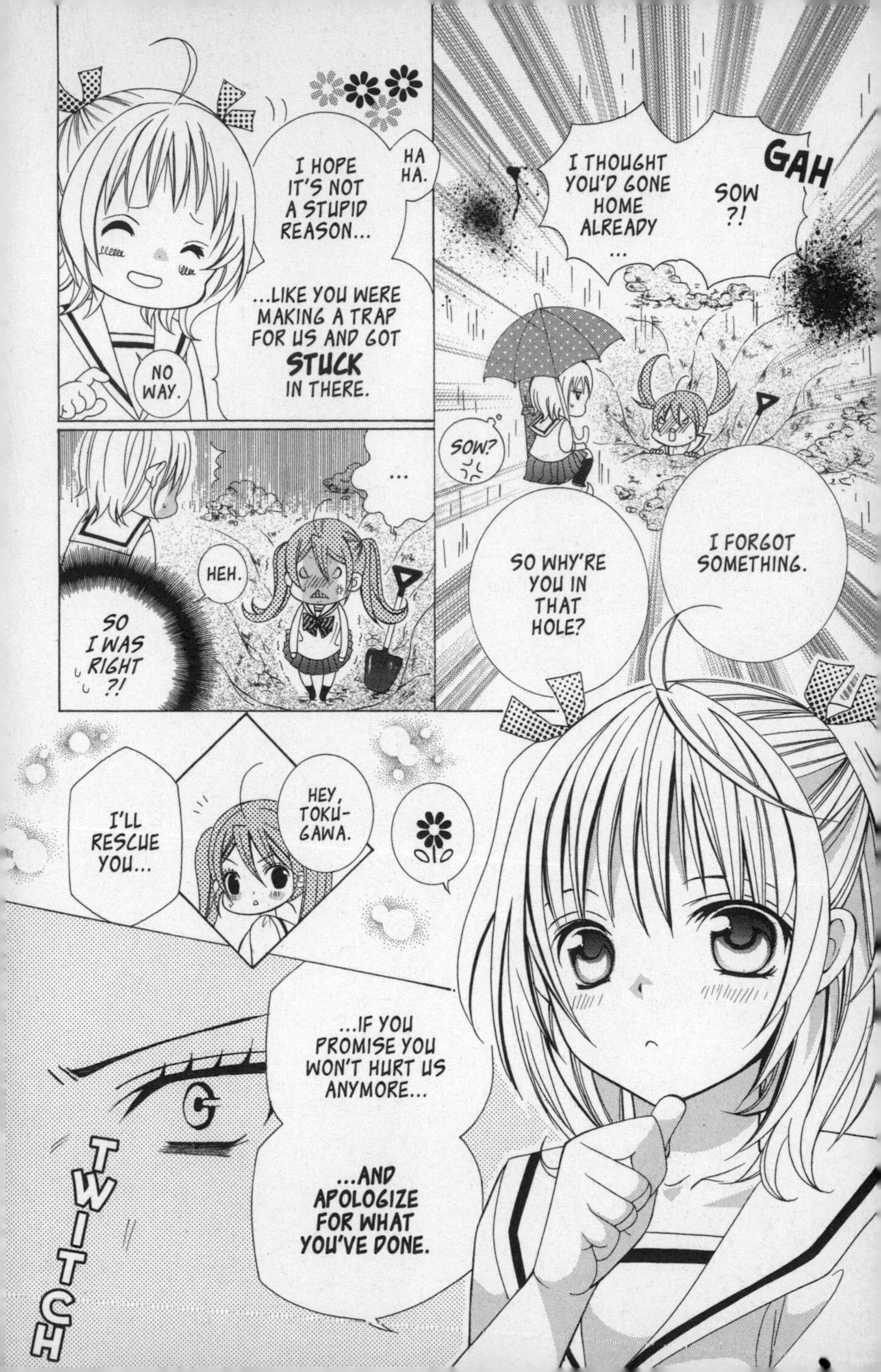
GAH
SOW ?!
I THOUGHT YOU'D GONE HOME ALREADY ...
SOW?
I FORGOT SOMETHING.
SO WHY'RE YOU IN THAT HOLE?
HA HA.
I HOPE IT'S NOT A STUPID REASON...
...LIKE YOU WERE MAKING A TRAP FOR US AND GOT **STUCK** IN THERE.
NO WAY.
...
HEH.
SO I WAS RIGHT ?!
HEY, TOKU-GAWA.
I'LL RESCUE YOU...
...IF YOU PROMISE YOU WON'T HURT US ANYMORE...
...AND APOLOGIZE FOR WHAT YOU'VE DONE.
TWITCH

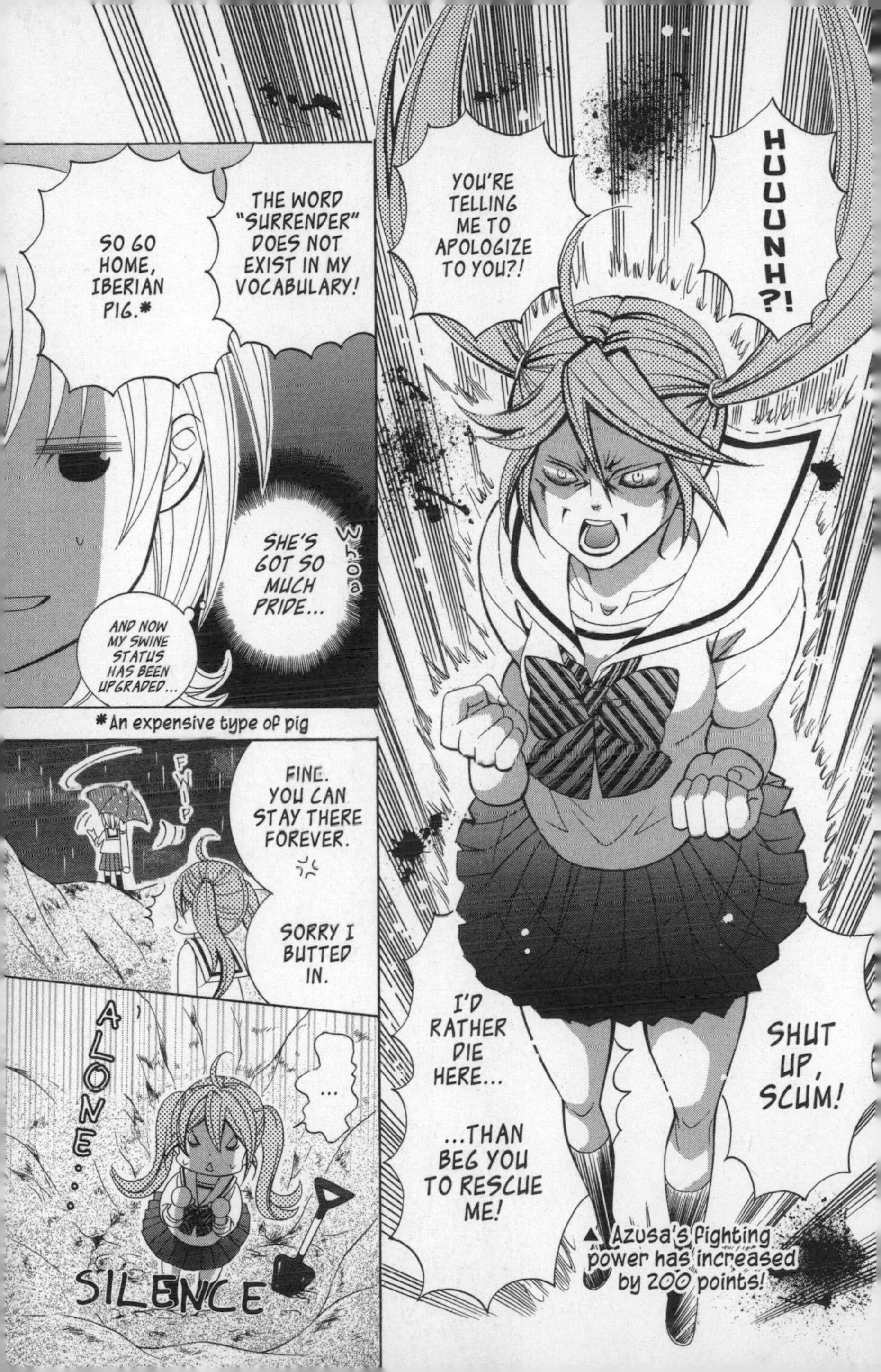
HUUUNH?!
YOU'RE TELLING ME TO APOLOGIZE TO YOU?!
SHUT UP, SCUM!
I'D RATHER DIE HERE...
...THAN BEG YOU TO RESCUE ME!
▲Azusa's fighting power has increased by 200 points!
THE WORD "SURRENDER" DOES NOT EXIST IN MY VOCABULARY!
SO GO HOME, IBERIAN PIG.*
Whoa
SHE'S GOT SO MUCH PRIDE...
AND NOW MY SWINE STATUS HAS BEEN UPGRADED...
*An expensive type of pig
FINE. YOU CAN STAY THERE FOREVER.
FWIP
SORRY I BUTTED IN.
...
ALONE...
SILENCE

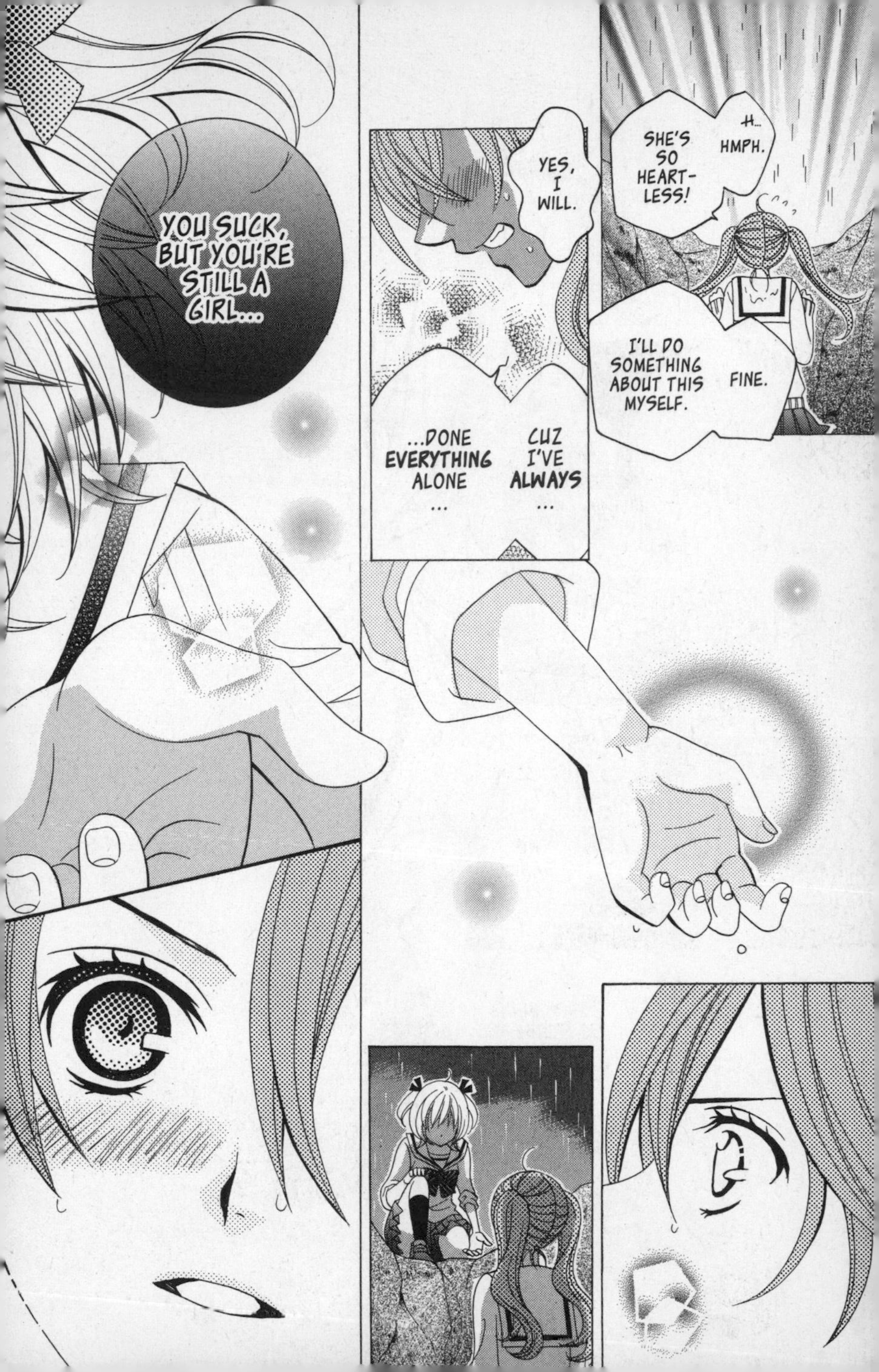
H... HMPH.
SHE'S SO HEARTLESS!
FINE.
I'LL DO SOMETHING ABOUT THIS MYSELF.
YES, I WILL.
CUZ I'VE ALWAYS...
...DONE EVERYTHING ALONE...
YOU SUCK, BUT YOU'RE STILL A GIRL...

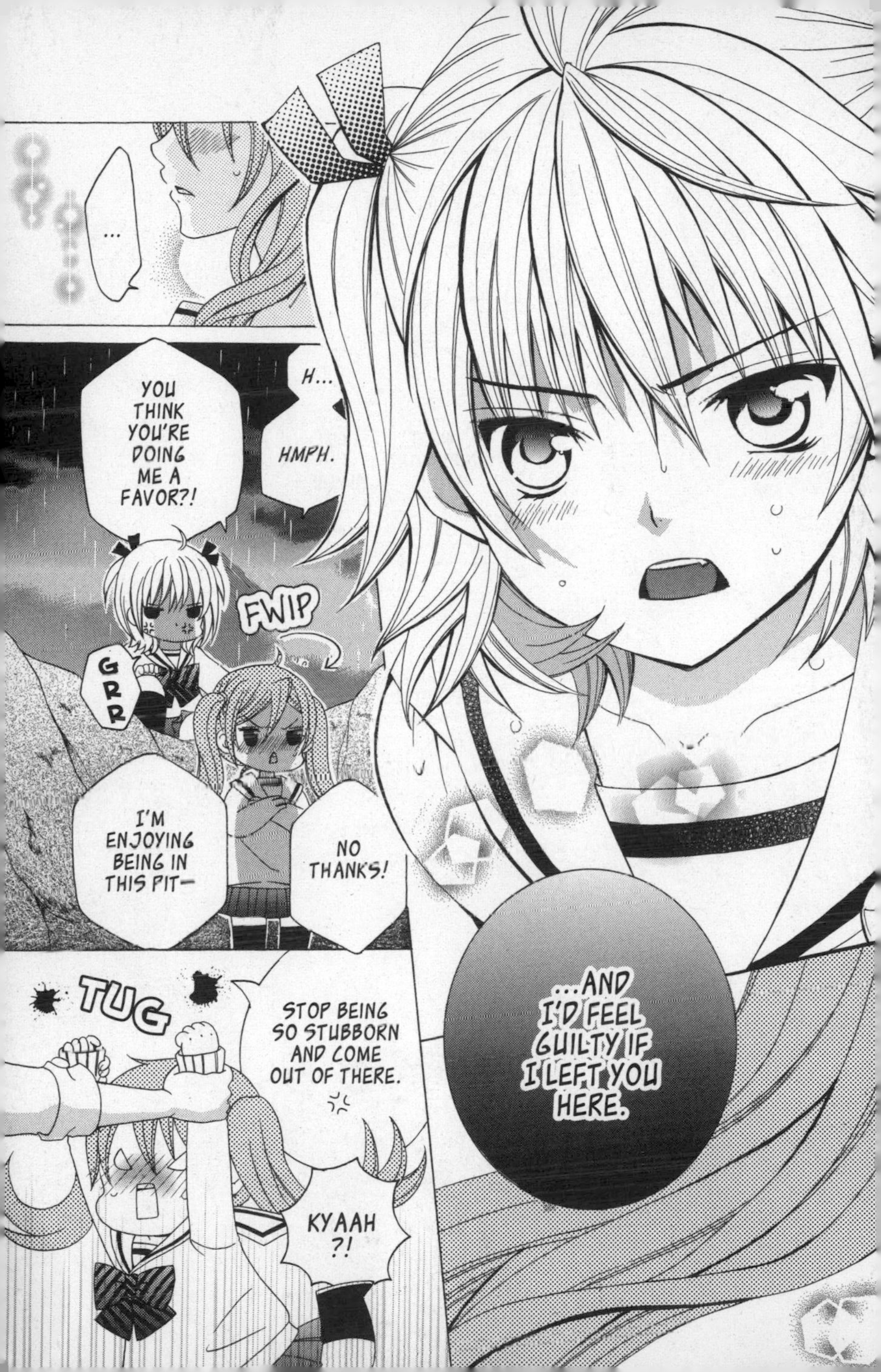
...AND I'D FEEL GUILTY IF I LEFT YOU HERE.
...
H...
HMPH.
YOU THINK YOU'RE DOING ME A FAVOR?!
FWIP
GRR
NO THANKS!
I'M ENJOYING BEING IN THIS PIT—
STOP BEING SO STUBBORN AND COME OUT OF THERE.
TUG
KYAAH ?!

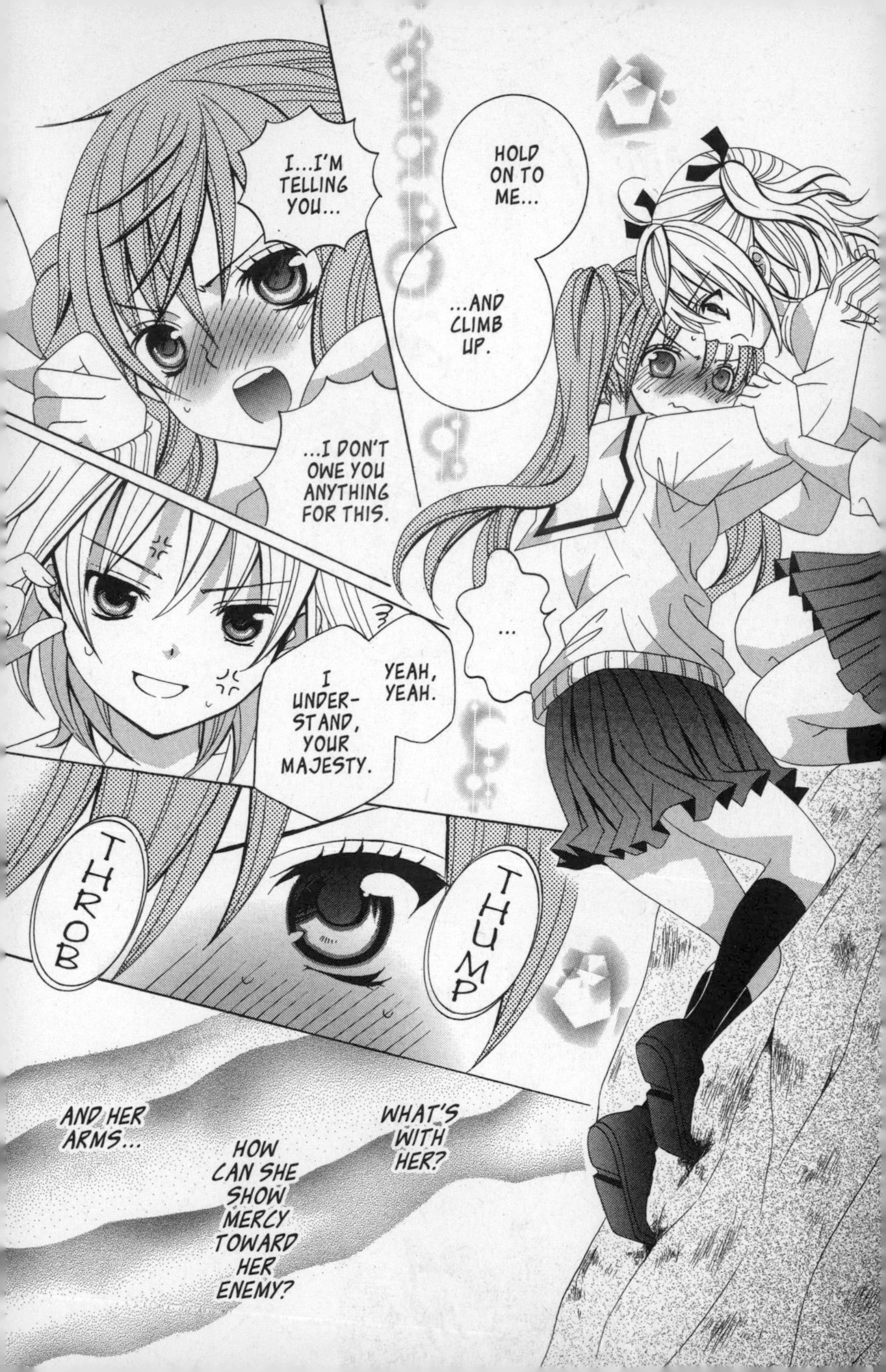
HOLD ON TO ME...
...AND CLIMB UP.
...
I...I'M TELLING YOU...
...I DON'T OWE YOU ANYTHING FOR THIS.
YEAH, YEAH.
I UNDER-STAND, YOUR MAJESTY.
THUMP
THROB
WHAT'S WITH HER?
HOW CAN SHE SHOW MERCY TOWARD HER ENEMY?
AND HER ARMS...

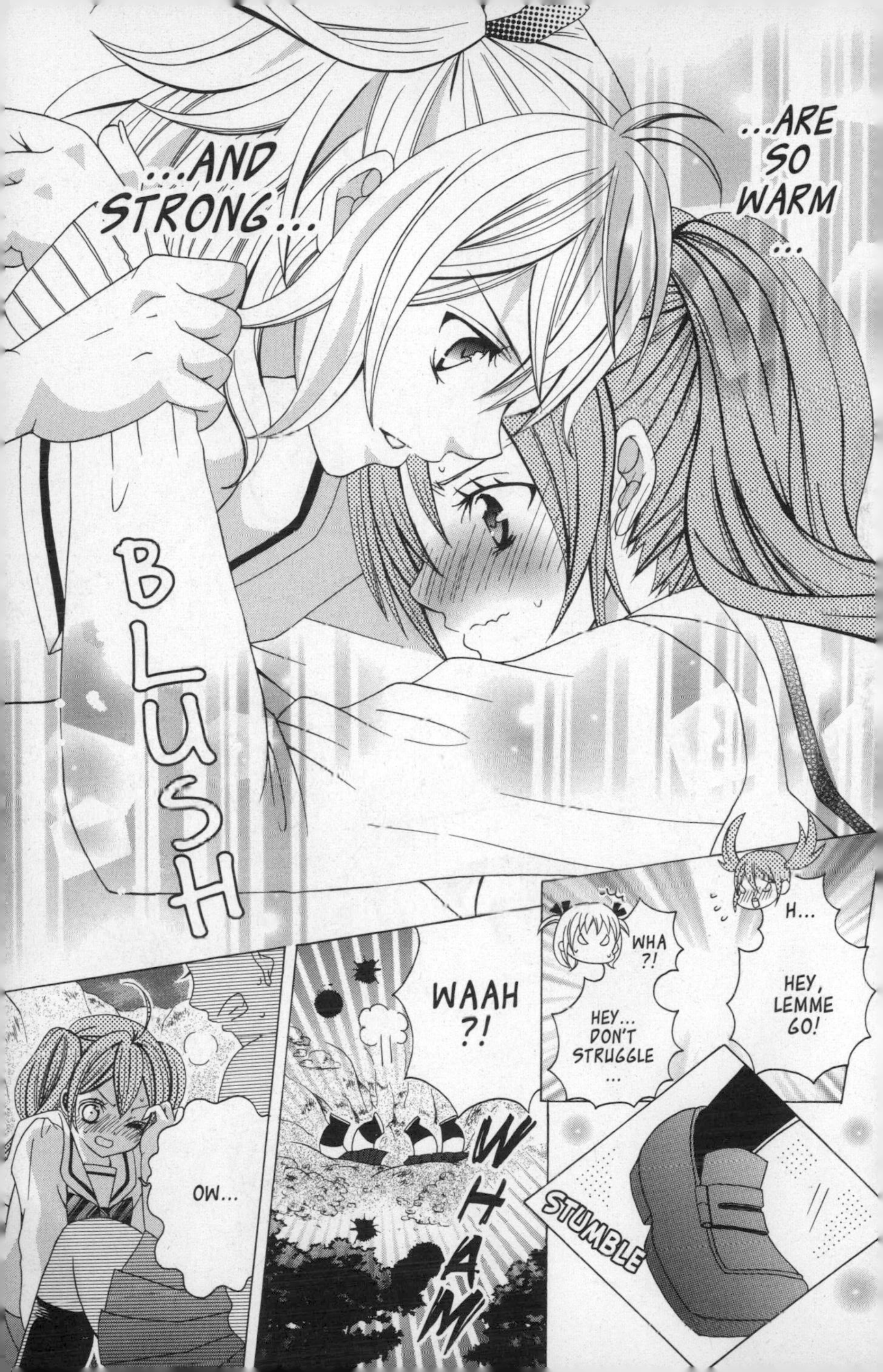
...ARE SO WARM ...
...AND STRONG...
BLUSH
H...
HEY, LEMME GO!
WHA ?!
HEY... DON'T STRUGGLE ...
STUMBLE
WAAH ?!
WHAM
OW...

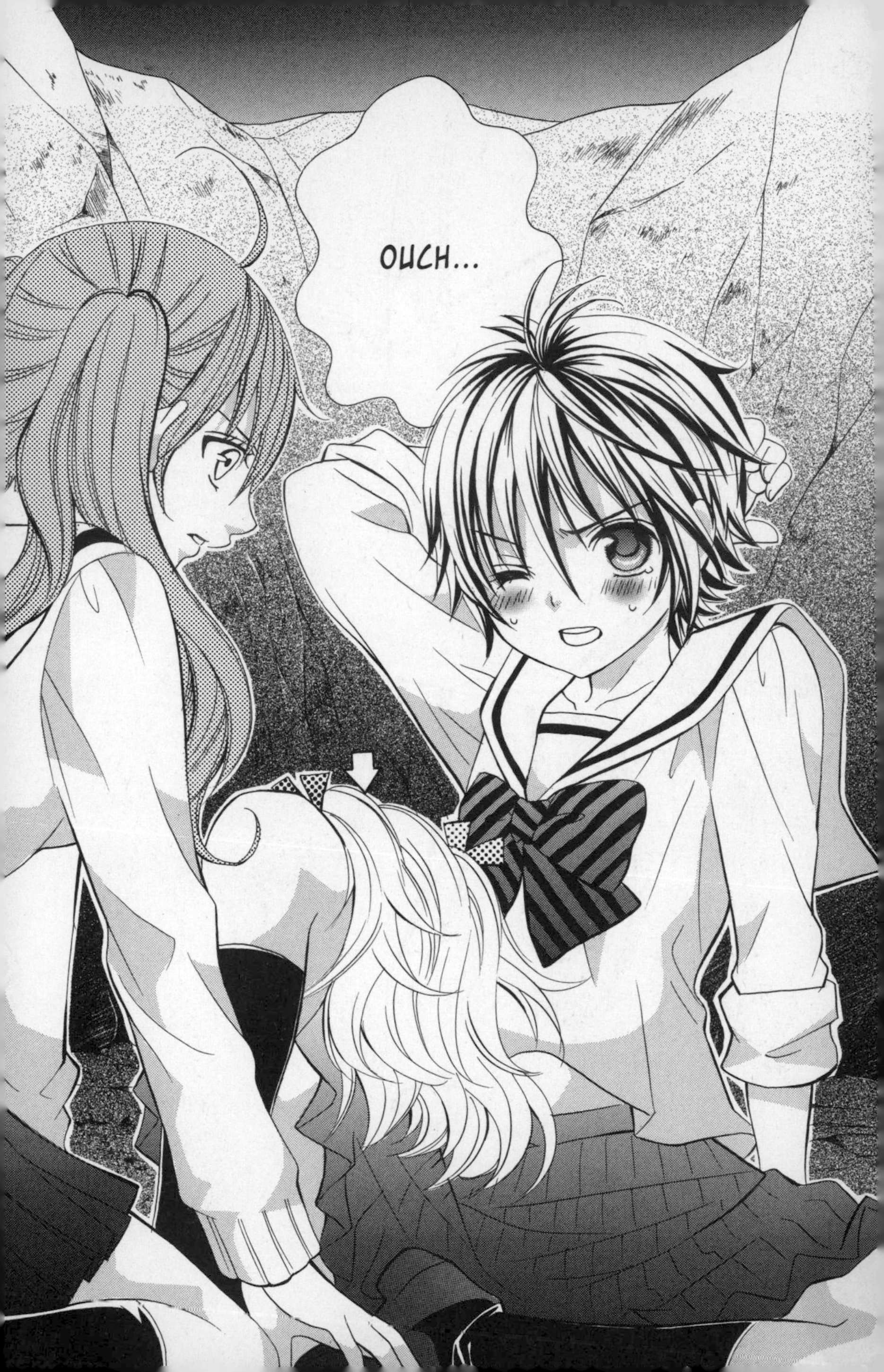
OUCH...

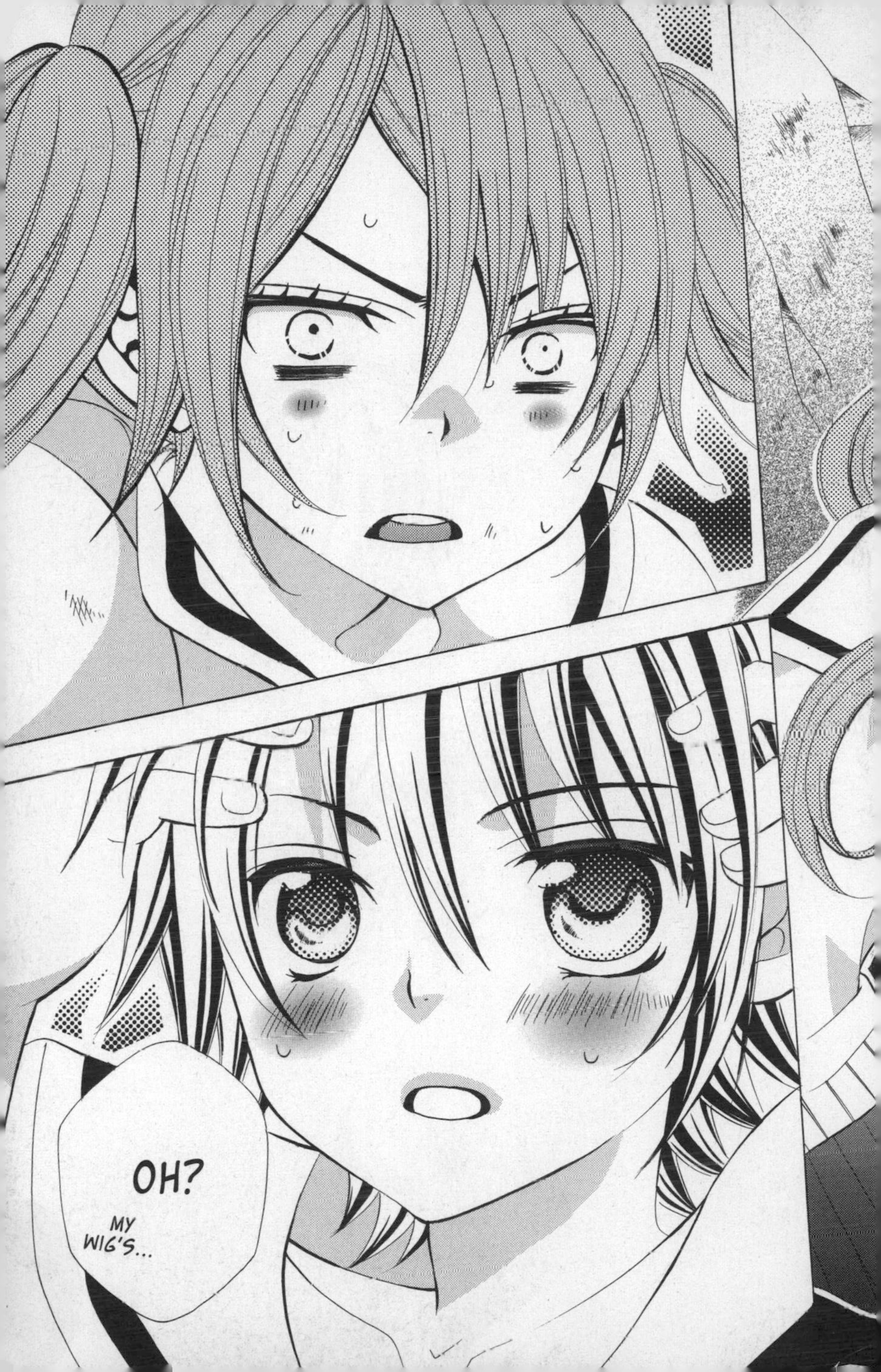
OH?
MY WIG'S...

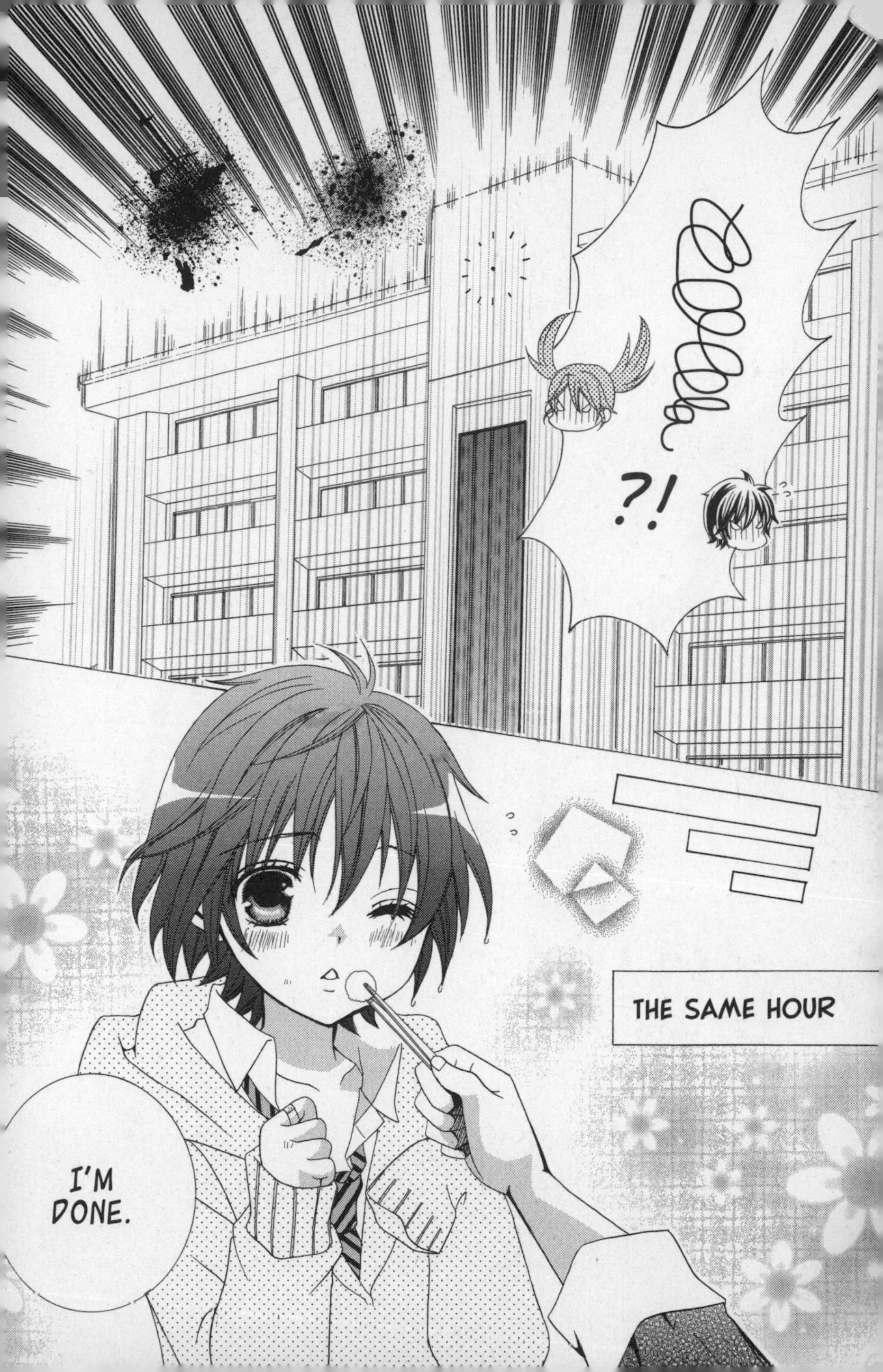
EWWWW
?!
THE SAME HOUR
I'M DONE.

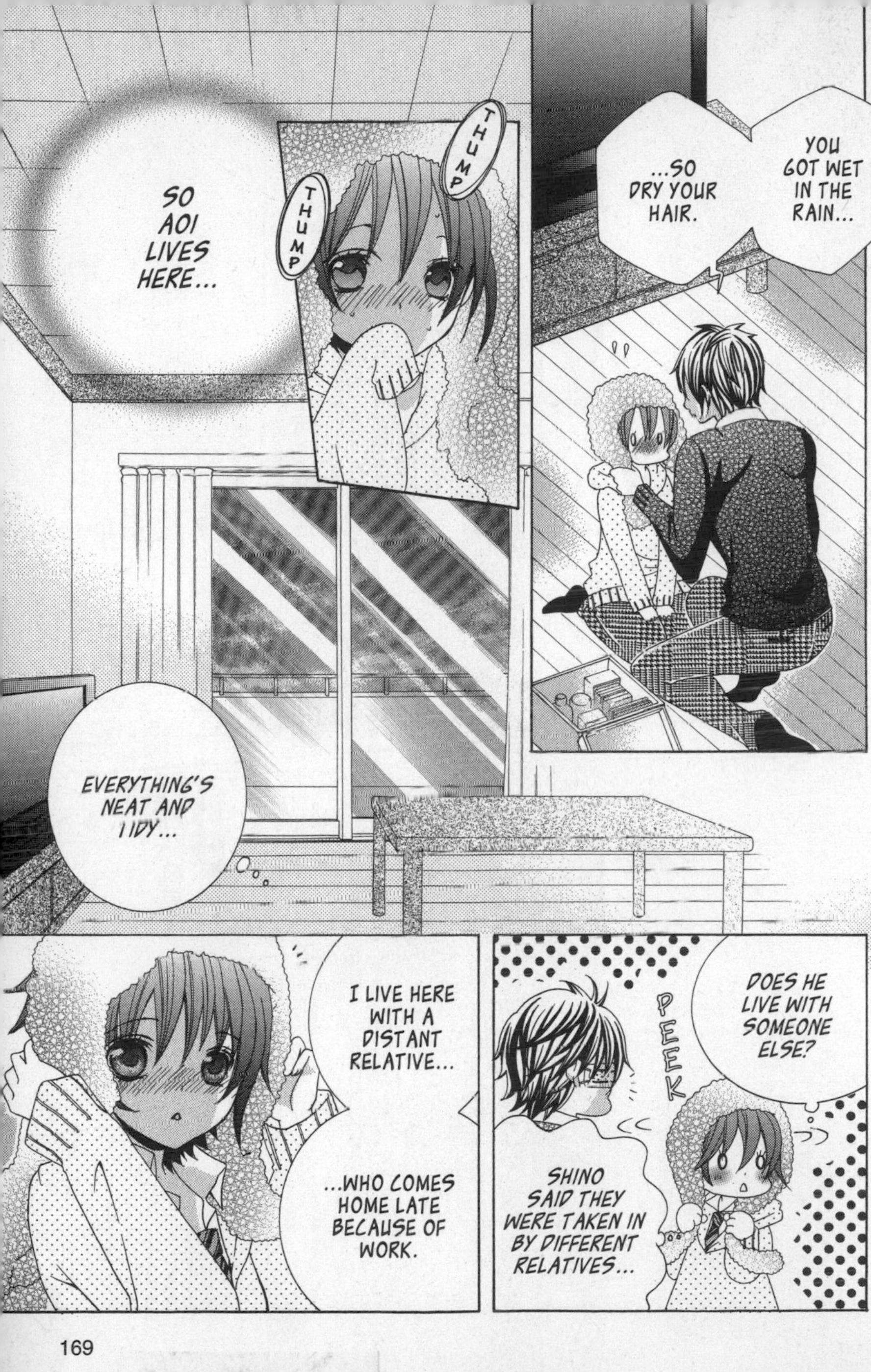
YOU GOT WET IN THE RAIN...
...SO DRY YOUR HAIR.
THUMP
THUMP
SO AOI LIVES HERE...
EVERYTHING'S NEAT AND TIDY...
DOES HE LIVE WITH SOMEONE ELSE?
PEEK
SHINO SAID THEY WERE TAKEN IN BY DIFFERENT RELATIVES...
I LIVE HERE WITH A DISTANT RELATIVE...
...WHO COMES HOME LATE BECAUSE OF WORK.

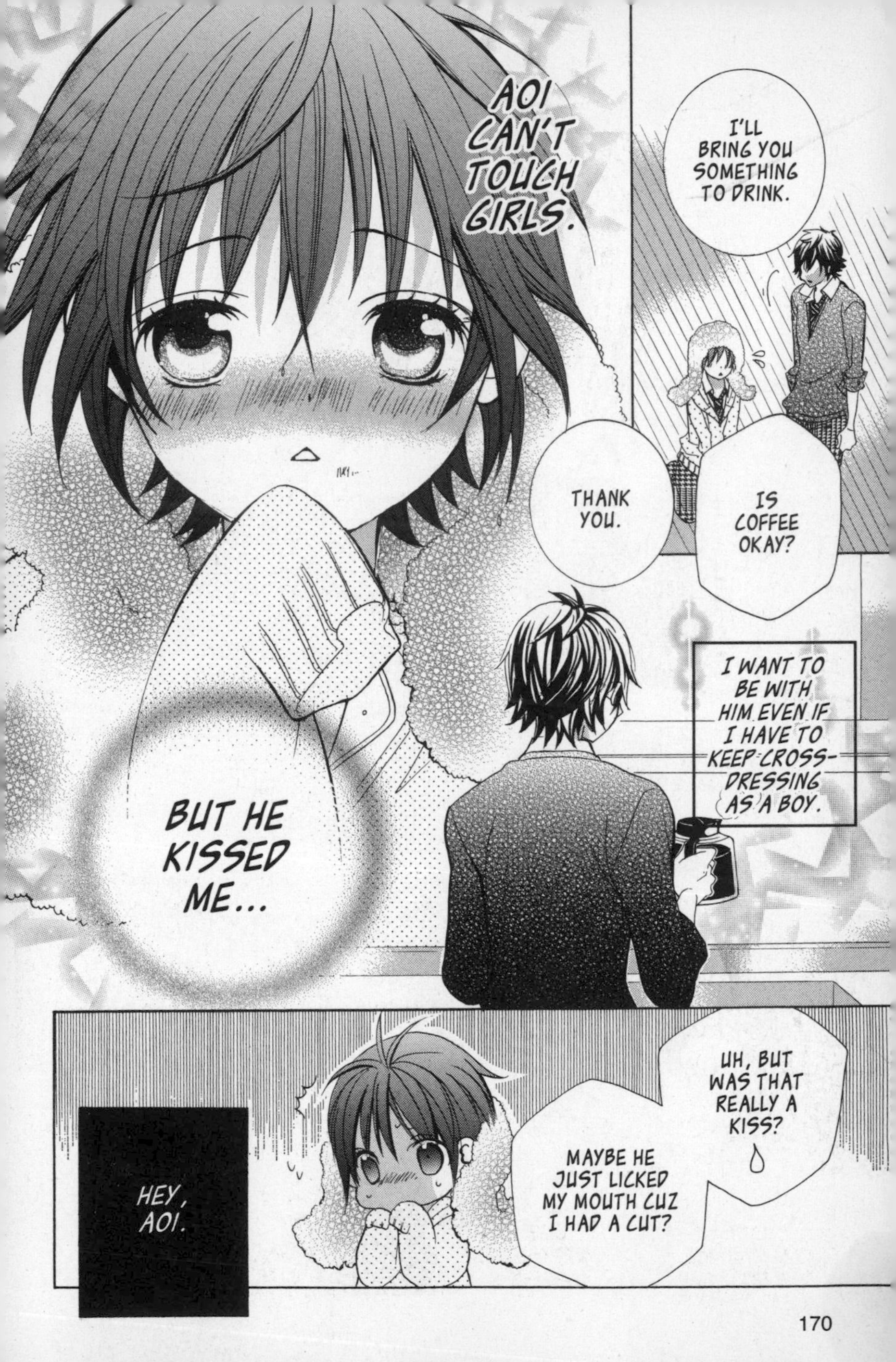
I'LL BRING YOU SOMETHING TO DRINK.
IS COFFEE OKAY?
THANK YOU.
I WANT TO BE WITH HIM EVEN IF I HAVE TO KEEP CROSS-DRESSING AS A BOY.
AOI CAN'T TOUCH GIRLS.
BUT HE KISSED ME...
UH, BUT WAS THAT REALLY A KISS?
MAYBE HE JUST LICKED MY MOUTH CUZ I HAD A CUT?
HEY, AOI.

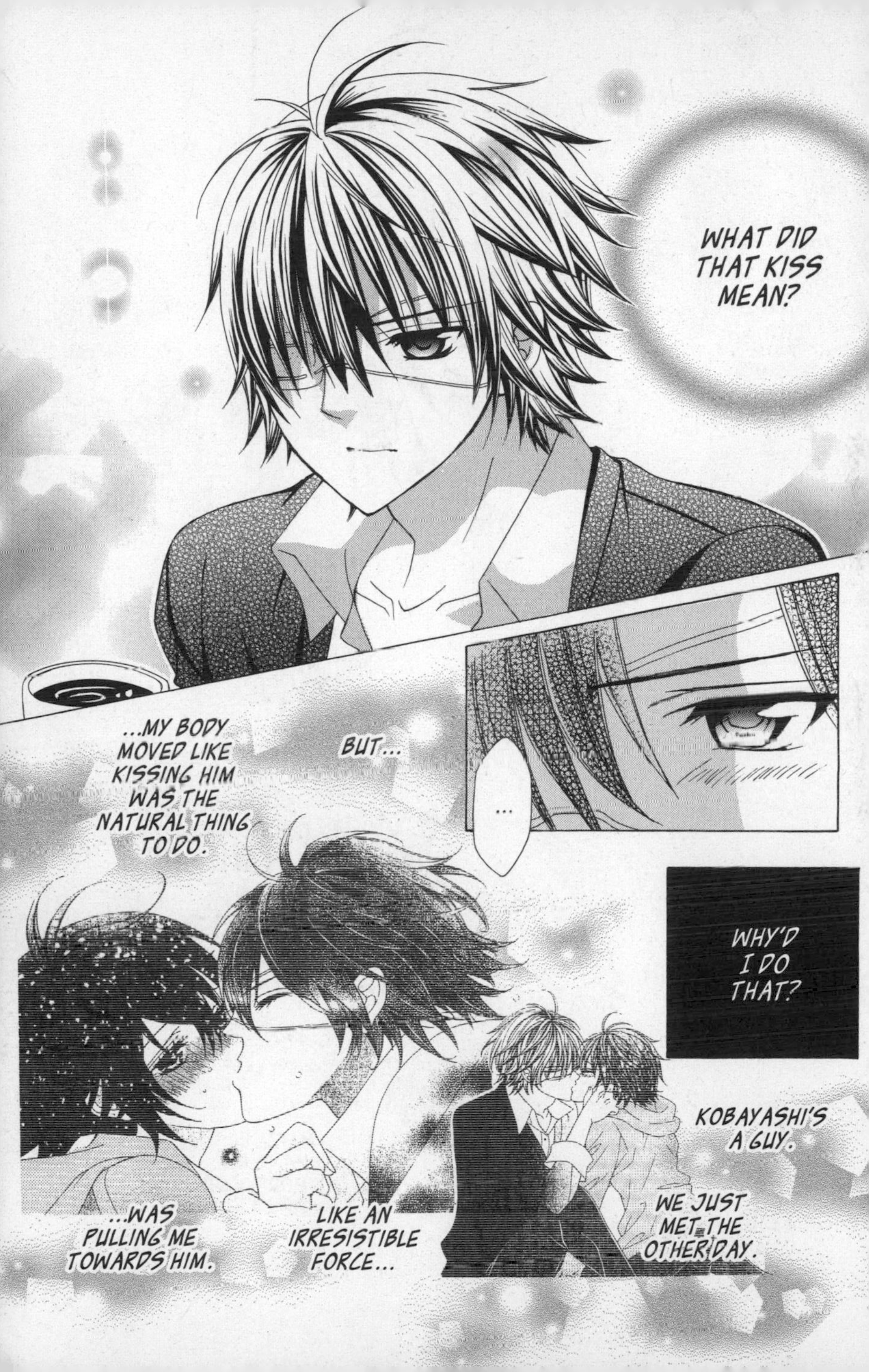
WHAT DID THAT KISS MEAN?
...
BUT...
...MY BODY MOVED LIKE KISSING HIM WAS THE NATURAL THING TO DO.
WHY'D I DO THAT?
KOBAYASHI'S A GUY.
WE JUST MET THE OTHER DAY.
LIKE AN IRRESISTIBLE FORCE...
...WAS PULLING ME TOWARDS HIM.

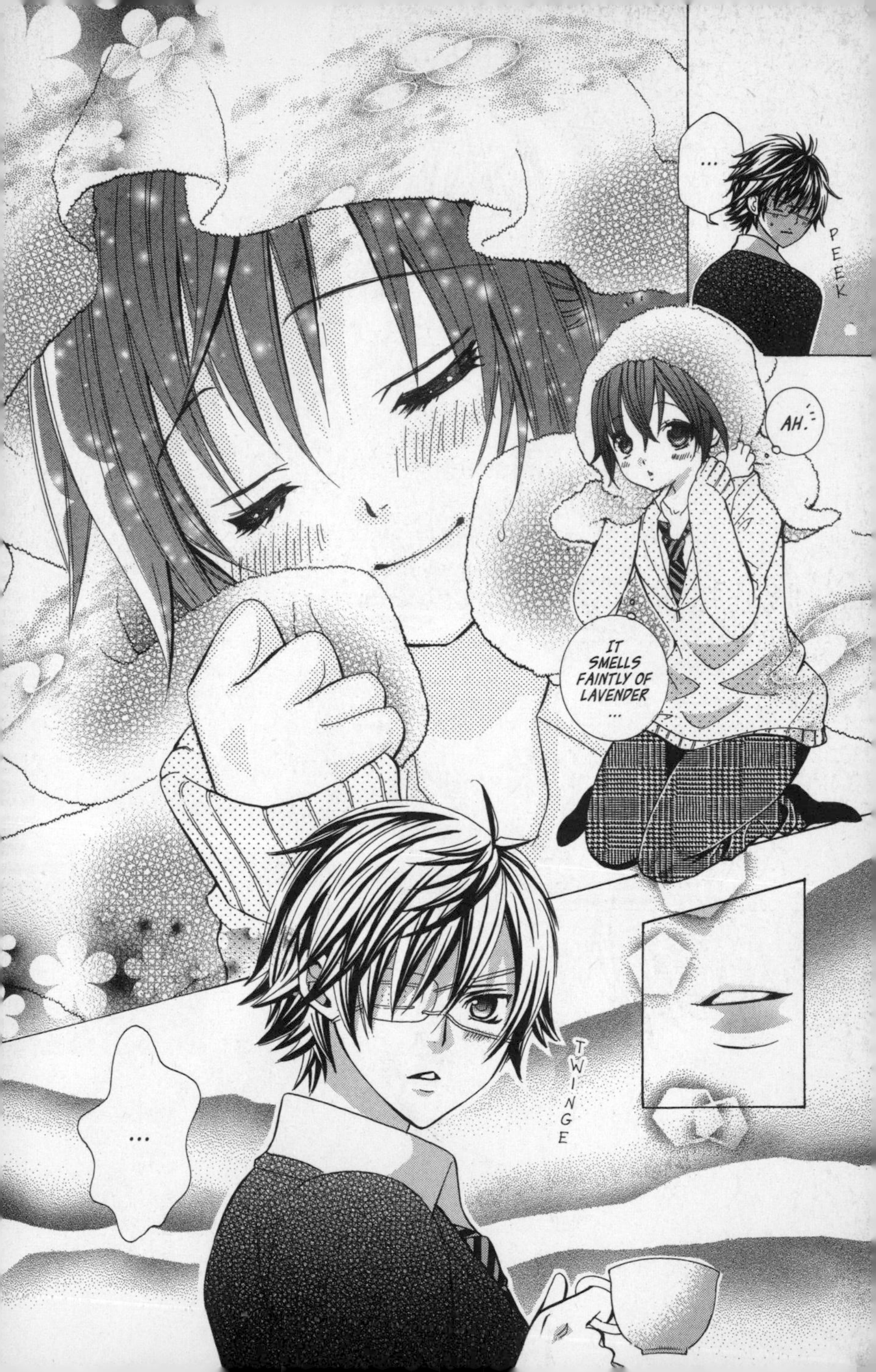
...
PEEK
AH.
IT SMELLS FAINTLY OF LAVENDER ...
TWINGE
...

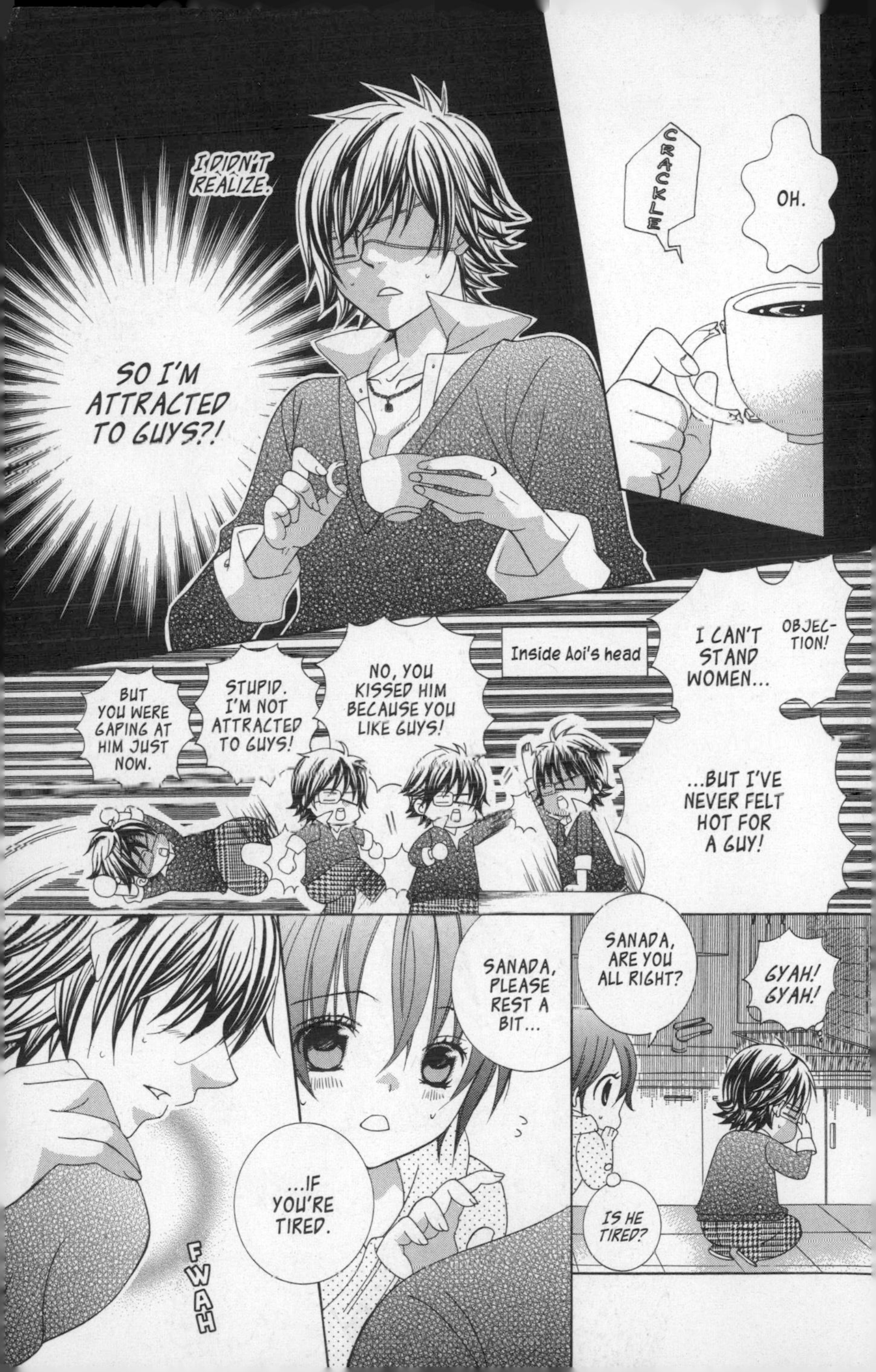
OH.
CRACKLE
I DIDN'T REALIZE.
SO I'M ATTRACTED TO GUYS?!
Inside Aoi's head
OBJECTION!
I CAN'T STAND WOMEN...
...BUT I'VE NEVER FELT HOT FOR A GUY!
NO, YOU KISSED HIM BECAUSE YOU LIKE GUYS!
STUPID. I'M NOT ATTRACTED TO GUYS!
BUT YOU WERE GAPING AT HIM JUST NOW.
GYAH! GYAH!
SANADA, ARE YOU ALL RIGHT?
IS HE TIRED?
SANADA, PLEASE REST A BIT...
...IF YOU'RE TIRED.
FWAH

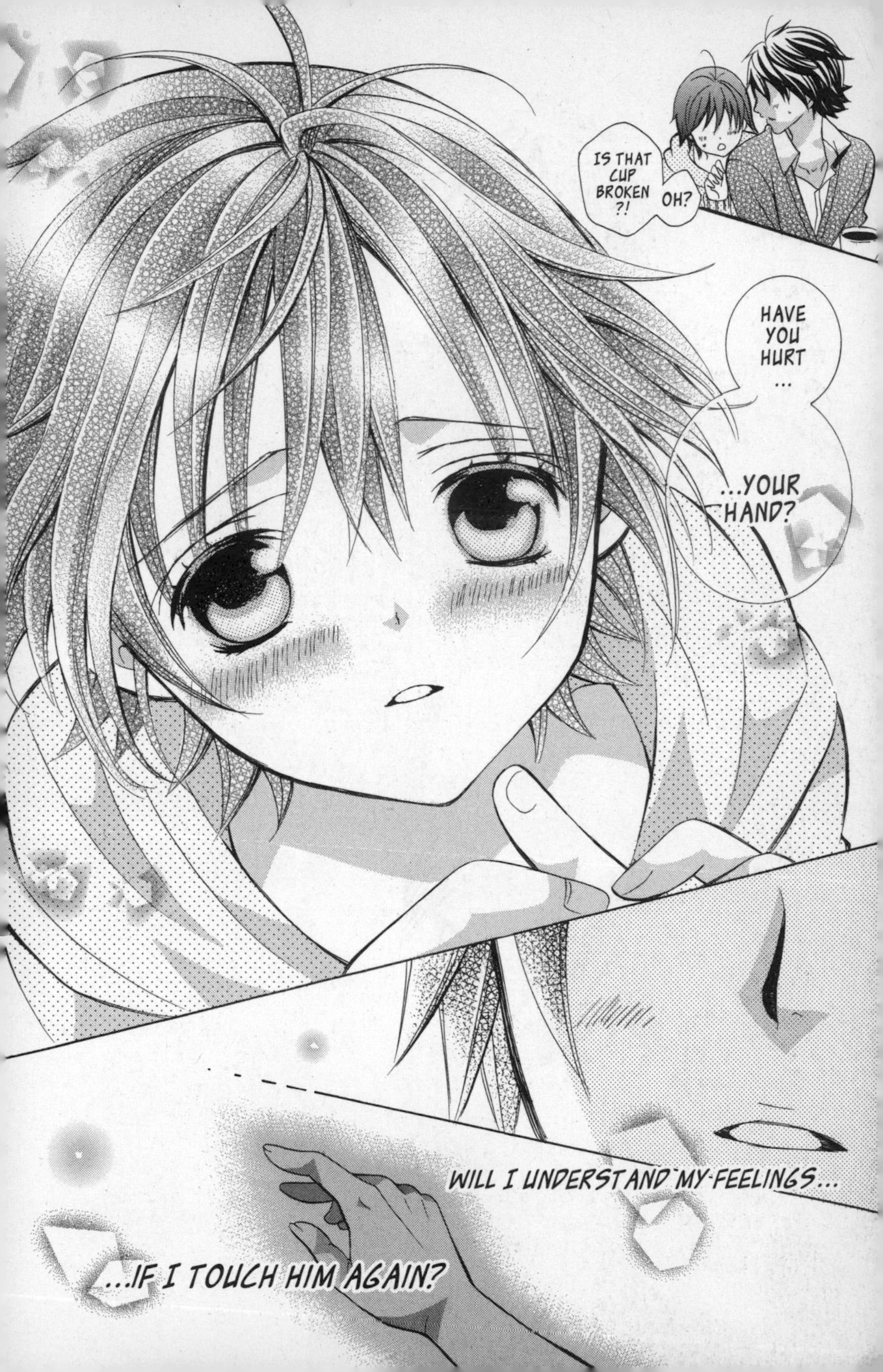

OH?
IS THAT CUP BROKEN ?!
HAVE YOU HURT ...
...YOUR HAND?
WILL I UNDERSTAND MY FEELINGS...
...IF I TOUCH HIM AGAIN?

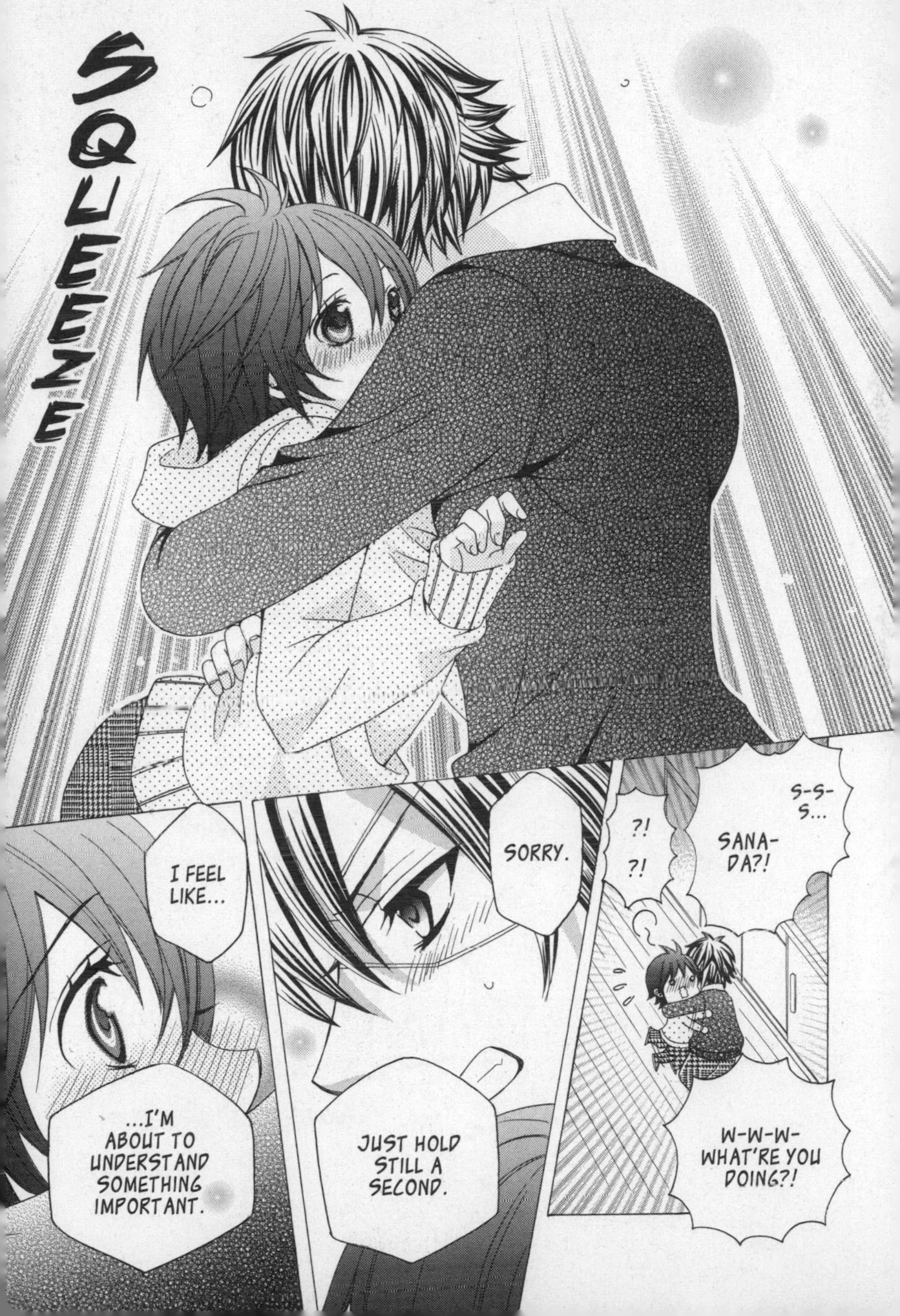
SQUEEZE
S-S-S... SANA-DA?!
?! ?!
W-W-W-WHAT'RE YOU DOING?!
SORRY.
JUST HOLD STILL A SECOND.
I FEEL LIKE...
...I'M ABOUT TO UNDERSTAND SOMETHING IMPORTANT.

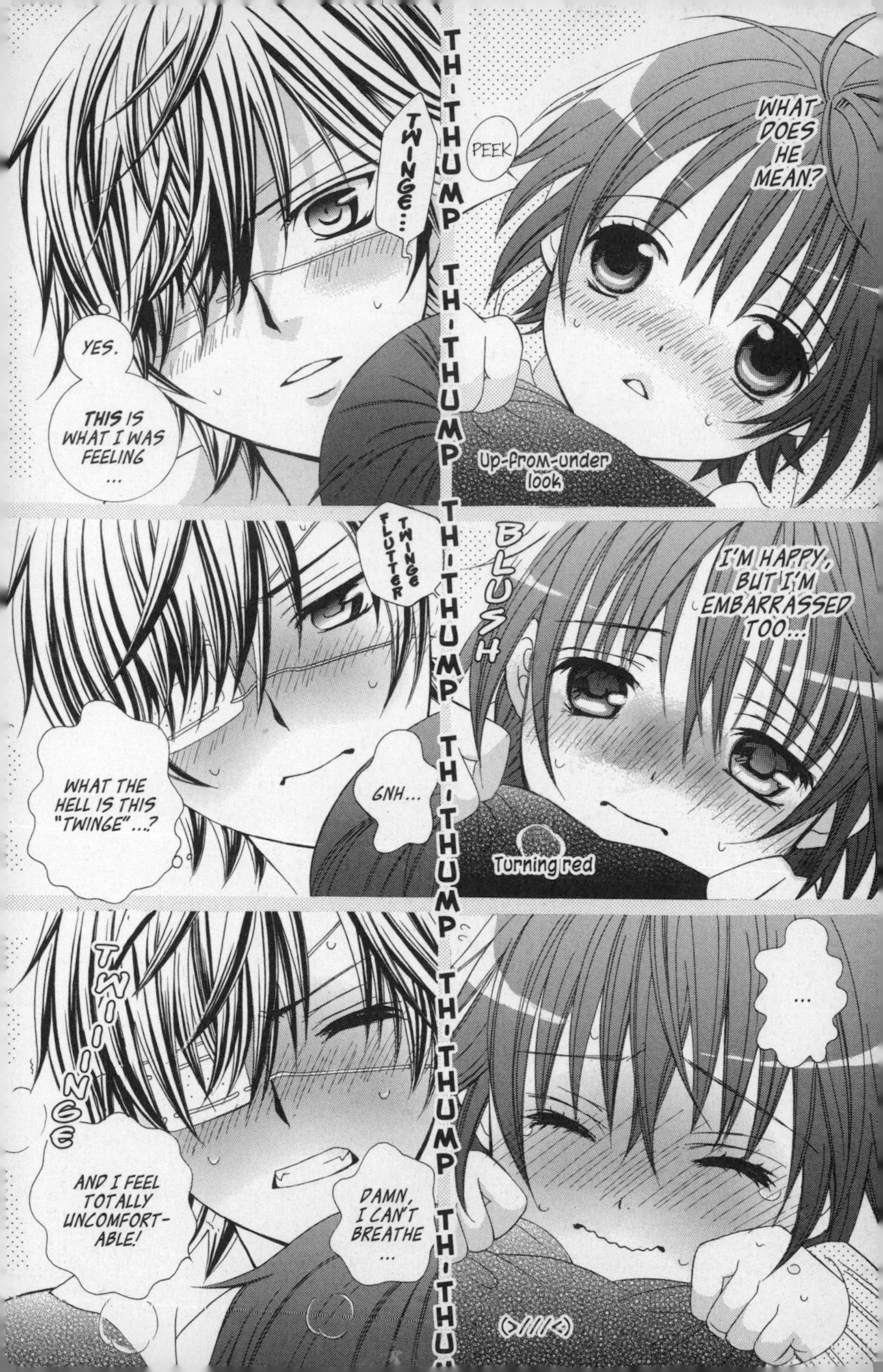
WHAT DOES HE MEAN?
PEEK
Up-from-under look
TH-THUMP TH-THUMP TH-THUMP TH-THUMP TH-THUMP TH-THU
TWINGE...
YES.
THIS IS WHAT I WAS FEELING ...
BLUSH
I'M HAPPY, BUT I'M EMBARRASSED TOO...
Turning red
FLUTTER TWINGE
GNH...
WHAT THE HELL IS THIS "TWINGE"...?
...
(>///<)
TWIIIINGE
DAMN, I CAN'T BREATHE ...
AND I FEEL TOTALLY UNCOMFORTABLE!

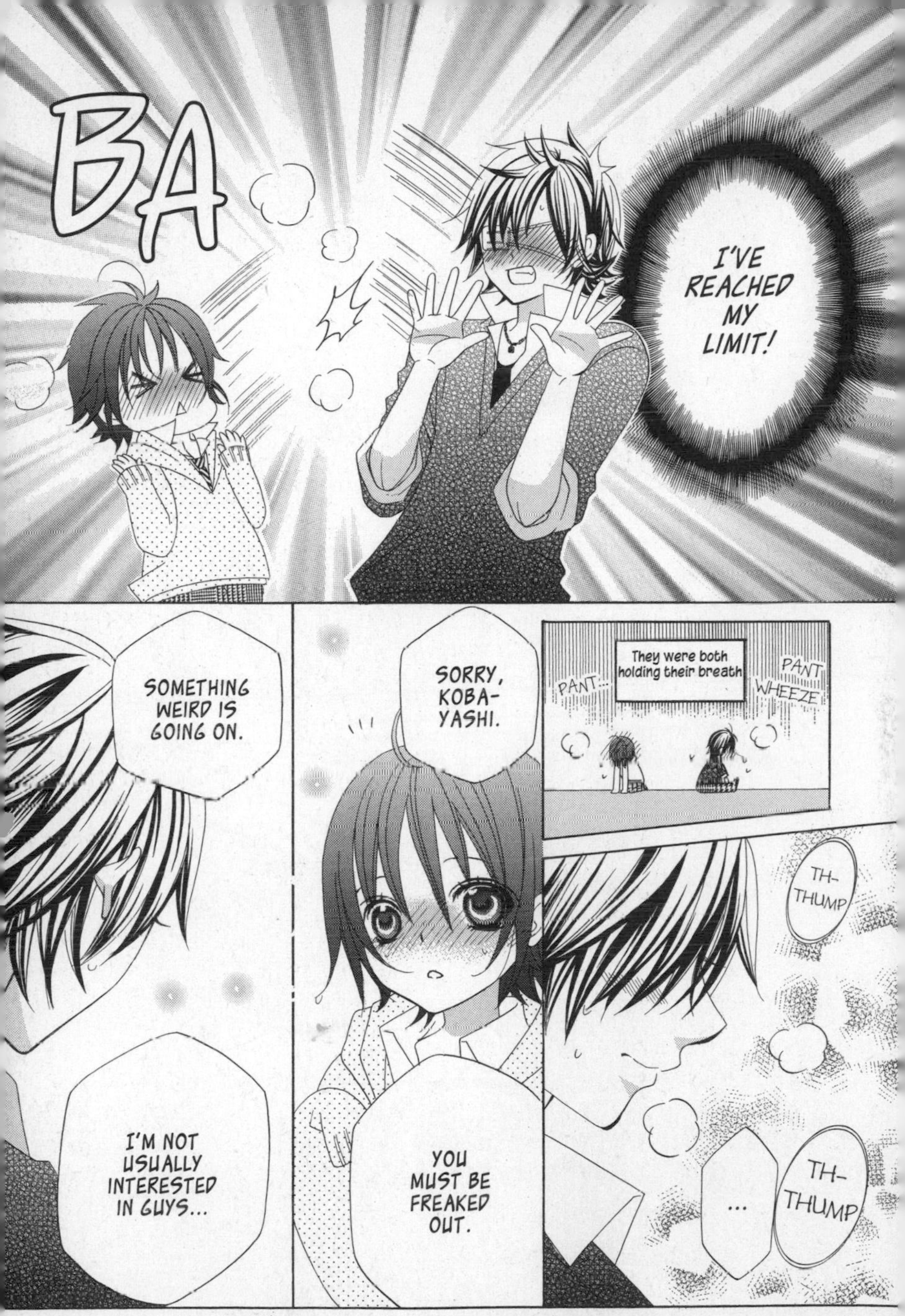
I'VE REACHED MY LIMIT!
BA
PANT
WHEEZE
They were both holding their breath
PANT...
TH-THUMP
TH-THUMP
...
SORRY, KOBA-YASHI.
YOU MUST BE FREAKED OUT.
SOMETHING WEIRD IS GOING ON.
I'M NOT USUALLY INTERESTED IN GUYS...

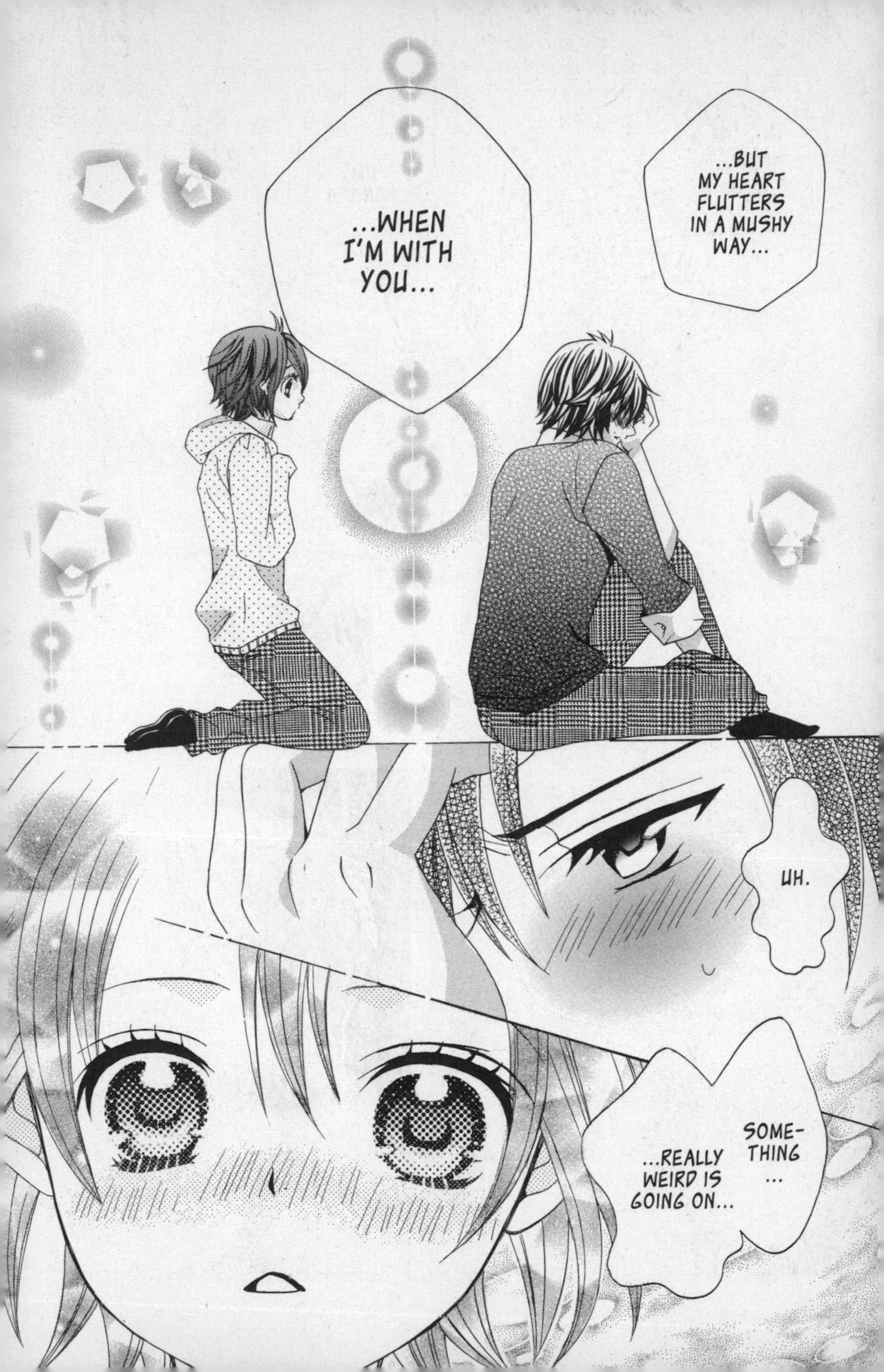
...BUT MY HEART FLUTTERS IN A MUSHY WAY...
...WHEN I'M WITH YOU...
UH.
SOME-THING...
...REALLY WEIRD IS GOING ON...

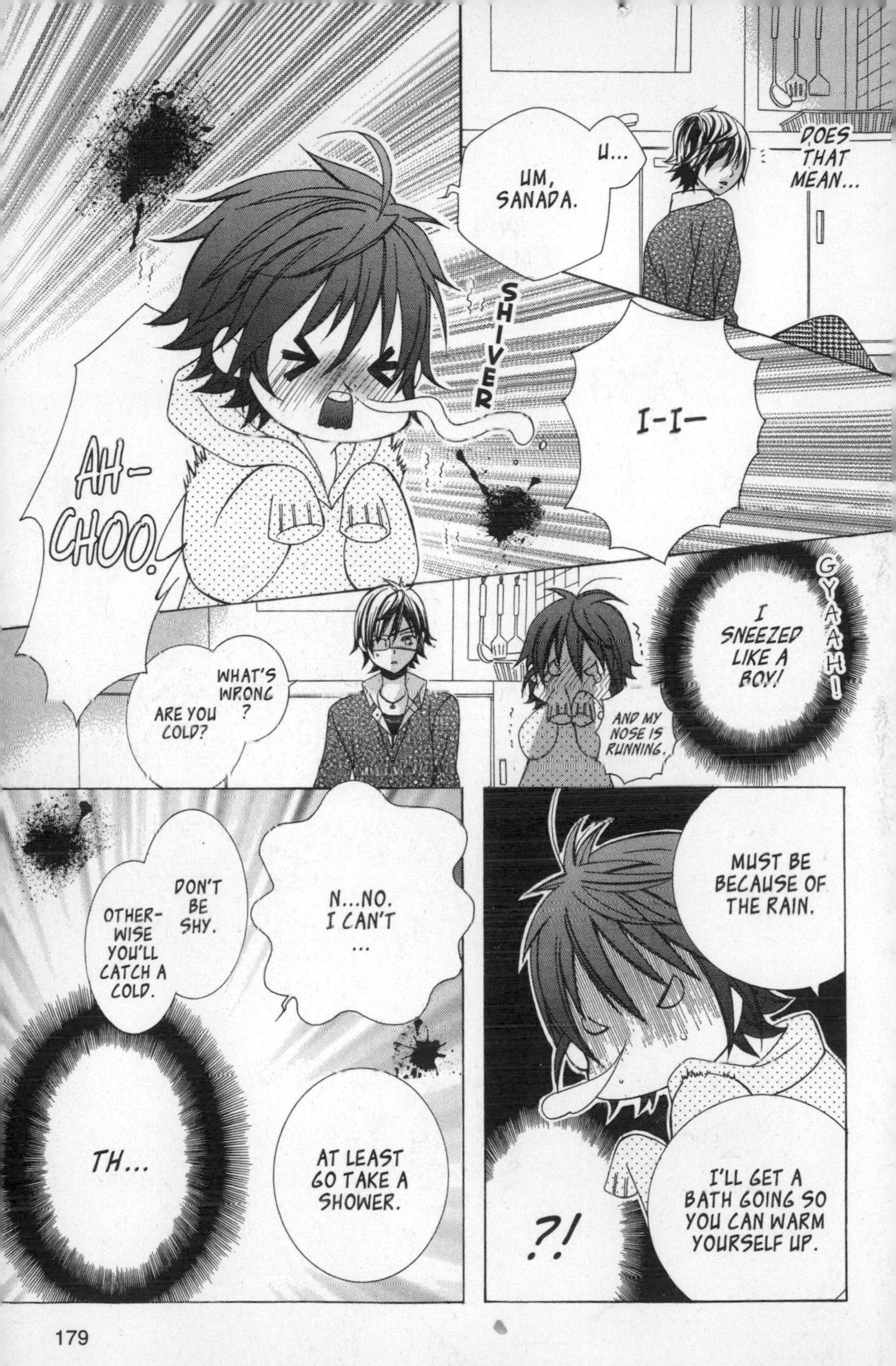
DOES THAT MEAN...
U... UM, SANADA.
SHIVER
I-I-
AH-CHOO!
GYAAH!
I SNEEZED LIKE A BOY!
AND MY NOSE IS RUNNING.
WHAT'S WRONG? ARE YOU COLD?
MUST BE BECAUSE OF THE RAIN.
I'LL GET A BATH GOING SO YOU CAN WARM YOURSELF UP.
?!
N...NO. I CAN'T ...
DON'T BE SHY.
OTHERWISE YOU'LL CATCH A COLD.
AT LEAST GO TAKE A SHOWER.
TH...

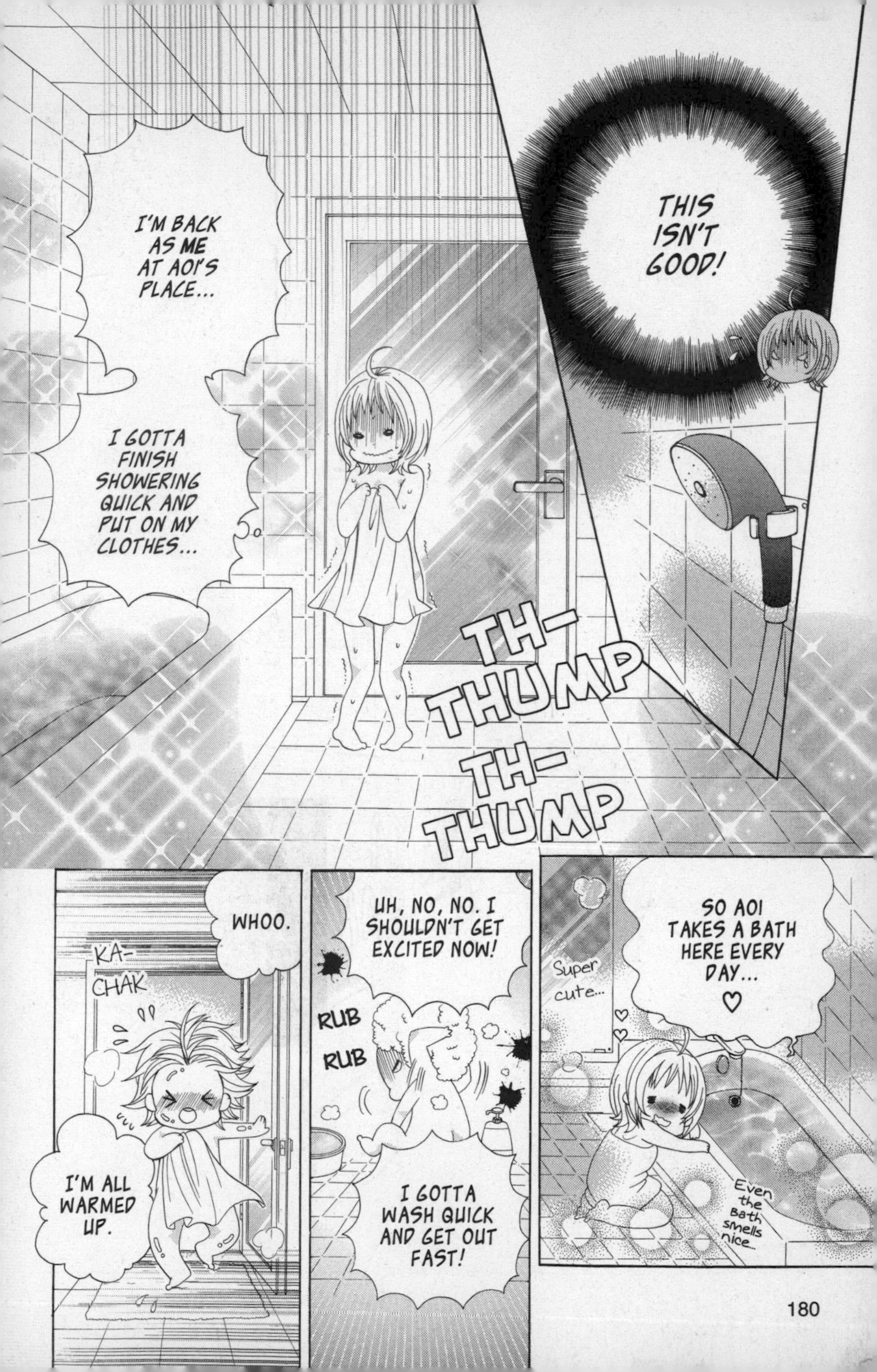
THIS ISN'T GOOD!
I'M BACK AS ME AT AOI'S PLACE...
I GOTTA FINISH SHOWERING QUICK AND PUT ON MY CLOTHES...
TH-THUMP TH-THUMP
SO AOI TAKES A BATH HERE EVERY DAY... ♡
Super cute...
Even the Bath smells nice...
UH, NO, NO. I SHOULDN'T GET EXCITED NOW!
RUB RUB
I GOTTA WASH QUICK AND GET OUT FAST!
WHOO.
KA-CHAK
I'M ALL WARMED UP.

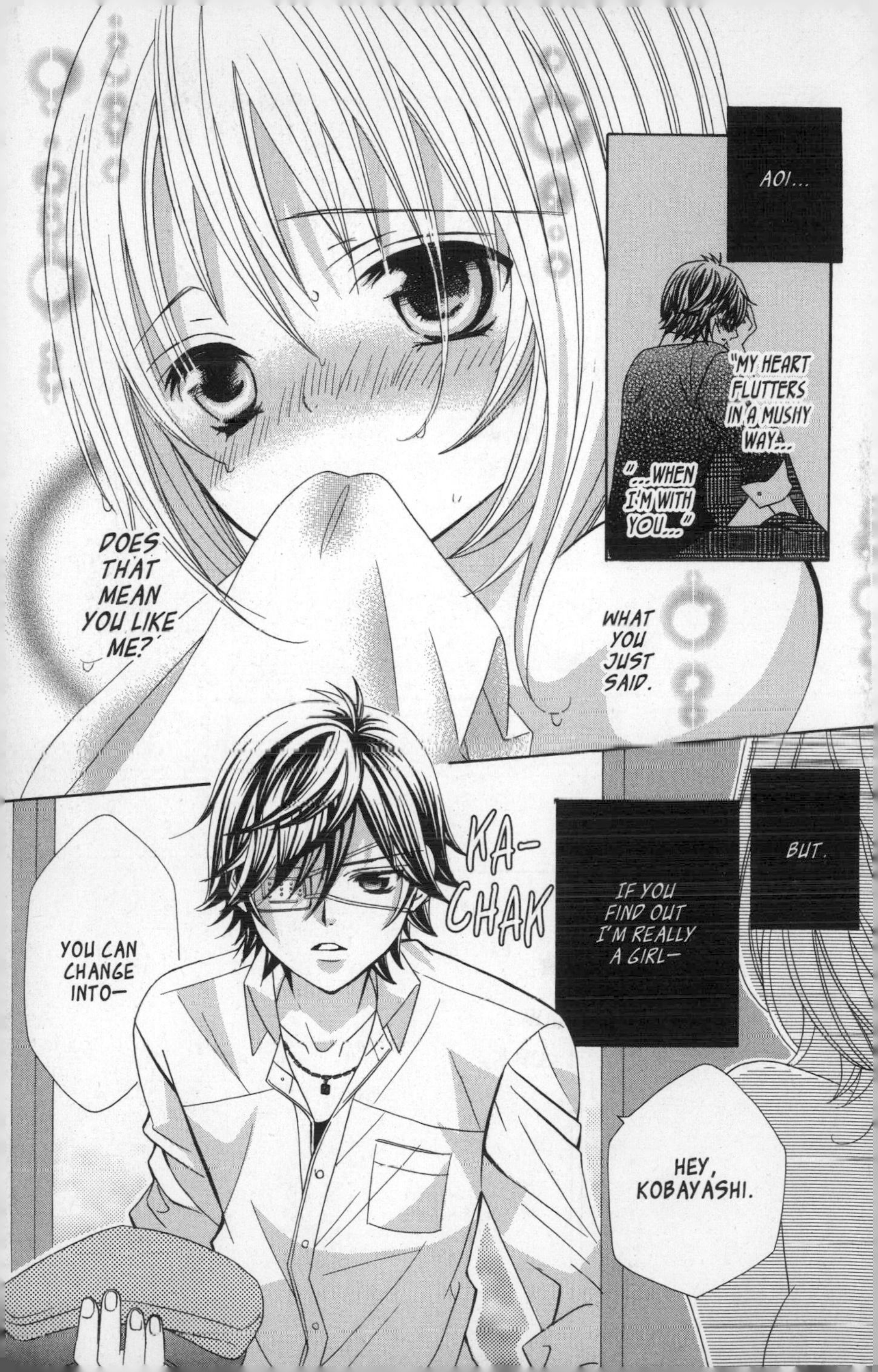
AOI...
"MY HEART FLUTTERS IN A MUSHY WAY...
"...WHEN I'M WITH YOU..."
WHAT YOU JUST SAID.
DOES THAT MEAN YOU LIKE ME?
BUT.
IF YOU FIND OUT I'M REALLY A GIRL—
HEY, KOBAYASHI.
KA-CHAK
YOU CAN CHANGE INTO—

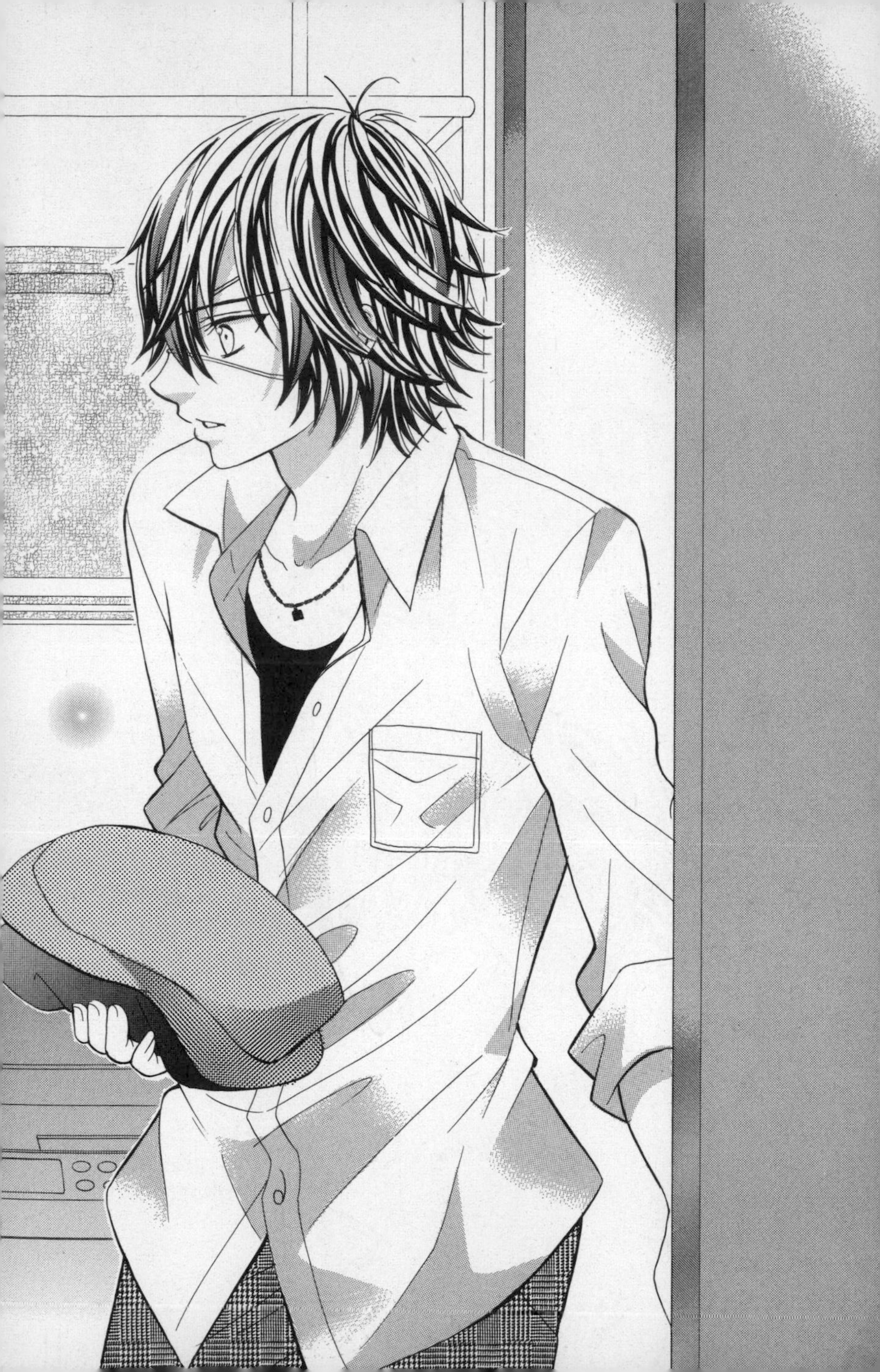

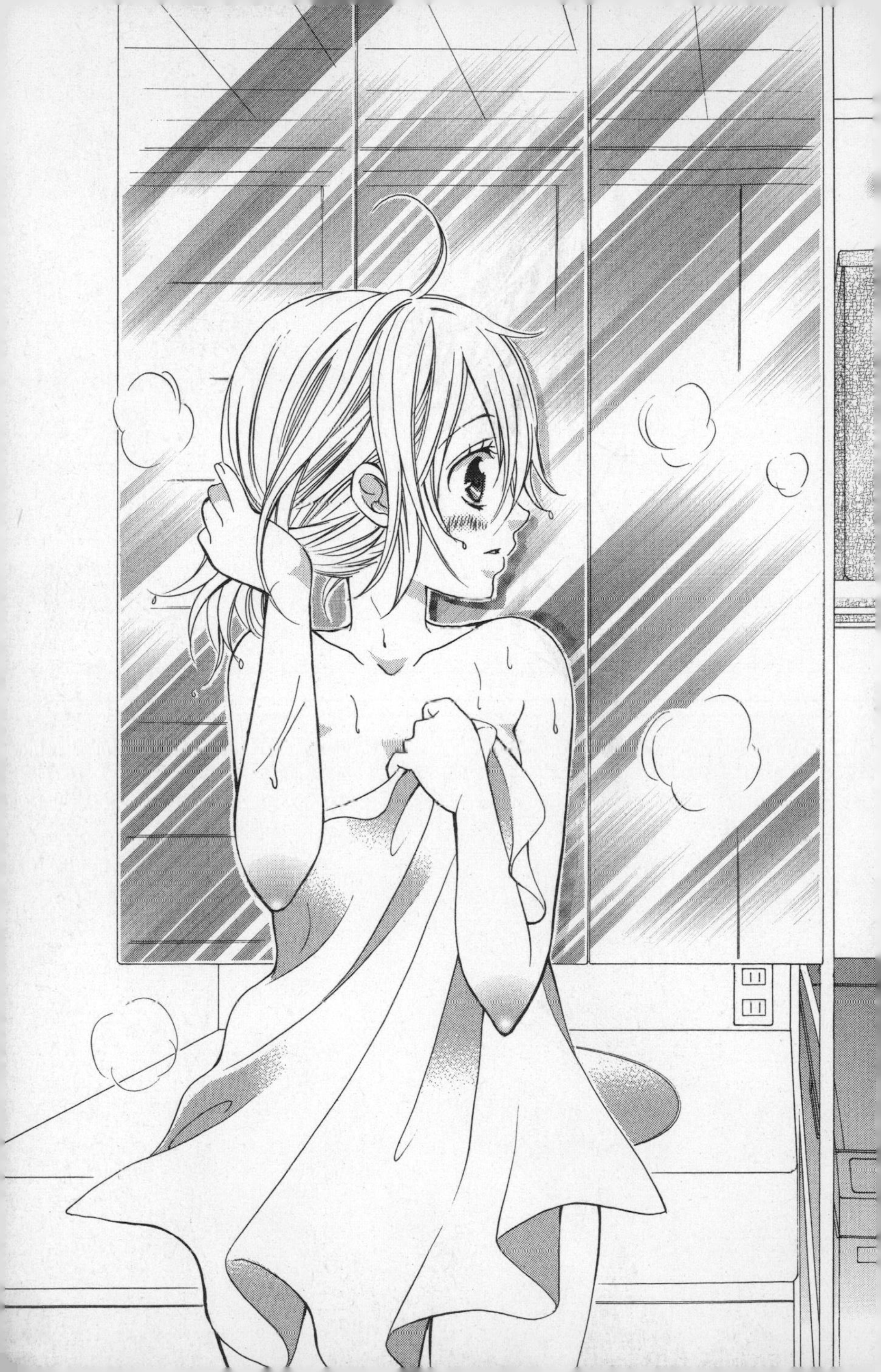

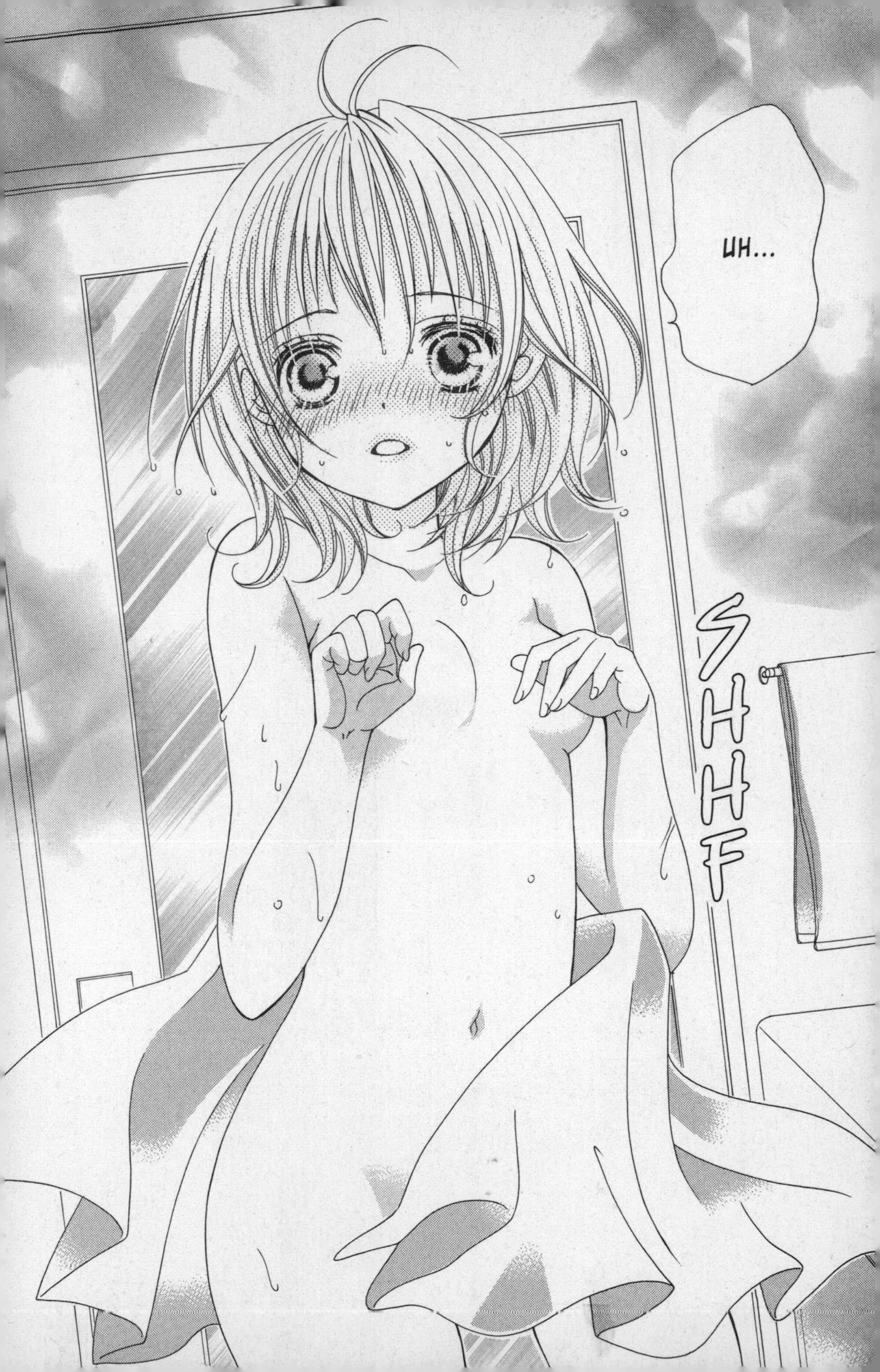
UH...
SHHF

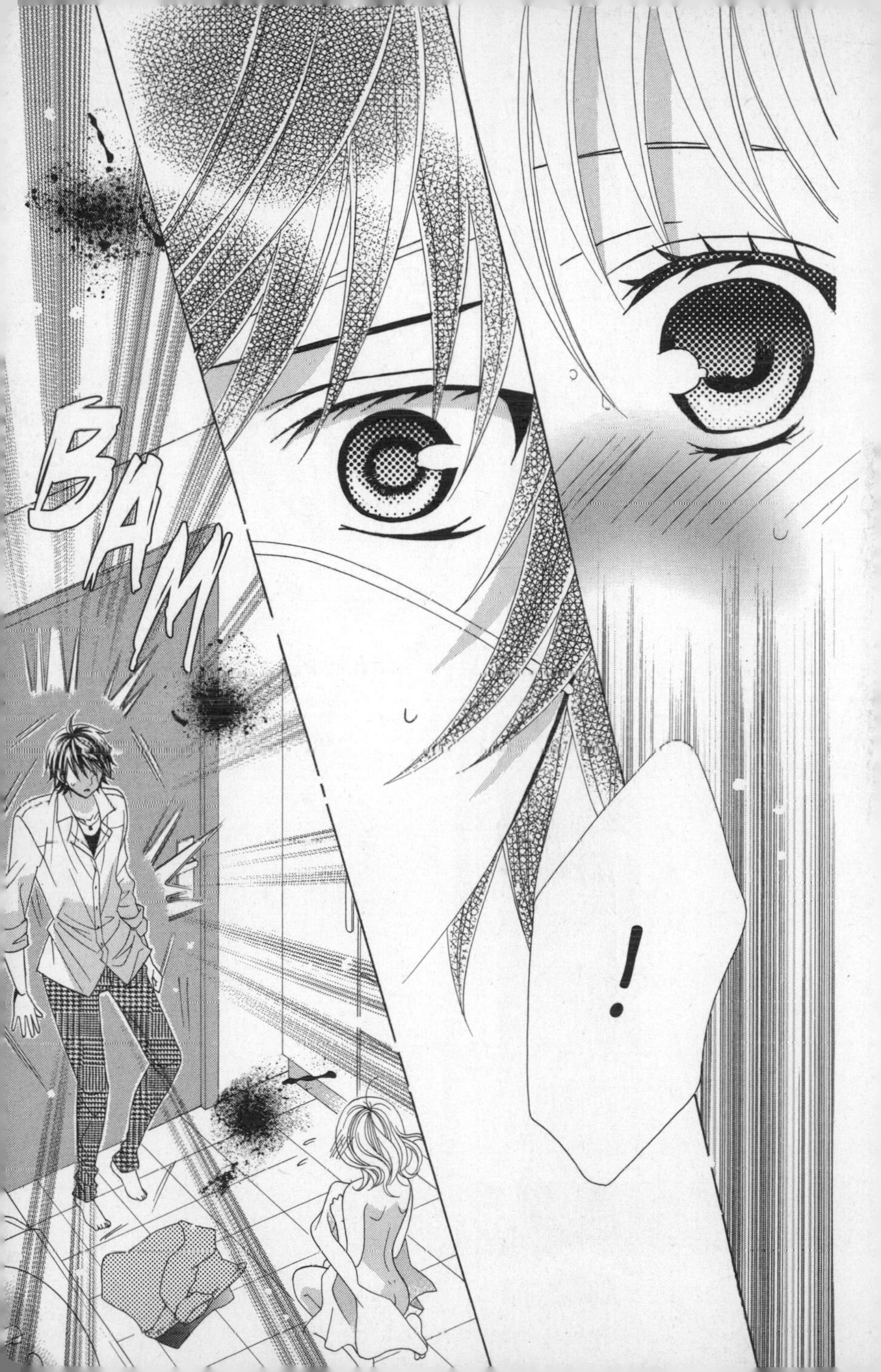
!
BAM

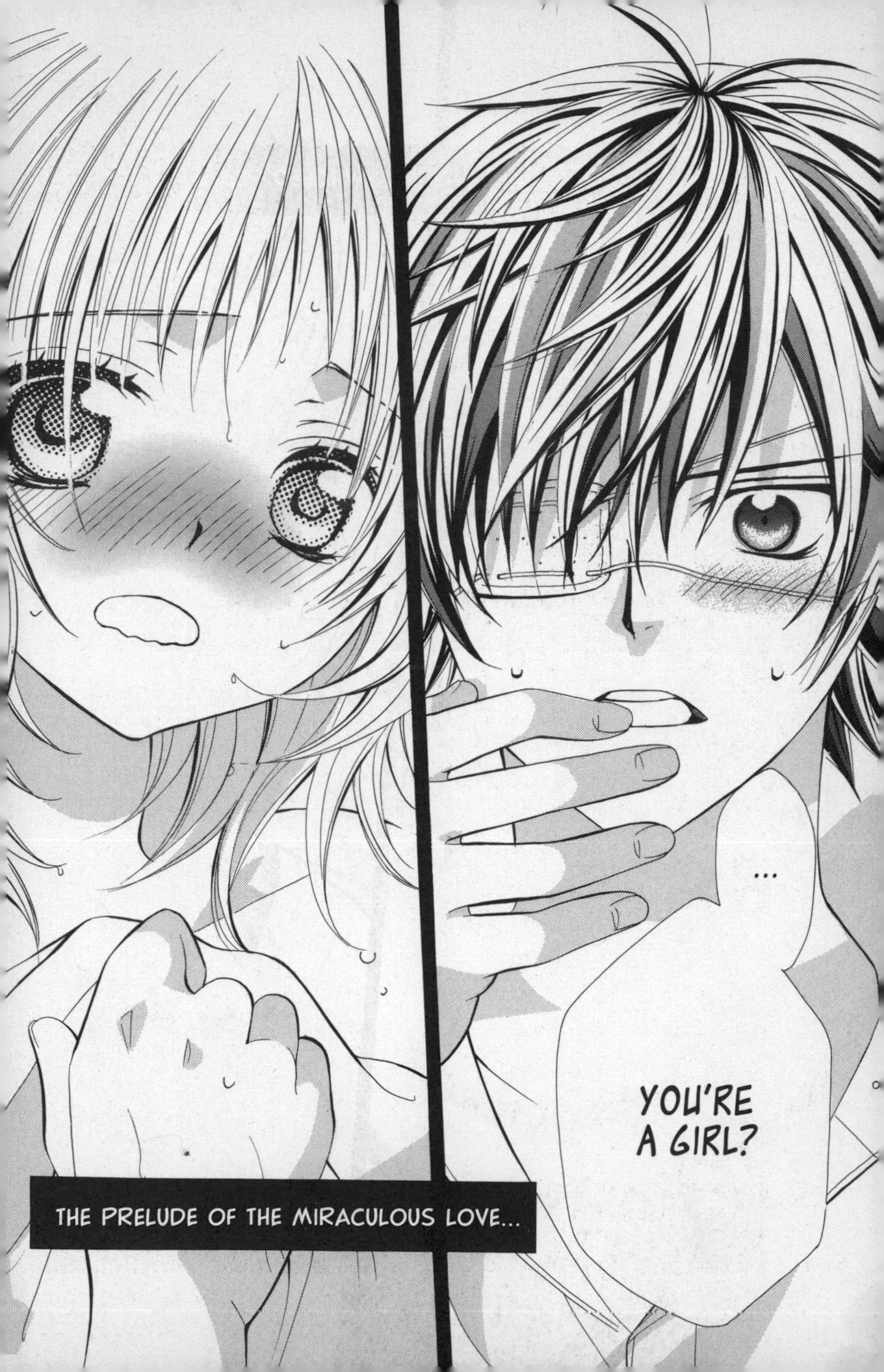
...
YOU'RE A GIRL?
THE PRELUDE OF THE MIRACULOUS LOVE...

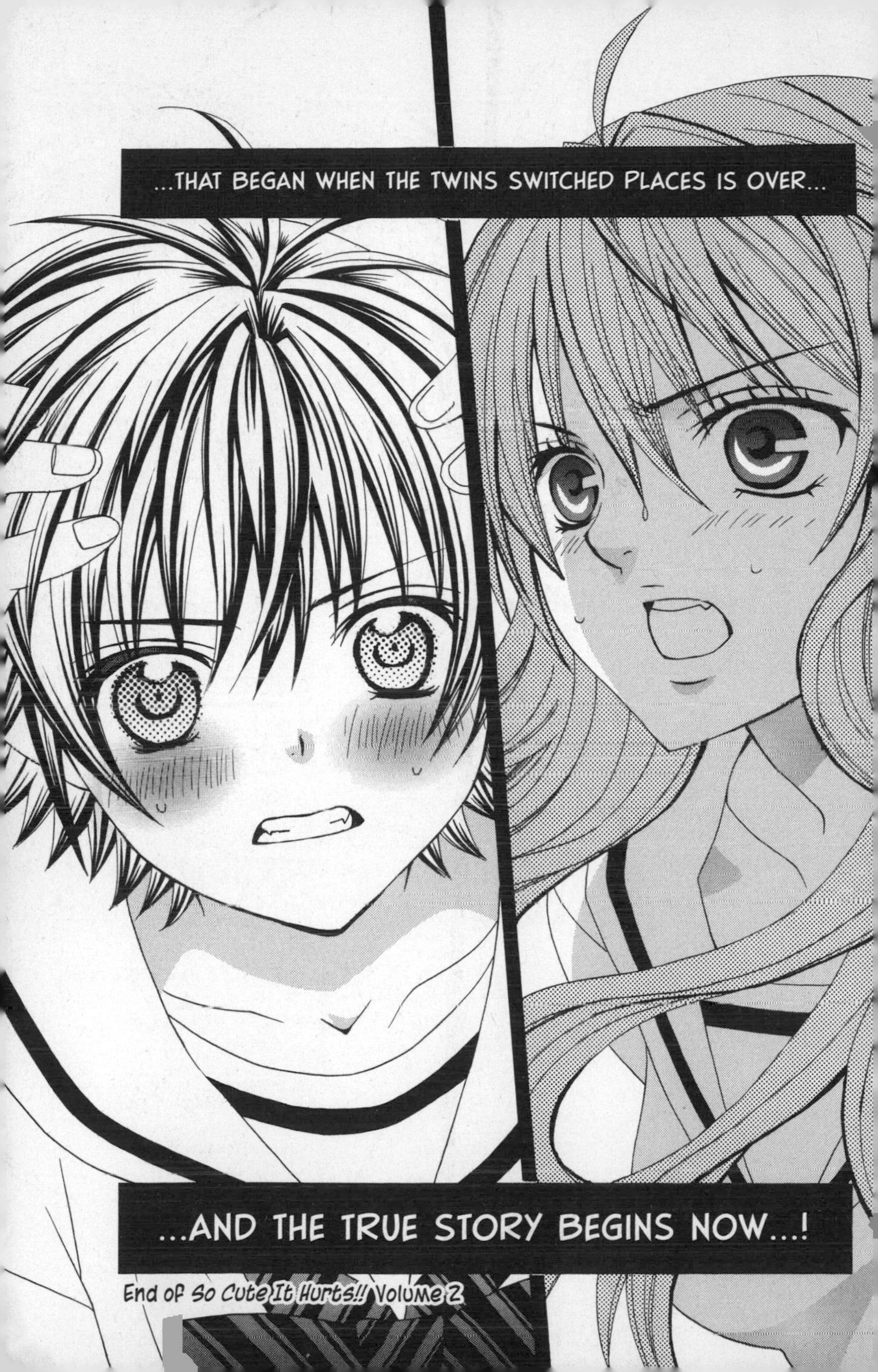
...THAT BEGAN WHEN THE TWINS SWITCHED PLACES IS OVER...
...AND THE TRUE STORY BEGINS NOW...!
End of So Cute It Hurts!! Volume 2

So Cute! Fan Art Feature ♥

EVERYONE'S DRAWINGS ARE SO CUTE, THEY HURT!!

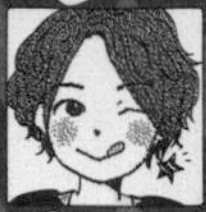

Shoojii

Editor Shoojii has commented on each one this time!!

Hana no Shizuku (Fukushima)

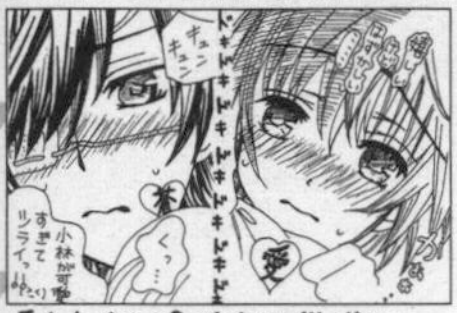

Ed: Lots of girls will die of cuteness if they see Aoi blushing like this. ☆

Azumi Shirasaki (Fukui)

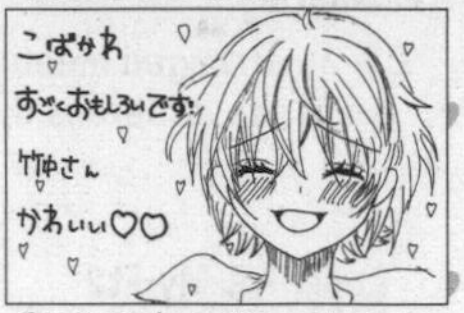

Ed: Shino's smile makes me smile too... (*^_^*)

Moyuyu's my fave

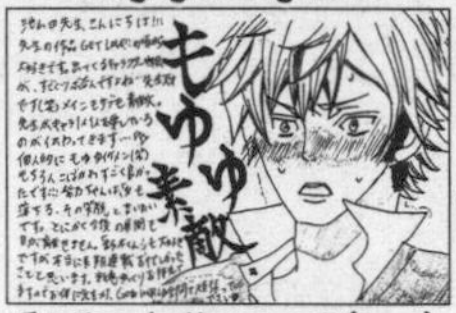

Ed: Here's Moyuuuu!! (>_<) Is he actually hot?!

AKC Satchan (Fukui)

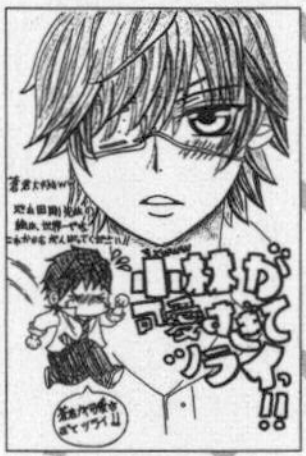

Ed: Yes, guys in eye patches are cool!!

Aoi Miyawaki (Aichi)

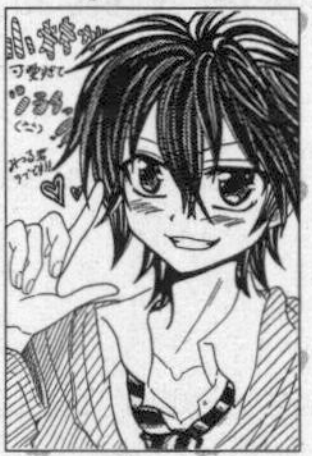

Ed: Mitsuru's smiling like a sweet devil! He does look cool in his male version!

Aoba Minamino (Kanagawa)

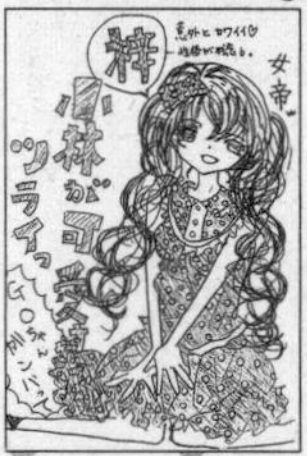

Ed: The Empress is here!! Everyone has suddenly begun to love her.

I love Mitsuru ♡ (Iwate)

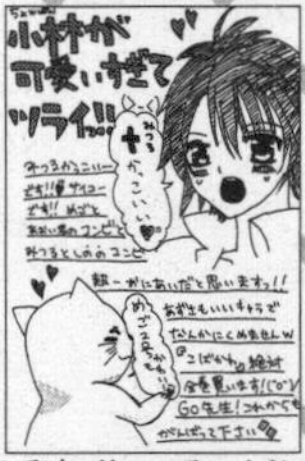

Ed: It's Mego Two! She's actually quite popular.♡

Kotone Sasaki (Chiba)

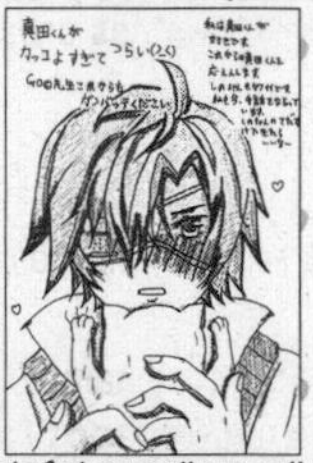

Ed: Cats really, really love Aoi!!

Momo Ogawa (Hokkaido)

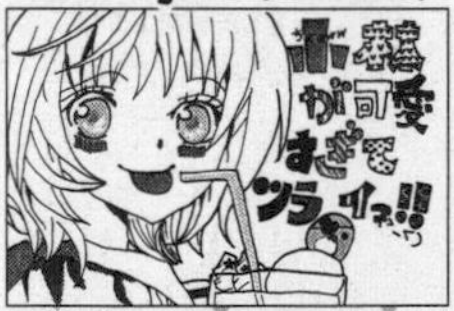

Ed: The super cute Mego & eye-patch penguin pair.♪

Hono (Tokushima)

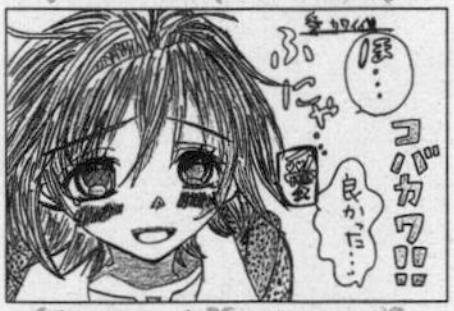

Ed: Mego's smile really makes you smile!

Send your fan mail to:

Go Ikeyamada
c/o Shojo Beat
VIZ Media, LLC
P.O. Box 77010
San Francisco, CA 94107

GLOSSARY

Page 8, panel 2: Tsundere
Tsundere is a term that combines two Japanese words—*tsuntsun* (which means "unfriendly") and *deredere* (which means "lovestruck"). It is used to describe people who can be unfriendly one second but sweet the next.

Page 15, panel 2: Marriage meeting
Called *miai* in Japanese, it is an arranged meeting between a prospective bride and groom to see if there is the possibility of a good match.

Page 81, author note: Sexy Zone, Kis-My-Ft2
Boy bands.

Page 81, author note: Yanki
A slang term for teen delinquents, bikers and dropouts.

Page 83, panel 2: Hand sign
Shino isn't flipping off Aoi—this is Japanese sign language for "brother."

Page 85, panel 3: Banzai
It literally means "ten thousand years" and can be used as an exclamation similar to "hurrah!"

Page 91, panel 4: Yaoi
Also knows as boys' love or BL. It refers to media about male-male romantic and sexual relationships created for a female audience.

Page 92, panel 3: Yuri
Similar to *yaoi*, but refers to female-female relationships.

Page 96, panel 6: Like the kanji in my name
The kanji for "shi" in Shino's name means "purple."

AUTHOR BIO

TOKYO Lithmatic created an eye-patch penguin figure!

It's so cute it hurts!! (*smile*) It's cute, but it's pretty big and weighs quite a lot, LOL. *Sho-Comi* magazine gave away 100 mini eye-patch penguin phone straps to readers!! ("Δ") Craftspeople hand painted (!) all 100 penguins with love. (*tears*) Thank you so much, Lithmatic!! (ToT)(^o^) I hope everyone who won a strap takes loving care of it. (* ⌒ ‿ ⌒ *) ♥

Go Ikeyamada is a Gemini from Miyagi Prefecture whose hobbies include taking naps and watching movies. Her debut manga *Get Love!!* appeared in *Shojo Comic* in 2002, and her current work *So Cute It Hurts!!* (*Kobayashi ga Kawai Suguite Tsurai!!*) is being published by VIZ Media.

SO CUTE IT HURTS!!
Volume 2

Shojo Beat Edition

STORY AND ART BY
GO IKEYAMADA

English Translation & Adaptation/Tomo Kimura
Touch-Up Art & Lettering/Joanna Estep
Design/Izumi Evers
Editor/Pancha Diaz

KOBAYASHI GA KAWAISUGITE TSURAI!! Vol.2
by Go IKEYAMADA
© 2012 Go IKEYAMADA
All rights reserved.
Original Japanese edition published by SHOGAKUKAN.
English translation rights in the United States of America, Canada,
United Kingdom and Ireland arranged with SHOGAKUKAN.

Printed in the U.S.A.

Published by VIZ Media, LLC
P.O. Box 77010
San Francisco, CA 94107

10 9 8 7 6 5 4 3 2 1
First printing, August 2015

www.viz.com   www.shojobeat.com

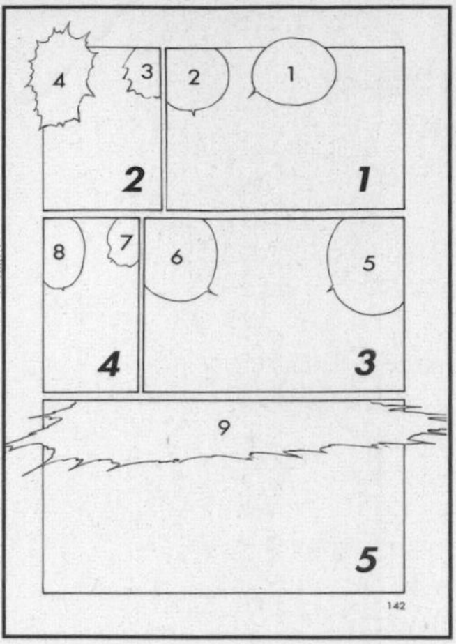
1
2
3
4
1
2
5
6
7
8
3
4
9
5
142

This is the last page.

In keeping with the original Japanese comic format, this book reads from right to left—so action, sound effects, and word balloons are completely reversed. This preserves the orientation of the original artwork—plus, it's fun! Check out the diagram shown here to get the hang of things, and then turn to the other side of the book to get started!

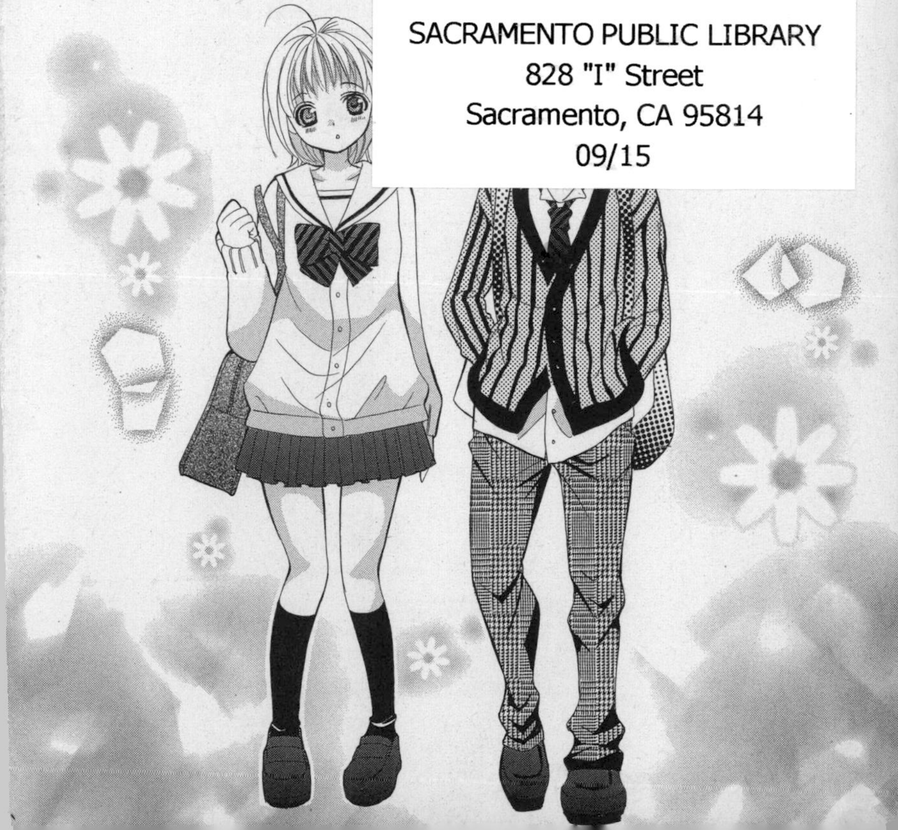